The Search
for National Integration
in Africa

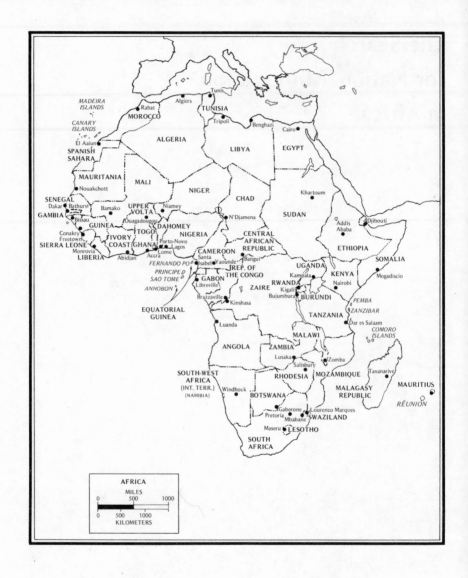

MADEIRA
ISLANDS

CANARY
ISLANDS

Tunis
Algiers
Rabat
TUNISIA
MOROCCO
Tripoli
Benghazi
Cairo
El Aaiun
ALGERIA
LIBYA
EGYPT
SPANISH
SAHARA

MAURITANIA
MALI
NIGER
CHAD
Khartoum
Nouakchott

SENEGAL
Dakar
Bathurst
Bamako
UPPER
Niamey
N'Djamena
SUDAN
Addis
Ababa
Djibouti
GAMBIA
Bissau
VOLTA
Ouagadougou
GUINEA
TOGO DAHOMEY
NIGERIA
CENTRAL
AFRICAN
REPUBLIC
ETHIOPIA
Conakry
Freetown
IVORY
GHANA
Porto-Novo
SIERRA LEONE
COAST
Lome
Lagos
Monrovia
Abidjan
Accra
CAMEROON
Santa
Bangui
UGANDA
SOMALIA
Mogadiscio
LIBERIA
FERNANDO PO
Isabel
Yaounde
REP. OF
THE CONGO
KENYA
PRINCIPE
SAO TOME
GABON
Kampala
Nairobi
ANNOBON
Libreville
ZAIRE
RWANDA
Kigali
PEMBA
ZANZIBAR
EQUATORIAL
GUINEA
Brazzaville
Kinshasa
Bujumbura
BURUNDI
TANZANIA
Dar es Salaam
COMORO
ISLANDS
Luanda
MALAWI
ANGOLA
ZAMBIA
Lusaka
Zomba
Tananarive
SOUTH-WEST
AFRICA
(INT. TERR.)
(NAMIBIA)
Windhoek
RHODESIA
Salisbury
MOZAMBIQUE
BOTSWANA
MALAGASY
REPUBLIC
MAURITIUS
RÉUNION
Gaberone
Lourenco Marques
Pretoria
Mbabane
SWAZILAND
Maseru
LESOTHO
SOUTH
AFRICA

AFRICA

MILES
0   500   1000

0   500   1000
KILOMETERS

The Search for National Integration in Africa

Edited by

David R. Smock
and
Kwamena Bentsi-Enchill

THE FREE PRESS
A Division of Macmillan Publishing Co., Inc.
NEW YORK

Collier Macmillan Publishers
LONDON

In Memoriam
Kwamena Bentsi-Enchill
1918–1974

The Free Press
A Division of Macmillan Publishing Co., Inc.
866 Third Avenue, New York, N.Y. 10022

Collier Macmillan Canada, Ltd.

Library of Congress Catalog Card Number: 74–33090

Printed in the United States of America

printing number

1 2 3 4 5 6 7 8 9 10

Library of Congress Cataloging in Publication Data
Main entry under title:

The Search for national integration in Africa.

    Includes bibliographical references.
    1. Africa, Sub-Saharan--Politics and government
--Addresses, essays, lectures. 2. Nationalism--
Africa, Sub-Saharan--Addresses, essays, lectures.
I. Smock, David R. II. Bentsi-Enchill, Kwamena.
DT353.S43   320.9'6'03   74-33090
ISBN 0-02-929560-2

Frontispiece map from Donald G. Morrison *et al., Black Africa: A Comparative Handbook* (New York: The Free Press, 1972), p. 2, used by permission of the publisher.

Contents

v

Part IV   Language Policy, Communications and Culture   **159**

Part V   The Current State of the Integration Process   **249**

Preface

THE GENESIS of this book lies in our shared interest in the process of nation-building in Africa. More particularly, we have been motivated by our distress over the dearth of thoughtful analytic and normative writing on the problems posed for African states by their ethnically fragmented character. Journalistic accounts of ethnic conflict in Africa appear all too frequently, but careful assessment of the dynamics of ethnic interaction and consideration of constructive governmental responses to these problems are rare. Foreign observers often facilely and inaccurately describe ethnic conflict in Africa as being primitive and tribalistic, and as posing insuperable obstacles to viable nationhood. In doing so they neglect the underlying commonality of politicized pluralism evident with increasing vigor in all parts of the world. Statements by many African leaders, on the other hand, tend to belittle the seriousness of the problems posed by the multi-ethnic make-up of their countries. When such conflict reaches levels of acuteness necessitating response, they often resort to exhortations against the evils of "tribalism." The question considered here is whether more effective policies and practices can be devised for reducing tensions and transforming conflict into cooperation or institutionalized competition.

It is our earnest hope that this volume will help stimulate a modest increment in the quality of discourse on this subject and the sophistication of policy formulation relating to national integration. This book should be of interest not only to students and scholars concerned with the diverse issues relating to ethnic pluralism in Africa, but to policy-makers in Africa as well. Such earlier studies as Gwendolen Carter's *National Unity and Regionalism in Eight African States* (Ithaca: Cornell University Press, 1966), James Coleman and Carl Rosberg's *Political Parties and National*

Integration in Tropical Africa (Berkeley and Los Angeles: University of California Press, 1964), Arthur Hazelwood's *African Integration and Disintegration* (London: Oxford University Press, 1967), Leo Kuper and M. G. Smith's *Pluralism in Africa* (Berkeley and Los Angeles: University of California Press, 1969), and Victor A. Olorunsola's *The Politics of Cultural Sub-Nationalism in Africa* (Garden City, N.Y.: Doubleday, 1972) have shed light on these issues, but this book deals with ethnic pluralism more explicitly and comprehensively than its predecessors have. It also devotes more attention to policy recommendations.

Rather than attempt to present comprehensive country profiles or exhaustively analyze the character of ethnic conflict, we have used a problem-oriented and comparative approach. Consequently, groups of chapters deal with education policy, economic planning, language policy, communications, cultural policy, and constitutional and political reform, whereas other chapters assess selected aspects of the dynamics of ethnic interaction and the current state of national integration in a sampling of African states. Even so, we have tried to add concreteness and realism to the discussion by analyzing each topic in terms of case studies of particular countries. We have naturally not been able to give equal attention to all the issues involved; nor could we achieve full geographic coverage. In selecting the countries to be treated we have sought to provide some geographic spread that would suggest the range of national experience. Yet we also wanted some geographic concentration so that the discussion of different phases of ethnic pluralism in one country would elucidate a similar discussion of another. We were also constrained in our selection of countries by the necessity of locating authors interested in the relevant issues, prepared to discuss them, and capable of writing in English. The end result is that we give special attention to four countries: Ghana, Nigeria, Cameroon, and Uganda, while individual chapters discuss selected aspects of Senegal, Somalia, Kenya, Zambia, and Tanzania.

The adoption of an interdisciplinary approach led to the selection of authors representing a wide range of professional specialties. They include political scientists, anthropologists, sociologists, legal scholars, educators, communication theorists, linguists, and an economic geographer. Although all the authors hold academic positions and many have published widely in academic media, two of the authors have also held public office, one having been a Supreme Court Judge and another a cabinet minister. We have been particularly anxious to have African authors address the issues covered in the book, and consequently 8 of the 16 chapters are authored by African scholars.

We are indebted to the Ford Foundation for providing funds to assist in meeting the costs entailed in this project. Naturally, that foundation is not in any manner to be held responsible for the views expressed by the various authors or the editors. Nor do we as editors necessarily share all the views of the other authors. They have been free to judge matters from their own perspective and experience, and we believe the end product is richer for the variety of viewpoints expressed. The same holds for the contributors themselves in the sense that they may not agree with all the ideas we have expressed as the editors and as the authors of the introductions.

We also wish to acknowledge our debt of gratitude to Audrey Smock, who helped us shape our thoughts on the issues discussed. Asha Mathur ably and good-naturedly handled the secretarial responsibilities. Finally, we are grateful to the publishers of the *Journal of Modern African Studies* for giving us permission to reprint in a different form I. M. Lewis's article on Somalia, and to the *Journal of Comparative Education* for allowing the republication in revised form of Bernard Fonlon's article on language policy in Cameroon.

February 1975

List of Contributors

David R. Smock—Deputy Head of the Middle East and Africa Program of the Ford Foundation, he has held a variety of posts with the foundation since 1964. He has also had academic appointments at the University of Nigeria and the American University of Beirut. His principal publications are *Conflict and Control in an African Trade Union, Cultural and Political Aspects of Rural Transformation,* and *The Politics of Pluralism.*

Kwamena Bentsi-Enchill—At the time of his death in 1974, Chairman of the Volta River Authority and Stool Lands Boundary Commissioner. He was formerly a Ghana Supreme Court Judge, Research Professor of Law at the University of Ghana, Dean of the Faculty of Law at the University of Zambia, and a practicing attorney. His most important publications are *Ghana Land Law* and *Institutional Challenges of Our Time.*

Billy J. Dudley—Professor and Chairman of the Department of Political Science at the University of Ibadan. A Nigerian, he is editor in chief of the periodical *Nigerian Opinion* and the author of *Parties and Politics in Northern Nigeria* and *Instability and Political Order.*

Abiola O. Ojo—Lecturer in the Faculty of Law at the University of Lagos, the author of many journal articles, and member of the Nigerian Bar.

A. Bolaji Akinyemi—Lecturer in Political Science at the University of Ibadan, and author of *Foreign Policy and Federalism: The Nigerian Experience* as well as of a forthcoming book entitled *Rhodesia: The Myth and the Reality.*

Ali A. Mazrui—Professor of Political Science at the University of Michigan, and formerly Dean of the Faculty of Social Sciences and Professor of Political Science at Makerere University in Uganda. He is the author of many books including *Cultural Engineering and Nation-Building, Violence and Thought,* and *Towards a Pax Africana,* and the editor of several journals and officer of several professional associations.

Kwamina B. Dickson—Dean of the Faculty of Social Studies, Associate Professor of Geography, and Chairman of the Department of Geography at the University of Ghana. His principal publications are *A Historical Geography of Ghana* and *A New Geography of Ghana,* and he is editor of the *Ghana Social Science Journal.*

Audrey C. Smock—Research Associate at Columbia University and Consultant to the Ford Foundation; she formerly held academic posts at Barnard College, University of Ghana, and the American University of Beirut. Her principal publications are *Ibo Politics: The Role of Ethnic Unions in Eastern Nigeria, Cultural and Political Aspects of Rural Transformation,* and *The Politics of Pluralism.*

Remi Clignet—Professor of Sociology at Northwestern University. His principal publications are *Many Wives, Many Powers: Authority and Power in Polygynous Families, The Fortunate Few: A Study of Secondary Students in the Ivory Coast,* and *Liberty and Equality in the Educational Process.*

Bernard Fonlon—Assistant Professor of African Literature at Cameroon University, and formerly Minister of Health, Minister of Transport, Posts, and Telecommunications, and Deputy Minister of Foreign Affairs in Cameroon. He was co-founder and subsequently director of the *Cameroon Bilingual Cultural Review, Abbia,* and studied at the University of Ireland, Oxford, and the Sorbonne.

Ayo Banjo—Senior Lecturer in English at the University of Ibadan. His principal publications are *Oral English* and *English in Action.*

William W. Neher—Dean of University College, Butler University and author of several conference papers and articles.

John C. Condon, Jr.—Associate Professor of Communication at International Christian University in Tokyo. He formerly taught at Northwestern University and is the author of several articles.

A. A. Mensah—Lecturer in Education, University of Cape Coast in Ghana and former head of the Music, Dance, and Drama Program at Makerere University in Uganda.

Donal B. Cruise O'Brien—Lecturer in Politics at the School of Oriental and African Studies, University of London. His principal publication is *The Mourides of Senegal: The Politics and Economic Organization of an Islamic Brotherhood.*

Victor T. LeVine—Professor of Political Science at Washington University in Saint Louis, and formerly Chairman of the Department of Political Science, University of Ghana. His principal publications are *The Cameroons from Mandate to Independence, Political Leadership in Africa,* and *The Cameroon Federal Republic.*

I. M. Lewis—Professor of Anthropology and Chairman of the Department of Anthropology at the London School of Economics and Political Science. Among his books are *Peoples of the Horn of Africa, A Pastoral Democracy,* and *The Modern History of Somaliland.*

Aidan Southall—Professor of Anthropology, University of Wisconsin at Madison, and formerly at Makerere University and Syracuse University, among others. His principal publications are *Alur Society, Townsmen in the Making,* and *Perspectives on Urban Anthropology.*

Introduction

The Problem: Subnational Loyalties in Africa and Their Threat to National Unity

In the decade since independence, most African states have made only modest progress toward consolidating the multitude of diverse and often discordant ethnic groups within their borders into stable national communities. Despite the commitment of most national leaders to instill a sense of national identity, the allegiance of a large portion of African peoples to particularistic ethnic groups still surpasses their loyalty to the national community. As a consequence, achievement of a greater degree of inter-ethnic accommodation and national integration constitutes the most critical political problem facing most African states today. President Julius Nyerere of Tanzania has stated that "if the present states [of Africa] are not to disintegrate it is essential that deliberate steps be taken to foster a feeling of nationhood. Otherwise our present multitude of small countries could break up into even smaller units—perhaps based on tribalism."[1]

The imploring faces of hungry Nigerian children reaching out from countless printed pages during the Nigerian civil war is the most stirring recent manifestation of ethnic friction and ensuing political disintegration. But similarly tragic situations have plagued other African countries. The insurrection of the Bantu and Nilotic peoples of southern Sudan against a government dominated by the Arabized northerners claimed up to a million lives and created virtual anarchy in the southern portion of the country for 15 years. Since achieving independence in 1962, Burundi has suffered from attempted coups, political assassinations, and even mass executions of Hutus as the result of conflicts between the politically dominant Tutsi minority and the Hutu majority. French troops fought alongside Chad soldiers to preserve the territorial integrity of that country in the face of a Toubou-led rebellion against the Sara-dominated government.

Although the worldwide politicization of primordial attachments in

3

recent times[2] has left even developed nations like the Soviet Union, Canada, Belgium, the United States, and Britain with rising ethnic tensions, the magnitude of the task of national unification in Africa is probably unequaled elsewhere in the world. Despite the relatively small populations of most African states (two-thirds of the countries of Sub-Saharan Africa have fewer than 5 million inhabitants), some contain more than 100 disparate ethnic groups. One indication of the extent of fragmentation in Africa is that one-half of the 2,000 languages of the world are indigenous to Africa, with more languages spoken per unit of population in Africa than in any comparable portion of the world. Only a few states, for example Somalia and Swaziland, have substantial cultural uniformity. The others face the problem of forging a sense of national accommodation and common citizenship amongst a large number of ethnic groups, whose languages, cultures, social and political institutions, and values differ significantly.

The artificiality of the political boundaries resulting from the European scramble for Africa in the late nineteenth century is well known to those familiar with Africa; national borders set by the colonial powers rarely followed geographic landmarks or reflected ethnic boundaries. Ethnic irredentism of groups attempting to overcome existing political divisions has sometimes caused internal conflict and created friction and occasional violence between states. The recent origins of many boundaries also complicate the task of forging a sense of unity. Effective national administrative amalgamation in British-controlled territories like Ghana, Nigeria, and Kenya occurred only after World War II, and the countries comprising French West Africa and French Equatorial Africa have only been governed as completely separate and distinct territorial entities since 1956. Somalia and Cameroon attained their present borders on the eve of independence through the incorporation of separate territories formerly under the control of two different colonial powers. Eritrea was joined with Ethiopia to constitute the present borders of that state in 1952, and Tanzania arose from the 1964 union of Tanganyika and Zanzibar subsequent to the independence of both.

Ethnic-based crises within African states may arise with greater frequency in the foreseeable future because, somewhat ironically, the processes of modernization tend to heighten ethnic awareness and in turn arouse ethnic tensions. Prior to the colonial period most ethnic groups — that is, communities bound together by felt ties of kinship or cultural similarity or both — and the numerous independent political units within them, lived in relative isolation. As these communities came into contact with a wide range of heterogeneous groups during the colonial era and particularly after independence, ethnic identification became more explicit.[3] Along with this intensified ethnic consciousness, ethnic boundaries have often been expanded to encompass larger populations simply because the small size of many traditional polities and ethnic groups made them ineffective units in the modern competition for economic amenities and political office. Some of the best-known large ethnic groups in Africa, like the Yoruba, Ibo, Sukuma, Kikuyu, and Kru people did not exist as self-conscious entities prior to the colonial period. The emergence of more comprehensive ethnic units does not, however, preclude the retention of more limited ethnic identifications.[4] For instance, in the face of certain competitive or threatening situations, all Yorubas may join in a united front, but under different circumstances the Oyo Yoruba and the Egba Yoruba can become competitors or even enemies.

The coming of independence aggravated ethnic competition and at the same time created a greater need for unity. National sovereignty at one stroke both eliminated the necessity of acting in concert against the colonial power and produced new national political prizes for which ethnic groups could compete.[5] Given their limited goals, colonial administrators could afford to neglect the promotion of a sense of national identity. Viable modern and independent states, however, require a certain minimum degree of cohesion and consensus.

Ethnic Identification

The preservation of some loyalty to particularistic groups is not necessarily incompatible with national integration. Ethnic loyalty and national integration do not represent two fixed and irreconcilable points on a continuum, for national identity is not an all-or-nothing proposition.[6] The experience of several nations, including the United States, Switzerland, and the Soviet Union, demonstrates that the maintenance of residual cultural values, attitudes, and commitments does not preclude the emergence of a strongly held national identity. National integration merely requires that identification with the national community supersede in certain situations more limited ethnic loyalties. National cohesion thus entails the development of an integrating strand among the networks of allegiances and commitments of the national community.

In several African states the ethnic situation is complicated by the special historical position of one dominant ethnic community. The historical ascendancy of the Amharas in Ethiopia, the Americo-Liberians in Liberia, the Tutsi in Burundi and Rwanda, and the Arabs in Zanzibar has significantly influenced the conditions of contemporary political and economic life in these countries. Colonial legacies also vested some newly independent states with one privileged community, like the Creoles in Sierra Leone, the Baganda in Uganda, and the Barotse in Zambia. The refusal of the once subordinate ethnic communities to continue to acquiesce to these unequal relations has already provoked violent changes of the political order in Rwanda, Zanzibar, and Uganda, and caused considerable instability in several other countries.

Primordial attachments also have a tendency to be mutually reinforcing in many African states so that ethnic boundaries often coincide with religious, linguistic, class, and sometimes racial distinctions. When government policy is predicated on maintaining these cleavages or penalizing minority communities, tensions are further exacerbated. The once desperate desire of the southern Sudanese to secede stemmed both from racial, religious, cultural, and economic differences between the two sections of the country and from the belief of the southerners that the more economically advanced and politically dominant Arabized northerners intended to acculturate them forcibly. South Africa represents the most extreme case of a nation not only rent by mutually reinforcing racial, cultural, and linguistic differences, but also of a government policy dedicated to the preservation of a racially and ethnically divided society. Ill-feeling between Africans and Asians in East Africa arises from their cultural, racial, linguistic, and religious differences, as well as from the economically and politically privileged position of the Asians prior to independence. Uganda's expulsion of most Asians has compounded intergroup tensions in East Africa as a whole.

Uneven patterns of development frequently follow ethnic boundaries so that significant economic and educational disparities exist between ethnic groups. Historical accidents in the siting of mission schools, together with culturally determined differences in receptivity to Western education, have propelled some ethnic groups far in advance of others. In 1970 in Nigeria, for instance, 80 percent of the eligible children attended primary school in the predominantly Ibo East Central State, while only 10 percent did so in the predominantly Hausa-Fulani Kano State.[7] Similarly, some ethnic groups have become relatively affluent because they were located near colonial administrative centers or had land suitable for cultivating cash crops introduced during the colonial period. To indicate the magnitude of disparities in some countries, in the Ivory Coast the per capita cash income in the long-established, eastern coffee-and-cocoa-growing areas is approximately five times that of northern farmers. Even when ecological differences are insignificant, cultural predispositions relating to entrepreneurial activity and adoption of innovations have led to economic advance for the more enterprising groups and relative stagnation for the others.[8]

When educational and economic advantages coincide so that one ethnic group or area within a country is significantly more developed, as in the case of the Baganda in Uganda, the less advanced groups often resent its achievements. An even more critical problem arises when the economically advantaged area refuses to share its wealth, as was the case with Katanga in the Congo in 1960. Instability also results when political power within a state is dissociated from economic ascendance, which occurred in Nigeria during the First Republic; the richer regions feared that the politically dominant poorer areas would force a redistribution of the wealth.

Aspects of Modernization Affecting National Integration

Virtually all the modern social forces impinging upon African nations, such as urbanization, the spread of education, economic growth, and social class formation, have implications for ethnic relations and the prospects for national integration. But the impact of these forces is usually sufficiently complex and multidimensional so that on one plane they contribute to improved ethnic relations while on another they aggravate ethnic tensions and conflict.

1. *Urbanization:* Analysts are inclined to look at Africa's growing urban centers as the great melting pots that will someday provide an environment conducive to the shedding of particularistic loyalties. The all-pervasive phenomenon of urban migration does lay potential groundwork for constructive social interaction across ethnic lines. The extent of ethnic mixing in Africa's cities is illustrated by Madina, a suburb of Accra, whose population of 2,000 speaks more than 80 different mother tongues. Urban residence, however, does not necessarily weaken primary ethnic allegiances. In many urban areas ethnic identification is sustained by the tendency for individual ethnic groups to live in self-segregated communities. The Ibos had their own residential area (*sabon gari*) in prewar Northern Nigeria, and the Hausa migrants to the south generally led secluded lives as well.

Rates of urbanization are generally too rapid to permit easy assimilation to new orientations and loyalties. Some cities have doubled in population over the past decade, and even those growing at more moderate rates are composed predominantly of first-generation residents. As a refuge from loneliness and other frustrations of urban life, newly arrived migrants tend to seek out members of their own ethnic groups and to organize themselves into associations based on their ethnic identity. Many of these associations maintain contact with their home communities in the rural areas, to which they make useful economic and social contributions. While playing this important role of forging urban-rural links and facilitating urban-rural communication, these associations also reinforce ethnic distinctions. Even when urban residents participate in social structures based on occupation and social class, they simultaneously retain these kinship networks for other purposes.

2. *Education:* In a continent where it is not unusual for governments to devote one-fourth of their budget to education and where universal primary education is the ambition of most countries, the commitment to education gives some observers the greatest ground for hope that Africa will be able to cope with its ethnic problems. Children who have passed through the educational system attain greater awareness of the world outside their own isolated communities and thus learn both about other groups in their country and about the world beyond. But, as discussed later in more detail, few African governments have consciously employed the educational system for purposes of fostering national unity and ethnic toleration. Moreover, it is the members of the educated elite who are in most direct economic and social competition with each other and are the most ethnically aware. One of Nigeria's leading intellectuals has described the educated Nigerian as the country's "worst pedlar of tribalism."9 Insofar as Christian denominational missions have controlled education in many countries and have usually concentrated their efforts in certain portions of the country, a tendency also exists for the educational system to create religious differences that in turn coincide with ethnic divisions.

3. *Economic Development:* Economic growth satisfies urges but it also whets appetites and increases competition. National economic integration with extensive links between the various ecological and ethnic sections of a nation can stimulate a sense of interdependence. But the different parts of a country rarely develop at a uniform pace, and regional discrepancies in both absolute economic terms and in rates of development probably provide the principal cause of regional and, in turn, ethnic conflict. Severely limited governmental resources mean that ethnic groups compete within the context of a "politics of scarcity" where the distribution of amenities or development to one area must of necessity deprive others. And economic competition can generate ethnic conflict. As Robert Melson and Howard Wolpe have described it, conflict and competition often produce "tribalism" rather than the reverse.10 Under such circumstances economic decisions have grave repercussions for ethnic harmony — as well as for development.

4. *Class Differentiation and Creation of National Interest Groups:* As Africa's economies grow and its educational systems expand, occupational differentiation occurs and socioeconomic classes develop. Though the devel-

opment of divisive class differences is something most countries try to minimize, divisions within a society based upon economic and occupational differences can to some extent serve a positive function in societies rent by ethnic divisions. To the extent that the new economic strata of a society bridge ethnic boundaries, they stimulate convergent self-interest among persons of divergent ethnic backgrounds, because in competitive situations an individual's self-interest may best be served by his joining forces with others in his socioeconomic group rather than with his ethnic brethren. Yet class formation can accentuate ethnic conflict when particular ethnic groups appear to dominate the upper economic strata, as the Kikuyu are coming to do in Kenya. In such instances class and ethnic divisions coincide rather than compete.[11]

Of more direct benefit in providing African societies with the kinds of multiple affiliations that can encourage inter-ethnic linkages are professional societies, farmers' organizations, and trade unions. At this point few are sufficiently strong to command firm allegiance, especially when ethnic considerations may be in competition,[12] but their steady development offers hope for the future. However, when a particular ethnic group dominates a trade union or professional society, or when ethnic conflict develops within such an organization, its potential contribution to societal strengthening is undermined. Examples of these two phenomena are the Nigerian Coal Miners' Union, which is basically an Ibo organization, and the Railway African Union (Uganda), which has been rent by internal conflict along ethnic lines.

5. *Development of National Governmental, Communication, and Trade Systems:* Less dramatic in their impact on ethnic relations but probably of greatest long-term benefit are the forces that begin to give even remote rural areas the sense that they are participating in a national system. The slow but steady penetration of central bureaucracies and governmental agencies to village level, the expansion of road systems and transportation networks that allow travel and movement of goods from one part of a country to another,[13] expanded distribution of national newspapers, wider use of transistor radios for listening to national stations, extended telecommunication networks, and television are giving people information not only about the state but about those living in other parts of it. All these forces encourage understanding of and sympathy for the problems and aspirations of different ethnic groups within a common border.

6. *Nationwide Cultural Patterns:* With increased communications and interaction among all parts of the country, national cultures slowly emerge. New forms of popular music and dance appeal broadly, even when the words for the music are in a language only spoken by people in one portion of the country. National holidays commemorating significant national events,

such as independence and the formation of a republic, become a part of this pan-ethnic culture. Forms of dress often spread from a particular ethnic group to the whole country, and in the same manner eating habits and recipes become national in character.

7. *Political Party Systems:* At the time of independence political parties seemed to offer the greatest hope for national cohesion based on cross-cutting affiliations,[14] but the illusion that African political parties were generally broadly mobilizing mass movements has been exploded; it is now clear that where multi-party situations exist most parties tend to have an ethnic base.[15] Moreover, politicians frequently capitalize on ethnic fears and sympathies. The most extreme case of ethnic-based party politics came at the time of independence in the Congo where many parties incorporated in their names reference to the ethnic group that provided their greatest support. The Nigerian federation came unstuck in part because the three major political parties were so closely tied to the three principal ethnic groups in the country.

Either one-party or military rule can give a facade of national unity, and in some cases, such as Tanzania, the appearance is more than a facade. Although the relative lack of ethnic conflict in Tanzania arises from several factors, the fact that the Tanganyika African National Union (TANU) Government has permitted competition for elective office without being subjected to the divisive pressures of full-scale party politics on an ethnic base has been significant. In Kenya on the other hand, the banning of the opposition Kenya Peoples Union was interpreted especially by its Luo supporters, as one more attempt by the Kikuyu-dominated ruling Kenya African National Union to further its own ethnic interests. If one-party rule is to succeed in containing conflict, cabinets must be carefully balanced in ethnic terms, and even top civil-service and military posts must be broadly distributed among the ethnic groups of the country. One reason for the instability of military rule in Dahomey has been the conflict within the army between northern and southern ethnic groups. On the other hand, military rule in Zaire has reduced ethnic conflict.

Action Programs to Encourage National Cohesion

Unfortunately, few African governments have fully exploited the mechanisms available to them to reduce tensions and promote national integration.[16] As the experience of other multi-ethnic states such as the Soviet

Union and the United States demonstrates, the development of a national community from heterogeneous ethnic groups can be facilitated through civic education, mass media, youth organizations, language policy, institutional arrangements and promotion of national ideologies and myths.

1. *Civic Education:* Despite massive outlays for education by most African governments, what has come to be called political socialization — or the use of the educational system to instill national identity and awareness in schoolchildren — has been largely neglected. Citizenship education including the civic ritual of singing the national anthem, exposure to national political leaders, and the study of other ethnic groups to increase toleration can significantly strengthen the fabric of national society. In their critical early years, schoolchildren can develop an emotional attachment to their country that will provide the foundation for the diffuse support necessary to maintain the nation in being.

While only limited use of the school system has thus far been made for this purpose in Africa, experiments with political socialization have been attempted with secondary and university students through the Young Pioneer movement in Kwame Nkrumah's Ghana, the National Service program in Tanzania, and the Ethiopian University Service in Ethiopia. A more recent experiment is Nigeria's Youth Corps, which, in addition to an intensive educational program to initiate new recruits, all of whom are university graduates, takes pains to see that members are posted to parts of Nigeria other than where they were born. In several countries the armed forces have been successful in indoctrinating young recruits to think in somewhat more national rather than in ethnic or more particularistic terms. The People's Educational Association and the Centre for Civic Education in Ghana represented attempts to offer adults citizenship training.

The failure to make greater use of the educational system to incubate national loyalty derives partially from the inherited colonial patterns of education. Education during the colonial period was predominantly a missionary undertaking and as such it stressed religion, character training, and academic subjects based on a European syllabus. As a consequence, effective use of the schools to inculcate national citizenship must await fundamental reforms in the structure and content of the educational system to make it more relevant to Africa. The inclination, even when reforms are being considered, is to look to Britain and France for models. The inappropriateness of these models for the study of civics in Africa derives from the fact that the British and French rely predominantly upon instruction in national history to impart a sense of national identity and pride to schoolchildren. In African countries, however, most history is particularistic and not national; it concerns the achievements of individual ethnic groups in precolonial times.

Some of the history texts currently in use in Africa present little more than a catalogue of tribal wars and conquests, hardly material likely to contribute to national cohesion.

2. *Achieving Regional Economic Parity:* Government efforts to encourage balanced economic and educational[17] development are essential if genuine national cohesion is to be fostered. Obviously, such an objective is not easy to attain because it usually involves spending the tax revenues collected in the wealthier portions of the country in the poorer sections, a process that rarely has the support of wealthier ethnic groups. Moreover, balanced development may necessitate sacrificing some national growth for the sake of regional growth because investments in the poorer sections of the country rarely yield the greatest returns. Unless an effort is made to achieve balanced growth, however, disparities in regional economic development will almost inevitably mean that certain ethnic groups within a country prosper while others feel themselves impoverished and neglected.

3. *Creating a National History, Culture, and Ideology:* As a result of the nonnational character of most African history, African states face the problem of choosing a suitable past. In an effort to forge a new national culture, some countries, like Mali, have chosen to glorify the achievements of ancient kingdoms or cultures that took place in only a portion of the present country. Other states, for example Uganda in respect to Buganda, have deemphasized the historical achievements of contemporary kingdoms for fear of stimulating divisive ethnic pride.

The struggle for independence gave most countries their first truly national heroes, who in turn came to represent symbolically a united nation.[18] Some of these heroes, like Nyerere of Tanzania and Kenneth Kaunda of Zambia, still effectively personify their countries' struggles for viability and cohesion. Other heroes of independence movements, like Nkrumah, had their reputations tarnished both by their own excesses and by their political opponents who have succeeded them in office. Still others have become too closely identified with a single ethnic group to be able to fully symbolize national unity. Even the venerable Emperor of Ethiopia, Haile Selassie, was seen by the Eritrean minority of that nation as a promoter of Amhara ascendancy.

An articulated ideology provides a framework for national cohesion in some countries, but this avenue has had only limited effectiveness in Africa. The ideologies expounded by the leaders of African states are usually broad and somewhat vague statements of principle or long-term objectives. Moreover, sophisticated philosophies like the humanism of Kaunda, the Negritude of Leopold Senghor, and the many versions of African socialism, at best inspire the educated elite.

4. *National Language Policy:* With the extreme linguistic fragmentation characteristic of the vast majority of African countries, language policy is a critical determinant of a country's ability to promote national unity. Even if other conditions were favorable for ethnic lines to become blurred and nations to coalesce, the overwhelming proportions of linguistic diversity in most nations create formidable obstacles to effective national communication and consensus formation. As many as 200 distinct languages, for example, are spoken in Nigeria, and in all of Sub-Saharan Africa only Somalia, Burundi, Swaziland, Lesotho, and Rwanda approach being monolingual states. The United States, Australia, the Soviet Union, and Indonesia have demonstrated the value of a country's promoting a common national language to foster communication, even if this language must be taught on a bilingual basis. Tanzania has adopted an East African language, Swahili, as its national language, and has benefited from the fact that Swahili constituted an effective lingua franca in Tanzania before it was selected as the national language. Obstacles elsewhere to the selection of an indigenous language are erected by the resistance on the part of most ethnic groups to accept as a national language the mother tongue of another group. Frequently no single indigenous language is spoken by even one-quarter of a country's population, and as a result most states still retain the language of their former colonial rulers as the national language, and some states, the Ivory Coast for one, vigorously promulgate the use of this European language.

5. *Balancing Political Power:* The distribution of political power has been recognized by most states as a key element in balancing pluralistic pressures against the need for national unity. The federal arrangement under which Nigeria gained independence was conceived as a means of satisfying the desires of the country's three largest ethnic groups to control their destinies while remaining part of a larger political unit. However, the almost perpetual stream of political crises during the life of the First Republic reflected the failure of the constitutional arrangements to distribute political power in an acceptable manner. At the national level the Northern Region was able to dominate at the expense of the Eastern and Western Regions, while within the regions the minority ethnic groups complained bitterly about the predominance of the larger ethnic communities. If the current division of Nigeria into twelve states had come earlier, it probably would have reduced political instability and forestalled the secessionist war.

Attempted solutions to these political problems usually reflect the political philosophies of key decision-makers. In his effort to deal with strong ethnic-regional affiliations in Ghana, President Nkrumah centralized power in Accra and undermined the authority and status of traditional rulers and decision-making bodies. Prime Minister Kofi Busia decided to try to decentralize governmental operations and decision-making as a means of placating traditional bodies and of assuring the country's ethnic groups that their interests would not be neglected. Thus two succeeding governments chose diametrically opposed approaches to achieving the same end, that of creating a viable and cohesive national unit.

Surpassing in significance the formulation and adoption of specific measures for the balancing of political power or the enhancement of national cohesion is the recognition of the deeply rooted character of ethnic identities and the necessity for nation-builders to come to terms with this fact. Though we are convinced that appropriate government initiatives can contribute to strengthening the national community, the most appropriate response in many situations will probably be the promotion of inter-ethnic reconciliation and equilibrium rather than an effort to obliterate ethnic distinctions and forge complete national unification. The institutionalization of various means for balancing political power among a state's constituent ethnic groups is part of what is required, along with sensitivity among government leaders regarding the implications for inter-ethnic relations of all government decision-making. The evolution of inter-ethnic equilibrium and commitment to a national community will not provide a panacea for Africa's complex developmental problems, but it could provide a more stable and viable context in which to approach them.[19]

In focusing this book on issues relating to national integration, we neither want to suggest that we consider the nation-state to be sacrosanct nor are we prepared to offer any simple definitions of what constitutes national integration. Use of the nation-state as the central unit of analysis reflects the present-day realities of African political life and contemporary African political philosophy. We by no means belittle the importance of dreams of pan-African unity or schemes for regional cooperation among African states. But the political problems of individual African states continue to hold center stage for most African leaders and political analysts. In discussing "national integration" we concern ourselves primarily with inter-ethnic relations, the viability of ethnically plural African states, and the interaction between ethnic and national identities. Beyond that, however, we hesitate to go because the kind of accommodation among the constituent ethnic groups that will provide the basis for the viability and functioning of one state may be quite different from the kind of national cohesion required or devised in another. Throughout this book we try to emphasize options and alternatives rather than ideal solutions, in recognition of the variety of national and ethnic configurations found in African states today.

In addressing the complex issues surrounding the search for national integration, we have employed four different rubrics. Part II discusses the constitutional, governmental, and political responses to the problems of ethnic pluralism in Africa. The four chapters in this section consider the following sorts of issues as they relate to national integration: the balance of political power, federalism versus centralization, the plurality of legal systems, the definition and concept of citizenship, political parties, political elite coalitions, military government, civic consciousness, and the impact of ethnic factors on interstate relations.

The three chapters in Part III consider the interconnections between education, economic development, and intergroup relations. Of particular concern are the tensions that result from disparities among ethnic groups in levels of economic status and educational achievement, and the extent to which these disparities can be rectified by state action. Two of the chapters in this part also discuss the role of the educational system in promoting political socialization for nation-building purposes and the inculcation by schools of intergroup tolerance.

Part IV, entitled Language Policy, Communications, and Culture, explores the issues of language policy and the mass media as facilitators of national communication. How can the multilingual states of Africa promote communication across language boundaries, and what language policies are best suited to achieving this goal? Two of the chapters in this section concentrate on the building of pan-ethnic national cultures and the utilization of the mass media to convey nation-building messages.

The final section contains an assessment of the current state of national integration in four African states, directing attention to both the idiosyncratic and general features that characterize ethnic conflict and national integration in particular African states.

Notes

1. Julius Nyerere, *Freedom and Socialism* (London: Oxford University Press, 1968), p. 209. Immanuel Wallerstein has pointed out that "every African nation, large or small, has its Katanga. Once the logic of secession is admitted, there is no end except in anarchy." Immanuel Wallerstein, *Africa: The Politics of Independence* (New York: Vintage Books, 1961), p. 88.
2. For discussions of this phenomenon see Samuel Huntington, Foreword to Eric A. Nordlinger, *Conflict Regulation in Divided Societies* (Cambridge: Center for International Affairs, Harvard University, 1972); and Walker

EDITORS' NOTE: In this and other introductory sections the editors have exercised restraint in citing sources because individual chapters offer extensive reviews of general and comparative sources.

Connor, "Nation-Building or Nation-Destroying," *World Politics,* Vol. 24, No. 3 (April 1972), pp. 319-335.

3. Clifford Geertz discusses this process in "The Integrative Revolution" in *Old Societies and New States,* ed. Geertz (New York: The Free Press, 1963), pp. 105-157. See also Abner Cohen, *Custom and Politics in Urban Africa: A Study of Hausa Migrants in Yoruba Towns* (Berkeley and Los Angeles: University of California Press, 1969), p. 1.

4. On the dynamics of ethnic identification see Fredrik Barth, Introduction, in *Ethnic Groups and Boundaries,* ed. Barth (Boston: Little Brown, 1969), pp. 9-38; Audrey C. Smock, *Ibo Politics* (Cambridge: Harvard University Press, 1971), pp. 4-7; and P. H. Gulliver, Introduction in *Tradition and Transition in East Africa,* ed. Gulliver (London: Routledge and Kegan Paul, 1969), p. 15.

5. The interconnections between modernization and ethnic competition are analyzed by Robert Bates in "Ethnicity and Modernization in Contemporary Africa," Social Science Working Paper 16; Pasadena: California Institute of Technology, November 1972.

6. According to Ronald Cohen and John Middleton: "We can view the plural society as having some degree of identity and meaning for all its members while subparts have theirs as well." [Introduction in *From Tribe to Nation in Africa,* ed. Cohen and Middleton (Scranton: Chandler, 1970), p. 9.]

7. Official statistics provided by the state governments.

8. Robert LeVine has written a controversial analysis of differential achievement motivation among Nigeria's major ethnic groups in his *Dreams and Deeds* (Chicago: University of Chicago Press, 1966). Abner Cohen among others has disputed LeVine's findings and interpretations in Abner Cohen, op. cit., pp. 188-189.

9. Gulliver, op. cit., p. 18.

10. Robert Melson and Howard Wolpe, Preface in *Nigeria: Modernization and the Politics of Communalism,* ed. Melson and Wolpe (East Lansing: Michigan State University Press, 1971), p. vii.

11. For a discussion of the frequent mutual reinforcement between class' and ethnic divisions, see James S. Coleman and Carl G. Rosberg, Jr., Conclusions in *Political Parties and National Integration in Tropical Africa,* ed. Coleman and Rosberg, Jr. (Berkeley and Los Angeles: University of California Press, 1964), pp. 690-691.

12. Nordlinger casts doubts on theories of integration based primarily upon the development of cross-cutting affiliations, arguing that the cross-cutting ties tend to be too weak to have much influence on behavior. (Nordlinger, *Conflict Regulation,* p. 96).

13. For elaboration of this idea see Edward Soja, "Transaction Flow Analysis and Political Integration in East Africa" (Paper delivered at the Association of American Geographers Annual Meeting, April 1967); and Ali A. Mazrui, *Cultural Engineering and Nation-Building* (Evanston: Northwestern University Press, 1972), pp. 280-282.

14. Immanuel Wallerstein, for instance, cited a nationalist party as the "most important mechanism to reduce the conflict between ethnicity and national integration." Wallerstein, "Ethnicity and National Integration in West Africa," in *Africa: Social Problems of Change and Conflict,* ed. Pierre L. Van den Berghe (San Francisco: Chandler, 1965), p. 482.

15. Aristide R. Zolberg, *Creating Political Order* (Chicago: Rand McNally, 1966), pp. 19-27; and W.J.M. MacKenzie and Kenneth E. Robinson, eds., *Five Elections in Africa* (Oxford: Clarendon Press, 1960).

16. See Gulliver, op. cit, p. 6.

17. Donald Morrison and Hugh Stevenson have demonstrated the interconnection between elite stability and intergroup balance in access to education. [Morrison and Stevenson, "Integration and Instability: Patterns of African Political Development," *The American Political Science Review,* Vol. 66, No. 3 (September 1972), p. 925.]

18. For discussions of charisma in relation to national integration see Claude Ake, *A Theory of Political Integration* (Homewood, Ill.: Dorsey Press, 1967), pp. 51-66; and David Apter, *Ghana in Transition,* 2nd ed. (New York: Atheneum, 1963), pp. 305-313.

19. It is well, however, for non-Africans to recall the following words of Aristide Zolberg addressed to an American audience: "That not all the rulers of Black Africa, whether civilians or men in uniform, possess the wisdom and skill to devise equitable solutions to the problems of political life in ethnically and racially heterogeneous societies is something which we, of all people, should understand." [Aristide Zolberg, "Tribalism Through Corrective Lenses," *Foreign Affairs,* Vol. 51, No. 4 (July 1973), p. 739.]

Government and Politics

Introduction

THE LEADERS OF African states face numerous dilemmas in trying to promote national integration. How do they construct governmental systems that will satisfy the desire of the state's constituent ethnic groups to have some control over their own destinies and well-being and at the same time meet the state's need for order and unity?[1] How far can a state go in seeking reconciliation, conflict resolution, and balance among its ethnic groups without paralyzing its efforts to promote economic and social development? If inter-ethnic consensus must be achieved before decisive government action is possible, can energetic development programs be formulated and implemented? On the other hand, can a state remain viable without institutionalized mechanisms for achieving equilibrium among its ethnic groups?

Some leaders have believed that political mobilization is the essential means of promoting national unity. Their aim is not merely peaceful coexistence among the state's ethnic groups, but ethnic homogenization. When Kwame Nkrumah in Ghana and Sekou Touré in Guinea eschewed federalism, undermined the authority of the chiefs, created a one-party state, organized the party on the basis of functionally defined subunits rather than ethnically defined ones, and by other means sought political mobilization, they were not only motivated by a desire for governmental effectiveness but also by the hope that they could thereby substantially reduce the salience of ethnic distinctions or even obliterate these societal divisions. They envisaged the political system serving as a melting pot and promoting an overarching sense of national identity.[2]

The critics of this approach point to the likely costs. This variety of mobilization usually entails loss of certain freedoms and the absence of open political competition. More fundamentally, given the tenacity of ethnic identities and the inevitable role they will continue to play in the political process, the question arises as to whether any effort at achieving homogenization is realistic. In his recent discussion of this issue, Eric Nordlinger contends that it is fruitless and even dangerous for government leaders in plural societies to vigorously attempt to inculcate a national identity. By Nordlinger's reckoning, plural states can only remain viable if their leaders emphasize conflict regulation and concession rather than mobilization.[3] Arend Lijphart's concept of consociational democracy calls for the formulation of nondivisive and accommodative solutions to most political issues facing plural societies, while recognizing the necessity of transcending cleavage lines on some critical occasions.[4]

Ali Mazrui is undoubtedly correct when he asserts that national integration necessitates both some depluralizing of society and the simultaneous establishment of mechanisms for intergroup conflict resolution — in other words, some homogenization but also accommodation to group differences.[5] Some concessions to the ethnically plural character of African states seems essential if their political systems are to remain viable. Only within a context of communal peace can national cohesion be enhanced and national integration proceed.

All those states that have attempted to promote homogenization have also made some concessions to the intergroup accommodation model, and the states at the other end of the continuum have expressed some interest in promoting depluralization. Wide variation, however, is evident in terms of the relative importance accorded these divergent approaches Naturally the most suitable approach for one state will not necessarily be the most suitable for another, and any prescriptions must explicitly recognize the wide variation of national and ethnic configurations found in Africa. But this variety of pluralisms does not imply that experience is not transferable and that states cannot learn from one another's experiments. The following chapters exemplify the extent to which most African states continue to experiment and agonize over what the proper mix should be between depluralization and conflict resolution.

In many respects the most logical response to pressures within a state for pluralistic autonomy is the federal system. Some African states, most notably Nigeria, have adopted federal systems, whereas several others continue to grapple with the problem of whether it is better to achieve a greater sense of local involvement and commitment to the state through the decentralization of power to ethno-provincial levels or to maintain centralized decision-making in order to avoid whetting even further the appetite for regional-ethnic autonomy. Billy Dudley demonstrates in his chapter some of the weaknesses and seeds of instability inherent in Nigeria's prewar federal system. But he asserts that the present 12-state system offers the potentiality for the conversion of Nigeria into what he terms an "amalgamated community." The 12-state system encourages the development of additional elite groups, thereby offering more possible combinations of elite coalitions, which could provide the basis for greater stability and intergroup accommodation.

The mere adoption of a federal system does not, however, necessarily assure the successful management of intergroup conflict; a federal system can generate more problems than it resolves.[6] In his chapter Abiola Ojo gives a historical account of the difficulties Nigeria has faced in working out a suitable and broadly acceptable division of power between the center and the states. Moreover, the granting of some autonomy to ethnically defined states does not substantially reduce the sharpness of ethnic competition for political control of the center. Ojo also describes the sharpness of conflict between majority and minority ethnic groups within individual Nigerian states; no matter how many states are created, minority ethnic groups will probably exert pressure within each state for the creation of additional states. Finally, one of the most persistent problems Nigeria has faced in operating its federal system is that of revenue allocation, with conflict between the poorer ethnic states who strive to have central revenue divided primarily on the basis of need, and the richer states who want to retain their wealth for their own development.

Although the respective merits and shortcomings of multi-party democracies, one-party states, and military rule range far beyond their import for national integration and inter-ethnic relations, the adoption of one or another of these forms of government has important implications for national unity as well. The multi-party parliamentary democracies that almost universally prevailed in African states at the time they attained their independence very frequently gave rise to intense ethnic conflict in the political arena, with party support frequently being heavily influenced by ethnic identity. In recognition of the divisive impact this phenomenon had on African states in the 1960s, Arthur Lewis advocated multi-party coalition cabinets as a means of assuring multi-ethnic leadership.[7] States face the dilemma of whether to opt for participatory democracy with its attendant difficulties for ethnic relations, or to impose more closed one-party or military systems, which limit ethnically divisive political competition. The one-party state has been advocated not merely as a means of limiting competitive politics on an ethnic base, but also as an institutional mechanism for creating national unity.[8] Frequently, however, a one-party system reduces ethnic conflict only through limiting political participation and even through repression. Where one-party systems have permitted broad political participation, ethnic conflict often occurs within the party apparatus, merely transforming what had previously been interparty ethnic conflict into intraparty ethnic conflict. Similarly, military regimes can often effectively suppress certain types of ethnic conflict, but as Dudley points out in his chapter, the armed forces frequently face severe problems of ethnic fragmentation within themselves. In his chapter Mazrui cites the military in

Uganda as being subject to ethnic fission and concludes that for military regimes to manage a state effectively, they must instill greater civic and national consciousness within their own ranks.

There appears to be rather widespread agreement in African states that it is important to achieve some semblance of ethnic balance within cabinets or ruling military councils. Even Nkrumah and Touré, who generally avoided making concessions to ethnic identity, employed ethnic arithmetic in forming cabinets. Despite basic agreement on the principle, rarely are all the constituent ethnic groups in a state satisfied that they are adequately represented in any given cabinet or ruling council. Their disgruntlement results from three factors. First, some heads of state give only token expression to the principle of ethnic balance within cabinets. Second, given the fact that the political party or military groups that control a government are often composed disproportionately of members of a particular ethnic group, it may be difficult for those in control to find capable and popular cabinet members from other ethnic groups who would be prepared to join them and accept their leadership. Finally, even under the best of circumstances it is difficult to arrive at a formula for the distribution of cabinet posts that all ethnic groups will find equitable.

By contrast, the achievement of proportional ethnic representation in parliaments does not constitute a difficult problem in most African states. In the rural areas ethnic groups tend to be differentiated geographically; consequently, electoral districts are largely ethnically homogeneous and in turn the ethnic make-up of parliaments roughly reflects the ethnic composition of the total rural population. In urban areas the situation is not so simple; urban areas tend to be ethnically mixed, and with increased rates of urbanization proportional representation is not as automatically assured as it was in the past.

Some political leaders have tried to promote a national instead of an ethnic orientation in parliament and undermine the assumption that members of parliament are primarily expected to represent the interests of their own ethnic group. President Milton Obote introduced an electoral law in Uganda designed to force a candidate to stand for election in several districts, with his electoral success dependent upon his doing well not only in his home district but in distant and ethnically alien districts as well. President Nkrumah encouraged some of his Convention Peoples Party members to present themselves as candidates in districts composed primarily of persons from other ethnic groups. When Ghana changed to a one-party state, members of Parliament were chosen as much for the occupational and other functional groupings they represented as for the ethno-geographic districts from which they came.

The plurality of traditional legal systems in most African states constitutes another sphere in which ethnic differences pose obstacles to national integration. The traditional laws governing land tenure, marriage, divorce, inheritance, and succession frequently differed from group to group, and most African states continue to accept the validity of these conflicting laws. The traditional diversity has usually been complicated by the adoption during the colonial period of British, French, or Belgian laws covering the same issues. As Ojo explains, the Nigerian approach to this diversity of legal systems has been primarily one of tolerance, displaying a preparedness to accept a plurality of systems even though this acceptance at times entails conflict between systems. The Ivory Coast, on the other hand, has adopted a unified civil code based largely on the French model, one that at least theoretically eliminates all diversity and conflict. Tanzania has tried to formulate a unified law governing the issues of land tenure and personal status by collating the common elements in the customary laws of the country's constituent ethnic groups.

Civil-service recruitment poses another type of problem for Africa's ethnically fragmented states. Most states have foregone the adoption of ethnic quotas in civil-service recruitment, but this eschewal has had the consequence of creating severe ethnic imbalances. Ethnic groups that are less modernized and less educated are at a serious disadvantage in terms of obtaining government employment, particularly higher level posts. Because the government is frequently the largest employer in these states, the underrepresentation of certain ethnic groups in the civil service means that they are severely disadvantaged economically. Furthermore, underrepresentation of certain groups in the higher echelons of the civil service can mean that their interests are not forcefully enough articulated — or that they are entirely neglected. Yet, as Ojo points out, the imposition of ethnic quotas carries with it inherent difficulties, not the least of which is that the quality of personnel must frequently be sacrificed if equity is sought.

Bolaji Akinyemi's chapter explores the implications of Nigeria's ethnic fragmentation in her relations with neighboring states. Internal ethnic conflict has several potential consequences for a state's external relations, and Akinyemi explores several of these in the case of Nigeria. The division of one ethnic group between two states, such as that of the Ewes between Togo and Ghana and the division of the Somalis between Kenya, Somalia, and Ethiopia, can lead to irredentist movements, as it has in both these instances. In the case of Nigeria, however, the delicacy of internal ethnic relations necessitated Nigeria's maintaining friendly and accommodative relations with neighboring states in order to assure that these states did not disrupt the internal situation. It is not unreasonable to anticipate that some states plagued by internal dissension might pursue aggressive foreign policies to arouse a sense of shared national interest among the state's various ethnic groups, but this has rarely occurred in Africa. As Akinyemi does point out, however, now that Nigeria has achieved a more effective basis for the management of inter-ethnic relations through the 12-state system, it is becoming more active in foreign affairs and is being somewhat more assertive of its national interests.

Surpassing in importance all the specific approaches to the promotion of national integration discussed in this and subsequent chapters is change in the sphere of political culture and values. The growth of inter-group tolerance and the preparedness to make compromises in the interest of maintaining a national life together are essential ingredients for the long-term viability of any plural state. Mazrui, in his chapter, explores the related subject of civic consciousness and the character of citizenship in the modern African state. He contends that one troublesome obstacle to national integration and to the development of modern states in Africa is the lingering (often unconscious) belief among many Africans that kinship and blood ties are the only legitimate bases for group membership — a concept that needs radical revision if the modern nation-state is to thrive in Africa.

Notes

1. This question is explored in Howard Wolpe and Robert Melson's Preface in *Nigeria: Modernization and the Politics of Communalism,* ed. Melson and Wolpe (East Lansing: Michigan State University Press, 1971).
2. For discussions of their respective approaches to political mobilization see David Apter, *Ghana in Transition,* 2nd ed. (New York: Atheneum, 1963); and Rupert Emerson, "Parties and National Integration in Africa," in *Political Parties and Political Development,* ed. Joseph La Palombara and Myron Weiner (Princeton: Princeton University Press, 1966), pp. 275-280.
3. Eric A. Nordlinger, *Conflict Regulation in Divided Societies* (Cambridge: Center for International Affairs, Harvard University, 1972).
4. Arend Lijphart, "Consociational Democracy," *World Politics,* Vol. 21, No. 2 (January 1969), pp. 207-225. Lijphart's approach is what Milton Esman terms balanced pluralism; the other five formulas for managing communal conflict enumerated by Esman are: institutionalized dominance; induced assimilation; syncretic integration; territorial autonomy; and legal/cultural autonomy. Milton Esman, "The Management of Communal Conflict," *Public Policy,* Vol. 21, No. 1 (Winter 1973), pp. 49-78.

5. Ali A. Mazrui, *Cultural Engineering and Nation-Building in East Africa* (Evanston: Northwestern University Press, 1972), pp. 283-288.

6. For a fuller discussion of the determinants of success of a federal system in a multi-ethnic polity, see Cynthia H. Enloe, *Ethnic Conflict and Political Development* (Boston: Little, Brown, 1973), pp. 89-107.

7. W. Arthur Lewis, *Politics in West Africa* (London: George Allen & Unwin, 1965), p. 83.

8. James Coleman and Carl Rosberg discuss what they see to be the value of the one-party approach to national integration in *Political Parties and National Integration in Tropical Africa*, ed. Coleman and Rosberg (Berkeley and Los Angeles: University of California Press, 1964), p. 691.

Chapter 1

Military Government and National Integration in Nigeria

by Billy J. Dudley

IT IS NOW commonplace to suggest that African states are highly pluralized and fractionalized. The societies within these states are split not only along ethnic and national lines, but also along religious, educational, and class dimensions. Confronted with crises of instability, the African states face the problem of how to create a viable state system. They face, in other words, the problem of how to achieve national integration.

A recent factor-analytic study of 32 African states has shown that instability within them can be categorized under three headings: elite, communal, and turmoil.[1] The study by Donald G. Morrison and Hugh M. Stevenson defines elite instability in terms of such events as plots, attempted coups, and coups d'états; communal instability is defined in terms of mutinies, civil wars, rebellions, irredentism, and declarations of protest; and turmoil. The authors of the study then showed the following relationship to hold between the three categories of instability during two time periods (Table 1-1).

From the table Morrison and Stevenson judged "that elite instability is very likely to recur in the African states, and that the incidence of plots, coups and attempted [coups] in 1960-64 is highly related to the incidence of those events for the period 1965-69. . . . The incidence of turmoil and communal instability in one period," they continued, "is likewise related to the incidence of the same forms of instability in the following period. [And] it is also clear, reading across the rows, that each type of instability is more likely to be repeated than to predict to another form of instability, [though],

TABLE 1-1 *Relationships between Types of Political Instability in Africa: Cross-lagged Correlations between Representative Indicators*

	SUMMARY INDICES FOR 1965-69		
SUMMARY INDICES FOR 1960-64	Turmoil	Elite instability	Communal instability
Turmoil	.53	.43	.25
Elite Instability	.73	.97	.40
Communal Instability	.39	.16	.47

SOURCE: "Political Instability in Independent Black Africa: More Dimensions of Conflict Behavior Within Nations," by D. G. Morrison and H. M. Stevenson reprinted from the *Journal of Conflict Resolution* 15 (Sept. 1971), table 8, p. 365 by permission of Sage Publications, Inc.

there are nonetheless some possible indications of the direction of diffusion effects. . . ."[2]

Though some writers, like D. E. Apter, would like to see the problem of instability as one of "modernization,"[3] we cannot really talk of modernization in any significant way in the absence of national integration. In fact, what the historical experience of African states has shown is that the modernizing process only serves as a catalyst for instability. When, however, we talk of national integration, it is often not clear how that concept is to be interpreted. Theories of nationalism and national unification, political development and nation-building, stability and federalism have all too frequently been subsumed under the general notion of national integration.[4] Sometimes, integration has been taken as an independent or intervening variable in the explanation of other dependent variables — for example, in some theories of political stability. Yet others have used the concept of integration as a dependent variable that is to be explained in terms of other independent variables. With such variations of usage, some preliminary attempt to explain what is meant by integration would seem to be called for.

Integration: Concept and Strategies

The literature on integration is replete with different definitions of the term. Thus James Coleman and Carl Rosberg define it as the "progressive reduction of cultural and regional tensions and discontinuities . . . in the process of creating a homogeneous political community."[5] For Leonard Binder, integration involves the creation of "a cultural-ideological consensus of a very high degree of comprehensiveness."[6] On the other hand, Amitai Etzioni has argued that a community is integrated when "(a) it has effective control over the use of the means of violence; (b) it has a center of decision making capable of affecting significantly the allocations of resources and rewards; [and] (c) it is a dominant focus of political identification for a large majority of politically aware citizens."[7] The list of definitions could be extended. Indeed, Myron Weiner has distinguished five different senses in which the term can be used: territorial, national, elite-mass, value, and behavioral.[8] Little purpose would be served, however, in expanding the typology.

Just as the definitions of integration vary, so do the proposed strategies for achieving it. E. H. Haas and P. C. Schmitter, for example, have suggested that the primary requisite for integration is that the political actors involved in the process behave rationally—rational behavior being defined as that which seeks to maximize the payoffs to individual participants.[9] This is the "free market model" which assumes that provided individual actors behave "rationally" not only will the individual's welfare be maximized, but the collective welfare will also be maximized since the gains and losses will cancel each other out leaving the collectivity better off. It was by such pragmatic calculations that the uniting of Europe (i.e., the Common Market) was brought about, Haas argues. As he puts it, in Europe, "self interest among governments and private groups has sufficed to weave webs and expectations of interdependence and mutual benefits."[10]

Because Haas's theory is set in the context of the integration of independent states, the question arises regarding its applicability to communities within a given nation-state. Once we see that different communities—as analogues of Haas's states—can coexist within the present states of Africa (in Nigeria, for example, there are supposedly more than 200 such communities), then it becomes patent that his argument can be generalized. Haas, in fact, saw himself as putting forward a generalized theory of integration, one that can be made applicable to any specific level of analysis if different values are substituted for the variable in his theory.

This is brought out quite clearly in Karl Deutsch's theory on political communities. Starting from the experimentally demonstrable fact that the greater the transactional exchanges between members of a group the greater the cohesiveness of the group, Deutsch has proposed a communications-transactional theory of integration, the essence of which is the suggestion that an intensive pattern of communication between national or communal units will result in a closer community, or what Deutsch prefers to call a "security community."[11] The underlying hypothesis that informs this theory can be put quite simply: given some balance between "loads" and capabilities of differing communities, if the rate of communications between groups within a community increases, an increase in elite responsiveness will result; and if elite responsiveness increases, then a security community will arise.

Deutsch defines a security community as one that attains a sense of unity "accompanied by formal and informal institutions and practices, sufficiently strong and widespread to assure peaceful change among members."[12] Hence, if an integrated community is desired, ways should be sought in which to increase the flow of transactional exchanges between and amongst its members.

A number of difficulties are inherent in the strategies proposed by Haas and Deutsch. In Haas, there exists an inferential jump in the postulation that the pursuit of individual rational calculations, as defined, will automatically lead to the creation of an integrated community. In fact, it can be shown, on game-theory grounds — using, for example, theorems deriving from the "Prisoner's Dilemma" — that far from such a rational calculus leading to the "members" being better off, both the members and the collectivity would actually be worse off.[13] If an integrated community is to be taken as a goal, therefore, the least desired strategy for achieving it would be the one proposed by Haas. As Mancur Olson has shown, an integrated community cannot be formed unless there are side benefits that accrue to the members and that are independent of the specific payoffs desired by the individual members.[14] From the experience of Nigeria, it can be demonstrated that it was the elite's pursuit of strategies like those suggested by Haas that all but led to the disintegration of the Nigerian federation.[15]

The difficulty with the Deutsch model is that it assumes we can talk of transactions independent of the perceptions and motivations of transacting actors. In putting forward his model, Deutsch did in fact add a number of postulates regarding such factors as trust, responsiveness, and complementarity, but he left unexplained when and how trust and responsiveness among the actors are to occur. As Haas, in a criticism of Deutsch, put it, "it is as if theorists of the balance of power need only worry about the application of the principles of mechanics to international politics and need not worry about how foreign ministers perceive themselves in this supergame."[16]

Unlike the authors of the two models we have considered, Coleman and Rosberg in their mammoth *Political Parties and National Integration in Tropical Africa* have put forward a much more limited strategy. Their strategy involves, first, the bridging of what they call an "elite-mass" gap, and secondly, the forging of what they term "territorial integration." The elite-mass gap, the gap between the modernizing political elite and the traditional mass, is, according to Coleman and Rosberg, "generic to the Afro-Asian world. . .[and] it is the core of the issue of national integration in these states."[17] Once the gap is bridged, the result will be "the development of an integrated political process and a participant political culture."[18] By territorial integration, Coleman and Rosberg refer to the problem that "stems from the persistence—indeed, the paramountcy—of 'primordial' attachments or ties."[19] In their analysis, however, little is said about how territorial integration is to be achieved other than the implied suggestion that the bridging of the elite-mass gap in itself will cause the primordial ties to be transcended. One is therefore left with what is, essentially, a single strategy.

In a way, this argument takes us back to the writings of Aristotle, Bentham, the elder Mill and even Hegel. For in the works of these authors are to be found suggestions that for social stability and integration to be maintained, it is necessary to create a sizable middle-class capable of mediating the conflicting interests between the elite and the masses. In this sense, then, the strategy proposed by Coleman and Rosberg — and it is also to be found in Leonard Binder and Edward Shils — has a long and respectable lineage. But in Aristotle and his followers, the prescription presupposes a homogeneous political culture, which, of course, is lacking in the new states of Africa. When Coleman and Rosberg talk of a "modernizing elite" and the "traditional mass" they are in fact assuming that both are relatively homogeneous groups. But, oddly enough, at hardly any point do they attempt to define what they mean by the elite. However, if we employ the term "elite" in a statistical sense,[20] to refer to those who enjoy more than a proportionate share of the distribution of wealth, power, and status in a society, then it becomes obvious that the term has recognizable referents. (Some writers have questioned the descriptive use of the term in African contexts.) So used, it is readily seen that in talking about the elite, the term should more appropriately be preceded by suitable adjectival prefixes that describe the existence of congeries of elites: economic, political, traditional, bureaucratic, and so on. There is little evidence to suggest that these groups have any sense of corporate being, and to talk of them as a "modernizing political elite" is seriously misleading indeed. A similar argument applies with reference to the use of the term "the traditional mass." If we cannot assume that the elite constitutes a homogeneous group in Africa, then little is left to be said for the prescription by Coleman and Rosberg, for as S. P. Huntington has noted, "if the elite divides among itself, its factions appeal to the masses for support. This produces rapid mobilization of the masses into politics at the same time that it destroys whatever consensus previously existed among the politically active on the need for modernization."[21] In other words, if the elite is divided and its factions are able to mobilize support among the masses, the mass itself is also not a homogeneous—or traditional—group. Moreover, the rapid mobilization of the masses, says Huntington, without a concomitant institutionalization of processes and structures, far from creating stability and integration leads instead to political decay and malintegration.

Though Huntington's thesis is not devoid of difficulties, his formulation does provide a possible alternative strategy to the question of integration in the new African states. Deutsch's definition of a "security community," it will be recalled, is in terms of minimal consensual ties holding a group together; his notion of an "amalgamated community" is hardly different from what Etzioni has defined as an "integrated community." Extending Deutsch's notion of a security community, we can describe the new states of Africa as "pluralistic security communities" — conglomerates of security communities within a given territorial unit. In these terms, we can then define the process of national integration as the conversion of a pluralistic security community into an amalgamated community.

From Huntington's thesis we can now suggest a possible model of a society capable of the conversion. We require for such a model only that there should be elite consensus and mass support for the elite. Such a model has been given the name "consociationalism" by Arend Lijphart[22] who stated that the "distinguishing feature of a consociational political system is the relative weakness of popular national sentiment and the overcoming of the weakness through the process of elite accommodation."[23] It is important to note that in this model, we do not require anything comparable to the "overarching comprehensive ideology" suggested by Binder, or the "symbolic outputs" of Gabriel Almond. The model accepts the existence in Africa of the relative weakness of popular national sentiment, and stipulates only that it is necessary and sufficient that there are processes within the society capable of effecting elite accommodation and that elite accommodation be reflected in mass support. We might also note that consociationalism fits the factor analytic findings of Morrison and Stevenson which were that:

> (1) turmoil, elite and communal instability are related types of violence in political systems; (2) turmoil is a localized response to the failure to achieve a significant redistribution of rewards in political systems which have experienced elite or communal instability; and (3) communal instability in Africa is a response on the part of communal groupings in national populations [i.e. our 'pluralistic security community'] to elite instability which either fails to bring about a reapportionment of ethnic representation in government, or which effects a too radical reapportionment.[24]

Instability, and hence malintegration, is thus a function of elite dissensus, the effect of which is magnified at the mass level.[25]

The radical or revolutionary activist might want to question our model of consociationalism and its built-in logic of elite consensus. He could argue that such a model merely preserves the status quo without attempting in any way to restructure the society. We can accept this argument and still point out that the incrementalism implied in the logic of accommodation is not incompatible with structural change in the society.[26] We can also accept the argument that the societies of the new African states belong to that class of societies which Durkheim called "segmentary societies," that is, societies characterized by the repetition of like aggregates in them. In this case, because we cannot logically predict what the unintended consequences of radical change would be, incrementalism and also its associated notion of accommodation constitute the only rational alternatives open to anyone concerned with the problem of national integration in these societies.

Elite consensus, we shall say, is possible when authoritative allocations are made by maximal coalitions. A coalition is maximal when it includes all possible winning coalitions in the society, and there is no winning coalition that is not a member of the maximal coalition. In other words, if S is the set of all possible winning coalitions, then the maximal coalition M is that coalition such that S is included in M.[27] The maximal coalition, by definition, is a winning coalition and it is characteristic of the maximal coalition that the value of the payoff to it is Pareto optimal. If it were not, then the disadvantaged member (S_i), would leave the maximal coalition and even though the other members would be better off, there would now be at least one member who would be worse off. Therefore, if a maximal coalition is to remain such, allocative decisions must be made in a way that no one member is left worse off. This would be the case, when, as a minimum condition, allocations are made in proportion to the relative size and bargaining skills of the different coalitions. Should the minimum condition be satisfied, we would expect the maximal coalition to hold together and the fact that the maximal coalition holds can be taken as evidence of a consensus amongst the members. By extension, given the minimal condition, the maximal coalition existing as a coalition would be sufficient grounds to expect that there would be mass support for the coalition.

It should be apparent that our consociational model is compatible with a variety of structural sociopolitical forms. It is compatible with the single-party state, provided the single party has a form structurally similar to the Mexican *Partido Revolucionario Institutional;* or with the multi-party system (with preferably some form of proportional representation). It is also compatible with a no-party state, the situation found in traditional societies —or even with a military regime where parties have been banned. It is, however, not compatible with the bi-party system where the two parties stand in counterposition and where governing takes on the characteristics of a zero-sum game; on conceptual grounds alone, such a system falls outside the domain of our model.

With the foregoing model in mind — one that takes in (the no-party) military regimes — we can now look at the integrative role of the military in one particular state: Nigeria.

The Military and the Integrative Process

In analyzing the literature on the army in the new African states, one cannot but be perplexed at the claims and counterclaims made on behalf of the military. One commentator, for example, seeing the military as an "agent of modernization," has suggested that in the underdeveloped countries it "can make a major contribution to strengthening essentially administrative functions" by producing skills not present elsewhere in the society, and that by recruiting the rising "middle classes" it can foster the development of a national consciousness.[28] As against this theory, it has also been argued that because of its conservative political outlook, the military has more often than not been an obstacle to political and social change rather than an agent of modernity and national cohesion.[29] Coleman and Belmont Brice have yet another approach:

> African states lack what many other states in the former colonial world had, an army which could be a modernizing and stabilizing source of organizational strength in society, a last stand-by reserve which could be called in, or could take over, to prevent external subversion or a total collapse of the political order.[30]

In the same strain, Aristide Zolberg has argued that African armies, far from being a model of hierarchical organization, are little more than "an assemblage of armed men who may or may not obey their officers"; they are not, says Zolberg, an institutional complex but more or less an armed rabble.[31] Fred Greene, however, claims that the armed forces of the African states were committed to modernity and to organization values incompatible with the value structure of the total society, a claim Zolberg would find meaningless.[32] Faced with such contradictory assertions, perhaps it is safer to examine a given situation involving the military and the issue of integration. We would then avoid making generalizations that cannot be ascertained, or be shown to hold true, beyond a given instance.

Civil-military relations in Nigeria typify what A. R. Luckham has called praetorian rule.[33] Luckham, who was following Rapoport, characterizes praetorianism, or the praetorian state, as a system in which (a) civil institutions are weak; (b) the coercive power of the military may be high or average; but (c) the organizational boundaries[34] of the military are fragmented. Civil institutions can be adjudged weak when (1) the allocative capability[35] of the state is low, which is true when effective para-political structures are able to compete with central institutions in the distribution of political (public) goods, and (2) "the degree of political mobilization, the extent of political communications and awareness of the government and the political issues surrounding it" are also minimal.

The military's coercive power is a function of a number of variables such as its size, its share of the national budget, its firepower. The pre-civil war military in Nigeria was an extremely small affair.[36] The total strength before the January 1966 coup was something on the order of 10,500. In terms of military/population ratio, the number in the military was about 1:5,500, which contrasted very favorably with countries like Sierra Leone, with a ratio of 1:2,500; Ghana, with 1:1,700, and Zaire, with 1:480.[37] Since the civil war, the size of the military has grown astronomically and now stands at approximately 250,000 to give a military/population ratio of 1:240. At that strength Nigeria has the largest number of men in uniform of all the states south of the Sahara. In fact, in terms of absolute numbers, Nigeria now has the second largest number of men in the armed forces in the whole of Africa, being second to Egypt with some 318,000 men.

Corresponding to the growth in size of the Nigerian military has been an increase in defense spending. Again, comparing the pre-civil war with the post-civil war patterns of expenditure, in 1965/66 total capital spending on the military amounted to no more than N£ 6.75 million (or 12.1 percent of the capital budget), whereas by 1970/71 it rose to something like N£ 100 million. On the recurrent budget, the government actually spent N£ 7.85 million (9.4 percent) on the military in 1965/66, and roughly N£ 129 million in 1971/72. All in all, the military accounted for approximately 35 percent of total federal government spending in 1971/72, or, expressed in terms of the gross national product, something like 5.6 percent of GNP. A comparison of Nigeria in terms of size and defense expenditure with certain other countries in Africa is shown in Table 1-2.

From Table 1-2 it is clear that Nigeria ranks third, after Egypt and South Africa, in terms of total defense spending. In terms of firepower, however, Nigeria is exceeded by all the North African states, South Africa, Ethiopia, the Sudan, and even Somalia, as a cursory glance at the Institute of Strategic Studies' *The Military Balance, 1971-72* will show. Even so, relative to the civil society, the Nigerian military has immense coercive power. As the experience of a number of African states has demonstrated, it requires little force to topple a government. But, perhaps, this circumstance is more a comment on the weakness of civil institutions than a reflection on the firepower of the military.

The notion of fragmented boundaries derives from thinking of the military in systemic terms, of regarding the military, institutionally, as a complex of elements that are related one to the other in a nonrandom

TABLE 1-2 *Armed Forces Size and Defense Expenditure of Some African Countries 1971/72*

Country	Total Population (million)	Armed Forces (000's)	Est. GNP ($billion) 1970	Est. Defense Expenditure ($million)
Sudan	16.0	37	1.83	133.0
Egypt	34.1	318	6.43	1,495.0
Zaire	21.3	46	1.9	84.0
Ethiopia	25.8	42.7	1.75	35.6
Ghana	9.0	18.6	2.57	44.4
Guinea	4.0	5.3	0.7	9.5
Ivory Coast	4.3	4.4	1.44	22.8
Kenya	11.5	7.1	1.58	24.5
Nigeria	62.0	252	9.1	243.6
Tanzania	13.6	11.1	1.1	26.6
Zambia	4.2	5.58	1.58	17.6
South Africa	20.5	44.2	17.6	442.4

SOURCE: Data from *The Military Balance 1971-72* (London: International Institute of Strategic Studies, 1971). Used with permission.

manner. The relatedness[38] then serves to demarcate one specific complex of elements — establishes the boundaries — from other complexes in the society, or the larger system. The boundaries of a given system may then be said to be fragmented to the extent that transactional exchanges between persons within the given system and the system's environment cannot be fully controlled by the key actors in the given system. The extent to which fragmentation occurs will obviously depend on such factors as the nature of the functions of the system, the nature of the socialization processes undergone by the actors, the skill and experience of the actors, and so on.

The Nigerian military was a product of the colonial inheritance; as such it was oriented more toward the maintenance of internal security than toward external defense. The military's self-image, however, tended to be that of protector against external aggression, which not infrequently caused it to resent being called upon to perform essentially internal security duties geared to keep politicians in power. For the six years of Nigeria's independent history before the civilian regime was overthrown, the military did little but help maintain the politicians in power, a situation hardly conducive to preserving its organizational boundaries. When, therefore, sections of the army intervened in January 1966, the surprise was not that they intervened at all, but that they waited so long before stepping in.

Though the role of the Nigerian army made it susceptible to inter-penetration by societal influence, the extent to which it was susceptible could have been minimized had military norms — such as the imperative to maintain the autonomy of the army — been sufficiently internalized. In other words, sources of cleavage and environmental factors contributing to boundary fragmentation have to be counterbalanced against possible cohesive forces, such as institutionalized norms of authority and command and the extent or degree of professionalism.[39] For the pre-civil war military, whose officer corps had been trained at such institutions as Sandhurst, Mons, and Eaton Hall, the degree of professionalism can be indicated by contrasting the experience levels of members of the officer corps with equivalent ranks from the civil bureaucracy and the police. Measuring experience levels in terms of years of service ranging from zero to 20 or more years, by the end of 1965 some 80 percent of those in the commissioned ranks of the military had had no more than four years' experience; by contrast, some 41 percent in the public service had had between five and seven years' experience. For the police, no less than 36 percent had been in service for nine years and more. These differences become more pronounced, particularly between the military and the public service, when other variables such as age and education are considered. Whereas 62 percent of the military fell within the age range of 20-24 years, the comparable figures for the civil bureaucracy and the police were 1 percent respectively. The contrasts in experience and age are shown in Table 1-3. In terms of education, 58 percent of the administrative class of the federal bureaucracy had a university degree, but 66 percent of the military (combat and noncombat officers) had no more than a secondary school education before being commissioned. In contrast with both, most of the police officers with the rank of Assistant Superintendent of Police and above (71 percent) rose from the ranks and had just a primary education. In the army (all officers) and the police (ASP and above) only 13 percent and 3 percent respectively had a university education.

It is highly unlikely that these characteristics will have changed significantly with the post-civil war military. In the first place, there was the considerable bloodletting in the two coups of January and July 1966, which resulted in the death of a large number of officers. Then to meet the demands of the civil war, a considerable number of noncommissioned officers were given commissions. As many of these had no previous formal education, or, at best, had only a primary education, it would be surprising if the educational level of the officer corps has risen in the interim. Even with the commissioning of NCOs, taking the normal average (for most African armies) of some 55 officers per battalion,[40] it has been estimated

TABLE 1-3 *Some Contrasts between the Military and other Services in Nigeria (in years)*

Variable	Measure	Military (Combat Officers) N=332	Police (Asst. Supt. and above) N=474	Federal Bureaucracy Admin. Class N=301
Experience	Median	2.4	4.2	6.5
	Mean	3.0	5.0	7.0
	Mode	2.0	2.0	7.0
Age	Median	23.6	41.2	33.8
	Mean	25.0	40.0	35.0
	Mode	22.0	42.0	32.0

SOURCE: Computed from data in Robin Luckham, *The Nigerian Military* (Cambridge: Cambridge University Press, 1971), pp. 96 and 98. Reprinted by permission.

that by 1974 Nigeria was to have produced only about 85 percent of the complement of officers it needed. In effect, by 1974 Nigeria was to have an officer corps with an average post-commission military experience of barely 18 months, a condition hardly conducive to the institutionalization of military norms.

If the level of professionalism in the pre-civil war military was not very high, the civil war did little to enhance it. Before the civil war, most officers had between 18 to 24 months of training before being commissioned. During the civil war, this period was shortened to 6 months. The situation with the other ranks was no different. For these, the training period was cut from between 6 and 9 months to a bare 2 weeks. However, the civil war did bring about one important result; it led to a broader class representation in the composition of the military, which now more accurately reflects the overall social composition of Nigeria. Nigeria's pre-civil war military has been likened to a three-layered cake, each layer representing a particular ethnic group. The top layer — the level of major and above — was made up largely of men of Yoruba and Ibo origin. In the middle layer — captains and lieutenants — the northerners predominated, men drawn almost equally from the far north and the Middle Belt; in the bottom layer — the "other ranks" — northerners, mainly men from the Middle Belt, were more in evidence. Before 1966, it was estimated that those from the Middle Belt formed about 75 percent of the other ranks. Whereas the structure of the top layer has not since been radically altered — though, of course, with the civil war and the coups fewer Ibos are to be seen at this level — a greater balance has been achieved in the middle and bottom layers.

Before the civil war there were perhaps not more than 600 men in the military ranks below lieutenant from the Yoruba-speaking areas. With the increased recruitment for the war, however, their number has grown, as Table 1-4 on recruitment at just one center, Abeokuta, shows.

TABLE 1-4 *Origin of Recruits into the Military: Nov. 1968-Dec. 1969 Abeokuta Center*

			STATE OF ORIGIN					
Date	Lagos	West	Mid-west	South-east	Rivers	North-ern Group of States	East Cen-tral	Total
Nov.'68	13	693	585	18	23	250	—	1,573
Dec.'68	50	478	327	16	18	357	4	1,250
Jan.'69	71	1,170	333	—	18	259	—	2,651
Feb.'69	9	386	33	—	23	123	—	574
Mar.'69	89	1,777	268	11	37	509	—	2,781
Apr.'69	29	651	98	8	8	212	—	1,006
May.'69	24	971	82	—	8	666	—	1,034
Jun.'69	58	1,137	177	1	35	316	—	1,724
Jul.'69	61	903	128	18	68	581	—	1,749
Aug.'69	48	1,027	76	3	38	501	—	1,673
Sep.'69	50	547	40	9	6	481	5	1,138
Oct.'69	32	534	57	12	5	399	4	1,043
Nov.'69	6	112	10	2	1	495	—	626
Dec.'69	47	546	126	54	10	366	—	1,148
TOTALS	557	10,932	3,240	152	278	5,535	13	20,707

Note: Recruits from the West and Lagos were Yoruba speaking.

The intake at the same center for the preceding year (August 1967-October 1968) was 27,820 men and showed roughly the same distribution. Though it might seem from the figures that more men from the West, primarily Yorubas, than other groups were recruited, it should be borne in mind that the data is for one center only. There were other recruiting centers at Zaria, Kaduna and Lagos, and for the states in the former Eastern Region recruiting took place in such places as Iguebe, Enugu, Calabar and Port Harcourt, where enlistment was carried out in such a manner as to even out the proportions between the different states.

If recruitment during the civil war did make the composition of the military bear a close correspondence to the relative distribution of population groupings in the society, the equilibrium so achieved is likely to carry with it certain costs. For one thing, proposals for demobilization and reorganization have not met with much success, largely, it is reported, because top military personnel are unable to agree on the basis for demobilization. Top personnel now see themselves in relation to the other ranks not unlike the way in which the politician sees himself with respect to his constituency. Put differently, the military hierarchy has become more or less a coalition (of interests), and like any coalition the payoff to the coalition leader is a function of his bargaining weight, that is, the size of the following. The outcome of this situation for discipline, command and control and military esprit de corps need hardly be spelled out. The Nigerian military does not fit Zolberg's description, an "armed rabble," but it certainly does not fit S. E. Finer's or Huntington's paradigm of the military either.

The above analysis of the Nigerian military provides a context within which we can now examine its role as it impinges on the integrative process. Earlier, we referred to Luckham's categorization of civil-military relations in Nigeria as praetorian. In such a system, as he put it,

> the military help civilian groups with which they have common interests into power and vice versa. . . . On the one hand, the military is a differentiated body with distinct group interests of its own, as well as those held in common with civilian groups. On the other hand, it acts like any other political elite, in pursuit of its own interests. It is prepared to cooperate with civilian groups to their mutual advantage, to trade off its own goals in return for support of other elites.[41]

These characteristics require elaboration and exemplification. We can examine very briefly, first, the role of the military during the regime of General J.T.U. Aguiyi Ironsi, and secondly, the military regime of General Yakubu Gowon.

The first military regime saw the integrative process in largely formalistic and symbolic terms. It reasoned that once the form of the "amalgamated community" is legislated into existence, the behavior that gives an ontological reality to the form should follow. It was in this spirit that the Ironsi regime abolished the federal structure and instituted in its place a unitary state. Elements from the bureaucratic-managerial elite were then recruited in an attempt at operationalizing the goal of the unitary state. In the process, the paradigm of managerial government was substituted for the politics of consensus and accommodation. The outcome was the alienation of those members of the elite who felt their interests were not sufficiently catered to. By communicating their own sense of deprivation to the mass, they succeeded in channeling the discontent thus created into withdrawal of support for the regime, thereby initiating the circular chain of turmoil-communal instability-elite instability-turmoil that finally ended in the civil war.

With the experience of the Ironsi regime before it, it was only to be expected that the successor regime of General Gowon would seek to reverse the policies initiated by the first military government. The decree establishing the unitary state was abrogated, and a 12-state federal system was created to replace the previous 4-region system. Not enough data exists as yet about the operation of the new 12-state system, and any judgment about it may be thought premature. Nevertheless, some claims could be made for the new system, if only on *a priori* grounds. If we liken the previous system to something of a 3-person game, we could by extension see the new structure in terms of a 12-person game. In the new structure, even if the strategies of play were to remain unaltered, we could still expect the 12-person game to be more perfectly competitive than the 3-person game. And by enlarging the possibilities of coalition formation, we could also expect the 12-person structure to be more stable than the 3-person game. Because coalition formation depends on the reciprocal expectations of coalition leaders, and because no one coalition likes to be left out of a winning coalition, we should expect in the 12-person game that attitudinal structuring would have wider possibilities and, therefore, that bargaining would be of the integrative variety.[42] In these circumstances, politics would take on the characteristics of a positive sum game and less of the zero-sum features that marked the political competition of the pre-intervention period. The 12-state system, consequently, should offer better prospects for the demands of competing elites being met than in the previous system and to the extent that they are met, then, in terms of our model, we would expect mass support for the regime and hence greater system stability.

Not only are elite demands more likely to be fulfilled under the new system, but the system itself, by broadening the base of political competition, should facilitate the emergence of new elites. Already the new states have established new bureaucracies, and with the greater opportunities thus offered a new bureaucratic elite has emerged to complement the old. The demand for more and better housing and other services by these elites has further spurred the growth of the contractor-business elite. Thus, more channels for demands are being created and new structures are emerging for the processing of demands. However, the capacity of the system to convert demands into outputs with adequate supportive effects is still to be determined. With a state of emergency and a decree banning strikes and lockouts still in force, the capability of the system to process demands must be regarded as indeterminate.

What we have discussed above are possibilities, not realities. The reality for the present is that, as indexed by the proportion of federal governmental spending allocated to the armed forces, the Nigerian military has become the dominant force in the society and the military elite has, by the same token, become the dominant elite. In most segments of Nigeria's society, competing elite demands have been subordinated to the demands of the military elite. Thus, these other elites — for example, the former political brokers and the top echelons of the intelligentsia — have become, in relation to the military, counter-elites. Admittedly, elements from the political elite and the intelligentsia have been recruited by the military into decisional roles. Essentially, however, it is the military that determines the goals of the society, and in the formulation of system goals, as a cursory analysis of present policies would show, the demands of the military have a prior claim in the allocation of resources. Translated into the terms of our model, in place of a maximal coalition, we have, in effect, a minimal winning coalition, and far from elite consensus, we have elite dissensus arising from the opposition between the military elite and the civilian counter-elite, though the opposition is as yet more latent than manifest.

Conclusion

Unlike the Mexican Army — to cite one example — that exploited the symbolism of the Mexican Revolution (civil war) for integrational and mobilizational ends, the Nigerian Army has been content since the civil war merely to carve out a privileged status for itself. The military appears to feel that Nigerian society owes it some kind of debt because it fought "to keep Nigeria one."[43] Thus, the military has tended to act in a way which suggests that whatever claims it makes cannot but be legitimate. Despite its hubris, however, the military has in the main equated its demands with the demands of the society and its goals with goals of the society. And for the military, the preeminent goal has become the preservation of the delicate balance of factions within the army.

The inflation in the size of the Nigerian Army necessitated by civil war brought with it both a lowering of the level of military professionalism and structural problems. Military leaders behaved more like political champions of factional groups rather than like members of a corporate, organic entity. In the uncertainty of the post-civil war period, the concern of the military with its internal coherence can easily be understood. But it is a concern that, while serving a utilitarian function with respect to the military, has resulted in an immobilization of Nigerian society. In the terminology of our model, this immobilization, in effect, means no more than maintaining the society as a "pluralistic security community." Though the predisposing conditions for the conversion of Nigeria into an "amalgamated community" may be said to have been instituted with the division of the country into 12 states, the structual incoherence of the military is such that it is unlikely to have the capacity to effect strategies required for the conversion. That task, it would now seem, must await the successors to the military.

Notes

1. Donald G. Morrison and Hugh M. Stevenson, "Political Instability in Independent Black Africa: More Dimensions of Conflict Behavior Within Nations," *Journal of Conflict Resolution,* Vol. 15, No. 3 (Sept. 1971), pp. 347-368.
2. Ibid., pp. 365.
3. See, for example, D.E. Apter, *The Politics of Modernization* (Chicago: Chicago University Press, 1965).
4. See the survey of the literature by Ernst H. Haas, "The Study of Regional Integration: Reflections on the Joy and Anguish of Pretheorizing" in ed. Leon N. Lindberg and Stuart B. Scheingold, *Regional Integration — Theory and Research* (Cambridge: Harvard University Press, 1971), pp. 3-42.
5. James S. Coleman and Carl G. Rosberg, eds., *Political Parties and National Integration in Tropical Africa* (Berkeley and Los Angeles: University of California Press, 1964), p. 9.
6. Leonard Binder, "National Integration and Political Development," *American Political Science Review,* Vol. 18, No. 3 (Sept. 1964), p. 630.
7. Amitai Etzioni, *Political Unification* (New York: Holt, Rhinehart & Winston, 1965), p. 4.
8. Myron Weiner, "Political Integration and Political Development" in ed. C.E. Welch, *Political Modernization* (Belmont, Calif.: Wadsworth Publishing Co., 1967), pp. 180-182.
9. E.H. Haas and P.C. Schmitter, "Economics and Differential Patterns of Integration: Projections about Unity in Latin America," *International Organization,* Vol. 18, No. 4 (Dec. 1964), pp. 711-719. Haas later qualified this to include an "ideological and philosophical commitment." See Haas, "The Uniting of Europe and the Uniting of Latin America," *Journal of Common Market Studies.* Vol. 5, No. 4 (Dec. 1967), pp. 327-328.
10. Haas, "Study of Regional Integration," op. cit., p. 13.
11. Karl Deutsch et al., *Political Community and the North Atlantic Area* (Princeton: Princeton University Press, 1957).
12. Ibid., pp. 5-7.
13. See, for example, W.G. Runciman and A.K. Sen, "Games, Justice and the

General Will," *Mind,* Vol. 74, No. 295 (April 1965). For an excellent review of the "Prisoner's Dilemma," see Anatol Rapoport, *Strategy and Conscience* (New York: Schocken Books, 1969), pp. 48-57.

14. Mancur Olson, Jr., *The Logic of Collective Action* (Cambridge: Harvard University Press, 1965).

15. See B.J. Dudley, *Instability and Political Order* (Ibadan: Ibadan University Press, 1973).

16. Haas, "Study of Regional Integration," op. cit., p. 23.

17. Coleman and Rosberg, op. cit., p. 686.

18. Ibid., p. 9.

19. Ibid., p. 687.

20. See the usage in Karl Deutsch, *An Analysis of International Relations* (Englewood Cliffs, N.J.: Prentice-Hall, 1968), pp. 63-64. On elites in general, Geraint Parry, *Political Elites* (London: George Allen & Unwin, 1969).

21. S.P. Huntington, "Political Development and Political Decay," *World Politics,* Vol. 17, No. 3 (Aug. 1967), p. 427.

22. Arend Lijphart, "Consociational Democracy," *World Politics,* Vol. 21, No. 1 (Feb. 1969), pp. 207-225; also, Lijphart, "Typologies of Democratic Systems," *Comparative Political Studies,* Vol. 1, No. 1 (March 1968), pp. 17-35.

23. Arend Lijphart, "Cultural Diversity and Political Integration," *Canadian Journal of Political Science,* Vol. 4, No. 1 (March 1971), pp. 1-14.

24. Morrison and Stevenson, op. cit., p. 366.

25. See Karl Deutsch, *The Nerves of Government* (New York: Free Press, 1963), pp. 192-194.

26. C.E. Lindblom and David Braybrooke, *A Strategy for Decision* (New York: Free Press, 1963).

27. George Kemeny and others differentiate between a "winning coalition" and a "minimal winning coalition" in *Introduction to Finite Mathematics* (Englewood Cliffs, N.J.: Prentice-Hall, 1966), pp. 79-80. It seems to me, however, that if we are to talk of a minimal winning coalition, then it makes sense equally to talk of a maximal winning coalition, which is a coalition of coalitions and a more inclusive coalition than a winning coalition.

28. L.W. Pye, "Armies in the Process of Modernization," in ed. J.J. Johnson, *The Role of the Military in Under-developed Countries,* (Princeton, N.J.: Princeton University Press, 1967), p. 89.

29. I.L. Horowitz, "The Military Elites" in *Elites in Latin America,* eds. S.M. Lipset and Aldo E. Solari (New York: Oxford University Press, 1967), pp. 151, 178-190. See also, S.P. Huntington, *Political Order in Changing Societies* (New Haven: Yale University Press, 1968), pp. 228-230.

30. J.S. Coleman and Belmont Brice, Jr., "The Role of the Military in Sub-Saharan Africa," in *Role of the Military,* op. cit., p. 359.

31. Aristide Zolberg, "The Structure of Political Conflict in the New States of Tropical Africa," *American Political Science Review,* Vol. 18, No. 1 (March 1968), pp. 70-87.

32. Fred Greene, "Toward Understanding Military Coups," *Africa Report,* Vol. 11, No.2 (February 1966), p. 10.

33. A.R. Luckham, "A Comparative Typology of Civil-Military Relations," *Government and Opposition,* Vol. 6, No. 1 (Winter 1971), pp. 5-35.

34. On the notion of system boundaries, see David Easton, *A Systems Analysis of Political Life* (Englewood Cliffs, N.J.: Prentice-Hall, 1965), pp. 25-26.

35. On "capabilities" see, G.A. Almond and Bingham Powell, *Comparative Politics, A Development Approach* (Boston: Little, Brown, 1966), pp. 190-212.

36. On the pre-civil war Nigerian military, see A.R. Luckham, *The Nigerian Military* (Cambridge: Cambridge University Press, 1971), and N.J. Miners, *The Nigerian Military, 1956-1966* (London: Methuen, 1971).

37. B.J. Dudley, "The Military and Development," *Nigerian Journal of Economics and Social Studies,* Vol. 13, No. 2 (July 1971), pp. 161-177.

38. For the notion that elements have to be related in a nonrandom way to form a "system," see M.A. Kaplan, *System and Process in International Relations* (New York: John Wiley, 1957), pp. 4-5.

39. S.P. Huntington, *The Soldier and the State* (Cambridge: Harvard University Press, 1957).

40. For a good account, see John Michael Lee, *African Armies and Civil Order* (London: Chatto and Windus, 1969).

41. Luckham, "A Comparative Typology of Civil-Military Relations," op. cit., p. 31.

42. On attitudinal structuring and integrative bargaining, see R.E. Walton and R.B. McKersie, *A Behavioral Theory of Labor Negotiations* (New York: McGraw-Hill, 1965).

43. Besides numerous other statements by top military personnel, see the announcement by the Army Chief of Staff, Major General David Ejoor, that servicemen who were in the forces during the civil war will be paid two months' salary for "leave" foregone during the war.

Chapter 2

Law and Government in Nigeria

by Abiola Ojo

National integration in Nigeria has proved a delicate and continuing process that broadly has involved the interplay of institutional and sociological forces. In more specific terms, it has witnessed the interaction of coercive (military), identitive (socio-psychological) and utilitarian (economic) factors. . . . The present level of integration of this community and the success of future attempts to accelerate integration will depend on the judicious use of any or several of these factors. . . .[1]

HARDLY DO ANY of the governors or the head of state make an important statement concerning Nigeria without emphasizing the need for national unity. Although in the past the need was recognized, greater emphasis is now given to integration because of the recent attempt to disintegrate the country. Prophecy may be a hazardous exercise in the fluid and ever-changing fields of law and government, but one may say that the continued survival of a Nigeria after military intrusions, which were further complicated by a bitter civil war, augurs well for the nation's future as an integrated and united whole.

The Precolonial Period (Pre-1862)

While it is appreciated that many factors—such as ethnic, educational, economic, and cultural divergencies, together with the sheer size of Nigeria — pose serious difficulties for integration and national unity, this is not to say that in precolonial times there had been no form of cooperation among the various societies now known as Nigeria. It is a falsification of history to emphasize war and conquest at the expense of the other more vital areas of cooperation and peaceful interrelationship among these societies.[2] An examination of the precolonial period of Nigerian history suggests that such peaceful contacts loomed larger than missionary stories of wars and conquest.[3] Though it is true that before 1914 there was no country called Nigeria, that fact does not mean that the various societies that have existed in this area do not have a history of interrelationship, which is generally considered necessary for knitting groups into a homogeneous whole. This intermingling of peoples throughout the area now known as Nigeria — brought about by slave trade, migrations, warfare, and peaceful trade relations — provides some basis for the forging of national unity in and beyond our own days.[4] Moreover, the physical features of the country — drainage system and vegetation zones — make it a single natural economic unit. Therefore, if British imperialism had not brought the inhabitants of the territory under one general government, some other social processes would have accomplished the same end.[5]

Indeed, every one of the great nations of today started as a mere geographical expression, and in time built upon its diverse cultures and ethnic strains to create its present peculiar national character.[6] No nation is completely homogeneous, either in its racial composition or in its cultural background. When Nigerians were struggling to become politically independent from Britain, they did not remember to fight as Ibos, Yorubas, or Hausa-Fulanis. Now that independence has been achieved, the lust for power, greed and personal aggrandizement have strengthened the myth of ethnic exclusiveness.

Integration in the Colonial and the Pre-Coup Period

In precolonial times, then, cooperation did exist before the arrival of the British between the societies living in the area that now constitutes Nigeria. It may be useful at this point to describe briefly the roles played by the British, taking into consideration the contributions of Nigerians themselves, in the search for national integration.

The Lagos Constitution (1862-1922) was the first of the colonial constitutions in Africa, and it was primarily an administrative instrument for the governance of the Lagos Colony. As the British further extended their jurisdiction over other areas of what is now Nigeria, the problem of holding together their territories had to be solved. In an effort to do so, the British created the two protectorates of Northern and Southern Nigeria on January

1, 1900. This division was arbitrary. It cut across peoples and cultures. For example, a substantial number of Yorubas were divided between the two areas. The two protectorates were "amalgamated" in 1914; the basic legal framework for the governance of this "unified" Nigeria was the Lugard Constitution of 1914-1922.[7] Again, this constitution was purely an instrument of colonial administration — then under the guidance of Sir Frederick (later Lord) Lugard. The Nigerian Council, the central institution created by this constitution was merely an advisory body.[8] The indirect-rule system initiated under the Lugard Constitution conceived of African institutions as local institutions that required a British administrative structure for their effective operation and rationalization. The native authorities thereby created were local institutions that affirmed existing cultural and ethnic diversities and not their reconciliation.[9] The result was not only uneven development among the various ethnic groups in Nigeria, but the isolation of the northern elements from the nationalist movement. Indeed, some practitioners of the indirect-rule system effectively discouraged inter-regional contacts and relations between the North and the South.[10]

Again, the next constitution, promulgated under Governor Sir Hugh Clifford, merely served the end of colonial administration.[11] The Clifford Constitution of 1922 further widened the gap between North and South because its jurisdiction was confined to the South and the North was ruled by proclamations issued by the governor-in-council. Although there were informal administrative links between the North and the South, in effect, the two areas were for the most part governed separately without any overriding common legal basis.[12] National integration or unity was not the aim of the Clifford Constitution.

The Richards Constitution of the mid-forties was the next constitution,[13] and it may be said that it provided the first instance in which serious thoughts were given to the problem of an integrated structure for Nigeria. In his proposals for constitutional development in Nigeria, Governor Sir Arthur Richards observed:

> The problem of Nigeria today is how to create a political system which is itself a present advance and contains the living possibility of further orderly advance — a system within which the diverse elements may progress at varying speeds, amicably and smoothly, towards a more closely integrated economic, social and political unity, without sacrificing the principles and ideals inherent in their divergent ways of life. The present system of government in Nigeria has many inconsistencies and by its nature is unsuited for expansion on a Nigerian basis. [14]

Accordingly, Governor Richards set forth three objectives in his constitutional proposals: first, to promote the unity of Nigeria; second, to provide adequately within that unity for the diverse elements which make up the country; and third, to secure greater participation by Nigerians in the discussion of their own affairs. In certain respects, the Richards Constitution had some impact on national integration and unity. It recognized that constitutional evolution in Nigeria must be conceived in the context of Nigeria's large size — more than three times as large as Italy — ethnic diversity, and uneven development. Its basic provisions pointed to the choice of federalism as a future constitutional and political guide for Nigeria. It also unified the dual system of government under the indirect-rule system into one stream by incorporating the native administration into the central government. Further, it created regions in place of provinces and through them linked the native authorities and other local institutions directly to the central government. The Richards Constitution thus attempted to create Nigeria-wide political relations on the basis of federation.

The 1951 Macpherson Constitution—Sir John Macpherson succeeded Richards—assumed the tripartite division of the country as under the 1946 Richards Constitution, but gave legislative powers to the hitherto purely advisory and deliberative regional councils.[15] It also provided for a list of legislative items on which the central government alone could act. The central government could also veto any regional law.[16] Under this constitution, only one Public Service Commission was provided for the whole country. The judiciary remained unified and the single Nigeria Police Force created on April 1, 1930, was retained. On the whole the government of the country was essentially unitary. Indeed, as one writer has appropriately remarked, "It would seem that in attempting to forge unity the 1951 Constitution had established a too closely-knit system of government."[17] Government under the 1951 Constitution, however, took a decisively new turn as the emphasis shifted from pure administration to politics. This trend started in the early forties with the growth of nationalist movements in the country. The Macpherson Constitution, unlike its predecessors, was drafted after consultation with people at various levels of society. Although federalism was the conscious choice of the people, the ultimate result of the consultation, as reflected in the constitution, was distorted to such an extent that it failed to represent a majority view.[18] The majority view would have required more states as constituent units of the federation than the three based on the largest ethnic groups — Hausa-Fulani, Ibo, and Yoruba.[19]

Another disintegrating feature of the 1951 Constitution was the relationship between the federal and regional executives. Each of the ruling parties in the three regions drew its strength from the majority ethnic group in the region. The electoral process for the federal legislators was such that the majority parties in the regions elected federal legislators from within themselves. And further still, no party or group of parties was designated as the government at the center. This process led to a delicate juxtaposition of antagonistic ethnic groups on the federal executive. Each group regarded itself as an agent of its ethnic base, and it was practically impossible to organize any concerted action at the federal level. In this circumstance, it needed only a fundamental point of disagreement to break the constitution. This point was provided by the split between the ruling party in the Eastern Nigeria Regional Legislature and executive and the central ministers.[20] Coupled with this conflict was disagreement over the date for independence.[21]

Viewed in the context of national integration and unity the 1951 Constitution was a failure. It failed to reflect the expressed wish of the people as to the type of federal structure they wanted. The arrangement whereby the representation of each unit at the center was based on population gave permanent ascendancy to the less developed North at the expense of the smaller but more developed East and West. Also the formula for determining the composition of the federal executive was too delicate to provide stability. And finally, its type of federalism was so centrally oriented that the regions had little influence over federal affairs. It was left to the 1954 Lyttelton Constitution[22] to make amends.

Under the Lyttelton Constitution — named after Colonial Secretary Sir Oliver Lyttelton — the federal structure defined by the 1951 Constitution was substantially retained but fuller recognition was given to the development of the regional government.[23] In providing for the shift of residual powers from the center to the regions, the constitution recognized and gave additional momentum to developing ethnic and regional forces, thereby helping to bridge the widening gap between institutions and popular sentiments.[24] But it also fostered the development of political parties in the regions around the major ethnic groups, and leaders in each region behaved as if government of each region must be controlled by the dominant group in the region. Political relations among the regions became sharply competitive; and appeals to tribalism were commonplace. Dual nationalism — ethnic and territorial — were freely called to service and convenience dictated priorities.[25] In reality, avowed macro-nationalism was used as a masquerade for the practice of micro- or ethnic-nationalism. The situation was further aggravated by acute imbalance in the levels of economic and educational development between the North and the South. The major problem in these circumstances was how to keep the country together. It was the shared desire for independence that saved the country from coming apart.

Certain other important events occurred before the 1960 Constitution was promulgated. At the 1957 Constitutional Conference the minority ethnic groups expressed fear of being persecuted by the larger groups in an independent Nigeria. Participants also indicated concern over the need for an equitable formula for revenue allocation. Two commissions were set up to look into these two issues. The Minorities Commission, while not underestimating the fears of the smaller ethnic groups, did not think it expedient to recommend the creation of new regions just for them.[26] To allay their fears, however, the commission recommended that a comprehensive list of fundamental human rights be included in the constitution.

In substance, the 1954 constitutional structure formed the basis of the 1960 Independence Constitution, which was later transformed into the 1963 Republican Constitution. We will now discuss the extent to which the provisions of this constitution, and the way in which they were operated, had a bearing on national unity and integration.

In spite of the often-proclaimed desire for unity among Nigeria's leaders, the principal trends of the last 20 years have pointed toward separation rather than unity. The problem of Nigerian political leaders was that while they advocated nationwide political parties based on social and economic ideologies, they always felt obliged to appeal to ethnic loyalties every time their political position was threatened by their rivals. Unfortunately, the country developed no national symbols strong enough to supersede regional loyalties.

In size and population the Northern Region was larger than the other regions combined, and in as much as the electoral laws were based on franchise for every adult Nigerian[27] and political behavior was basically ethnic, it was a foregone conclusion that the North would have a majority in the federal Parliament. A constitutional structure that predetermines election results in favor of one ethnic group can hardly be said to promote national integration and unity; on the contrary, it can result in the misuse of federal powers for partisan—and therefore ultimately disruptive—purposes.

To ensure the integrity of the federation, the constitution gave certain powers to the federal government to deal with any unit or units that might attempt to disrupt the federation.[28] Disturbances occurred in the Western Region in 1962 and 1965. The 1962 situation was less serious than that of 1965. Surprisingly, however, though the federal government was quick to declare a state of emergency in the less serious situation, it remained unmoved by the graver 1965 crisis. [29] The truth was that whereas the federal government acted in 1962 to undermine a political party in the West irrevocably opposed to it, in the 1965 situation it refused to act, to save and entrench an unpopular party that was its ally in the federal government. The stability and interest of the federation was not a factor in either decision. An objective commentator clearly saw the 1962 action of the federal government as a means of ensuring the entrenchment of a regional government supportive of those in power at the center, and concluded that, "such an action would have been manifestly unconstitutional in Canada and Australia."[30]

A federal government that exercises its coercive powers with evident partiality can hardly be said to be mindful of the need for stability and unity. By its actions, the Nigerian Government in the 1960s sparked a chain of events that eventually led to the demise of the First Republic. As aptly put by B. A. Williams, "The problem of national unity under the Independence Constitution and the failure of the First Republic were linked more with policy and the caliber of leadership than with institutions."[31] The attempt to impose an unpopular government in the West was resisted and serious violence continued. The federal government refused to act, and on January 16, 1966, the Army intervened.

On taking over the government of the federation, the federal military government promulgated a constitutional decree by which the offices of president, regional governors, prime minister, federal and regional ministers, the federal Parliament and regional legislatures were all suspended.[32] The judiciary, the public services, the armed forces and the police were not affected. The country remained a federation. The two principal organs of government became the Supreme Military Council and the Federal Executive Council, replacing the suspended Parliament and the Cabinet. In the four regions, all powers of government, aside from judicial authority, were vested in newly appointed military governors.[33]

After a short time the federal military government set up a number of study groups to consider the advantages and disadvantages of a unitary system of government as opposed to the existing federal arrangement. Before the groups reported, another constitutional decree[34] was promulgated under which Nigeria was to become a unitary state. The decree had the effect of increasing the fears of the non-Ibo communities that the military coup had been an attempt by the Ibos to dominate the other ethnic groups. A wave of rioting and violence broke out in many parts of the North. The northern emirs sent a memorandum to the newly created national military government in Lagos expressing the fears of their people over unification, although the government assured them that the change was merely in response to the need to run the government more efficiently.[35]

The upshot of the these events was a counter-coup on July 29, 1966. Lieutenant Colonel Yakubu Gowon assumed the position of head of the national military government and supreme commander of the Armed Forces. He announced that the unifying decrees had clearly failed and that the country would revert back to a federal structure. Accordingly, another constitutional decree was promulgated, effective September 1, 1966, that again federalized all the institutions and agencies of government.[36] What is apparent from Nigerian history, particularly of the 1960s, is that although Nigerians desire to be united, they do not wish their government to be run on unitary lines.

The story of the Nigerian "police action" that escalated into a civil war is too well known to be repeated. The crux of it was the attempt by the government of the Eastern Region of Nigeria to secede from the federation and the firm resistance of the federal military government to preserve the integrity of the federation. The move by the Eastern Region to break away came two days after a federal decree restructured the federation into 12 states.[37] This 1967 decree has rightly been hailed as the most momentous event in the constitutional history of Nigeria. It not only broke up the overwhelming size and population of the former Northern Region, but also substantially succeeded in structuring the federation in such a way as to satisfy the desires of some minority groups in Nigeria for their own states. Even so, agitations have continued for the creation of more states.[38] The truth is that no matter how many states had been created, still further demands for more would have been made because there will always be some minorities within each state. The present 12-state structure should be given time to develop, especially as the 1967 decree creates machinery for making boundary readjustments where the demands are strong and reasonable.[39]

Division of Powers and Its Effect on National Integration

The problem of division of powers between center and periphery stems from the federal nature of the constitution. The federal approach aims to give each unit of the federation its own identity and to reduce the power of those controlling the center to the point where they cannot completely dominate the country's other constituent groups. The first problem that arises here, of course, is to determine how much power can be given to the units consistent with the preservation of national unity.

The first real experiment relating to this issue came with the 1951 Macpherson Constitution. Under it, three regions were given competence over a limited range of matters, but the federal legislature could enact laws on all matters, including those within regional competence. It also provided that the central government could veto any bill passed by a region.[40] Curiously, one provision stated that if any inconsistency occurred between a federal law and a regional one, the latter in time was to prevail;[41] the force of this provision, however, was negated by the veto power of the central government.

Obviously, the 1951 Constitution did not give sufficient recognition to regional and group interests. The governmental structure under the Macpherson Constitution was quite at variance with the political, social, and cultural realities of Nigeria, and did not significantly contribute to the achievement of consensus. It fomented undue friction between the regions as well as between the regions and the federal government.[42] As the secretary of state for the colonies remarked before the British House of Commons:

> Recent events in Nigeria. . . have shown that it is not possible for the Regions to work effectively in a federation so closely knit as that provided by the present constitution. Her Majesty's Government in the United Kingdom, while greatly regretting this, consider that the constitution will have to be redrawn to provide for greater regional autonomy and for the removal of powers of intervention by the center in matters which can, without detriment to other Regions, be placed entirely within regional competence. . . . [43]

In an attempt to correct this weakness of the 1951 Constitution, the 1954 Constitution can be said to have moved to the other extreme by granting substantial powers to the regions and at the same time leaving the residual powers in their jurisdictions. It was this pattern that was extended in all the subsequent constitutions except the current one. Nigeria's current Constitution, the 1963 Republican Constitution, enumerates two legislative lists, the Exclusive and the Concurrent. The Exclusive contains items on which only the federal government can legislate whereas the Concurrent is for both the federal and the regional governments. All other matters not specified in the two lists fall under the jurisdiction of the regions.[44] As a means of ensuring integrative forces in the federation, it is provided that where there is conflict between a federal law and a regional one, the federal one prevails to the extent the two are inconsistent.[45]

It would be tedious to enumerate all 44 items on the Exclusive List. Suffice it to say that the inclusion of certain items on the list is highly desirable, such as jurisdiction in matters of external affairs, including extradition; immigration and emigration; currency and coinage; defense, including the police, naval, military, and air forces and nuclear energy; aviation, airports, mines, and minerals; regulation of interregional and foreign trade; taxation on companies; and banks and banking. We would suggest, however, that for the integration of the country and its fuller development, certain items in the Concurrent List be transferred to the Exclusive List. For example, central jurisdiction over arms and ammunition; labor, including conditions of labor, industrial relations, trade unions, and labor welfare; industrial development; and higher education would seem more appropriate. All these items require uniformity of standards. They are also capital expenditure items and therefore should be made a charge against the relatively superior finances of the center. The suggested change would also serve to strengthen the hand of the federal government for the purpose of ensuring integration and unity. In the field of industrial development particularly, the wasteful duplication and competition among the 12 states in the establishment of projects could thereby be eliminated.

One common misconception about federal constitutions is that the balance of power in the federation is determined by which unit or level of government is granted residual powers. This misconception prompted the Nigerian regions to insist on controlling residual matters. But the significance of residual powers depends on the scope and importance of the items that are residual, on how imaginatively the powers are employed, and the extent to which the federal government is weakened by not controlling them. Just how weakened the central government is in this connection depends on its commitment to total national economic and industrial development. In Nigeria, it was the central government, through its superior financial resources, that has weakened the capacity of the regions to move independently. The crucial factor in Nigeria, aside from finance, has been the coercive powers of the center, which we discuss later.

The unitary nature of the Nigerian Army and its tradition of a vertical hierarchical chain of command substantially affected the policy and manner of distribution of powers in the federation. Section 3 of Decree No. 1 under the present constitution provides that "the Federal Military Government shall have power to make laws for the peace, order and good government of Nigeria or any part thereof with respect to any matter whatsoever."[46] The governor of a region (now state) still has no power to make laws with respect to any matter on the Exclusive List, but now he cannot even legislate on a matter on the Concurrent List without the prior consent of the federal military government. The significant feature of this new division of powers is that the federal military government is no longer restricted to the Exclusive and Concurrent Legislative Lists; it can also enter residual matters hitherto reserved to the regional (state) governments. This arrangement has a striking resemblance to the 1951 Constitution, which had been condemned as bringing the units of the federation into too closely-knit a relationship. Though this arrangement is understandable in a military regime, it is not likely to be received favorably during a period of civilian control.

Constitutional Provisions Relating to Ethnic Relations and National Integration

Today, the principal constitutional provision relating to ethnic relations and national integration in Nigeria is the federal system of government itself. Nigeria, as a large, diverse and multilingual state, is naturally resistant to uniformity in government and administration. Even while a colony, it was found necessary at the early stages of British administration to decentralize so as to allow the various groups to grow along their own lines and to permit more effective local administration. As noted, the two attempts to concentrate powers at the center in 1951 and 1966 encountered strong communal opposition.

The coercive powers of the federal government, as provided in the 1963 Constitution, are also designed to ensure that the federation does not disintegrate. Section 65 (1) of the constitution provides that:

> Parliament may at any time make such laws for Nigeria or any part thereof with respect to matters not included in the Legislative Lists as may appear to Parliament to be necessary or expedient for the purposes of maintaining or securing peace, order and good government during any period of emergency. . . .

Again Section 86 of the 1963 Constitution provides that:

> The executive authority of a Region . . . shall be so exercised as not to impede or prejudice the exercise of the executive authority of the Federation or to endanger the continuance of Federal Government in Nigeria.

And Section 71 empowers Parliament to take the necessary corrective action to save the federation when Section 86 is violated.

The above provisions are designed not only to ensure the continuation of the federation as an integral whole, but also to establish the constitutional supremacy of the federal government.[47] Although the word "secession" is nowhere mentioned in the constitution, the provisions outlined above are obviously adequate to cover any such contingency. It must, however, be remarked that the provisions impose an onerous responsibility on the federal authority to exercise its will with great care and responsibility, attributes not characteristic of the government's response to the crises of 1962 and 1965.

Another constitutional provision that has fostered a common sense of national belonging pertains to citizenship. Prior to independence on October 1, 1960, the peoples of Nigeria were classified as either (a) British subjects and citizens of the United Kingdom and Colonies (if born within the colony of Lagos and its environs) or (b) British protected persons (if born within the protectorate, which comprised the remainder of Nigeria). The Independence Act of 1960, however, provided that the colony and protectorate should, from October 1, 1960, together form part of Her Majesty's dominion, thus abolishing the dichotomy. All peoples of Nigeria now have a common citizenship, regardless of location. However, in effect this common citizenship is more apparent than real.

The cumbersome and rigid procedure to be followed before a new state can be created under the Republican Constitution is designed primarily to discourage the Balkanization of the country.[48] It can be argued that this expectation is based on a false and unrealistic premise in the sense that the communal fragmentation that stamped Nigeria as an unmistakably plural society was ignored in the delineation of the original three regions. The substantial settlement of the problem had to await a military solution, when the military government decreed the establishment of 12 states.

The 12-state structure has been lauded as a major step toward ensuring healthy ethnic relations, national integration, and stability in Nigeria. Agitation for state creation in Nigeria has been intrinsically interwoven with the question of ethnic identity and fear and suspicion by the ethnic minorities of the major ethnic communities. As rightly remarked by Arikpo, "The minority problem, more than any other single political issue, was at the root of most of the friction between and within political parties, governments and administration since Independence."[49] Yet it is open to question whether any sound federation in Nigeria can be based solely on ethnic units. Other factors, such as compactness of geographical area, administrative convenience, the facts of history, the wishes of the people, political realities, and the viability of the units, need be considered. Ethnicity should be one of the factors, but undue emphasis on it can contribute to considerable systemic stress. Dual loyalty is a prerequisite of federalism, but in a young federation like Nigeria the danger of ethnic loyalty prevailing over national loyalty is very real. And its results, as the civil war demonstrated, can be disastrous.

An additional critical factor in shaping ethnic relations and national stability in Nigeria has been the formula for revenue allocation among the various units of the federation. The distribution of funds collected by the central government has always been a source of controversy among the units of the federation, and no allocation formula has ever been universally acceptable.[50] Historically, revenue allocation in Nigeria has revolved around the four basic principles of need, derivation, independent revenue, and national interest, and the various commissions that have been appointed to resolve the issue have recommended use of the four principles in varying degrees.[51] However, for a revenue allocation formula to be realistic it must be consistent with the character of the federation. The recent experience of a civil war has convinced most Nigerians of the need for a strong center, as well as the need for unity among the states. To achieve these twin objectives, sufficient resources must be left to the center to give it strength, and the manner of dividing the remaining resources among the states must be equitable. These considerations argue in favor of the new formula for allocating the funds that go to the states (the Distributable Pool Account) on the basis of 50 percent equally among the states and 50 percent according to population.[52] This formula not only ensures equality of shares among the states, but also gives consideration to the peculiar needs of each state. The way in which this formula is being used, however, is already being attacked,[53] which lends credence to the assertion of K. C. Wheare that, "There is and can be no final solution to the allocation of financial resources in a federal system."[54]

Legal Prohibitions of Ethnic Discrimination

As already mentioned, in response to the demands of minority groups that additional regions be created, the British colonial administration wrote into the constitution a detailed enumeration of Fundamental Human Rights. These in fact did not guarantee or safeguard the rights of minorities *qua* minorities; they safeguarded enumerated rights of individuals, be it those in the minority or the majority.

While the human rights provision of the Nigerian Constitution could be said to be meant to protect the liberty of the individual, nonetheless it does contain certain provisions specifically directed toward the protection of particular ethnic groups. Section 27, for example, guarantees the freedom of every Nigerian to move freely throughout Nigeria and to reside in any part of the country; but exceptions are attached to it to protect certain ethnic groups. Subsection 3 says nothing in Section 27 shall invalidate any reasonably justified law that imposes restrictions on the acquisition or use of land or other property in Nigeria. This provision was designed to give constitutional validity to the 1962 Land Tenure Law of the northern states, which places Nigerians from the southern states on the same footing as foreigners with respect to landholding in any part of the North. The unfairness of this provision has been pointedly brought out by Professor T. O. Elias.

> It is suggested that the Constitution should not have entrenched the continued discrimination against Southern Nigerians in this respect. This is all the more so in view of the express provision in another section of the Constitution which provides that the enjoyment of the fundamental rights shall be secured without discrimination on any ground such as race, tribe, language, religion, political opinion or place of origin. There would appear to be some inconsistency here unless words have lost their meaning. But the issue is a sensitive one for the Northern leaders who fear the possible expropriation of many peasant landholders by sophisticated Southern property speculators. Yet the same might justifiably be said of some Northern merchants and property dealers in relation to land in certain areas of the South.[55]

Section 28 of the constitution provides that a citizen of Nigeria shall not be discriminated against on the grounds that he is from a particular community, tribe, place of origin or belongs to a particular religion or holds a particular political opinion. Subsection (a) further provides that he shall not be subjected to any disabilities or restrictions to which all other citizens of Nigeria are not made subject. And Subsection (b) provides that he shall not be accorded any privileges or advantages either by reason of his community, tribe, religion, place of origin, or political views. But some of the exceptions attached to Section 28 are so far-reaching as to nullify its substance. For example, Subsection 2(a) exempts any law that prescribes qualifications of service in a state office, the armed forces of the federation, a police force, or any federal corporate body.

The upshot of all these exceptions is that virtually all forms of discrimination in public life that emphasize the state of origin, tribe, or ethnic affiliation of a Nigerian are legal under the constitution. Only in rare cases are persons from one region or state employed in responsible public positions in other regions or states. In fact, until very recently the policy of the then Northern Region was to recruit foreigners, rather than southerners, into its public services.

If Nigerians are serious about building an integrated nation, future exercises at constitution-making must expunge these obnoxious provisions from the laws. Yet there is ground for hope. In 1972 Governor Audu Bako of Kano State in the North announced that Nigerians who choose to work in Kano can now do so on a permanent basis, rather than on contract.[56] The Federal Public Service Commission has also indicated that it would underwrite the security of tenure of Nigerians who opt to serve outside their states of origin. Unfortunately, the reaction of some Nigerians to this announcement has been that they would only go if they were treated as expatriates. As the Daily Times pointed out correctly in an editorial: "Meaningful national unity can only be forged if Nigerians can live and work in any part of the country—as Nigerians and not as expatriates in their own country. Free mobility of high level manpower is a major factor in forging a new national loyalty in the country."[57]

Efforts to Achieve Ethnic Balance in the Public Services

While it is difficult to come across any declared policy on the question of achieving ethnic balance in the public services, it is apparent that the Nigerian Government is well aware of the problem. Indeed, it is essential in a federation that a single group should not dominate the Federal Public Services. The crucial problem is how each unit can gain a sense of participation in federal affairs. The "quota system" has been widely discussed recently. Even if the principle is accepted, its universal application would be detrimental to governmental effectiveness, particularly in the judiciary.

Dr. Ishaya Audu, then vice chancellor of Ahmadu Bello University, strongly urges the adoption of the quota system in the sphere of education. He suggests that it would close the vast gap in educational achievement among Nigeria's various ethnic groups. Quotas could be applied both for the admission of students and for appointment and promotion of staff. Says Audu: "All the universities should make a determined effort to help underrepresented areas and groups. No basic university requirements should be set aside. But requirements should be thought out flexibly. And all the universities should endeavour to remain as multi-ethnic as possible."[58]

True, the ethnic imbalance in education is glaring. But the proposed solution of the problem by means of a "quota system" would obviously lower standards. We suggest that the ideal solution to "bridging this gap" is for the federal and state governments to increase educational facilities and make education free at all levels to all Nigerians. It might take time to achieve this goal, but the best interest of the federation would have been served in the end.[59]

In the other sectors of Federal Public Service, particularly the public corporations, the chairman of the Federal Statutory Corporations Service Commission has said that the policy of the commission would be equal representation of all the states in all the federal corporations. Speaking to the governor of the Benue-Plateau State, he said: "If there are vacancies to be filled all the States in the Federation must be equally represented without any bias to educational qualifications."[60] Another commentator has recommended the adoption of a constitutional provision requiring ethnic quotas in all types of government employment.[61] On the one hand, Swiss arrangements in this regard are worth examining; on the other, the experience of Cyprus, where communalism gallops with constitutionalism, might well suggest caution.[62]

An area in which the quota system could be practiced with much benefit to the federation is in the armed forces.[63] Every ethnic group would then be afforded the opportunity of participating in the defense of the nation. More important, because the constitution gives exclusive control of the army to the federal government, the government, even if it were controlled by one or two ethnic groups, would hesitate to misuse the coercive powers of the army on the nation if it knew that all the ethnic groups were proportionately represented in the armed forces. Before the civil war, the origin of about 75 percent of the infantry force was northern Nigeria; 60 to 70 percent of technicians and officers were of eastern origin, and the higher percentage of those from the East came from one ethnic group.[64] It took Nigeria the lesson of a bitter civil war to learn the danger of ethnic imbalance in so vital and delicate a sphere as the military.

Dissonance in Customary Law and Attempts at Reconciliation: Need for a Common Law?

There appears to be general agreement among scholars that there is considerable disparity — and ample sources of conflict — in the customary law of Nigeria's various ethnic groups. How great the diversity is a matter of debate. Despite the diversity, however, many common principles run through Nigeria's customary law, particularly in such spheres as family law and inheritance.[65] Professor Elias has written that "it would be better to have a set of well-established common rules of customary laws having universal acceptance and application than to continue to revel in a welter of particularistic customs sought to be preserved only on the ground of purely ethnocentric considerations."[66] Professor B. O. Nwabueze has also noted: "It should be explained that customary law is not a single body of law throughout the country. Far from that being the case, customary law is as various as the number of independent communities comprised in Nigeria. This is not of course to say that the contents of any two customary laws are necessarily different in every particular. On the contrary a measure of basic uniformity of content does exist over a considerable range of matters."[67]

Today, a major anxiety of all African countries, including Nigeria, is nation-building. Most efforts, at least in theory if not in practice, are directed at building economically virile and politically integrated nations. Accordingly, areas of government with divisive tendencies must be streamlined to attune them with the ultimate objective of national unity. Even in countries with a federal system of government like Nigeria, the desire to achieve unification, or at least integration, of laws and the legal systems is clear.[68] Indeed, a unified body of customary law will minimize, if not totally eliminate, the problems of legal conflict within the various customary laws.

Even if a unified body of customary law is presently beyond achievement, there are certain areas in which uniformity of customary law is urgently needed. Uniformity in criminal law and in the substantive civil law of obligations (especially commercial law and contractual law) is highly desirable. Indeed, uniformity in criminal law is being promoted in Nigeria. One of the fundamental rights in the 1963 Constitution states that no one can be convicted in any court except for an offense against written law.[69] And Section 3 of the Penal Code Law says that no person shall be liable to conviction under any native law and custom (which in this case includes Islamic law) in the northern states.

However, a potent warning that must be sounded is that unification of customary law should not be sought merely for its own sake. It is important to ask to what extent variations in local customary law are necessary and justifiable. The key factor in determining whether variations are necessary or should give way to uniformity is the attachment that communities feel toward their individual variations of law. A uniform system that reflects biases in favor of the customary law of a particular ethnic community could be highly offensive to the other communities.[70]

Assuming that uniformity of the customary law is the ideal, the crucial question is how do Nigerians achieve it? There has not been in Nigeria any national policy or effort to reconcile or unify its various bodies of customary law. There have been, however, ad hoc attempts on state and local levels to streamline divergencies, where possible. In our view, the judicial process is certainly too slow to make any significant impact on uniformity. Awaiting declarations by traditional authorities has its drawbacks, the major one being the danger of possible distortion of customary law. The textbook approach suffers from the same weakness, if not more so, as the judicial process. The ideal approach, it seems to us, is for the authorities to set up a Customary Law Revision Committee of people knowledgeable and interested in the development of customary law who would investigate Nigeria's bodies of customary law and make recommendations to the appropriate legal and legislative bodies for eventual embodiment in legislation. A beginning could be made by setting up these committees on the state level. A compilation of the works and findings of these bodies could eventually lead to a common customary law for Nigeria — one of the many steps required to enhance national integration in Nigeria.

Notes

1. B. A. Williams, "Constitutions and National Unity in Nigeria: A Historical and Analytical Survey," *Journal of Business and Social Studies,* Vol. I, No. 1 (September 1968), p. 71.
2. Even then, most advanced countries of today have had to fight wars for one reason or another to maintain the integrity of their various communities. For example, Great Britain is composed of England (which in Anglo-Saxon times

was a heptarchy of kingdoms), Wales, and Scotland. The Swiss Federation, the United States of America, and Canada are examples of multi-national states.

3. See, for example, G. O. Olusanya, "The Historical Basis for National Unity — An Analysis" (Paper read at the *Conference on Integration and National Unity in Nigeria,* December 14-19, 1970); Hugh Clapperton, *Journal of a Second Expedition into the Interior of Africa from the Bight of Benin to Ooccaloo* (Sokoto, 1829; reprinted ed. London: Frank Cass & Co., Ltd., 196), p. 136; K.O. Dike, *Trade and Politics on the Nigerian Delta, 1830-1885* (London: Oxford University Press, 1956), p. 183; and G. O. Gbadamosi, "The Growth of Islam among the Yoruba, 1841-1908" (Ph. D. diss., University of Ibadan, 1968).

4. See Olusanya, op. cit., p. 6. For the international aspects of such cooperation, see T. O. Elias, *Africa and the Development of International Law* (Leiden: Sijthoff, 1972), chap. 2.

5. See Okoi Arikpo, *The Development of Modern Nigeria* (London: Penguin African Library, 1967), p. 13.

6. See Olusanya, op. cit., p. 2; Arikpo, op. cit., pp. 142-145.

7. Note, however, I. F. Nicholson's comment in *British Administration in Nigeria: Men, Myths and Methods* (London: Oxford University Press, 1969), p. 180, that "the most remarkable thing about Lugard's amalgamation of Nigeria is that it never really took place."

8. Order-in-Council No. 165 of November 1913, par. 18, cited in *Nigeria's Constitutional Story 1862-1964* (Lagos: Federal Government Printer, 1954), p. 5.

9. Williams, op. cit., p. 54; and Olusanya, op. cit., p. 10.

10. For example, Sir Percy Girourd, Sir Graeme Thompson, and C. L. Temple. See paragraphs 17-20 in the *Nigerian Gazette Extra-Ordinary,* Nov. 21, 1920, and republished with amendments in *Nigerian Gazette Extra-Ordinary,* March 2, 1926. See also *Indirect Administration* (Kaduna: Secretariat, 1926), chap. 4.

11. Nigeria (Legislative Council) Order-in-Council, 1922; SRO, 1922.

12. T. O. Elias, *Nigeria: The Development of Its Laws and Constitution* (London: Stevens and Sons, 1967), p. 27.

13. Nigeria (Legislative Council) Order-in-Council, 1946; SRO, 1946.

14. Cmd. 6599, "Proposals for the Revision of the Constitution of Nigeria," March 1945, par. 2.

15. Nigeria (Constitution) Order-in-Council, 1951, Sec. 91 and Sch. 3.

16. Ibid., Sec. 96.

17. Elias, *Nigeria,* op. cit., p. 41; and O. I. Odumosu, *Nigerian Constitution* (London: Sweet and Maxwell, 1963).

18. See "Nigerian Constitutional Review," *Journal of African Administration,* Vol. 2, No. 1 (January 1950), pp. 11-14.

19. Ibid. See also Henry Swanzy, "Quarterly Notes: West Africa," *African Affairs,* Vol. 49, No. 194 (January 1950), pp. 4-10.

20. Henry Swanzy, "Quarterly Notes: West Africa," *African Affairs,* Vol. 52, No. 208 (July 1953), pp. 216-217; idem, "Crisis at the Centre," *West Africa,* Vol. 37, No. 1884 (April 4, 1953), p. 289.

21. See Nigerian *House of Representatives Debates,* April 1, 1953, pp. 1050-1053.
22. The Nigeria (Constitution) Order-in-Council, 1954.
23. For example, by providing for two legislative lists, by leaving residual matters with the regions, and by regionalizing the judiciary and the public services.
24. Williams, op. cit., p. 63.
25. Odumosu, op. cit., pp. 74-77.
26. See (1958) Command Paper, 505.
27. Women in the North were, however, disenfranchised.
28. See Sec. 65, 70, 71 and 86 of the 1963 Republican Constitution.
29. For a comparative account of the two events, see Arikpo, op. cit., pp. 127 and 134-143; see also Odumosu, op. cit.
30. S. A. de Smith, *The New Commonwealth and Its Constitutions* (London: Stevens, 1964), p. 268.
31. Williams, op. cit., p. 67.
32. Decree No. 1 of 1966.
33. Ibid., Sch. 2.
34. Decree No. 34 of 1966.
35. Press Release No. F. 686 by the National Military Government, June 8, 1966.
36. Decree No. 9 of 1966.
37. States (Creation and Transitional Provisions) Decree No. 14 of 1967, Sec. 1(1)(2)(3).
38. See, for instance, G. B. A. Akinyede, "Emergence of Two Soldier Rulers is the Greatest Thing That Ever Happened to the Ekitis," *Daily Times,* Oct. 22, 1969; "Olubadan's Council Recommends Central Yoruba State," *Daily Times,* Oct. 13, 1969; Omolade Adejuyigbe, "Dr. Aluko's Panacea Had Once Failed," *Daily Sketch,* June 25, 1970; and R. O. A. Akinjide, "The Path of Peace in the West Is to Let Each Group Go Its Way," *Daily Times,* Oct. 28, 1969.
39. States (Creation and Transitional Provisions) Decree No. 14 of 1967, Sec. 6(1).
40. Nigeria (Constitution) Order-in-Council, 1951, Sec. 96.
41. Nigeria (Constitution) Order-in-Council, 1951, Sec. 107.
42. See Williams, op. cit., p. 62.
43. See *House of Commons Debates,* Vol. 1, Cols. 2263-64 (May, 21, 1953), quoted from Odumosu, op. cit., pp. 90-91.
44. Note, however, that certain powers, not enumerated in either of the Lists, are given to the center: see section 69(3) of the 1963 Republican Constitution where such powers are enumerated.
45. The Republican Constitution, 1963, No. 20, Sec. 64(4).
46. Constitution (Suspension and Modification) Decree, No. 1 of 1966.
47. For a more comprehensive discussion of these sections, see Elias, *Nigeria,* op. cit., p.. 284-296; O. Ohonbamu, *The Psychology of the Nigerian Revolution* (Devon: Arthur H. Stockwell, 1968), pp. 135-151; and B.O. Nwabueze, *Constitutional Law of the Nigerian Republic,* (London: Butterworth, 1964), pp. 167-174.
48. Decree No. 20 of 1963, Sec. 4(3)-(6).
49. Arikpo, op. cit., p. 94.
50. See Elias, *Nigeria,* op. cit., p. 250; P. C. N. Okigbo, *Nigerian Public Finance*

(Evanston: Northwestern University Press, 1965); A. A. Adedeji, *Nigerian Federal Finance* (New York: Africana, 1969); and R. O. Teriba, "Nigerian Revenue Allocation Experience, 1952-1965: A Study in Inter-governmental and Financial Relations," *Nigerian Journal of Economic and Social Studies,* Vol. 8, No. 3 (November 1966), pp. 361-382.

51. "Administrative and Financial Procedure under the New [Richards] Constitution: Financial Relations Between the Government of Nigeria and the Native Administration," (Lagos: Government Printer, 1947); "Report of the Commission on Revenue Allocation," (Lagos: Government Printer, 1951; Command Paper 9026, December 1953; Command Paper 481 (Nigeria Report of the Fiscal Commission); *Report of the Fiscal Review Commission* (Lagos: Federal Ministry of Information, 1965), p. 17.

52. Constitution (Distributable Pool Account) Decree No. 13 of 1970, Sec. 5.

53. *New Nigerian,* July 21, 1972, p. 4.

54. K. C. Wheare, *Federal Government* (London: Oxford University Press, 1968), p. 117.

55. There are two types of landholding in the northern states: statutory and customary rights to occupancy. The latter, which is the more secured, is reserved for northerners. Southern Nigerians are, for this purpose, defined as foreigners.

56. *Daily Times,* July 14, 1972, p. 3.

57. Ibid.

58. Ishaya Audu, "The Role of Universities in National Integration" (Lecture delivered at the Nigerian Institute of International Affairs, Lagos, July 14, 1972). As proof of ethnic imbalance in Nigeria's universities, Audu cited Ibadan University as an example. Between 1948 and 1966, 2,706 Yoruba students, 1,974 Ibos, 395 Edo and 138 Urhobo were admitted, but only 31 Hausa, 17 Fulani and 6 Tiv.

59. The federal military government has rejected the "quota" system on this same ground, that it would lower government personnel standards. (See *Daily Times,* July 2, 1972.)

60. *Daily Times,* Aug. 17, 1970, p. 7.

61. Ohonbamu, op. cit., p. 130.

62. See de Smith, op. cit., chap. 8.

63. Note, however, the statement in the *Daily Times,* July 26, 1972, of Major General Adeyinka Adebayo that ethnic balancing is not being contemplated in the army.

64. Ohonbamu, op. cit., p. 194.

65. This statement stands qualified by the existence of Islamic Law in the northern states.

66. T. O. Elias, "Law in a Developing Society" (Inaugural lecture delivered at the University of Lagos, January 17, 1969), p. 18.

67. B. O. Nwabueze, *Machinery of Justice in Nigeria* (London: Butterworth, 1963), p. 3.

68. For example, all judges of the higher courts in the federation are now appointed by a central body. The objective is to promote commonality and uniformity in judicial and legal matters.

69. Sec. 22(10), 1963 Constitution. See also the case of *Taiwo Aoko* v. *Adeyemi Fagbemi and the Director of Public Prosecutions* (1961), Western Nigeria Law Reports 147.

70. See, for example, Nwabueze, op. cit., pp. 43-44, and the A. N. Allott, ed., *Future of Law in Africa* (London: Butterworth, 1960), pp. 10-11.

Chapter 3

National Unity Within the Context of Regional Relations: The Nigerian Experience

by A. Bolaji Akinyemi

NIGERIA SHARES its international boundaries with Dahomey on the west, Niger on the northwest and north, Chad on the far northeast, and Cameroon on the east. To the south is the Gulf of Guinea—the Bights of Biafra and Benin. The international boundaries cut across certain ethnic groups. The frontier between Dahomey and Nigeria splits the Yoruba, leaving the majority in Nigeria, and the old Borgu Kingdom, again leaving the bigger section in Nigeria, although its capital stayed in Dahomey. The boundary between Niger and Nigeria cuts through the Hausa-Fulani and the Kanuri. The Chad-Nigeria frontier also divides the Kanuri, and the Cameroon-Nigeria northern frontier again splits the Hausa-Fulani.

The first question that comes to mind is: What effect did these environmental factors have on the Nigerian drive for national unity? But one has to define one's terms. Minimally, "unity" can be defined in terms of Nigerian politics, as agreement among the political actors to operate within one physical unit: to maintain the territorial integrity of the state. Maximally, "unity" can be defined in terms of loyalty, as the achievement of the transference of loyalties from subnational primordial units to the state.

Minimal Unity and Regional Cooperation

Within the minimal context, there is no episode so far to show that any of the Nigerian ethnic groups conceived of a pan-ethnic state with its kin and kith across the border as an alternative to a Nigerian state. It is true that certain elements in the Action Group, the ruling party in the then Western Region, at one time intervened in the politics of Dahomey. Chief Obafemi Awolowo, the leader of the Action Group, was alleged to have given £40,000 to a political party in Dahomey in 1959,[1] while John West, a columnist in the Action Group party press and a high-ranking member of the party, advocated that Dahomey should join Nigeria because of the shared ethnic groups.[2] Nothing came of these moves, and what the £40,000 was supposed to have achieved is obscure. It could have been to secure electoral victory for a Dahomey party with influence among the Dahomey Yoruba; presumably the party victory could then, if need be, have led to a unification of Dahomey and the Western state. Or its purpose could have been to buy electoral victory for a party in Dahomey that would be friendly with the Western state. When the Action Group lost the 1959 Federal elections, there was a debate over the future of the Western Region. According to Chief Anthony Enahoro, one of the Action Group leaders, "Ever since Independence Day, debate had raged within the party over the future of the Western Region and of the party. Some members wanted the Action Group to join an all-party coalition government at the centre. Others suggested that the Western Region should secede from the Federation."[3] Whatever the motives, they were not pursued, because by December 1960 the Action Group had rejected secession as the solution to the problems of the Western Region.

Until the 1963 census fiasco, which was one of the events that eventually led to secession in 1967 by the Eastern Region, the Ibo were the most committed to Nigerian unity and had not previously toyed with the idea of secession. The Hausa-Fulani in the Northern Region were the least committed. That their participation in the Nigerian political system was contingent on northern control of the system was made glaringly clear by this threat made by Ahmadu Bello, then the northern premier:

> The North has half the seats in the House of Representatives. My party might manage to capture these, but it is not very likely for the present to get any others: on the other hand, a sudden grouping of the Eastern and Western parties. . . might take power and so endanger the North.

> This would, of course, be utterly disastrous. It might set back our programme of development ruinously; it would therefore force us to take measures to meet the need. . . .[4]

Since the Northern People's Congress was in power in Nigeria until the military take-over in 1966, it is impossible to say whether the alternative to Nigeria for the NPC would have been sought in a merger with Niger or Cameroon. Bello's only declaration on this issue was clearly irredentist rather than secessionist. When irked by the torrent of abuse directed by the Cameroon Government against Nigeria because the Trust Territory of Northern Cameroons voted to join Nigeria instead of Cameroon, he said he had ambitions to recover for Nigeria those parts of the Cameroon Republic that were part of the former Fulani Empire.[5]

To the extent, then, that the various ethnic groups in Nigeria had domestic reasons for being reconciled to the minimal unity of Nigeria, the existence across the frontiers of ethnic groups with kith and kin in Nigeria did not in any significant way threaten this unity. At the same time, no issue arose that could lead to the conclusion that it promoted or forced the Nigerian groups to be more attached to this unity.

If one reverses the question to ask for the effect on these countries of the state of the relationship among Nigerian ethnic groups, one gets a slightly different answer. We have already mentioned the fact that the North's commitment to Nigeria's unity was conditional—it depended on its electoral supremacy. There is circumstantial evidence to show that this consideration of electoral supremacy influenced Nigeria's relationships with its immediate neighbors. Between 1959 and 1961 Nigeria was faced with the problem of the Trust Territory of the Cameroons. After the First World War, the German colony of the Kamerun was divided between France and Britain. The French administered its part as one colony, while the British divided its own into two parts: the Northern Cameroons as part of Northern Nigeria and the Southern Cameroons as part of Eastern Nigeria. In 1954, partly out of what the Southern Cameroonians regarded as economic exploitation by the Ibo, the Southern Cameroons demanded and was granted a separate regional status by the British.

As Nigeria drew near independence, agitation started in both the Northern and Southern Cameroons about their own political future. Opinion was divided between those who wished for a future with Nigeria and those who desired a future with the Cameroon Republic (the original French section of the colony).[6] The United Nations, which had ultimate authority over the territory, decided to hold separate plebiscites in the North and the South to determine the wishes of people. While the Nigerian Government and most of the Nigerian press maintained a studied indifference to both plebiscites, one can distinguish differences in the way both northern and southern Nigerians reacted to them. All the Nigerian parties allowed their local branches in North Cameroons to form a consortium to campaign for integration with Nigeria. When at the first plebiscite in Northern Cameroons in 1959, the people voted to defer their decision, Bello took this as a slap directed at the North and flew into a rage, demonstrating an untypical anti-British feeling.[7] On the other hand, it was only the Action Group that gave indirect help to those in the Southern Cameroons campaigning for integration with Nigeria. When Nigeria lost the plebiscite in the Southern Cameroons, there was no outburst comparable to Bello's 1959 anti-British tirade. The all-party effort for the integration of Northern Cameroons with Nigeria was seen as a national duty, although the importance which the North attached to Northern Cameroons lay in the presence of the Hausa-Fulani there: if they were integrated with the North, they would add to the electoral strength of the NPC. In the Southern Cameroons, though, the pro-Nigerian elements were primarily supporters of the Action Group, although they were not Yoruba.

If the Action Group had prevailed and the Southern Cameroons had joined the federation as a separate region, it would have changed the pattern of Nigerian politics. As a separate region, the Southern Cameroons would have been entitled to 12 representatives in the Nigerian Senate. Under the 1960 Constitution, each region contributed an equal number of senators; bills approved by the House of Representatives had to receive the assent of the Senate before they could go to the governor-general for signature. After the 1959 elections, the National Council of Nigerian Citizens (NCNC) and Northern People's Congress (NPC) formed a coalition government — the Action Group ended up in the opposition. In the Senate, a combination of northern (NPC) and eastern (NCNC) senators also dominated the western (Action Group) senators. Hence, if the 12 senators from the Southern Cameroons had teamed up with the Action Group, the Senate would have been divided 24-24 with the four senators from the Federal Territory (also divided) and the four appointed by the governor-general holding the balance. To the North, this would have raised the specter of southern domination in the Senate if the Southern parties should ever team together. To the opponents of the Action Group, it raised the specter of a dead-locked Senate to the advantage of the Action Group. In view of these considerations, it was no surprise that the Action Group — and the nationally conscious *Sunday Times*[8] — were unhappy about the rejection by the Southern Cameroons of integration with Nigeria.

Another issue was the problem posed for Nigeria by the ill-treatment of Nigerian workers on the then Spanish island of Fernando Po.[9] Following disclosures in the *Sunday Times* about the maltreatment, demands were made for annexation of the island by the Zikist National Movement, the *West African Pilot* (both auxiliaries of the NCNC), the Nigerian Trades Union Congress, and the *Sunday Times,* especially its editor, Peter Enahoro. The NPC as a party was silent on it, although members of the party were to be found on both sides of the issue. The NCNC as a party was also silent on the issue, but allowed its two auxiliaries to spearhead the cause for annexation. The NCNC was part of the federal government, and therefore could not espouse an issue opposed by its senior partner (the NPC) in the government. But it could not write off the Nigerians on the island either, because the overwhelming majority of them were easterners — hence the use of its auxiliaries. Of course, any annexation would have benefited the easterners specifically, and the southerners generally — hence the attitude of the NPC. The Action Group as a party also remained silent on the issue because its private soundings among the nationalist elements in Fernando Po had revealed no desire to join Nigeria. The Action Group would have been prepared to come out for annexation for the same reason it supported the unification of Southern Cameroons with Nigeria.

Once again, Fernando Po was an issue on which Nigeria's regionally and ethnically differentiated parties took different stands — even when this amounted to silent opposition — for reasons related to their electoral fortunes. The conclusion to be drawn here is that the state of political conflicts existing among Nigerian ethnic groups has served to diffuse irredentist situations, thereby serving the cause of regional cooperation by discouraging situations that could have led to international ruckuses.

Maximal Unity and Regional Cooperation

We have earlier defined maximal unity in terms of achieving the trans-ference of loyalties from subnational primordial units to one nation state. The fundamental method for achieving this maximal unity and its feasibility in the case of a developing state like Nigeria, is much too complicated to be tackled within the limited confines of this chapter. What should be clear is that the sum differences among the Nigerian ethnic groups really constitute deep and basic cleavages. In a way, it is really irrelevant whether or not these differences constitute basic cleavages. Politically, the relevant factor is that the political elites that represent these ethnic groups see the conflicts as constituting basic cleavages. Under these circumstances, the only rational interpretation that should be given maximal unity is one that approximates minimal unity. In other words, this maximal unity would manifest itself not only in operating a system based on the recognition that these conflicts exist, but in designing policies that would lessen their most abrasive tendencies and eventually remove the root causes of the cleavages.

In terms of regional cooperation, maximal unity means pursuing policies that are seen to serve the interests of the whole state rather than a section of it. Put another way, it means pursuing policies in which the sum total of benefits derived from regional cooperation are seen to have incidence on all sectors of the country without any particular regional area being more favored than others in terms of closer relationship. This policy, in fact, is what the Balewa government of the First Republic pursued. When its ban on French shipping and aircraft following the French atomic tests in 1961 created economic difficulties for Dahomey and Niger, the government exempted French shipping carrying goods to these two countries.[10] In May 1962 Nigeria signed an agreement on a radio telecommunications link with Cameroon. In August 1962 it was announced that Nigeria and Dahomey were linked by phone, which by September 1962 was extended to Togo. In July 1962, a draft convention establishing a common customs frontier between Nigeria and Dahomey was signed in Lagos. The announcement of the signing was coupled with another that a delegation from Cameroon was also in town to discuss a similar draft convention. By January 1963, a common customs station had been established along the Nigerian-Niger border. One could go on enumerating examples of this balanced policy, but the point has been made.

A corollary of this policy was Alhadji Balewa's preference of a low profile in the pursuit of certain Nigerian interests abroad. Of particular concern was the presence of Nigerian minorities abroad and the consequent need for their protection. Nigerians were expelled in large numbers from the Ivory Coast, Niger, Cameroon, and Sierra Leone while Balewa was in office from 1960 to 1966. The Ivory Coast case is typical. Three years after the 1958 riots in the Ivory Coast, the expelled Nigerians and those remaining in the Ivory Coast were still petitioning the Nigerian government to demand compensation from the Ivory Coast Government for damages both to persons and property during the riots. The Nigerian Government, however, simply was not prepared to do more than protest the treatment of these people.

During this period Nigeria bent over backward to demonstrate acts of friendship of one type or another toward its neighbors. In 1963 it was announced that 80 non-Nigerian Africans were employed in executive positions in the Nigerian federal civil service. The countries represented were the Cameroon Republic, Dahomey, Gambia, Ghana, Sierra Leone, Togo, South Africa, and Southern Rhodesia.[11] In 1965 the Nigerian Government banned the Sawaba Party of the Niger Republic (the outlawed opposition party in Niger) from operating in Nigeria on the ground that the party was not in the interest of good government in Nigeria. Even in 1960, at the height of the crisis between Nigeria and the Cameroon Republic, Nigeria put on trial a member of the *Union des Populations du Cameroun* (UPC), which had been banned in Cameroon. In 1958 it was revealed that without reciprocity Nigeria was training at its own expense non-Nigerian nationals in educational institutions in Nigeria and elsewhere. The only possible explanation is that the Balewa government might have felt that because Nigerian unity was vulnerable to disruptions from external forces, it was in Nigeria's interest to maintain good relationships with its neighbors, even in the face of provocation. The support given by countries such as Cameroon, Chad, and Niger to Nigeria during the latter's civil war seems to have justified Balewa's caution.

The Civil War, Unity, and Regional Cooperation

While the pre-civil war unity of Nigeria was a conditional one, the post-civil war unity is a definitive one in the sense that none of the states is strong enough to pose a threat to the physical existence of the nation as a unit. Once this capability is missing, the commitment of the actors to turn the system into a going concern is increased beyond whatever former level existed. In essence, then, the minimal unity of Nigeria is at a higher level than that of the First Republic. This does not imply an absence of problems, but this new level of minimal unity is reflected in the way these problems are solved.

The new confidence of the federal government has already been manifested in the centralizing in federal hands of all external relations. For example, under Balewa it was not unknown for the heads of some neighboring states to visit the northern premier in Kaduna without visiting Lagos, while it was not unknown also for the northern premier to offer technical assistance to some neighboring states.[12] In post-civil war days, such conduct would be unthinkable and unacceptable. The new state of unity has also enabled the federal government to pursue different levels of cooperation with neighboring states without feeling the need to duplicate with other neighbors what is done for one neighbor. The financial and economic relations between Nigeria, Dahomey, and Togo have been rather closer than and of a different nature from those between Nigeria and Niger. Also, the military assistance to Niger when it was under Hamani Diori has not been duplicated, and so far there have been no complaints.

Under both Balewa and Yakubu Gowon, many intelligentsia felt that Nigeria was not doing enough to assert itself on the African scene. Some maintained that Nigeria should be more comprehensively involved in African affairs; others went so far as to suggest that Nigeria should impose its will on others because of its potentially dominant military and economic position. As long as the energies of the political actors were directed toward internal problems, the pressure on the government for external involvement could be deflected. However, the newly acquired sense of national unity has led to national pride and increasingly insistent and loud demands for policies commensurate with Nigeria's size.What these demands will ultimately mean is not clear. But if assertive policies on the part of Nigeria should be seen by her neighbors as contrary to their interests, if they should be seen as Nigerian interference in their internal affairs, then the cause of regional cooperation will be damaged. It was precisely this kind of bully foreign policy that damaged Ghana's relationships with her neighbors when Kwame Nkrumah was in power.

National pride and integration, of course, need not always have unfavorable consequences on regional cooperation. If the state is small, in fact, the opposite could well result. But in the case of a wealthy and big state, it is probably inevitable because the logic of size and wealth imposes its own quantum of involvement. It is surely debatable whether the role of the Ivory Coast in the *Conseil d'Entente* has always been positive. It does seem that a happy middle ground would be achieved if the state with the physical and economic capability to dominate a region interprets its role in terms of advancing proposals while leaving the course and content of the regional cooperation to the determination of the majority of the states in the region. This course looks like the one Nigeria has been following and should continue to follow.

Notes

1. *Report of Coker Commission of Inquiry into the Affairs of Certain Statutory Corporations in Western Nigeria, 1962*, vol. I (Lagos: Federal Ministry of Information, 1962), p. 39.
2. John West, "Dahomey Should Join Nigeria," *Daily Service*, March 10, 1960.
3. Anthony Enahoro, *Fugitive Offender: An Autobiography* (London: Casell, 1965), p. 177.
4. Ahmadu Bello, *My Life* (Cambridge: Cambridge University Press, 1962), pp. 228-229. The Action Group had also threatened to take the West out of the federation in 1953.
5. *West Africa*, March 11, 1961, p. 271.
6. For a detailed account see Victor T. LeVine, *The Cameroons: From Mandate to Independence* (Berkeley and Los Angeles: University of California Press, 1964).
7. See *Daily Times*, November 11, 1959: "Now that the British had succeeded in breaking the ties between Northern Nigeria and the Northern Cameroons,

the British Chancellor of the Exchequer would no doubt go ahead with the suspected plan of building the Trust Territory into an earthly paradise for the Whiteman as well as a strategic military base for Britain."

8. Feb. 26, 1961.
9. Bolaji Akinyemi, "Nigeria and Fernando Po, 1958-1966: The Politics of Irredentism,"*African Affairs,* Vol. 69, No. 276 (July 1970), pp. 236-249.
10. *Daily Times,* Jan. 20, 1961.
11. *House of Representatives Debates,* April 23, 1963.
12. *West Africa,* Jan. 1, 1966, p. 23.

Chapter 4

The De-Indianization of Uganda: Who Is a Citizen?

by Ali A. Mazrui

FROM UGANDA'S own point of view, perhaps the most fundamental question that arose following President Idi Amin's decision to expel noncitizen Asians was, quite simply, what the economic life of Uganda would be like without the Asians. Would there be a smooth adjustment after initial dislocations? Were black Africans likely to be as effective in commerce and the professions as the Asians had been? Or were there fundamental cultural and sociological differences between the two races that would make it very difficult for the Asians to be effectively replaced?

The Origins of Indophobia

This chapter does indeed start from the premise that the Asians attained their levels of economic and professional success not only because of historical factors, which favored them in the colonial period, but also because of cultural factors, which were relevant to their business success even though their status was that of a minority. As so often happens with immigrants in new societies, a preselection is involved. Many of the Indians who came to Uganda were, almost by definition, drawn from the more ambitious and the more enterprising sectors of the population in the Indian subcontinent. Their readiness to uproot themselves from their ancestral soil, and try their fortunes in lands fundamentally different from their

77

own, implied that the Indians who came started off with a high degree of ambition and enterprise.

The Indians of East Africa might, therefore, be said to have evolved for a time a distinct subculture of their own, different both from the culture of their immediate neighbors in East Africa, and from the dominant value systems of the Indian subcontinent itself. Again, such a process is not unusual for a minority group that transplants itself to another part of the world. Differences eventually begin to emerge between the minority group and the parent entity from whose womb it sprang. The Indians of East Africa were no exception; they developed an economic subculture that was more enterprising than the dominant cultures of the Indian subcontinent, but that also drew, of course, a good deal from the parent culture.[1]

The British colonial authorities sharpened the entrepreneurial factor in the local economic subculture of Asian immigrants. They did so by forcing the Asians away from certain areas of endeavor, especially farming and food production. In Kenya, for example, the white settlers monopolized the field of cash crops and kept the Asians at bay. In Uganda some Indian participation became crucial in selective cash crops, but the principle of maintaining black ownership of land drastically reduced the potential for Asians in agriculture and diverted their energies even more purposefully into commerce and the professions.

The Asians did become successful in the business world, the liberal occupations, and in the clerical, managerial, and administrative areas of specialization. Indeed, they became too successful for their own safety in the long run. Not long after independence, measures were being considered by the new government of Uganda to reduce the Asian factor in the national economy. The policy of drastically curtailing the Indian presence in East Africa was by no means invented by General Amin.

It became clear quite shortly after independence that three distinct elements were involved in this entire endeavor. First, there was the deep race consciousness that had been building up for half a century, and that emphasized people's awareness of each other's color of skin; second, there was the fragile but growing territorial nationalism attached to the new entity called Uganda; and third, there was a genuine desire to create an effective African entrepreneurial culture and a successful African business class.[2]

The race consciousness made Asians vulnerable, whether or not they adopted local citizenship. The territorial nationalism exposed black Africans from neighboring countries working in Uganda, while at the same time protecting those Asians who had adopted Ugandan citizenship. In other words, when Uganda adopted policies based on territorial nationalism,

Rwandese, Kenyans, and Tanzanians, however black, were more exposed than Asians who had adopted local citizenship. This circumstance certainly applied in the last 18 months of President Milton Obote's rule; his new labor policies resulted in a large exodus of black Kenyans, many of whom had lived and worked in Uganda for many years. Obote seemed to be embarking on policies similar to those adopted by Dr. Kofi Busia when he was prime minister of Ghana. Busia in 1969 and 1970 initiated a series of measures under which thousands of Nigerians and other non-Ghanaian West Africans trekked forth, uprooted from their normal areas of residence, often impoverished in the very act of removing themselves from Ghana. Similarly, in Uganda under Obote, cooks, porters, houseboys, large numbers of whom were from Kisumu and surrounding areas in Kenya, were forced out of the country, whereas the future of Asians who were citizens remained secure for the time being.

The third factor in this entire Asian question was the ambition to create a local entrepreneurial private enterprise system. Independence had brought effective African participation in government, administration, university life, managerial work, the clerical professions, law, and, increasingly, medicine and other professions. But African participation in the higher reaches of the commercial life of the country was still modest. Again, Obote's government, partly following Kenya's lead, started a series of measures to promote the Africanization of commerce in Uganda. The measures ranged from special loans to enable Africans to enter the commercial world to a request by the Uganda Government to Makerere University that a School of Business be established as quickly as possible. In 1969 the Trade Licensing Act was passed in Uganda, and a new Immigration Act was also passed under Obote's government, both of which were designed to contain and circumscribe the Asian presence in business and to promote more rigorously an effective African entry into this area of national endeavor.

Then in January 1971 the army overthrew Obote, and before long Indophobia entered a new phase. We define "Indophobia" as a tendency to react negatively toward people of Indian extraction. Cultural Indophobia is a reaction against aspects of Indian culture and normative habits; economic Indophobia in East Africa has been a resentment of Indians as a successful economic group.

By August 1972 General Idi Amin had decided to push the logic of Indophobia to its extremity. Why not throw out the Asians altogether? Original estimates placed the total number of Asians in Uganda at 80,000 — less than 1 percent of the entire population. Of the 80,000, about 23,000 were thought to be Uganda citizens. The rest were mainly British Asians (once estimated at more than 50,000) plus a few thousand from India,

Pakistan, and Bangladesh. The noncitizens were given 90 days, beginning August 8, 1972, in which to wind up their businesses and depart. The Uganda citizens had their papers subjected to a new scrutiny — and many lost their Uganda citizenship.

In the wake of the expulsion of Asians, can black Ugandans now take over and continue successfully? Much depends upon whether they are capable of evolving an economic culture as relevant to success as was the Indian subculture among the immigrants. If there are unfavorable cultural factors in their systems of values, adequate success in the economic sphere could presumably presuppose some basic cultural changes. Can these cultural changes be brought about without a major "educational revolution"?

We would argue that a major educational revolution is needed if the Asians are ultimately to be effectively replaced in their roles and functions. By the term "educational revolution," however, we mean more than just changes in schools, colleges, and the university. Important changes in the formal educational institutions may indeed be needed for this purpose, but even more fundamental is the double task of making structural changes in the wider society and promoting new forms of economic acculturation in the population as a whole. The changes in the wider society must include new attitudes toward acquisition and consumption, new perspectives on economic risk-taking as against bureaucratic security, a more modernized form of citizenship, and a transformation of the values themselves.

From Kinship to Citizenship

Let us attempt to understand both the strengths and the limitations of General Amin's conception of citizenship in a wider anthropological context. When the British arrived in Uganda, they found a number of societies, some of which had state structures. Among the more developed, and certainly one that developed even further under colonial rule, was Buganda. Bunyoro was also a highly structured polity. The concept of citizenship in these societies was inseparable from the concept of kinship. All the Baganda together were deemed to be descended from a single ancestor. The state rested on a principle of political consanguinity, a presumed descent from a shared forefather.

At its most literal, consanguinity implies a blood tie, but in fact there were other ties connected either with marriage and adoption or with cultural assimilation. New citizens of an African society did not become full citizens until they mixed their blood with the original members of that society, or adopted more fully the language and culture of that society. Biological intermingling and cultural assimilation were the most effective ways by which foreigners could enter the mainstream of African citizenship. President Amin's response to the cultural and sexual exclusiveness of the Asians of Uganda rested in part upon a primordial African conception of true citizenship. The Asians, by being distant culturally and by being reluctant to mingle their blood with black Ugandans, remained alien by this criterion. They could no more become Ugandans than could an Acholi who refused to intermarry with the Baganda and resisted the adoption of the Ganda cultural ways ever be deemed a Muganda.

Among communities to the north, on both sides of the Sudan-Uganda border, political ideas sometimes went to the extent of regarding all those who were not kinsmen as basically potential enemies. The distinction between a foreigner and an enemy could be very thin indeed, which did not necessarily mean that the groups automatically attacked strangers and foreigners who came in contact with them. But it did mean that they regarded them with the kind of reserve and deep suspicion usually accorded to traditional enemies.

It is possible to be adopted as a kinsman fictionally, or be given protection in terms of presumed kinship, but the stranger is then expected to behave like a kinsman, permitting himself to be assimilated into the system of rights and duties of that society. In the words of E.E. Evans-Pritchard in his study of the Nuer:

> If you wish to live among the Nuer you must do so on their terms, which means that you must treat them as a kind of kinsman and they will then treat you as a kind of kinsman. Rights, privileges and obligations are determined by kinship. Either a man is a kinsman, actually or by fiction, or he is a person to whom you have no reciprocal obligations and whom you treat as a potential enemy.[3]

General Amin is in some respects deeply African in his attitudes and presuppositions, but his values are those of an African receding into the past. His demands on the Asians echoed some of these anthropological findings about traditional political societies in Africa. Amin has been primordial in his demand for cultural identification and biological intermingling; he has also been primordial in his tendency to regard complete aliens as basically potential enemies; and thirdly, he has been primordial in his distrust of private choice in matters of public concern.

African societies within themselves are an impressive cluster of mutual obligations and responsibilities, an impressive system of fellowship based on the solidarity of kinship. That is why President Julius Nyerere virtually equated the English word "socialism" with the Swahili word *Ujamaa*. The latter is a term denoting the bonds of kinship, the obligation of young people to look after the old and of the old to care for the young, the readiness to extend hospitality, the presumed duty of whoever is better off among kinsmen to look after those who are not quite as well off. Nyerere saw in Ujamaa the roots of socialism.

By contrast, Amin saw in Ujamaa the roots of *citizenship*. Just as Nyerere moved on from tribal solidarity to the solidarity of socialistic fellowship, so Amin sought to move from the bonds of the clan to membership in the nation-state. Amin could see this easily enough where all the groups were black in color. Racial identification permits the psychological leap from tribal pride to black ethnicity.

Soon after assuming power in January 1971, Amin emerged as someone within the classical tradition of viewing the nation as a family writ large. His adoption of the title Dada, patriarch, confirmed his image of the role of the president as being in some fundamental sense a father figure. His view of marriage as a device of tribal intermingling was also in a classical tradition of its own. Intermarriage becomes part of the foundation of national integration, simply because kinship was part of the foundation of citizenship. The general himself began to take pride in having one wife drawn from the Lugbara, one from the Basoga, one from the Langi, and later, one from the Baganda. Not all his marriages have survived since then, but Amin's approach to social integration has remained profoundly African.

Yet there is always a problem when, in the context of modern sensibilities, a head of state sees himself as the father of the nation. The logical problem in terminology arises when he is unable to refer to his fellow citizens as "my children." If he had been a very old figure, like Mzee Kenyatta, the term "my children" could have aroused an indulgent response from the population. Mzee Kenyatta is after all a real "Mzee"—an old man, an aged elder, enjoying widespread, though not universal, reverence among Kenyans. General Amin, however, is relatively young as a head of state. In his role as a Dada, or patriarch, he must at the same time refrain from the condescension of treating his fellow citizens as children.

And yet the general still likes to think of Uganda as in some sense a large Kakwa family, and all Ugandans as being to some extent his kinsmen. And so, although the general himself is a father, he calls his children "my brothers and sisters." By calling his children "brothers and sisters" he maintains an egalitarian relationship with them, at least in vocabulary and tone. It is like those Western parents who now permit their children to call them by their first names, and have abolished the term "daddy" and "mummy" from the vocabulary of the family. The philosophy behind this Western innovation is an attempt to establish a kind of parity of esteem between children and their parents from an early age, and prepare the ground for a relationship of equality. Similarly, General Idi Amin Dada, while viewing himself as the head of the family, prefers to use the vocabulary of fraternity, rather than of filial relationship.

The general can see himself as a father figure for all black Ugandans. But he continues to have great psychological problems in seeing himself as a father figure for brown Ugandans (there are some still left). The racial exclusiveness of the Asians aggravated the general's incapacity to see the Asians in kinship terms.

And yet in the ultimate analysis Africa must move away from conceptions of citizenship based on kinship to conceptions of citizenship that, though retaining some link with descent, also allow for contractual rights and obligations. The modern nation-state must, in fact, respect even more the person who is a citizen by act of will than the one who is a citizen by biological accident.

Before independence most Asians enjoyed the same colonial status as most Africans—colonial subjects or "British protected persons". But when Uganda attained independence the Asians had in effect three choices: they could become British, adopt Ugandan citizenship, or return to the Indian subcontinent. A similar choice confronted the Asians of Kenya, and less clearly the Asians of Tanzania. The majority of Asians in East Africa chose to invest in British citizenship. But those Asians who adopted local citizenship were, from the point of view of the modern rational basis of social arrangements, greater East Africans precisely because they had a choice to be something else — and yet decided to commit themselves to the soil of their adoption.

Very few indigenous East Africans (i.e., black Africans) had any choice in their citizenship. To some extent their predicament was classical in African terms, as it was derived from the biological accident of descent. Of course, these East Africans ought to retain full rights as citizens. The modern state ought not to move in the direction of victimizing indigenous citizens, simply because in their case they had no choice. But it is especially important to protect the rights of the non-indigenous citizens—those Asians in East Africa who looked at that ominous question mark hanging over the continent at independence, and decided by a conscious act of will that they would throw in their lot with the social groups among whom they lived.

When these non-indigenous citizens were ordered in Uganda in August 1972 to go and stand in queues to confirm what they thought was already confirmed, they responded with impressive conformity. I know of Uganda Asians who accidently happened to be abroad thousands of miles away when they were required to report at the Kampala Immigration Office to confirm their citizenship. Some traversed half the globe in order to join those queues. Because the notice was so short, the queues outside the Immigration Office used to assemble from the previous night, sleeping on the pavement, waiting for the offices to open at eight o'clock the following morning. And then when they got to the counter the following noon, they perhaps stood there anxiously awaiting the verdict. A little irregularity, a wrong numbering here, and an unclear signature there, or a birth certificate of one's grandfather long lost, was sometimes enough to lead to a declaration that they had never been citizens at all—that their papers were false and their status null and void. Those Asians are quite apart from those who renounced British citizenship after the 90-day deadline.

Citizenship in the modern sense has often as strong a moral content as kinship solidarity. Administrative or legalistic irregularities should indeed necessitate further scrutiny of individual cases, carefully considered with a readiness to give the benefit of the doubt to the person who is a citizen. Only concrete proof of fraud could justify the cancellation of citizenship. The discovery of administrative delays, or wrong pagination, or unclear official stamps, or clerical delays from London may justify further thought on the matter, but on no account do they justify a frivolous game with people's moral commitments.

The general's final decision not to expel Asian citizens after all was a decision of political courage, considering that he had previously pronounced otherwise. But the meaningfulness of the decision required a seriousness of purpose further down the administrative hierarchy to prevent technicalities and irregularities from being invoked as a mode of trivializing solemn contractual obligations.

In historical terms, more is at stake in the citizenship adventure than the fate of a few thousand Asians. What is at stake is Uganda's capacity to modernize herself, and move efficiently from a world of pure kinsmen to a world of compatriots, from a morality of clan to a legality of contract, from primordial ethnicity to modern nationhood. The few thousand remaining Asians should get extra protection—at least as much for the sake of Uganda as for themselves.

But economically and professionally, will Uganda survive the departure of all the others? It is too early to conduct an adequate cost-benefit analysis of the de-Indianization of Uganda. There have been societies in history that never fully recovered from the consequences of their intolerance toward minorities. Spain is one such society. But Ugandans have a duty to try and salvage what they can. Even natural disasters can sometimes be put to creative purposes, where there is a will to do so.

The Commercialization of the Military

Leaving aside for the moment the unfortunate aspects of the expulsion of much of Uganda's Indian population, we now turn to consider one way in which the new economic opportunities offered by their departure might provide an opportunity to promote national integration and stability. Because foreigners are traditionally regarded in some African societies as potential enemies, and because different ethnic groups within the same society continue to regard each other as foreigners even when they are all black, an acute danger does persist in the relations between these ethnic groups. And these relations in times of stress could degenerate into a militarized confrontation.

African soldiers tend to be recruited from those strata of society that are still bound by such traditionalist values. The Africans that have undergone a process of de-traditionalization are those who have either moved physically for a long time to situations where they have no kinsmen nearby, or those who have undergone a system of secular education, usually of the Western style. The armed forces in Africa recruit from strata of societies different from the more highly educated. It could be argued that the real problem with soldiers in Africa is not that they are very politically conscious, but that they are underpoliticized. The level of political consciousness among recruits is often frighteningly low, and there is a marked lack of sensitivity to the political implications of their actions. President Nyerere of Tanzania staggered onto this fact after the 1964 mutiny, and Tanzania then took active steps to raise the level of political education among the rank and file of its reconstituted army.[4]

When President Obote of Uganda was shot at and wounded on December 19, 1969, roadblocks were set up around Kampala to control the movements of some of those who might have been implicated in the attempted assassination, and to contain any civil strife which might follow the attack. The soldiers had a job to do, and many of them performed their task with competence and humaneness. But there were also reports of the senseless brutalization of people stopped at roadblocks, and even of the pointless killings of innocent civilians.[5]

These incidents in some ways echoed the experience of the previous month. When the ex-Kabaka of Buganda died suddenly in exile in London, the government of Uganda was presented with a delicate problem. Because the Kabaka was the leading opponent of the regime there could be no question of officially recognizing his death as an event of any importance, and yet to prevent the Baganda from mourning their late leader would have been to run the risk of serious popular disturbances. The government adopted a conciliatory stance, and mourning was permitted. However, when large crowds assembled outside the Royal Tombs at Kasubi, they were dispersed by the army, and for several days afterward soldiers molested civilians going about their business in the area. The government may have been involved in the original decision to prevent the formation of large crowds of emotional mourners, but there can be little doubt that it was embarrassed by the way in which the decision was implemented. The actions of some elements in the armed forces were counterproductive in terms of the realization of government policy.

Uganda has not been unique in these problems concerning discipline in the armed forces. Several other African governments have encountered comparable difficulties. Uganda experienced some of the stresses of having created rather rapidly a new army for independence, which was then allowed to expand quite quickly. The rawness of some of the recruitment aggravated the difficulties of socializing the troops.

Throughout much of Africa there is the phenomenon of a rugged militariat, relatively unsophisticated politically, and unaware quite often of the possible consequences of its acts. These are compatriots who are under-politicized in the sense of not having been subjected to a process of socialization that would have made them conscious of the nature of citizenship and its rights, the meaning of individual protection, the boundaries of authority, and the concept of national interest.[6]

In a sense the most fundamental of the processes of political socialization are those that relate to national integration on the one hand and to consolidation of political authority on the other. Soldiers become nationally integrated when they become capable of recognizing the bonds of shared nationality and respecting the rights of federal citizens. Soldiers become absorbed into the system of authority when they learn to measure physical force against legitimate need, when they recognize their place in the pattern of roles and functions within the social system, when they learn to respect socially sanctioned frontiers of authority, and when they are sensitized to the broader concept of national welfare.[7]

In addition, the training of soldiers during the colonial period presupposed a pattern of military duties that would involve dealing with distant foreigners as enemies. The techniques transmitted were techniques of maiming and killing. Whereas soldiers of the developed countries in the West may indeed have their primary military duties defined in terms of foreign wars, soldiers in much of Africa find themselves dealing most of the time with fellow citizens of the same country. Here are people drawn from traditionalist norms, tending often to regard total foreigners as potential enemies, inadequately sensitized as yet to regard people from other ethnic groups as compatriots. And yet these same people were trained by the colonial authorities not in the soft arts of dealing with troublesome fellow citizens within, but in the harsh skills of destruction. A paramount educational revolution from the point of view of the soldiers is a revolution that would at last recognize that the previous philosophy of military training inherited from the imperial power is inappropriate in countries that have very few foreign wars to fight, and few international alliances to maintain. The most immediate duties of soldiers in a country like Uganda involve relations with their own compatriots.

But the process of politicizing the soldiers in terms of moral sensibilities to their new political systems may not be separable from a process of economicizing those soldiers. The two processes are indeed substantially different. The consequences of soldiers becoming political animals are to be distinguished from the consequences of their becoming significant economic agents. Nevertheless, it may well be that the two processes, like politics and economics at large, need each other for mutual reinforcement.

In the Ugandan situation, the issue that arises is whether the entry of soldiers into the world of business and commerce will create among them new perspectives concerning the value of stability. Where soldiers regard themselves as a group apart, in a relationship of economic warfare against the bourgeoisie, the soldiers' interest in commercial stability would not be paramount. For them, other issues would intrude and demand more immediate attention. But, to use fictitious names, when Lieutenant Colonel Multindo and Captain Hamisi become, in addition to their military roles, shareholders in this industry, or actual owners of that shop, these two military figures will evolve a productive interest in commercial stability in its own right. And commercial stability is often an aspect of general political stability.

Not all the businesses and shops previously owned by Asians will in fact be bought or acquired by the soldiers. The soldiers are likely to become only a fraction of the total size of the national bourgeoisie. There will be many civilian businessmen to every one military entrepreneur. But the economic interpretation between the civilian and economic sectors of society should help to reenforce the bonds between them. That old sociological theory of cross-cutting loyalties, as Lugbara soldiers find a point of affinity with fellow shareholders among the Baganda, could help both to demilitarize ethnic confrontations and reinforce the trend toward the bonds of modern citizenship.

For the time being, General Amin himself has categorically asserted that he would not personally go into business. Some of his statements also seem to encourage civil servants and soldiers to enter business, but as an alternative career to their present one. In the actual operation of the Africanization of commercial activity in Uganda, however, the possibility of civil servants and soldiers being at the same time investors can hardly be ruled out.

As soldiers enter the culture of calculating profits and loss, their attitudes toward the virtues of procedure and predictability, together with the whole system of analyzing in terms of cost and benefit, might indeed undergo a change. Through the commercialization of the soldiery, a process of re-stabilizing Uganda might be set in motion.[8]

Conclusion

We have attempted in this paper to see beyond the heartaches of the present situation in Uganda. We have accepted the drastic de-Indianization of Uganda as a *given,* and then sought to discern both the signs of hopes and the lines of future reforms demanded by the situation. Uganda must continue to live with herself, even after the Indians have departed.

But although the de-Indianization of Uganda is now, on the whole, irreversible, reservations remain regarding the way in which it was done. It is true that General Amin invented neither the psychology of Indophobia nor the policy of economic de-Indianization in East Africa. His measures to expel Asian noncitizens were an acceleration of the policies of his predecessor, Obote. But in that very acceleration lay the special dangers of the policies. A phased de-Indianization program could have been conducted without an excessive dislocation of services and needs of Uganda, and without too much disruption of the lives of the Asians involved. Indeed, the de-Indianization program should have been accompanied with a manpower program for Uganda. Uganda should indeed have refused the unilateral British quota system, devised by London under the Commonwealth Immigration Act to control the number of British Asians who could enter Britain in any one year. Uganda should simply have introduced a quota system of its own about how many British Asians may remain in Uganda based on some rough manpower projections, oriented toward helping Uganda to realize its policies without dislocating some of its own services. The Uganda Government could have said that one particular category of British Asians (e.g. bank managers) should leave, say, by June 1973; another category (e.g. lawyers) should leave by December 1973; a third category (e.g. shopkeepers in specified cities) should leave by August 1974; and the bulk of the rest of the population of Asians from Britain, India, Bangladesh and Pakistan should leave by, say, December 1975. But the government of Uganda should still have allowed for a system of exemptions, even after December 1975. These exemptions could have been either on the basis of Uganda's continuing need for some particular categories of manpower (e.g. doctors and teachers), or for humanitarian considerations in special individual cases. These latter humanitarian exemptions would surely include Asians too old to be expelled to a new and strange environment.

If by 1975 the Asian population of Uganda had been reduced from the peak of 80,000 to a mere 10,000, and the latter figure consisted overwhelmingly of Uganda citizens themselves, the government could have proceeded to use creatively these very gifted people as citizens, and at the same time promote a new indigenous business class. The Asians who have adopted citizenship in East Africa are basically greater East Africans, as we mentioned earlier. They have made the impressive move from kinship to citizenship.

In any case, it makes sense that they should be regarded as simply one additional African ethnic group. Kinship culture should be used in a new way. If Indians are overrepresented in commerce and some of the professions, so are the Baganda in the civil service, and northern peoples of Uganda in the security forces. There is a case for restoring the balance in commerce and the professions, just as there is a case for such a restoration of balance in the armed forces and the civil service. The methods used in that restoration should be as considerate as those that might be devised to deal with other problems of ethnic arithmetic in the nation.

Another balance also needs to be struck — a healthier balance between race consciousness and human toleration; between territorial nationalism and the larger African view; and between the promotion of an indigenous private enterprise system and the dictates of economic and social justice.[9]

But even this balance cannot be effectively struck without social reform and new modes of economic acculturation. The educational institutions have to respond with a new emphasis on *free* secondary education and *expanded* vocational training. It is hoped that the civil service may never again become a fortress of complacent security, devouring disproportionately the skilled manpower of the country. Above all, ethnicity in Uganda needs to be demilitarized, and the soldiers have to acquire a new awareness of the costs and benefits of what they do. The partial politicization of the soldiers may indeed need to be accompanied by a partial commercialization.

The owl of Minerva hovers over Uganda's dark hours — while the cockerel of Masaka is waiting to announce a new dawn.

Notes

1. We use the adjective "Indian" in this paper mainly to refer to the Indian sub-continent as a whole, including Pakistan and Bangladesh, rather than just the Republic of India alone. The more popular word in East Africa for this group of people is, of course, "Asian."

2. I have discussed this third ambition more fully in Mazrui, *Cultural Engineering and Nation-Building in East Africa* (Evanston: Northwestern University Press, 1972), especially chap. 12 and 13. See also Mazrui, "Sex and Indophobia" Lecture delivered at Markerere University Main Hall, Kampala, Jan. 26, 1972).

3. E. E. Evans-Pritchard, *The Nuer* (Oxford: Clarendon Press, 1940), p. 183.

4. For details of some of the problems involved see Henry Bienen, *Tanzania: Party Transformation and Economic Development* (Princeton: Princeton University Press, 1967), pp. 374-481.

5. These issues are discussed in a related context by John D. Chick and Ali A. Mazrui in "The Nigerian Army and African Images of the Military" (Paper presented at the Seventh World Congress of the International Sociological Association, Varna, Bulgaria, September 14-19, 1970).

6. Refer also to Mazrui, "Political Science and Social Commitment across Two Republics of Uganda" (Paper delivered at the Universities Social Science Conference of Eastern Africa, Makerere University, Kampala, December 1971).

7. For a neo-Marxian interpretation of the Uganda coup consult, Michael F. Lofchie, "The Uganda Coup — Class Action by the Military," *Journal of Modern African Studies,* Vol. 10, No. 1 (May, 1972), pp. 19-35.

8. Consult also my paper "The Lumpen Proletariat and the Lumpen Militariat: African Soldiers as a New Political Class" (Seminar Paper No. DSP6/72-73, Department of Political Science and Public Administration, Makerere University, August 1972), mimeographed.

9. This critique of Amin's style of de-Indianization was first published in Uganda in my feature article, "Exodus, 1972," *The People* (Kampala) (September 9, 1972).

Part III

Economic Planning and Education

Introduction

IT MAY not be immediately apparent why economic planning and education should be considered together in this section. Obviously, in some respects these two subjects relate to national integration in quite different ways. Yet in one central regard they are closely related. Disparities in the economic status and economic prospects of a state's constituent ethnic groups stand among the most widespread and serious sources of ethnic tension and conflict. At times these economic disparities arise from the fact that certain ethnic groups have enjoyed educational opportunities that in turn have given them an edge in competition for government posts and private employment. Thus, many economic disparities have their source in the educational sector. Some ethnic groups may also be economically disadvantaged because their traditional homelands suffer from insufficient natural resources, poor farmland, or inadequate infrastructure, such as roads, railways, electricity, and communications systems.

Disadvantaged groups frequently point to the evil machinations of the opposition ethnic group that controls political power to explain why they have fared poorly in intergroup economic competition. Such charges often have substance. In the majority of situations, however, the causes of economic disparities are more complex and cannot so lightly be attributed to ethnic discrimination or political factors. Kwamina Dickson's chapter is particularly illuminating in describing the historical background to disparities in economic well-being among Ghana's ethnic groups. In planning infrastructural development in Ghana, the British colonial administration took two major factors into consideration: first, the location of exploitable and exportable resources, whether mineral or agricultural; and second, the character and placement of existing trade routes and population concentrations. Most of the road and rail routes the British built benefited those areas, and in turn those ethnic groups, that were already ascendant economically. These routes, therefore, had the consequence of further improving the economic situation of certain advantaged groups, not only absolutely but also relative to those who were historically disadvantaged. Some readjustments naturally occurred as commodities that had not been previously exploitable were marketed, but for the most part economic development during the colonial period in Ghana meant that existing economic strengths were capitalized upon and existing intergroup disparities became more severe. The few efforts made to rectify these regional-ethnic imbalances, like the cotton scheme in the north, were poorly planned or encountered technical obstacles and ended as failures.

Some of the continuing economic disparities among African ethnic groups can be rectified, however, or at least brought into closer balance, and the political problems to which they give rise can to that extent be ameliorated. Despite built-in difficulties, much of this task can be accomplished through greater attention to regional planning and to the economic potential of every geographic and ethnic region. Although regional planning has gained some respectability among economic planners in recent years, interest in it has prompted more talk than action.[1] In large measure this inactivity results from the unfortunate fact that economists' comprehension of how to assess and exploit resources on a regional basis is still very limited.

The viability of some African political systems may hinge upon governments making strides toward the promotion of greater regional-ethnic equity in levels and rates of economic growth. Yet it must be readily conceded that paying serious attention to the spatial aspect of economic development poses some very hard choices for African governments. To give prime consideration to the equitable distribution of development projects and to plan the positioning of development not solely in terms of economic cost-benefit ratios means abandoning the use of national growth rates as the measure of successful planning. Hence, governments that adopt a planning strategy in the interests of intergroup equity must be prepared to make some national economic sacrifices. Even with effective regional planning, perfect equity can never be attained. As Dickson asserts, "The issue here is not how to attain uniform areal development throughout the country, for that would be unrealistic. There will always be spatial variations in development. Rather, the issue is one of stimulating development in poor areas while at the same time maintaining a fair rate of national development." Dickson warns that to do otherwise is to court serious social and political unrest in Ghana, and the same can be said for most other African states.

The level of economic prosperity and the character of economic opportunities available in a geographic area largely determines the economic well-being of its indigenous ethnic group. But the economic status of an ethnic group also depends upon the jobs held by those members who migrate to urban areas. How successful these migrants are in competing for jobs is largely dependent upon their educational achievement. Thus the degree of educational development contributes substantially to the economic standing, and the bureaucratic and institutional power, of ethnic group members. Levels of educational attainment are thus decisive factors in the inter-ethnic competition for wealth and power, and sharp intergroup disparities often create serious social and political tensions.[2] Such disparities were certainly among the factors that caused the Nigerian civil war, and inasmuch as the educational gap among Nigeria's ethnic groups remains vast, it continues to be a potential source of political conflict and national instability.[3] Although intergroup imbalances are not quite as great in most other African states as they are in Nigeria, such disequilibriums certainly pose very real problems for both Ghana, as described by Audrey Smock, and for Cameroon, as discussed in the chapter by Remi Clignet.

Some of these discrepancies in educational attainment among ethnic groups are attributable to contrasting traditional values or perspectives. Most, however, derive from a variety of factors quite extraneous to ethnic differences per se. Some groups, for instance, have enjoyed special educational opportunities because of their proximity to urban centers or because of early missionary contact. Educational attainment, of course, usually provides the basis for socioeconomic mobility—and socioeconomic status influences the degree of access to educational opportunities. This circular and mutually reinforcing relationship between economic status and educational opportunity makes it especially hard to rectify intergroup imbalances once they have developed. The chapters on Ghana and Cameroon describe the difficulties the governments of these two states have had in trying to intervene in this cycle and overcome some of the disparities among their ethnic groups.

Aside from the very considerable practical problems entailed in trying to surmount intergroup educational disparities, efforts to rectify them provoke other serious issues. For instance, in states where education is considered a universal right, opposition will naturally be voiced to any government action that imposes ethnic quotas on admission to educational institutions or that favors certain groups over others in admissions. For states that conceive of their educational system as primarily serving the ends of national economic development, ethnic calculations bring extraneous and dysfunctional factors into the educational equation. Any government that bases its educational planning solely on manpower considerations faces many such difficulties.[4] And as James Coleman has written, "A premature and excessive effort to impose or to realize equality may so disperse meager resources that system capacity is gravely weakened, if not destroyed."[5]

Clearly, educational development has often exacerbated intergroup differences and engendered heightened intergroup tensions in Africa.[6]

Nevertheless, the educational system constitutes the most effective instrument available to governments to promote various dimensions of national integration. The chapters in Part IV discuss the close relationship between the educational system and those aspects of a state's language policy that influence the process of national integration. Similarly, the success of efforts to promote a national culture and an improved national communications system depends heavily upon promulgating new cultural forms and creating a literate and informed citizenry through the educational system.

Two other potential functions of an educational system have equal import for national integration. The first is the contribution the educational system can make to the process of political socialization; the second is the opportunity if offers for ethnic mixing. More than 2,000 years ago, Plato and other political theorists were already aware of the crucial role of education and childhood training in instilling national loyalty and appropriate citizenship values. The emphasis in the last decade on the systematic and comparative study of social systems has called attention once again to political socialization, or the process through which members of society acquire politically relevant orientations and patterns of behavior. Although most of the political socialization research has dealt with American and Western European children, some of the findings regarding the transmission of national identity and loyalty have significant implications for the states of Africa. Five relevant findings are as follows:

1. The school can be employed as the central agent of political socialization.[7]
2. Countries with multi-ethnic populations have been able to socialize students to a national identity through the system of public education in a relatively brief period of time without sacrificing cultural pluralism.
3. The amount of emphasis on social and political subjects,[8] the content of the social studies curriculum,[9] the teaching methods, and the composition of the student body[10] affect the process and success of political socialization by schools.
4. The critical period for imparting the foundations for national loyalty and respect for political authority is early in childhood.[11]
5. Political socialization in early childhood involves the personalization and idealization of political authority, most notably the central executive figure in the political system.[12]

States with multi-ethnic populations, such as the United States, the Soviet Union, and Israel, have consciously employed the public educational system as the paramount nationalization agent with considerable success.

The large-scale influx of immigrants from Europe and Asia to the United States during the second part of the nineteenth century, the Soviet inheritance of the multi-ethnic and disunited czarist empire, and the settling of Jews from throughout the world in Israel subsequent to its creation confronted these states with problems of national integration comparable in many respects to those faced by the new states of Africa. These three countries have placed an extraordinary emphasis on civic education for the young through the schools.[13] Immigrant schoolchildren in the United States not only assimilated an American identity and democratic norms, they frequently transmitted them to their parents.[14] In a relatively brief period of time, the United States achieved a sense of national identity among its citizens without seriously undermining the cultural heritage of its diverse immigrant groups.[15] It remains a nation of nations, a composite of many different ethnic groups embracing a common national identity along with a strong sense of patriotism and national loyalty.[16] Likewise, the Soviet Union has created a strong sense of patriotism among its multi-ethnic population.[17]

Clignet indicates in his chapter some skepticism regarding the extent to which schools in Africa can serve as effective instruments for political socialization. Although in her chapter on Ghana, Audrey Smock recounts the difficulties that Ghanaian schools have had and will continue to have in this sphere, she stresses the opportunities available to Ghanaian and other educational systems in Africa for instilling a sense of national identity, for promoting intergroup tolerance, and for augmenting the legitimacy of the state.

The other potential role of the schools in promoting national integration that both Audrey Smock and Remi Clignet discuss in detail is the opportunity schools offer for children to mix with students and teachers of different ethnic groups. Research done previously in other countries[18] underscores the great contribution schools can make in this regard. Unfortunately, the fact that most schools in Ghana and Cameroon tend to be relatively homogeneous ethnically, because of the geographic concentration of ethnic groups, means that schools do not provide as much opportunity for interethnic exposure as would be desirable for the purposes of national integration.

Notes

1. For a discussion of regional planning in relation to sectoral planning, see Jos G. M. Hilhorst, *Regional Planning* (Rotterdam: Rotterdam University Press, 1971).

2. This is an interesting and important illustration of what Philip Foster refers to as the unanticipated, unintended, and dysfunctional consequences of the introduction of Western education in Africa. See his *Education and Social Change in Ghana* (London: Routledge and Kegan Paul, 1965), pp. 7-8.

3. This aspect of the Nigerian situation is discussed by L. Gray Cowan, James O'Connell, and David G. Scanlon, eds., *Education and Nation-Building in Africa* (New York: Praeger, 1965), p. 20.

4. Manpower factors in relation to educational planning in Africa are analyzed in Adam Curle, *Educational Strategy for Developing Societies* (London: Tavistock Publications, 1963), pp. 131-139; Frederick Harbison and Ibrahim A. Ibrahim, "High-level Manpower for Nigeria's Future," *Investment in Education* (Lagos: Government Printing Office, 1960), pp. 50-72; W. Arthur Lewis, "Education and Economic Development," *Social and Economic Studies*, Vol. 10, No. 2 (June 1961), pp. 113-127; "Report of the International Conference on Regional Planning and National Development in Tropical Africa," University of Ibadan, Ibadan, Nigeria, March 20-25, 1972, mimeographed; and W. Arthur Lewis, *Development Planning* (London: Unwin University Books, 1966), pp. 103-104.

5. James S. Coleman, ed., *Education and Political Development* (Princeton: Princeton University Press, 1965), p. 32.

6. A careful and insightful analysis of some dysfunctional consequences of educational development in Nigeria is presented in David Abernethy's *The Political Dilemma of Popular Education* (Stanford: Stanford University Press, 1969), pp. 253-277.

7. Robert Hess and Judith Torney, *The Development of Political Attitudes in Children* (New York: Doubleday, 1968), p. 120; and Gabriel A. Almond and Sidney Verba, *The Civic Culture* (Boston: Little, Brown, 1965).

8. George Z. Bereday and Bonnie Stretch, "Political Education in the U.S.A. and U.S.S.R.," *Comparative Education Review*, Vol. 7, No. 1 (June 1963), pp. 9-16.

9. Edgar Litt, "Civic Education, Norms, and Political Indoctrination," *American Sociological Review*, Vol. 28, No. 1 (February 1963), pp. 69-75.

10. Kenneth P. Langton, *Political Socialization* (New York: Oxford University Press, 1969), p. 171.

11. David Easton and Jack Dennis, *Children in the Political System: Origins of Political Legitimacy* (New York: McGraw-Hill, 1969), p. 398; and Fred I. Greenstein, *Children and Politics* (New Haven: Yale University Press, 1965), p. 56.

12. Easton and Dennis, op. cit., pp. 391-393; and Hess and Torney, op. cit., p. 36.

13. Jeremy R. Azrael, "Patterns of Policy Directed Education: The Soviet Case," in Coleman, op. cit., pp. 233-271; Frederick C. Barghorn, *Politics in the USSR* (Boston: Little, Brown, 1966); and Melford E. Spiro, *Children of the Kibbutz* (New York: Schocken Books, 1965).

14. Richard E. Dawson and Kenneth Prewitt, *Political Socialization* (Boston: Little, Brown, 1969).

15. Lawrence Fuchs, ed., *American Ethnic Politics* (New York: Harper & Row, 1968); and Milton M. Gordon, *Assimilation in American Life: The Role of Race, Religion, and National Origins* (New York: Oxford University Press, 1964).

16. Michael Parenti, "Ethnic Politics and the Persistence of Ethnic Identity," *American Political Science Review*, Vol. 61, No. 3 (September 1967), pp. 716-726.

17. Alex Inkeles and Raymond A. Bauer, *The Soviet Citizen* (Cambridge: Harvard University Press, 1959).

18. Dawson and Prewitt, op. cit., pp. 168-169.

Chapter 5

Development Planning and National Integration in Ghana

by Kwamina B. Dickson

AMONG THE NUMEROUS problems faced by development planners everywhere, and especially in developing countries, is that of choice between the sectoral approach and the regional approach.[1] Under the former, planners' attention is initially focused on those sectors of the economy that promise to yield reasonable returns to investment. The sectoral approach is not aspatial, however. Whichever sectors of the economy are selected for investment and rapid development will not necessarily involve every part of the country, for the simple reason that some parts of it will always appear to be more suitable as locations for the sectoral activity chosen. If export agriculture is the activity picked for development, for instance, the focus will be on those areas in the nation deemed most suitable, from the point of view of ecological and infrastructural conditions for development of export agriculture. In adopting the sectoral approach, the hope is that revenue from the developed sector will be available for the development of complementary economic activities whose spatial distribution will initially overlap with that of the activity of major concern. Essentially, therefore, the sectoral approach is likely to lead to marked spatial variations in development within a country. By contrast under the regional approach planners divide a country into a number of areas on the basis of a certain criterion, and then decide whether to develop some regions in preference to others or to spread development evenly over all the regions.

Nevertheless, the two approaches, the sectoral and the regional, are not mutually exclusive, for pursuit of the sectoral approach should lead to a spatial structuring of the country into regions on the basis of the degree to which the activity or service of major concern could be developed. Problems arise where a country is divided into administrative (political) units with each unit having a well-developed sense of identity; no central development planning agency can then ignore the sensibilities of the constituent administrative units. So far as Ghana is concerned, an important question to ask at this stage is: To what extent do its administrative regions exhibit this sense of identity and of territoriality? Or, to put it another way, what is the background of regional administration in the country?

Administrative Regions

From the 1880s to the beginning of World War I, two European colonial powers controlled what is now Ghana: Britain and Germany. The British were in control of practically the whole country, except for a narrow, full-length strip of land at the eastern end that was the domain of the Germans. This narrow strip formed part of the German colony of Togoland, which included the present Republic of Togo. After the war German Togoland was shared between the British and the French and, down to 1921, the British portion was known as the British sphere of Togoland. In 1946 British Togoland became a United Kingdom Trusteeship, and six years later the southern section was designated Trans-Volta Togoland; the northern section was regarded as part of the Northern Territories. After a plebiscite in 1957, the Trans-Volta Togoland opted to unite with independent Ghana, where it is now known as the Volta Region.

For more effective administration of its portion, the Gold Coast, the British at first divided the coastal portion of the country, which was called the Colony, into provinces, which in turn were subdivided into districts. The division into provinces was, as nearly as possible, made on the basis of ethnic groupings.[2] Central Province included predominantly the Fante and Assin speaking peoples who formed a fairly distinctive cultural group from the standpoint not only of language but also of political ties and history of settlement. Western Province similarly had a cultural identity based on language that, though belonging to the same linguistic grouping with the Fante, is phonetically rather distinctive and is closer to the languages in the eastern coastal portion of neighboring Ivory Coast. Again, the peoples of the Western Province have in their history interacted with one another at a more intimate level than with the neighboring Fante to the east of them. Finally, there was Eastern Province, which included two large and recognizable cultural groups, the Akim in the interior and the Ga-Adangbe along the coast. The Akim language, together with the languages of the Central and Western provinces, belongs to the Akan group of languages; but the Akim have, at least since the Adanse-Denkyira war around the beginning of the seventeenth century, always formed a distinctive body of people, held together by the brutal necessity to maintain the integrity of their newly settled home in the face of repeated attacks by hostile neighbors. Recognition of the Ga-Adangbe as a distinct cultural group came with the delimitation of the Greater Accra Region. The Ada and the Krobo, who share many cultural traits with the Shai, were included with the Akim and the Kwahu in the Eastern Province. Thus, the principle was accepted that although cultural groups were recognized as such, it would be unrealistic to constitute the territory of each cultural group as an administrative province. Hence, different cultural groups were sometimes put together in the same province, although care was taken that such groups were not too dissimilar in their essential characteristics.

Ashanti, which was formally annexed to the British Crown in 1902, was, by every criterion, a distinctive region of the Gold Coast. As constituted, the province included the neighboring Brong, who were intimately involved in the history of the Ashanti and were, indeed, for many years under the political domination of the Ashanti.

North of the Ashanti Province were the Northern Territories, which included two major cultural groups: the Mole-Dagbani peoples and the Grunshi. The boundary between the Northern Territories and Ashanti was not firmly fixed until 1907. Also, in that year, the Northern Territories were divided into three provinces, Northeastern, Northwestern, and Southern. In 1921 these provinces were reduced to two, Northern and Southern, and 11 years later the two were merged to form a single province: the Northern Territories of the Gold Coast. For several reasons, the Northern Territories were not considered to be important enough to warrant the additional expense of stationing more than one provincial commissioner there.

On the whole the major administrative units into which the country was divided by the British recognized large cultural groupings. Even so, in each administrative province outside the Northern Territories were several minor cultural groups that did not share the same tradition with the major cultural group. Yet it is true to say that, except for the Northern Territories where large ethnic groups with markedly different traditions were thrown together, the administrative provinces of the British Gold Coast recognized as much as possible the territorial extent of the dominant cultural groups.

After political independence in 1957, the administrative provinces were simply renamed regions. The northern half of Trans-Volta Togoland was already attached to northern Ghana while the southern half became known as the Volta Region. The present boundaries of the administrative regions do not exactly coincide with the boundaries of the provinces, for adjustments have been made here and there to accommodate the wishes of peoples who would rather belong to a different region. The most spectacular changes occurred during the First Republic, when in 1959 Brong Ahafo was constituted a separate administrative region from Ashanti proper. The Brong claim for a separate identity was based on the nature of their historical relations with the Ashanti. They do not form the same cultural group with the Ashanti, but their separate identity was submerged under Ashanti power. Northern Ghana was also split into two administrative regions in 1960: Upper Region, which took in the two most densely populated areas of northern Ghana, and Northern Region, which included the rest of northern Ghana. This division was made not on ethnic grounds, but rather for the sake of more efficient administration.

Inequalities in Regional Development

The British, after dividing the country into administrative units, then proceeded to invest more heavily in some units than in others. Their principal guideline was the presence of exploitable resources that could be exported — gold, diamonds, manganese, timber, and cocoa. Areas with these resources received more attention from the colonial administration. It should be noted, however, that only those resources were exploited for which there was ready demand in industrial Europe, and whose export from the country would not conflict with British colonial interests elsewhere. Thus bauxite, which had been known since 1914 to occur in the country in large quantities, was not exploited because no immediate market or uses could be found for it. For the same reason, limestone and barite were not prospected until after 1915.[3]

As a factor in the development of particular administrative units, the value of economic quantities of the requisite resources was further determined by consideration of distance from the seaports in the South. Resources too far removed from the coast were generally ignored. A case in point was the gold deposit discovered at Nangodi in the Upper Region in 1933 whose exploitation ceased soon afterward because of the high cost of transporting imported machinery to the mine and of sending the ore to the ports. The gold deposits at Nangodi would have had to be extra-ordinarily large and rich to have justified their continued exploitation. Deposits located near the ports with size and quality characteristics comparable to those at Nangodi would not have been abandoned so readily. A similar factor of distance from the ports and of inaccessibility explains the lack of interest in the large iron ore deposits of reasonable quality in the Shiene-Tweleba area in extreme eastern Gonja, first reported by the Geological Survey Department in 1928. In any event, Britain had numerous alternative sources of iron outside Ghana.[4]

A factor of primary importance therefore in the choice of an area for development by the colonial administration was the availability there of minerals. Consequently, parts of Ashanti and Western Regions, with their gold deposits, were some of the earliest areas to receive large inflows of capital. The first railway in Ghana was begun in 1898 from Sekondi with the express purpose of tapping the rich gold deposits of Tarkwa and, later, of Obuasi, which it reached in 1901. The line was continued to the Ashanti capital of Kumasi in 1903 for purely administrative (military) reasons. Again, the eastern railway from Accra to Kumasi, constructed between 1900 and 1923, was meant to serve the thriving cocoa-growing industry that had spread from the Eastern Region to Ashanti and the Central regions. Yet again, the central railway from Huni Valley to Kade, begun in 1923 and completed in 1927, was built to tap the timber, cocoa, and diamond resources of parts of the Central and Eastern regions. Feeder roads leading off from the railway increased its range of effectiveness.

Several other railway lines were proposed during the colonial period, all for the areas west of the Volta. The Volta Region was excluded because it had not yet come under the full control of the British. None of these other railway lines were constructed, however, owing principally to the uncertainty of obtaining enough of the desired freight to justify their operation. The most ambitious of the proposed railways was the one from Kumasi to Navrongo, through either Wa in the west or Tamale in the east.

Similarly, the construction of roads, which preceded that of railways and was more widespread, was guided by the availability of agricultural exports, principally palm oil at first, and by the importance of the need to link up the major settlements. In a sense, the roads were not new. They were no more than improvements of the old trade routes or pathways that had long since been trodden within areas of economic dominance. Thus the trade-route network at the beginning of the eighteenth century bore close similarity to the road network at the end of the colonial period, and, indeed, still bears to the contemporary road network.

Roads, railways, and other items of infrastructure thus came to be found within those areas of the country that were *already* in a dominant economic position. Ashanti and the Central Region were the most prosperous, politically the most advanced, and generally the most developed parts of the Gold Coast by the middle of the nineteenth century, and their prosperity was based principally on the export trade in gold. Equally prosperous were those parts of the Western Region where gold was mined. Less wealthy were the Volta Region, from which slaves were regularly marched down to the seaports, and the Eastern Region, whose gold mining industry was controlled by Ashanti.[5] Northern Ghana may have been less wealthy generally, but the contrast between its more wealthy eastern portion and, say, the Central Region could not have been as stark as it is today. The eastern half of northern Ghana was engaged in a thriving middleman trade between the western Sudan and Ashanti. Salaga was justly famous for its international market, which was the largest in the country during the mid-nineteenth century.

Ghana's present regional inequalities in development thus arose from a combination of circumstances: the discovery of precious minerals in the existing areas of dominance; the ease with which cocoa, rubber, and other tree crops grew in the same areas; the consequent development there of infrastructure; and the pull of population from other regions into these areas. Northern Ghana suffered the full backwash effects of the strengthening of these core areas. Its middleman trade practically disappeared when the country's trade as a whole became reoriented from northward to the western Sudan to southward to the seaports. Efforts made subsequently by the British administration to develop commerical agriculture in northern Ghana, based on the cultivation of cotton, failed, not so much because of the physical environmental circumstances but because of the British failure to diagnose correctly the cultural constraints on cultivation for commercial purposes. The situation of northern Ghana worsened with the years as the south became more powerful economically and the British took measures that conspired to keep the north less developed.[6]

A similar, though slightly different, sequence of events occurred in the Volta Region. As a mandated territory after World War I, the Volta Region was generally ignored by the British administration and no serious efforts were made to develop it. The social and economic infrastructure created by the Germans during the period of their administration was on the whole maintained in its previous state but not extended. The region, like northern Ghana, therefore became an area of out-migration, a periphery to the more vigorously developing core areas to the west of the Volta.

Since 1957, however, when the Volta Region became part of Ghana, more positive efforts have been made to develop it.

It is not easy to measure the level of development of an area. Per capita income, a popular measure, is a crude one, but useful. Unfortunately, regional per capita income figures are not available. Table 5-1 shows several indexes of a region's possession of certain essential socioeconomic elements critically needed for development. Based on a simple arithmetical procedure, the administrative regions are ranked according to their possession of infrastructure, and the ranks added and averaged. Greater Accra Region easily stands out as the one best supplied with the infrastructural bases for development. The remaining regions, in descending order of degree of development, are Ashanti, Eastern, Central, Western, Volta, Brong Ahafo, Northern, and Upper.

Admittedly, this simple arithmetical procedure gives only a rough picture; it lacks the precision, for example, of factor analysis. Nevertheless, it is beyond dispute that the Greater Accra Region, centered around the country's capital, Accra, and its premier industrial city, Tema, is the one that is best supplied with infrastructure. Nor can it be doubted that the three least developed regions in the country are Brong Ahafo, Northern, and Upper. The Brong Ahafo Region is proportionately less richly endowed with infrastructure than the Volta Region. This circumstance is not surprising because at no time did Brong Ahafo Region receive as much attention from the British administration as did Volta Region from the German administration. By contrast Ashanti proper, to which Brong Ahafo was an adjunct, received every attention from the British administration after 1902, and Brong Ahafo suffered the effects of accelerated development in the Ashanti core area. Ashanti's capital, Kumasi, is second only to Accra in economic, social, and political importance. The Western Region's development is narrowly centered around Sekondi-Takoradi and the mining towns, while development is more widespread in the Central Region. As a major locus of colonial activity, the Central Region developed early. It is more urbanized than the Western Region and has a better transport network. The Eastern Region is even more highly urbanized than the Central Region and also has richer and more varied resources. Moreover, it has made more successful adjustments in its agriculture than the Central Region following the devastation of cocoa by swollen shoot disease. The problem of depressed rural areas is more serious in Central than in Eastern Region. Northern and Upper regions do not need to be commented upon specifically; they are by every index the least developed parts of Ghana.

Within each administrative region there are spatial variations in the

TABLE 5-1 *Some Socioeconomic Indexes by Administrative Region*

REGION	1 POPULATION DENSITY PER SQ. MILE (1970)	2 NUMBER OF SETTLEMENTS OF 5,000 OR MORE (1970)	3 NUMBER OF SECONDARY SCHOOLS AS OF 10/31/72	4 POPULATION PER DOCTOR IN GOVT. HOSPITAL (IN THOUSANDS)	5 PERCENT OF REGIONAL POPULATION CONSUMING ELECTRICITY	6 GALLONS OF WATER PER HEAD IN 1969 (IN THOUSANDS)	7 NUMBER OF MANUFACTURING INDUSTRIES	8 LENGTH OF STANDARD ROAD PER 100 SQ. MILES	9 OVERALL RANK IN DEVELOPMENT
Greater Accra	853	8	21	9.1	6.0	11.6	526	21.6	1
Eastern	164	32	26	63.0	0.7	0.5	36	5.6	3
Volta	119	15	20	55.1	0.3	0.4	6	4.0	6
Central	234	22	15	81.0	1.0	1.1	17	8.7	4
Western	83	14	13	32.0	1.6	2.1	35	2.3	5
Ashanti	157	17	30	38.0	1.3	1.2	119	4.3	2
Brong Ahafo	50	19	11	95.3	0.2	0.4	6	2.2	7
Northern	27	8	5	61.0	0.4	0.9	2	0.8	8
Upper	81	3	8	143.0	0.1	0.3	1	1.4	9

SOURCE: Column 4:   Annual Report, Medical Services of Ghana, 1967.
      "   5:   Annual Report, Electricity Corporation of Ghana, 1971.
      "   6:   Annual Report, Water Works Department, 1967; or *Economic Survey*, CBS, 1967.
      "   7:   Ministry of Industries and Tourism.
      "   8:   Public Works Department, 1972.

potential for development, and it is these variations that reduce the usefulness of static measures of development levels such as the one above. The concept of potential development is itself tricky, for one measures potential development only after making such simplifying assumptions as unchanging technology and perception of resources, and ready mobility of capital and labor. For example, northern Ghana could well be the country's bread basket if certain technological and social problems facing agriculture could be solved. Mechanized cultivation is more easily carried on in northern Ghana than elsewhere in the country, but the inadequacy of water supplies will always be a serious constraint to agricultural development there. The dramatic effect of irrigation on agricultural productivity is already well demonstrated in limited areas in northern Ghana. Within the context of existing technological and other conditions, one of the most promising areas for agricultural development is what has been referred to as the Pioneer Fringe, an area belonging to both Brong Ahafo and the Western regions.[7] It is now being actively colonized by cocoa farmers and per capita income there is bound to rise.

ATTITUDES TO INEQUALITIES IN
REGIONAL DEVELOPMENT

Awareness of the regional disparities in development certainly exists in Ghana; but how far this awareness is or will be a divisive force in the country is not easy to evaluate. Many of the popular opinions expressed on the issue are not based on careful scientific assessment. Some facts are nevertheless clear. First, if ethnicity is a divisive force, it has got nowhere near the level it reached in Nigeria where it exploded into a hot, tragic civil war; and one cannot foresee the situation in Ghana deteriorating to that dangerous point. Secondly, the spatial aspects of the voting pattern in the 1969 general elections are yet to be fully analyzed, but a few correlations are possible. It is true that all the representatives of the National Alliance of Liberals (NAL) who stood for election in the Volta Region, in Ewe territory, were returned, while the overwhelming majority of the Progress Party nominees in the predominately Akan regions won convincingly.

The Progress Party was voted into power while NAL and two other parties, whose strongholds were in the Akan areas, later came together to form a single opposition party, Justice Party. During the election campaigns, it was not unusual for party candidates to ask for support on the grounds of ethnic affinity, but on the whole it would be hasty to attempt to explain the spatial pattern of voting solely in terms of ethnic groupings because the pattern is a complex one, inspite of the apparent broad correlations between NAL stronghold and Ewe territory and Progress Party stronghold and Akan territory. Events in Parliament after the election show the readiness with which political parties with an allegedly ethnic base can merge to form a single national opposition party.

While one should not go so far as to see a meaningful correlation between ethnicity and political affiliation, it cannot be denied that the politicians or the educated leaders in the poorer administrative regions are keenly aware of the need to develop their regions and will demand that the national government invests more in them. As I have written elsewhere:

> The northerners are now openly distressed over the great disparity in the economic development in their area and in the south, and view with a certain amount of concern the many development schemes that are being drawn up to strengthen further the economy of the south. There was even a suggestion in the Constituent Assembly, which is now [in 1966] discussing the draft constitutional proposals for the country, that a government ministry should specially be set up to deal with problems of economic development in northern Ghana, and that the ministry should remain in existence so long as the south continued to be so much more developed than the north. This suggestion was made by a northern Ghanaian, and it underscores the possibility of political tension arising between the south and the north if the latter, about half of which belongs to the Middle Belt, was allowed to remain relatively undeveloped. It is true that the Ashanti and the Brong also have sizeable stretches of territory belonging to the Middle Belt, but they have no grievance on that score since the remaining portions of the territories produce more than 50 percent of the country's exports of cocoa and gold. [8]

GOVERNMENTAL REACTION TO INEQUALITIES IN REGIONAL DEVELOPMENT

Perhaps the earliest overt governmental reaction to this problem of inequities in regional development, especially the problem of northern Ghana, came in 1918 when Sir Gordon Guggisberg, the governor, proposed a plan for a railway to northern Ghana from Kumasi: "The career of the Northern Territories as the Cinderella of the Gold Coast is nearing its end: as Cinderella she had done good and unobtrusive work; her reward for that . . . is in sight."[9] Subsequent governors occasionally referred to the problem of northern Ghana, but the whole issue of deliberately promoting faster economic growth in northern Ghana and the Volta Region so that they could catch up with the rest of the country was never seriously discussed.

The Seven-Year Development Plan (1963-1970) proposed by the government of the First Republic, pronounced on this issue as follows:

> The development of Ghana has hitherto not been sufficiently balanced between different parts of the country. It is the deliberate policy of this Plan to correct this imbalance. Naturally we must develop in each part of the country the type of economic activity to which it is best suited by reason of natural resources and geographical location. But a special effort has to be made in order to ensure that the rate of progress in the less favored parts of the country is even greater than the rate of progress in those sections which have hitherto been more favored. It is only by this means that we can achieve a more harmonious national development.
>
> In the present Plan period it is proposed to pay special attention to the modernizing of agriculture in the savannah areas of the Northern and Upper Regions. It is hoped, through secondary industries based on agricultural raw materials, to turn the Northern areas into major sources of food supplies for the whole country. [10]

From the point of view of its declared objective, the plan was fairly realistic. Pond water was to be provided for every village in northern Ghana; state farms were to be located there as well as two factories, and so forth. Nevertheless, it is doubtful if the rate of economic growth in northern Ghana would have surpassed that of the more developed parts of the country, for planners also realized that the location of industries would present a problem in the drive to even out the inequalities in regional development. "In general industrial projects will be sited so as to make the maximum use of the infrastructure facilities that Ghana has already built up at such great cost instead of being sited where this will necessitate more of such nonproductive investment."[11] The point here, of course, was that most of the proposed industrial projects would be located in the more developed areas. The number of manufacturing enterprises and employees in 1963 and the expected distribution by region of capital to be invested in planned state and private enterprises during the seven-year plan period are indicated in Table 5-2.

At first glance, columns 3 and 5 or 6, for example, would suggest that the better developed areas were to be more favored than the less developed ones. This is true in terms of the absolute numbers of industrial establishments and the amount of money to be invested. Nevertheless, there is a significant inverse correlation between column 1, the number of enterprises in 1963, and column 5, the amount of money to be invested in 1970, which tends to support the claim that the poorer areas were on the whole to receive more, proportionately, than the richer areas. Also, calculation of the mean number of employees per enterprise, as proposed for the period 1963-1970,

TABLE 5-2 *Number of Manufacturing Enterprises and Employees by Region in 1963 and Projected for 1970*

	1963		1970			
	1	2	3	4	5	6
REGION	NO. OF ENTER-PRISES (STATE AND PRIVATE)	NO. EMPLOYED	EXPECTED NO. OF NEW ENTERPRISES	EXPECTED NO. OF EMPLOYEES	AMOUNT TO BE INVESTED IN £G'000	PERCENT OF AMOUNT TO BE INVESTED
Western	373	41,365	20	8,641	31,404.8	9.82
Central	256	8,571	9	4,458	106,604.0	33.32
Greater Accra	461	28,568	51	16,899	83,690.8	26.16
Eastern	612	16,765	14	5,602	74,359.3	23.24
Volta	472	16,080	3	2,946	7,700.0	2.41
Ashanti	634	26,726	11	4,648	6,356.7	2.00
Brong Ahafo	186	6,476	4	432	717.0	0.22
Northern	51	1,228	5	2,394	6,505.3	2.03
Upper	96	3,053	6	906	2,571.0	0.80
Total	3,141	148,832	123	46,926	319,908.9	100.00

SOURCE : *National Physical Development Plan, 1963-1970* (Accra: State Publishing Corp., 1965), Tables 21 and 26.

shows that some of the largest enterprises were to be located in the Volta and Northern regions, although Upper and Brong Ahafo regions were to have some of the smallest enterprises.

Whether the Seven-Year Development Plan would indeed have reduced the glaring disparities in regional development is hard to say, for it was obvious that the distance factor and the distribution of the principal markets in the country would seriously have affected, at least in the short run, the cost of operating the manufacturing enterprises, and therefore the success of the establishment. Be that as it may, the Seven-Year Development Plan did not really get under way before it was scrapped immediately after the overthrow of the First Republic in 1966.

Subsequently, few explicit references have been made to the problem of spatial inequalities in Ghanaian development. Indeed, the official view immediately after the military coup of 1966 appeared to be that the economy of the more developed areas should first be strengthened before the problems of underdevelopment elsewhere were tackled. The new regime's reasoning was based on the desperately weakened state of the economy at the time Nkrumah was overthrown. The Second Republic, instituted in 1969, began a massive program of providing water and electricity for the rural areas, and a similar program is apparently contemplated by the present military regime, the National Redemption Council,[12] which succeeded the Second Republic in 1972. But the current regime has not addressed itself directly to the problem of disparities in regional development. As before, the main concern appears to be with the lessening of the rural-urban differential in development.

Nevertheless, there is now in each administrative region a planning committee entrusted with the task of development. These planning committees were set up by the government of the Second Republic in its efforts to decentralize administration and decision-making. In regular contact with all regional planning committees is the National Economic Planning Office in the capital, Accra.

Potentially, these committees are a means of stimulating development in consonance with the resources of every administrative region in the country. But the work of the committees is to a large extent hamstrung by the close supervision exercised by the National Economic Planning Office, which seeks to reconcile regional with overall national interests. Thus the regional committees have to submit their development plans and budgets to Accra for approval, and it is not unusual for individual items in the regional development plan to be eliminated without reference to their expected function in the plan. In effect, therefore, the regional planning committees cannot plan and program development in an *integrated* way. In practice each department within a region—for example, education, agriculture, electricity, water—proposes its own budget and plans without reference to the other departments, and the regional planning committee is not able to coordinate and fuse these individual departmental plans with different objectives into a unified program with a single purpose.

Possible Lines of Action

A tragic truth about development planning in Ghana is that since political independence from Britain no serious and sustained effort has been made to examine the spatial implications of economic development policies. Fiscal and investment policies have been proposed and implemented without any thought being given to their differential regional impact, and several of these policies have failed for this very reason. The pattern of areal variations in development is one that should be studied with care, for development policies that are not based on a clear appreciation of spatial variations in resource endowment and of patterns and dynamics of spatial interaction will have little chance of succeeding.

The issue here is not how to attain uniform areal development throughout the country, for that would be unrealistic. There will always be spatial variations in development. Rather, the issue is one of stimulating development in poor areas while at the same time maintaining a fair rate of national development. What may be considered to be a fair rate of national development is a matter for a country to decide, but there can be no doubt that a national policy that ruthlessly ignores some parts of Ghana while vigorously pushing development in others will create serious social and political unrest. For this reason, it is important to assure a pattern of areal development that does not unnecessarily slow down the pursuit of a declared national objective.

The following suggestions on development planning in Ghana are proposed in outline, the details of which can always be worked out:

1. The present system of regional planning committees and a single national planning committee should be retained, but:(a) the composition of the national committee should be altered to include a representative or two from each regional planning committee; (b) the regional planning committees should be given legal recognition; (c) both the national and the regional planning committees should have a core of salaried professional planners with facilities for research and collection of data.

2. There should be *programming* of *national* development in terms of

a *clearly defined objective*. This requirement is one that has not always been fully met in post-independence Ghana. A development plan is not of much use if all it does is list production and other targets that do not add up to the achievement of a declared national objective.

3. The declaration of the overall national objective should be accompanied by the identification and careful study of those other sectors of the economy whose functioning will be of major importance to the achievement of the national objective. A system of relationships should be worked out, based on results of pilot projects and past experience in Ghana and elsewhere, to establish the implications of the national objective on other sectors of the country's life.

4. The sectoral approach implied in (3) must be translated into "spatial action" where ecological regions, not administrative regions, are identified as being suitable or potentially suitable for investment. Thus, investment might be channeled into a well-populated area with the requisite infrastructure or into a thinly populated area with desirable resources and requisite locational coordinates. Such decisions or actions would be taken by the national planning committee on which representatives of the regional planning committees serve.

5. The regional planning committees will then draw up development plans whose objective is defined within the broad context provided by the national objective. Where the nature of the national objective would discourage heavy investment in a given administrative region, a certain amount of money should in any case be set aside by the national planning board to be used by the regional committee for purposes of maintaining and improving existing infrastructure and to aid, however indirectly, the attainment of the national objective. The regional development plan would be discussed by the national planning board, which would approve it as an entity. Whatever changes are suggested should be in light of the declared objective of the regional plan.

6. All such plans, including the national one, should be reviewed periodically, say at three to five-year intervals, to make sure that Ghana as a whole does not fall out of step with the changing system of relationships with other countries of the world.

The suggestions above mean that the opportunities for spatial interaction within the country should be increased, and a vital step in this direction is to link up more effectively the clusters of road networks that exist in the country. Roughly speaking, there are five major clusters, each with subclusters, in the Western Region, the Central and Eastern regions, the Volta Region, the Ashanti and Brong Ahafo regions, and northern Ghana. Also, the effectiveness of each cluster should be extended and strengthened with feeder roads that tap known productive areas.

Conclusion

The suggestions made in the preceding section are meant to stimulate development in every administrative region in the country while at the same time assuring steady progress towards the national development goals. Pursuit of these suggestions could, on the other hand, slow down both regional and national development if the suggestions are not implemented rigorously and professionally. It is essential to underscore this point, for the continuance of glaring disparities in regional development in any country will serve as a basis for political discontent.

Disparities in spatial development in Ghana existed for centuries before the colonial era and still exist at a time of nation-wide political consciousness. They will continue to exist and may indeed be a necessary condition for rapid national development. But every effort should be made to change the present concept of disparity to one of variation in development, where every major areal unit in the country sees itself as contributing, in its own way, toward overall national development and integration.

Notes

1. A discussion of the two approaches will be found in, for example, Jos G.M. Hilhorst, *Regional Planning* (Rotterdam: Rotterdam University Press, 1971), chap. 1.
2. For major ethnic groupings, see B. Gil, A.F. Aryee, and D.K. Ghansah, *Special Report E: Tribes in Ghana, 1960 Ghana Population Census* (Accra: Census Office, 1964), chap. 2 and 3.
3. K.B. Dickson, *A Historical Geography of Ghana* (Cambridge: Cambridge University Press, 1969), p. 196.
4. Ibid., p. 198.
5. A good account of spatial variations in development in the southern half of the country in the 1860s will be found in J.A.B. Horton, *West African Countries and Peoples* (London: W.J. Johnson, 1868).
6. R.B. Bening, "The Evolution of the Administrative Boundaries of Northern Ghana, 1898-1965" (Ph.D. diss., London University, 1971).
7. K.B. Dickson and George Benneh, *A New Geography of Ghana* (London: Longmans, 1970), p. 144.
8. K.B. Dickson, "The Middle Belt of Ghana," *Bulletin de l'I.F.A.N.*, Vol. 31, Ser. B, No. 3 (1969), pp. 714-715.

8. K.B. Dickson, "The Middle Belt of Ghana," *Bulletin de l'I.F.A.N.*, Vol. 31, Ser. B, No. 3 (1969), pp. 714-715.

9. K.B. Dickson, "Background to the Problem of Economic Development in Northern Ghana," *Annals of the Association of American Geographers*, Vol. 58, No. 4 (December 1968), p. 694.

10. *Ghana Seven-Year Development Plan, 1963-64 to 1969-70* (Accra: Office of the Planning Commission, 1964), pp. 14-15.

11. Ibid., p. 107.

12. See, for example, *Daily Graphic*, October 14, 1972, pp. 1 and 3.

Chapter 6

Education and National Integration in Ghana

by Audrey C. Smock

ALL STATES face a continuing need for inculcating a sense of national identity in their citizens and for strengthening the legitimacy of institutions embodying political authority. In longer established countries, such as France and Great Britain, many factors operate as effective socialization agents to meet this need. They derive primarily from their histories of common government and united struggle against foreign foes, their long possession of unitive symbols and facilities such as language, literature, heroes, and social and political institutions. These factors supply much of the content and atmosphere of the education system of such countries and are themselves powerfully reinforced by the national educational system.

In the new states of Africa this requirement for instilling national loyalty and appropriate citizenship values is obviously more pressing. Political institutions are fragile, and ethnic fragmentation, which in all its manifestations means strong particularistic loyalties, manifests itself in two ways: (1) a majority of the members of the political system do not have a sufficient sense of national citizenship to mobilize their allegiance to the national community in times of crisis and conflict; (2) the values, aspirations and expectations of the citizens of the state reflect the widespread structural and cultural divergencies in the traditional social and political systems into which they have been socialized, so that the common social and political orientations on which a wider community could possibly be founded have yet to be achieved.

Colonial administrators did not see it as their business to foster any sense of allegiance to the common nation made possible by the arbitrary imposition of their rule on diverse peoples and polities. Thus, by the various colonial policies of indirect rule, the traditional socialization agents of each such constituent people or polity were left substantially intact and even encouraged to operate in their inevitably parochial or particularistic manner. With the approach to independent nationhood, therefore, a revision of the policies affecting these endemic particularistic tendencies became impera- tive, though it cannot be said to have received the necessary conscious response. Obviously, in the absence of the other effective socialization agencies that reinforce the sense of national identity in longer established countries, the formal education system must assume a more decisive role as a factor promoting attachment to the larger national unit beyond the village and beyond the ethnic group.

As an expression of their faith in education, many of the African states, including Ghana, invest a significant portion of their revenues in it. But despite these considerable investments in mass education, the educational systems of virtually all African states are unable to socialize students effective ly. Their inability to do so results from the nature of the colonial educationa. system and the failure to undertake fundamental reforms after independence Colonial education embodied the inadequacies of the metropolitan systems combined with the prejudices of the colonial overlords as to what con stituted a proper education for Africans. Ministries of education have not often embarked upon a drastic reordering of the approach, objectives, and curriculum inherited from the colonial period, sometimes because adminis trators do not perceive how serious the deficiencies of the present curriculum are and sometimes because of the very great difficulties drastic reform entails Moreover, throughout the continent the initial focus of ministries of educa tion has understandably tended to be on the expansion of the educational system rather than on the quality.

As the first Sub-Saharan African state to achieve its independence Ghana provides an interesting example of the dilemmas of educational reform. For the first years of its independence the Ghana government under the leadership of Kwame Nkrumah, was explicitly committed to utiliz- ing the educational system for the purpose of instilling a sense of loyalty to Ghana and its ideals. The Ministry of Education moved quickly to unify an educational program split between the various Christian missions and the government into a national education system, to expand it, and to introduce Ghanaian history. Nevertheless, 15 years after independence the educationa system still very much reflects the colonial mold, and the curricula often exhibit the patterns and biases inherited from the colonial period. This remains so notwithstanding the fact that with the installation of the Nationa Liberation Council after the overthrow of Nkrumah in 1966, Ghana estab lished a Curriculum Research and Development Unit within the Ministry of Education, one of the first such governmental agencies in Africa.

The ethnic fragmentation of Ghana into primary ethnic groups, none of which comprises a majority of the population, makes it typical of most countries in Africa. Like other African states, the political history of Ghana attests to the strength of particularistic ties. However, Ghana has not been subjected to the eruption of ethnic tensions into mass violence, as have some of its neighbors. Recently, the strategy adopted by some of the politicians during the period of political competition in the Second Republic, 1969 to 1972, intensified ethnic awareness and aggravated certain ethnic hostilities. Neither Nkrumah's exhortations for the paramountcy of nationalism and pan-Africanism nor the educational curricula have succeeded in creating a sufficiently strong sense of Ghanaian citizenship to countervail ethnic loyalty.

Two major cleavages in Ghana are the Akan/non-Akan ethno-linguistic groupings, and the North-South division, which reflects ethnic, historical, and economic disparities. At the time of the 1960 census the various ethnic groups speaking an Akan dialect, all of whom resided in the southern part of Ghana, constituted 44 percent of the population. Historically, however, the Akan subgroups, particularly the Ashanti (with 13 percent) and the Fante (with 11 percent of the population), have been rivals of one another. The perception of Akanness as a common bond and as a basis for political and social alignment is of relatively recent origin and is perhaps an ephemeral phenomenon. Widespread adoption of elements of the Akan social and political organization by other communities, particularly the Ewe and the Ga in the South and the Gonja, Dagomba, and Mamprusi in the North, have decreased some of the social distance between Akan and non-Akan. Major non-Akan ethnic groups in the South include the Ga-Adangbe (8 percent of the population) and the Ewe (13 percent of the population). The Mole-Dagbani ethno-linguistic community comprises the largest single unit in the North (with 16 percent of the population).[1] In contrast with the pyramidal social structure characteristic of the Akan, most of the units in the North were traditionally much smaller in scale and had little centralized political authority.

Even more important than these traditional differences, though, is the fact that the patterns of development in the country have left the North far behind the South. During the colonial period the North suffered both from neglect and from isolation imposed by the administration which preferred to keep the more quiescent northerners quarantined from southern political activists. Few of the commercial enterprises or cocoa cultivation, which provided the major impetus for the economic development of the South, reached the North. Christian missionaries were not allowed to proselytize or to open schools in most parts of the North until after independence. Because Ghanaian regimes since independence have evidenced only limited concern over these regional imbalances, the pattern of investments and allocations has tended to accentuate these economic inequalities.

Ethnic and Regional Disparities In Educational Development

For education to be an effective instrument of national integration, the public system should reach all parts of the country and provide approximate equality of opportunity. In many parts of Africa, including Ghana, ethno-regional disparities in educational development can both weaken the potential role of education as an agent of national socialization and lead to tensions between the more and less educationally advantaged areas. An analysis of the educational achievements of the ethnic communities in Ghana underscores the vast gap between the North and the South. A look at the number of males aged six years and over who were attending school at the time of the 1960 census shows that among the southern Ghanaians the figure averaged about 50 percent whereas only 7 percent of the Mole-Dagbani males were attending. At least 20 percent of the female members of the southern ethnic groups were attending school, but only 2 percent of the Mole-Dagbani. The same relationship held for the relative progress of groups in finishing at least a middle school education of 10 years. Among the males in southern Ghana, the percentage of those with any education who went on to complete middle school ranged from 75.3 percent for the Ga-Adangbe to 62.8 percent for the Ewe. In contrast, only 30.5 percent of the Mole-Dagbani males who started school remained in school for that length of time.[2]

Because the 1960 census results, taken only three years after independence, reflect the discrepancies in development inherited from the colonial period, it is relevant to assess the progress made during subsequent years. Unfortunately, at the time of this writing the publication of the relevant data from the 1970 census is still unavailable. Therefore, the tables presented rely on regional statistics prepared by the Ministry of Education. It is likely, however, that some of those attending school in the Northern and Upper regions, the two regions comprising the northern portion of Ghana, were of southern Ghanaian origin and only temporarily residing in the North. Because northern male migrants frequently leave their families behind, the incidence of northern children in southern schools is lower.

TABLE 6-1 *Public Schools by Region in 1960 and 1970*

Region	Population, 1970*	Primary Schools, 1960	Primary Schools, 1970	Middle Schools, 1960	Middle Schools, 1970	Secondary Schools, 1960	Secondary Schools, 1970
Accra	9.9%	8.7%	6.4%	10.5%	8.9%	20.4%	18.6%
Eastern	14.8	16.9	18.3	17.2	20.7	11.9	14.8
Central	10.4	12.1	10.7	14.4	11.2	18.6	12.0
Western	9.0	10.2	11.3	9.8	9.8	11.9	11.1
Volta	11.1	16.7	13.0	14.9	13.7	13.5	14.8
Ashanti	17.3	20.1	19.5	22.3	19.3	15.2	16.4
Brong Ahafo	8.9	8.2	9.2	6.6	9.5	3.4	6.5
Northern	8.5	2.6	5.3	1.8	2.0	3.4	1.9
Upper	10.0	4.5	6.3	2.5	4.9	1.7	3.8
Total	100.0	100.0	100.0	100.0	100.0	100.0	99.9

*Based on provisional 1970 figures
SOURCE: *Educational Statistics, 1968-1969* (Accra: Ministry of Education, 1971), p. 71; and *Education Statistics* (Ministry of Education, 1970).

With regard to the regional development of educational facilities, in 1950 the Northern Territories (now the Northern Region and Upper Region) had only 3 percent of the total number of primary and secondary school facilities.[3] By 1970 the same area had 10 percent of the public primary, middle, and secondary schools.[4] Although this proportion was still far below the 18.5 percent of the population that the 1970 population census attributed to the two regions, it represents a substantial improvement in educational opportunity, especially when it is remembered that the educational system as a whole expanded rapidly after 1960. For a more detailed analysis of the progress of the Northern and Upper regions as well as other parts of the country, see Tables 6-1 and 6-2.

TABLE 6-2 *Growth of Enrollments in Public Schools by Region, 1961-1970*

REGION	PRIMARY SCHOOL, 1961	PRIMARY SCHOOL, 1970	MIDDLE SCHOOL, 1961	MIDDLE SCHOOL, 1970
Accra ⎤ Eastern ⎦	149,894*	93,984 194,586	45,310*	39,989 79,007
Central	63,145	109,848	20,689	47,125
Western	50,643	96,543	15,499	42,578
Volta	82,263	121,726	24,066	54,371
Ashanti	106,213	207,342	35,168	97,583
Brong Ahafo	36,982	85,373	9,562	31,774
Northern	10,427	30,974	2,893	10,183
Upper	20,459	35,293	4,496	15,821
Total	520,026	975,669	157,683	418,431

*In 1961 Accra was part of the Eastern Region; therefore, the statistics do not separate the attendance for each.
SOURCE: *1963 Statistical Year Book* (Accra: Central Bureau of Statistics, 1966), p. 180; *Education Statistics* (Accra: Ministry of Education, 1970).

In comparing the expansion of educational facilities with the growth of enrollments, it is clear that despite government efforts to favor somewhat the Northern and Upper regions in siting schools, attendance has not kept pace with the increase in institutions. The overall improvement in the position of the Northern Region from 1961 to 1970 was from 1.9 percent to 3.2 percent of the proportion of Ghanaian primary school students and from 1.8 to 2.9 percent of those in secondary school. Primary school enrollments in the Upper Region did not advance as rapidly as the other regions; indeed, it actually fell from 3.8 to 3.6 percent during the same period while middle school figures improved slightly, from 2.9 to 3.7 percent. The lower rate of educational achievement in the northern portion of the country, therefore, cannot be compensated for merely by the opening of more institutions.

Despite an apparent lack of general anxiety about balanced regional growth, the government has evinced a concern over the disparity in the progress of education in the northern and southern parts of the country. As mentioned, one sign of this concern has been the siting of schools. In a period in which the number of primary schools almost doubled from 3,574 to 7,293 and the middle schools increased from 1,234 to 3,201, in order to accommodate the influx of students resulting from the introduction of 10 years of universal free education, both the Northern and Upper regions improved their relative positions. Unlike its policy in other portions of the country where the cost of school construction is a local responsibility, the government has borne the entire cost of constructing new primary and middle schools in the North. Moreover, the government has favored this area in allocating trained teachers. When fees for school texts were reintroduced after the 1966 coup, the primary and middle school students in the Upper and Northern regions continued to receive theirs free. The government has given secondary school students from these two regions scholarships for tuition and full board; the students have had to pay only for their uniforms and books. Northern university students also receive special living and travel allowances.

Students from the southern part of the country have often taken advantage of the growth in educational opportunities in the North. Despite a ruling that only southern children whose parents were working in the North were eligible to attend the secondary schools there, other southern students have been admitted. Similarly the Ministry of Education has not always rigorously applied the formula that 50 percent of the intake of the training colleges in the Northern and Upper regions should be reserved for candidates originating in the area.[5] The Ministry of Education has had to face the dilemma of reserving places for northern candidates in these secondary schools and training colleges or of having to lower standards for admission in order to fill them. Alternatively, the ministry can violate the purpose for which the schools were constructed by filling the openings with southern students. What it has done, however, is close some of the newer primary and middle schools in the North for lack of pupils. Perhaps a more vigorous effort by the Ministry of Education or the Department of Social Welfare in going to northern towns and villages and promoting school enrollment would have made a difference, but clearly factors other than the lack of opportunity now hold the North back. Traditional cultural values contribute to the reluctance to attend school, but there are other reasons as well. The slower rate of social change and economic development has limited the utility of formal education. For families who assume that their progeny will follow in their footsteps, it sometimes makes more sense for them to keep the children in the fields helping their fathers than to send them to school to acquire a literary education they may not use. The slower rate of change has meant that traditional life patterns and socialization agents have greater strength and relevance in the North. For the parents there, the choice is perceived not simply as between school attendance or no education, but between a somewhat foreign, potentially alienating education and the traditional forms. Economic incentives, mainly the lure of a white-collar job in an urban center, have played a significant role in other parts of the country in attracting children to schools. Even as these job openings decline in number, southern students continue to hope for them, and both these sometimes unrealistic aspirations and the habit within a community of school attendance keep the southern schools filled.

Degree of Ethnic Heterogeneity in Schools

In bringing students into contact with members of other ethnic groups, heterogeneity in the classroom can foster toleration and lead to friendship across ethnic boundaries. Unfortunately, the widespread expansion of the educational system at all levels since 1960 has made the schools more homogeneous in ethnic composition. For primary-age children, Ghana has achieved something close to the American concept of the neighborhood school. In ethnically heterogeneous neighborhoods in urban centers, the composition of the primary school reflects that of the neighborhood, Most of the population, however, still resides in the relatively homogeneous rural countryside. Middle schools draw their student body from a somewhat broader area, but the pupils are usually still from the same ethnic group. The one exception is in the northern part of the country where some of the middle schools are boarding institutions that bring together many different ethnic groups in order to have enough students to keep their doors open. Older, elite secondary schools still recruit the best students from all ethnic groups, though many of the more recently opened ones with lower standards attract students only from the region in which they are located.

Some heterogeneity in the composition of the student bodies of all schools does result, however, from a high level of internal migration within Ghana. In a nation where only 58 percent of the population enumerated in 1960 were residing in the place they had been born and in which only one-fourth of the local authority areas had a homogeneity index higher than 75 percent, population movements themselves assure a certain element of heterogeneity.[6] Many of the migrants prefer to leave their children behind with relatives, but some take their children along. In a 1970 survey by the author of 300 schoolchildren in five Ghanaian communities, each one in a different region, only 58 percent of the schoolchildren had been born within the village in which they were interviewed. When asked about their ethnic origins, 83 percent of the children identified themselves as members of the subgroup of the ethnic group dominant in the local community, 5 percent belonged to another subgroup of the same ethnic group, and 11 percent came from other ethnic groups.

The three universities in Ghana, like the elite secondary schools from which they disproportionately recruit their students, remain heterogeneous. A survey the author conducted of students at the University of Ghana in 1970, in which the sample was randomly selected from lists provided by the residence halls, showed that the composition of the student body roughly reflected that of the country's population. The major differences came in the overrepresentation of students from the Volta Region and the underrepresentation from the Northern and Upper regions. Despite the long-term problem of educational development of the North, 7 percent of the sample (as compared with 18.5 percent of the population) came from the two northern regions. Thus it is possible that a narrower gap exists at the more elite levels of education than amongst primary and middle school students.

The survey of university students also pointed to one of the major advantages of having heterogeneous educational institutions. When students were asked to list their three closest friends and their home regions, for only 13 percent of the sample did all three friends come from the same region as the respondent. Thirty-three percent had one friend from outside their own region, 43 percent had two friends, and 11 percent had three friends from other parts of Ghana. Moreover, 81 percent said that they had met their friends at school.

The Ministry of Education generally posts teachers without reference to their ethnic background or home community. This policy has derived primarily from the attempt to equalize the number of trained teachers throughout the country. With more than half of the present teachers now holding the minimum qualifications prescribed by the ministry and with teacher training facilities established in every region, it is becoming increasingly feasible to regionalize assignments while maintaining some balance with regard to trained teachers. At the present time the Volta Region has the largest surplus of trained teachers and Brong Ahafo the greatest deficit.[7] Along with the desire of teachers to work nearer to their home, the greater emphasis on the vernacular (another recent policy development) will probably put pressure on the Ministry of Education to take ethnic factors more into account in placing teachers. In 1971 the ministry switched to the use of the vernacular in the first three years of primary education. These early grades usually have the highest proportion of trained teachers, some of whom serve outside their own language area and are not fluent in the local vernacular. Thus, the need for primary school teachers to be able to converse in the vernacular of the child conflicts with the earlier decision to achieve an element of integration in the posting of teachers, a policy that increased the exposure of students to adults of other ethnic groups.

Curriculum

The content of the curriculum to a great extent determines the effectiveness of the educational system. A uniform curriculum explicitly devoted to instilling a sense of national citizenship would facilitate the socialization of students into a national political perspective. Since 1958 the Ministry of Education has prescribed the content of the curricula and prepared the list of recommended texts for all primary and middle schools in Ghana. Previously, head teachers had either been provided with syllabi by the general manager of their educational unit or they had drawn up their own.[8] Although the ministry had intended to offer a choice between several acceptable texts for each subject, in actuality the yearly list has merely mentioned a single book. All schools in Ghana, therefore, irrespective of their location or whether they are managed by a local authority or a church agency, follow the same program. While the government does not directly control the secondary schools, students prepare for uniform examinations set by the West African Examinations Council (WAEC), an autonomous agency composed of educators nominated by the Ghanaian Government in conjunction with representatives similarly chosen from Nigeria, Sierra Leone, and the Gambia.

Shortly after independence, the Ministry of Education incorporated many Ghanaian-oriented teaching materials at all levels of the educational system.[9] At the time of independence the schools did have a few Ghanaian-oriented geography books, but they did not emphasize Ghanaian history. There was a series of texts entitled *Tropical Africa in World History* written by a colonial educational officer along with other books unrelated to Africa. By the 1961-1962 school year, the ministry had introduced two Ghanaian history texts for primary school and one for middle school, and virtually all of the geography books were oriented toward Ghana or West Africa. In civics, however, which is a more sensitive and, for the purpose of fostering a sense of national citizenship, a more significant subject, the Ministry of Education has not done as well. The only civics text currently in use was written before independence by a colonial education officer for all of West Africa; it contains no material specifically oriented to the Ghanaian political system or experience. Under the auspices of the WAEC, secondary school examinations at both the ordinary and advanced levels in history and in the social sciences assumed a more African orientation by 1967. At that time the council replaced examinations on the British Constitution with tests on government, much of which dealt with West Africa. Economics and economic history also became more African centered.[10] At the university level Ghana pioneered the concept of African studies centers; university students still take a compulsory interdisciplinary course in African studies during their first year.

The Ministry of Education offers two forms of guidance to schools for the teaching of social studies: a syllabus outlining the program and its objectives and a list of approved texts. It also prescribes how many hours each week should be devoted to each subject. According to ministry materials, the study of history and geography begins in the fourth year of primary school and continues through the last year of middle school. The number of hours assigned to history and geography, though, suggests that the Ministry of Education considers it less important than religious instruction, arithmetic, physical education, or Ghanaian languages. Only 105 of the 1,620 hours in each term are reserved for history and geography whereas language studies (English and the local language) receive 630, physical education 370, and arithmetic and religious instruction 150 each. Although the Curriculum Research and Development Unit has prepared a syllabus for civics at the primary level, the time sheet circulated by the ministry does not allocate any periods to it. Moreover, up to 1972 the civics title for primary schools that appeared on the list of recommended texts had never actually been published due to the poor quality of the draft version of the book that the State Publishing Corporation received. Hence, no book for primary civics existed. Interviews with teachers confirmed that civics was not then taught in primary schools and presumably never had been.

Out of a total of seven years of history, four and one-half of them focus exclusively on Ghana. An analysis of the contents of these texts, however, reveals that despite the fact that all but one of them were written by Ghanaians, a schoolchild is still exposed to an interpretation of Ghanaian history that strongly reflects European biases.[11] Ghana is described as an artificial creation of British colonial rule composed of disparate peoples whose precolonial contacts were in the form of military conflict. Historical chronologies focus on the establishment of European settlements, European relations with Africans, intertribal wars, and the British contribution to Ghana's development. The books, therefore, portray Africans as passive subjects of European actors. These textbooks never seek to demonstrate that some basis for Ghana's nationhood preceded the imposition of colonial rule. Nor do they dwell on the cultural achievements of African people. The very superficial descriptions of the ethnic groups in Ghana, which are often little more than a catalogue of physical traits, together with the continuous mention of the intertribal wars, might lend themselves to aggravating rather than mitigating stereotypes and ethnic chauvinism. History books mention common elements of Ghanaian society only briefly and then usually in the context of the mythological origin of the Ghanaian population in the Empire of Ghana or the coming together of the groups during the colonial period to constitute the contemporary state of Ghana.

Other deficiencies include the emphasis on the divisive years prior to the twentieth century and, particularly, the failure to deal with the independence movement in any detail. During the first four years of the study of history, the texts devote a total of eight pages to the period subsequent to the imposition of colonial rule over what is now Ghana. In the last two years of the study of history, half of one of the six books and 16 pages in another describe the developments in the twentieth century. Consequently, it is quite conceivable that a Ghanaian schoolchild attempting to comprehend the deficiencies of the colonial period and the basis of the demand for independence would have some difficulty. Colonial figures, like George MacLean and Sir Gordon Guggisberg, receive more detailed and sympathetic attention than the architects of Ghana's independence, whether they were Nkrumahist or anti-Nkrumahist. The only twentieth-century Ghanaian who successfully competes with colonial governors for space is the educator Dr. James E. K. Aggrey, the first vice principal of Achimota College. In editions published after Nkrumah's downfall, two books mention his role as the leader of the independence movement as a background for discussing his faults and failures. Similarly, evaluations of colonialism attempt to be so balanced that the number of lines discussing its bad effects are then followed by a dissertation of equal length on the good results. Moreover, this extremely important topic is given only a single page in the fourth-year history book for primary seven. At the middle school level the scramble for Africa and the resulting colonial system get nine pages. In response to a textbook inquiry as to why Africans disliked colonialism, middle school students are told that: "Africans had been used to ruling themselves and doing things in their own way for centuries. They did not like to break with the ways of the past and be ruled by white men."[12] Particularly with regard to the grievances leading to the anticolonial movement and the extent of its support, the texts fail to clarify the motives of the leaders or even to provide much information about the manner in which the Ghanaians convinced the British to grant them independence. Instead, the superficial treatment generally outlines the steps the British followed in the final stages of decolonization. For example, in the history book for primary seven only 10 pages in the section on "Ghana Prepares for Self-Rule" relate to the independence movement in comparison with 34 pages that relate changes in governmental forms. This inadequate treatment of the independence movement deprives students not only of knowledge of important events but of a source both of a sense of belonging to a nation and of pride in their national identity.

The origin of the civics book as a colonial textbook for British West African colonies itself constitutes an indictment against its relevance for Ghana 15 years after independence. Furthermore, it is unrealistic to expect that the teachers will be sufficiently knowledgeable, creative, and motivated to teach a civics course unrelated to the only textbook they are given. Rather, it is probable that the only civics course that Ghanaian schoolchildren are exposed to begins and ends with this quite inadequate book. The text never discusses the subject of national unity, nor does it make explicit reference to the Ghanaian political system. It typifies the English approach to civic education, which concentrates on character training and includes little direct effort to inculcate a sense of national citizenship. Despite the obvious differences between Britain, a country that was able to achieve a large degree of national identity and loyalty in its population even before the inauguration of a mass educational system in the nineteenth century, and Ghana, where the very study of history reactivates divisions in the society, the Ministry of Education continues to follow the British approach of emphasizing history and character training.

Only one book, the history text for the eighth year of primary school, discusses the contemporary Ghanaian political system. In that book 14 pages are devoted to Ghana after independence and an additional 18 to the organization of the political system and the duties of the citizen. An evaluation of Nkrumah's contribution and why he failed receive three additional pages.

Along with the misplaced emphasis on the early period of Ghanaian history and the lack of attention to civics, the Ghanaian curriculum also fails to deal with other parts of Africa or modern European history. Surprisingly, almost no mention is made of the history or contemporary situation in other African countries. Most of the classroom time devoted to world history, one and a half of the two and a half years, deals with ancient Greece and Rome, hardly a historical epoch that has much relevance for a Ghanaian schoolchild.

Formulation of Policy

At all times since independence there have been educators in the Ghanaian Ministry of Education, and many others in the government, aware of
the inadequacies of the nation's education system. In recent years it has
been quite fashionable to issue wholesale indictments of the irrelevance of
the system of education for the country. Initially the attention of the Ministry
of Education focused almost exclusively on the enormous problems of implementing Nkrumah's directive to establish comprehensive, universal primary
and middle school education, and then after 1963 it had to cope with the
additional burden of distributing free textbooks. Later a solution to the
fundamental deficiencies were sought in structural changes. Few voices have
been raised, though, suggesting the need to reconsider and improve the content of the curriculum generally or in specific subjects. The nature of the
curriculum has generated little interest. Aside from a few specialists in
curriculum work, most of the personnel within the ministry rarely concern
themselves with the content of social studies education.

According to one of the early principal secretaries of the Ministry of
Education, Nkrumah was aware of the deficiencies of the educational
system and instructed the ministry to collect samples of the syllabi and
curricula from other countries, including Eastern European countries and
perhaps Israel, with a view to making recommendations for changes. However, the ministry never followed up this request with any concrete proposals.[13] Then in 1959 Nkrumah sent a memorandum to the Cabinet calling
for the creation of the Young Pioneer Movement to replace existing youth
movements. When officially established in 1960, the Pioneer Movement was
placed under the jurisdiction of the Ministry of Education, although it was
later moved. Theoretically, every primary, middle, and secondary school in
Ghana was to have a branch of the organization, but in actuality the movement never achieved such universal scope. A 1961 survey of 39 schools in
Accra, for example, showed that only 11 percent of primary and 10 percent of
middle school students were members. Letters from the national head-
quarters of the Young Pioneer Movement to the districts continuously
reminded the Ministry of Education of its responsibility to set up branches.
According to the statistics issued by the Young Pioneers themselves, before
its dissolution they had 569,601 members of which 19,577 were "militants"
with uniforms. The general membership constituted 43 percent of the then
schoolchildren and 20 percent of the total primary and middle school-age
population. Activists numbered only .7 percent of the eligible children.[14]

At its inception the Young Pioneer Movement seems to have been conceived as an instrument of national integration. However, it quickly became a vehicle through which its leaders attempted to indoctrinate children with the ideology of Nkrumahism. The pledge of the Ghana Young Pioneers began: "I sincerely promise to live by the ideals of Osagyefo Dr. Kwame Nkrumah, Founder of the State of Ghana and Initiator of African Personality."[15] The published aims of the Young Pioneer Movement included both training in civic responsibilities and fostering Nkrumahism. They were:

1. To train the mind, the body and soul of the youth of Ghana.
2. To train them to be up to their civic responsibilities so as to fulfill their patriotic duties.
3. To train their technical skills according to their talents.
4. To foster the spirit of voluntarism, love and devotion to the welfare of the Ghana nation.
5. To inculcate into the youth "Nkrumahism" — ideals of African Personality, African Unity, World Peace, Social and Economic reconstruction of Ghana and Africa in particular and the World in general.[16]

For understanding the limited impact of the Young Pioneer Movement, it is important to remember that it was always an extracurricular organization whose activities were limited to after-school hours. The Ministry of Education successfully resisted any intrusion by the Young Pioneers into school time. The movement also suffered from the absence of skillful leaders to create and maintain a viable organization. According to the author of one study of the Young Pioneers, "Even though they had the potential to organize all Ghanaian school students, the Pioneers never achieved the level of involvement envisioned originally by the party for them. Although the Pioneers were the only officially recognized youth group they were not able to obtain in the schools the widespread support they wished."[17] Because most of the leaders were selected on the basis of their party loyalty rather than their organizational ability, they lacked the experience or the knowledge for founding and running a large-scale youth movement. Originally the Young Pioneers sought to recruit leaders from secondary school teachers, but the Ministry of Education quickly discouraged the teachers from joining. Reports of the auditor general showed continuous instances of corruption and mismanagement of Pioneer funds. The fears of the organizers as expressed in internal correspondence that the whole movement might collapse had some basis.[18]

Nkrumah also turned his attention to the social studies curriculum itself. After Nkrumah's secretary simplified his autobiography to make it suitable for schoolchildren, Nkrumah pressed the Ministry of Education to adopt it as a required text. The ministry resisted for a time, then put it on the list as a supplementary reader, which in effect consigned the book to oblivion inasmuch as not even all required texts were provided to schools. On being told that the book had been placed on the official list, Nkrumah was satisfied, however. But he also grew impatient when the Ministry of Education failed to produce a new history and civics syllabus more relevant for Ghana's needs as a newly independent nation. Again the members of the educational service perceived the issue as political meddling with their professional integrity. It was not until late in 1964 that the Saltpond Unit, then responsible for curriculum development, completed "Education for Citizenship," the new history and civics syllabus. When the March 1966 coup ousted Nkrumah, however, the "Education for Citizenship" curriculum had not yet been distributed to all of the schools, and it never was put into use.[19]

Nonetheless, the "Education for Citizenship" curriculum recognizes — to a far greater extent than any other syllabus adopted in Ghana — the significant contribution that history and civics can make to fostering national unity. Had it been adopted, it could have improved the teaching of these subjects. For example, one of the first instructions to teachers states that

> Teachers should note that in dealing with this syllabus, they are required to teach CITIZENSHIP with all the emphasis at their command. Citizenship in the widest sense implies behavior that is consistent with the values of our society and proper appreciation of those values. Since habits formed in the tender years are often those that become permanently ingrained in us, it is in the early classes at school that the foundation for good citizenship be firmly laid.[20]

At another point teachers were reminded that

> Many leading persons in authority including the Head of State himself have given expression to the concern of the nation for a responsible citizenry in Ghana. There is general agreement that the prosperity of this nation depends on loyal, industrious, self-less and honest citizens. It is hoped that this syllabus, if handled conscientiously by devoted classroom teachers, will help to produce future citizens that will help to build a prosperous Ghana.[21]

With its focus on the contemporary Ghanaian, "Education for Citizenship" incorporated studies on the political system of Ghana at that time, but it also covered such subjects as the nature of traditional society, societal duties and obligations, current events, character training, international organizations, and national symbols, some of which were commendable innovations. Moreover, the syllabus called for a factual presentation of the institutional elements of the one-party state without the express ideological indoctrination of Nkrumahism for which many people have criticized the Young Pioneers.

With the overthrow of Nkrumah and the installation of the National Liberation Council in 1966, the Ministry of Education no longer faced "political interference." But five years later proposals designed to make the content of the educational system more suitable for instilling a sense of national citizenship were still immediately suspect because of their association with the efforts of Kwame Nkrumah. Ironically, although Nkrumah never succeeded in bringing about the innovations he desired, the ritualistic pledges of loyalty to Nkrumah and Ghana of the Young Pioneers tainted many later reforms because officials could claim that they had already been tried and rejected as contrary to the Ghanaian way of life. A small group of educators, who had been trained in Canada to conduct the functions of the new Curriculum Research and Development Unit, constituted the major exception to this outlook. With the creation of the CRDU in 1967, the Ministry of Education overcame one of its major deficiencies, namely, the absence of educators professionally trained and responsible for curriculum revision.

Prior to 1967, the unit at Saltpond in the Central Region was theoretically vested with the responsibility for supervising curriculum development. But the staff there had neither the time nor the skill to do so. In 1952, the year the Accelerated Development Plan for education was promulgated, the Ministry of Education assigned to this Central Region Unit the responsibility for the content of primary and middle school education and professional staff development through in-service training courses. According to the staff's own conception of its role, curriculum research and revision did not constitute one of its major functions. Nine years after the creation of the unit, an internal memorandum listed 15 functions, the most important of which were the in-service training of education officers, seminars for inspecting officers, preparation of professional materials for teachers, and supervision of demonstration schools. Designated unit duties included the preparation of the list of recommended textbooks and school materials and the distribution of syllabi and timetables to all schools. However, there was no explicit mention of curriculum development.[22] According to the incumbent head of the Saltpond Unit, the only revisions in the social studies curriculum in the past, other than "Education for Citizenship," came about when the Ministry of Education decided to change the length of the regular primary school course from eight to six years.[23] An official report of the Ministry of Education itself states that the Saltpond Unit lacked the facilities for curriculum research because all of its work was based on practical classroom experience.[24]

The decision to establish a curriculum research center originated within the ministry after it was stimulated by a UNESCO conference on curriculum reform. UNESCO had started an Educational Information Center for all of Africa in Accra with a Ghanaian on secondment from the Ministry of Education being groomed for the directorship. After a UNESCO inspection team gave an adverse report on the information center, UNESCO withdrew and donated the building to the Ghanaian Government. The building became the CRDU's, and the Ghanaian educator formerly on secondment to UNESCO became its director.[25] The new unit received assistance from the Canadian Government, the British Ministry of Overseas Development, the British Council, and the Centre for Curriculum Renewal and Educational Development Overseas in Britain (CREDO). Several Ghanaian university graduates were sent to Canada for graduate programs in the field of curriculum development and until they returned the unit was staffed by four Canadians and one British specialist.

Shortly after their return, the few Ghanaian curriculum specialists decided to revise fundamentally the entire history, civics, and geography program for primary and middle school. They were initially influenced by methodological considerations and innovations in social studies teaching methods, but they soon also became aware of the potential contribution that the social studies curriculum could make to national integration. They proposed to unify the social studies subjects along with the natural sciences in a new integrated course entitled "environmental studies." As part of the background research, a nationwide survey of civic attitudes of school-children at all levels of the school system was designed and administered in the spring of 1972. The attitudes that the environmental studies course sought to foster were:

1. To develop in the individual an appreciation of the need for changing the environment or adapting to it.
2. To maintain the child's sense of wonder and stimulate and broaden his interests in the world around him.
3. To inculcate in the individual a moral responsibility for the preservation and improvement of the Ghanaian natural and cultural heritage.
4. To develop in the child positive feelings toward the state.
5. To help the child appreciate the need to cooperate with other sub-groups within the nation.
6. To develop in the child an appreciation of the importance of cooperation and tolerance among nations.[26]

The work of the curriculum specialist on the environmental studies program constitutes a big step in the right direction, but it by no means resolves all of the problems related to making the content of Ghanaian education relevant for instilling a sense of national citizenship. First of all, to contemplate such an undertaking as constructing a completely new edifice based on an original synthesis of the social and natural sciences obviously involves enormous preparation. Those responsible for the new program estimate that it will take a minimum of 10 years to plan the new syllabus and test it. In the interim the Ministry of Education will proceed with the present inadequate curriculum.

Another set of problems derives from the distance between the progressive innovations proposed by the Curriculum Research and Development Unit and the conservative bias of the top educational officers in the Ministry of Education. On paper the unit is an integral part of the ministry under the direction of a deputy chief education officer, and the ministry automatically incorporates its reforms. However, after a review of the environmental studies program in late 1971, the chief education officer informed the CRDU that it could continue with the project, but its adoption was by no means assured.

No thoroughgoing reform of Ghana's education system can be assured unless the ministry modifies its policy of refusing to commission the preparation of textbooks. Since independence the ministry has followed the British practice of reviewing texts written by private individuals for possible use in the classroom after they have been published. Without prior assurances that the text will be adopted, Ghanaian educators have been reluctant to invest the time in writing a text. And because no civics textbook was forthcoming to replace the colonial-inspired book in use since 1959, the ministry continued to endorse it as the official choice. Most of the textbooks now in use in Ghanaian schools were written in response to the overtures of a representative of the Macmillan Publishing Company who came to Ghana in 1962 to recruit Ghanaian authors,[27] and in 1963 Macmillan was given a virtual monopoly on the production and marketing of textbooks in Ghana. A commission of inquiry appointed after the 1966 coup concluded that "it does not serve the best interest of the country to have one publishing firm, Macmillan, publishing all the textbooks in use in our schools."[28] They recommended that the monopoly be broken in order to encourage competition in the academic content, the price, and the quality of production.[29] Although the Ghanaian government's White Paper issued in January 1969 supported this recommendation,[30] the same texts still appear on the list of approved books. Apparently no other alternatives are forthcoming.

The functions of the Curriculum Development and Research Unit could usefully be expanded, therefore, to include the preparation of textbooks and other teaching materials. Otherwise the new syllabi it produces will never be reflected in the books assigned to schoolchildren. However, unless the staff of the unit is expanded or university and secondary teachers are hired on a part-time basis to write books under the direction of the unit, it will be impossible to produce the needed texts.

In Ghana, as in most other African states, educators have not been fully aware of the critical impact of the content of the curriculum or the effectiveness of the system of education in promoting national integration. With the massive efforts to expand primary and middle school enrollments, the Ministry of Education has usually concerned itself with the number of children in schools almost to the exclusion of what these students learn. The Ghanaian experience demonstrates that the mere inclusion of national history in the curriculum far from resolves the intricate problems of utilizing education for the purpose of promoting national unity. The road to a relevant education must traverse both the reinterpretation of history toward a more African perspective and the preparation of a new civics curriculum focused on the contemporary political system and the problems of political development. The time has arrived for the interpretation of Ghanaian history in school texts to be de-colonialized. Furthermore, an anthropological and sociological orientation has more relevance and utility than the current emphasis on history. The study of history in new countries generally, and as it is now taught in Ghana particularly, tends to reinforce divisions in society. Study of traditional cultural and institutional patterns would better enable children to comprehend and appreciate the heritage of their country than a compendium of dates and historical incidents. A comparative analysis of the social and political organization, goals, values, and cultural symbols of the major ethnic components of the Ghanaian national community could emphasize the similarities as well as note the differences. Through such a study of the country's traditional heritage, students could develop respect for their past and tolerance for other groups. But most important of all, the Ministry of Education in Ghana could usefully evince a greater concern with the role it can play in national integration.

Notes

1. B. Gil, A.F. Aryee, D.K. Ghansah, *1960 Population Census of Ghana, Special Report 'E,' Tribes in Ghana* (Accra: Census Office, 1964), p. 33.
2. Ibid., pp. 58-65.
3. Philip Foster, *Education and Social Change in Ghana* (London: Routledge and Kegan Paul, 1965), p. 117.
4. Ministry of Education, *Educational Statistics, 1968-1969* (Accra: Ministry of Education, 1971), p. 1.
5. See for example, *Report of the Education Review Committee Appointed by the National Liberation Council* (Accra: State Publishing Corp., 1967), pp. 34-35, 137-138.
6. Gil, Aryee, Ghansah, op. cit., pp. 34-35.

7. Interview with D.A. Brown, then principal secretary, Ministry of Education.

8. Ministry of Education, *Education Report for the Years 1958-1960* (Accra: Ministry of Information and Broadcasting on behalf of the Ministry of Education, 1962), p. 49.

9. Information about required books is from an analysis of the yearly lists published by the Ministry of Education from 1956 to 1971.

10. *The West African Examinations Council Annual Report for the Year Ended 31 March, 1968* (Accra: WAEC Printer, 1969).

11. The textbooks used in this analysis are, for civics: J.R. Bunting, *Civics for Self-Government* (London: Evans Brothers, 1959); for primary school history: F.K. Buah, *An Elementary History for Schools, Book 1*, 1st and 2nd eds. (London: Macmillan and Co., 1963 and 1967); idem, *History for Ghanaian Schools, Book 2* (London: Macmillan and Co., 1964); idem, *An Elementary History for Schools, Book 3, Africa and Europe* (London: Macmillan and Co., 1966); idem, *An Elementary History for Schools, Book 4, Ghana and Europe*, 1st and 2nd eds. (London: Macmillan and Co., 1963 and 1967); and idem, *An Elementary History for Schools, Book 5, New Ghana* (London: Macmillan and Co., 1968). For middle school history: Godfrey N. Brown and Philip M. Amono, *An Active History of Ghana, Book 1, From Earliest Times to 1844* (London: George Allen & Unwin, 1961); George N. Brown, *An Active History of Ghana, Book 2, Since 1844* (London: George Allen & Unwin, 1964); M.I. Potts, *Makers of Civilization, Book 1*, 3rd ed. (London: Longmans, 1961); idem, *Makers of Civilization, Book 1* (London: Longmans, 1953); C.S.S. Higham, *Landmarks of World History* (London: Longmans Green and Co., 1947); C.M.O. Mate, *A Visual History of Ghana*, 2nd ed. (London: Evans Brothers, 1968). It should be noted that on the required textbooks lists, the ministry divides them into those for up to primary eight and then form three and form four of middle school. All the authors of Ghanaian history texts, except Godfrey Brown, are Ghanaians. None of the authors of European history books or the civics texts are Ghanaian.

12. Brown, op. cit., pp. 42-43.

13. Interview with E.A. Winful, former principal secretary, Ministry of Education.

14. Emily Card, "The Politics of Underdevelopment: From Voluntary Associations to Party Auxiliaries in Ghana" (Ph.D. diss., Columbia University, 1972), pp. 292-299.

15. At the time the research for this chapter was undertaken, the files of the Young Pioneers and all other related materials had either been destroyed or put in the archives, where they were to remain inaccessible for 20 years. A copy of the Young Pioneer Pledge is reproduced in the appendix of Charles A. Ballard, Jr., "A Contemporary Youth Movement: The Ghana Young Pioneers" (M.A. Thesis, Institute of African Studies, University of Ghana, 1967), p. 105.

16. A copy of the aims of the Ghana Young Pioneer Movement is reproduced in the appendix of Ballard, op. cit., p. 106.

17. Card, op. cit., p. 299.

18. Ibid., pp. 305-308, 344-362.
19. Interview with Service Addo, deputy chief education officer and first Ghanaian head of the Saltpond Unit.
20. Ministry of Education, "Education for Citizenship" (Saltpond: Ministry of Education, 1964), p. 12, mimeographed. Emphasis in the original.
21. Ibid., p. 2.
22. Ministry of Education, "Functions of Saltpond Office," Aug. 21, 1961.
23. Interview, E.I. Benyarko, head of the Saltpond Unit. The reorganization of the course of studies was never universally implemented.
24. *Education Report 1963-1967* (Accra-Tema: Ministry of Education, n.d.), p. 16.
25. Interview with D.A. Brown, who was chief education officer of Ghana in 1966.
26. Curriculum Research and Development Unit, "Objectives of the Environmental Studies Course" (Accra: Ministry of Education, 1970), p. 1, mimeographed.
27. Interview with D.A. Brown.
28. *Report of the Commission into the Affairs of the Distribution Division of the State Publishing Corporation* (Accra-Tema: Ghana Publishing Corp., 1968), p. 26.
29. Ibid., p. 27.
30. *White Paper on the Report of the Commission of Enquiry into the Affairs of the Distribution Division of the Erstwhile State Publishing Corporation*, No. 1, 1969, (Accra-Tema: Ghana Publishing Corp., 1969), p. 6.

Chapter 7

The Impact of Educational Structures and Processes on National Integration in Cameroon

by Remi Clignet

ACCORDING TO the most usual definition, the aim of educational enterprises is the inculcation of values and the transmission of knowledge from one generation to the next. However, the specific historical forces underlying the emergence of most African nation-states make this definition problematic on a number of counts. First, although nation-building requires temporal integration and, more specifically, a justification of the present by reference to the past, it also demands a projection of the present into the future. In the educational field, this requirement leads schools to face conflicting sets of demands. On the one hand, educational institutions are expected to facilitate mobilization of the masses by extolling the merits and virtues of traditional cultures, that is, of traditional cognitive, expressive, and normative styles. On the other hand, the same institutions are expected to forge new elites, able to compete successfully with their counterparts in industrialized nations.[1] The first demand implies that educational curricula should be turned toward the past and should ensure a continuity between yesteryear and today; the second demand implies that educational curricula should be shaped by the demands imposed by institutions of higher learning in Europe, America, China, or Russia.

Second, even though African schools pay increasing attention to tradition, the relevance of traditional prescriptions to the demands of modernization in Africa appears to be questionable. For example, should schools teach their students about traditional patterns of family organization? In this regard, what is the content of the courses that teachers should teach

139

about polygyny? Should they view this particular institution favorably, because it is a legacy of the past and because references to the past are supposed to facilitate political mobilization? Should they alternatively take a negative stance, because it is often assumed that modernization cannot take place as long as familial roles are not sufficiently individualized and as long as a Western type of nuclear family has not emerged?[2] In other words, it is not clear that the entire knowledge of past generations is consistent with the demands of a current and ever-changing situation. Which element of traditional culture, then, should be stressed in the educational context? Which element should be minimized, and for what reasons?

The third problem results from the large number of ethnic groups present in most African nation-states. Contrasts in the patterns of social organization or in the historical experiences of these groups raise difficult questions about the nature of the knowledge that should be transmitted by local schools. Should we assume that the only knowledge worth transmitting pertains to the *common* sets of rules that various ethnic groups share with regard to cognition, arts, and ethics?[3] But how are these common qualities supposed to be identified? Should we assume conversely that the knowledge to be transmitted by schools is that of the dominant ethnic groups? But here again, we are still confronted with serious dilemmas. The concept of dominance might refer to sheer numbers, in which case the dominant ethnic group is defined as the most numerous. Alternatively the concept could refer to the most politically and economically powerful people. In brief, the concept of ethnicity is eventually divisive in the effects that it has on educational curricula and programs. Yet, ethnicity might have other divisive effects on educational institutions. Insofar as schools are expected to contribute to national integration, they should recruit their students evenly from the variety of ethnic groups present in a country. The problems raised by ethnic factors in the field of education, therefore, pertain to the functions that schools are expected to perform. They also pertain to the allocation of resources.

In the present chapter, we will discuss these two problems as they arise in the context of the Republic of Cameroon. The Cameroon — twice the size of Ghana and half that of Nigeria — offers excellent opportunities in this respect, insofar as the implications attached to the diversity of ethnic groups are complicated by the diversity of colonial experiences to which the various parts of the country have been subjected. In the first of the five parts to this chapter, we will summarize the dimensions along which Cameroonian ethnic groups differ from one another, and we will also indicate in what terms the variety of colonial legacies affect the educational scene. The second part analyzes the extent to which there are ethnic inequalities in the recruitment of students, and the third part examines variations in the ethnic representation of teachers in public and private educational institutions of East and West Cameroon. In a fourth part, we will assess the impact of ethnic factors on educational curricula and techniques. In the final part, the implications of the findings for the Cameroonian educational scene will be assessed.

Cameroonian Ethnic Diversity: Its Educational Implications

The Cameroonian population of nearly 6 million — less than one-tenth that of Nigeria — is comprised of 136 distinct ethnic groups.[4] Although these various peoples can be regrouped into a significantly smaller number of clusters, they still differ markedly from one another in terms of their traditional patterns of social and economic organization.

In the southern part of the country is concentrated one-third of the total population, which belongs to the large Bantu family. Initially at least, these peoples were scattered among small villages located in the heart of the tropical forest, on the shores of lagoons and rivers, or on the coastal line. Further, these peoples did not migrate to Cameroon at the same time. Both the geographic dispersion of these ethnic groups and their contrasting migratory experiences have been associated with differential reinterpretations of their initially similar cultural patterns. On the whole, these peoples are characterized by patrilineal rules of descent, which facilitate a spatial and social segmentation of familial groups. Insofar as these arrangements are accompanied by a growing individualization of social and economic rights they should also stimulate individual participation in educational structures.[5] Many of these peoples had a system of age classes, the significance of which has declined as a result of social change. In general and with the partial exception of the Duala, none of these ethnic groups is characterized by a significant level of political integration. The competition in which they are opponents of one another results from their different areas of settlement and, consequently, from their uneven opportunities of being exposed to colonial influences and of participating in modern activities.

The Cameroonian highlanders constitute another third of the entire population. Although they share the same Bantu origin as coastal groups, their modes of social and economic organization are quite different. The nature of their habitat in the western part of the country has enabled them to engage in more intensive and more diversified subsistence activities. The peoples of this particular part of the country are characterized by a high degree of political and social integration — an integration, however, involving forces that exert divergent influences on the processes of modernization. The Bamileke, who constitute the major and most visible ethnic group of the area, are characterized by patterns of social organization (notably with regard to rules of inheritance and to participation in voluntary associations) which stress the significance of individual achievement.[6] But this group has also an ascription-based system of age classes that accentuates interdependence between alternate generations (grandparents and grandchildren) and as such is most likely to slow down participation in modernizing processes. Thus, the Bamileke seem to have been able to retain certain traits of their traditional structures while participating intensely, albeit lately, in modernizing structures. As a result, they are particularly visible and stir many ambivalent feelings on the part of the remaining segments of the population.

Finally, northerners constitute over one fourth of the whole Cameroon population. These northern populations are divided into three distinctive subgroups. The highly Islamized Fulani were initially engaged in pastoral activities and characterized by a system of sharp social stratification based on religion. The initially agricultural Hausa were early on subjected to the power of the Fulani and imitated them. Lastly, there are the Kirdi, a mosaic of distinct ethnic groups that were pushed back from the plains toward the mountains as a result of the Fulani invasion. The Kirdi are agriculturalists, have animist religious orientations and have always occupied a marginal position in the traditional as well as the modern structures of Cameroon.

To summarize, ethnicity is likely to influence educational structures and processes in three significant ways. First, ethnicity reflects the differential intensity and duration of the contacts established by local peoples with European colonial powers. In this regard, the Duala should have higher school enrollments than other peoples because of their earlier involvement in the colonial experience. At the other end of the continuum, the Hausa and Fulani should have lower enrollments because of their overt opposition to colonization.

In addition, ethnicity reflects the differential congruence between the value system imposed by Western schools and the cultural orientations characteristic of distinct ethnic groups. For example, the lower enrollments of northern peoples in public schools may reflect conflicts between European and Islamic values and more simply the preference of such peoples for a Muslim type of education.[7] They could also result from the conflict between a system that stresses achievement as the major criterion for placement in the social structure and a system that emphasizes ascription as a legitimate basis for social stratification.

Finally, ethnicity reflects the differential visibility of the various local peoples. Certain peoples stir negative feelings on the part of the remaining segments of the population. Such is the case of the Bamileke, who perceive formal schooling as the most appropriate mechanism for coping successfully with the discriminatory treatment imposed upon them in urban areas.[8]

As noted, however, the potential influence of traditional ethnicity in Cameroon is made more complex by the multiplicity of European influences to which the various parts of the country have been exposed. After having been colonized by the Germans, the country was divided into two parts: East and West. The eastern part was subjected to French authority, while the western part was placed under British tutelage.[9] These two powers had different educational ideologies and organizational patterns. In turn, these contrasts affected the potential influence of traditional ethnic factors on formal schooling.

According to the French pattern, formal schooling is a fundamental right guaranteed by the state to the children of a particular age group.[10] This view implies that the government must control the exercise of such a right. Indeed, the underlying stress placed upon equality requires authorities to achieve a maximal standardization in the procedures followed for the recruitment of students, as well as in the definition of educational goals and programs. In other words, the system aims at a maximal centralization. Insofar as the government is religiously neutral, learning processes are defined primarily in cognitive and universalistic terms. As a result, schools in the East are expected to recruit their clientele on the basis of both geographic location and academic potential.

By contrast, the British pattern defines formal schooling as a privilege to be privately exerted by the parents of a relevant age group. Because this view implies a stress upon individual liberty and initiative, schools were not initially tuition-free. In addition, educational institutions remain differentiated not only in terms of the quality of the services that they render, but also in terms of their ideological orientations. Thus, schools in the West are expected to recruit their clientele according to a larger number of criteria than those used by their counterparts in the French-speaking part of the country. The clientele of these schools tends to be attracted for economic and cognitive as well as ideological reasons.

One can, therefore, expect that ethnic inequalities are less marked in the more centralized and universalistic French-speaking East. Further, one can expect that these ethnic inequalities are more independent of other social and cultural inequalities in the East, in view of the lesser importance attached to financial factors in the recruitment of students.

Both parts of Cameroon have private and public schools, the functions and importance of which are different. In the French-speaking part, public schools tend to have a higher standing than the private and tend to recruit their students from among the more academically talented segments of the population.[11] In the English-speaking part, conversely, it is the private institutions that are deemed to be the most prestigious and that, correspondingly, tend to attract the best students. Further, disparities in the cultural orientations of French and British cultures are associated with parallel contrasts in the nature of private institutions. In the French-speaking area, both Catholic missions and secular schools attract the overwhelming majority of students enrolled in private educational institutions. In contrast, the share of Protestant schools is significantly greater in the western part of the country.

Clearly enough, these cleavages in the organizational patterns of educational institutions should have some effects on the extent and the form of the educational competition among ethnic groups. Thus, one can expect that private schools in the East may be used to relieve ethnic competition and recruit their clientele from the academically marginal Cameroonian peoples. In the West, on the other hand, such a role will be more likely to characterize public institutions. Moreover, the extent of the integrative functions performed by private institutions along these lines should be different in the two areas. Insofar as Catholic missions that are more universalistic and broadly encompassing, are proportionately more numerous in the East, the severity of ethnic competition should be less pronounced in that region than in the West.

Ethnic Inequalities in the Recruitment of Students

Unfortunately, figures concerning the relative size of school enrollments by ethnic orgin are not systematically available for the country as a whole. Yet, insofar as the various Cameroonian peoples are located in distinct parts of the country, regional data approximate ethnic distributions and suggest sharp contrasts in the level of participation of Cameroonian peoples in educational structures. Further, the same data suggest that the relative magnitude of such contrasts is not necessarily declining over time. While the school enrollments of the population between 6 and 13 years of age have increased for the whole country from 51 to 61 percent between 1965 and 1970, disparities between regions have tended to remain the same. During this particular period, rates in the North have increased from 19 to 22 percent. Those of the western section have moved from 77 to 80 percent, while in the center southern area (Yaoundé and its surroundings), they went up from 92 to 94 percent. In short, during this five-year period, ethnic inequalities are most likely to have persisted.[12]

Nonetheless, an analysis of regional disparities in the level of participation in educational structures remains insufficient. Regions are inhabited by various ethnic clusters with distinct orientations. Table 7-1 shows that within the Center South of East Cameroon, there are significant differences in the relative enrollment rates of smaller areal units. For example, in the Mbam, an area occupied by the Bafia, the Baboute, and the Beti, enrollments are significantly lower than in the Mefou or the Lekie parts of the country predominantly occupied by the Eton, the Bane, and the Ewondo. Table 7-1 also shows that variations in relative enrollments are associated with parallel disparities in the relative representation of the two sexes in educational structures. Indeed, such disparities are significantly more marked in the areas of Lom and Kadei than in the Mefou. In short, the low participation of a particular ethnic group in the school system induces an accentuated selectivity in the recruitment of students along sex lines. In turn, the minimal participation of girls in educational structures is most likely to perpetuate the marginal involvement of the entire ethnic group in modernizing processes.[13]

Table 7-2 suggests that the overall level of participation of a particular ethnic group affects other forms of selectivity as well. Whereas enrollments are uniformly higher in the larger cities of West Cameroon than in the rural hinterland, the magnitude of the corresponding increases varies along ethnic lines. On the whole, ethnic contrasts are more marked in urban than in rural areas. In other words, the places where social change is most manifest are also the places where social differentiation is the most marked. Ethnic disparities in enrollment rates often increase in cities because of accentuated differences in the occupational status of adults, which in turn accentuates differences in the resources they can devote to the education of children.

Table 7-3 — based on an analysis by Joyce Sween and myself of the 1964 census — shows significant contrasts in the educational level (and, hence, indirectly, in the occupational level) of the adult residents of the city of Douala with distinct ethnic origins. As expected, it is among the Duala and the Pahouin-Betis ethnic groups that one finds the highest percentages of individuals who have at least completed a primary education. Such percentages, as expected, drop sharply among the Bamileke and among the northern people.

By way of summarizing this array of observations, let it be noted that

TABLE 7-1 *School Enrollments for the Male and Female Population, 6-17 Years of Age, by Area in the Southeast Region of East Cameroon*

AREAS	BOYS	GIRLS
Center South		
Mefou, Lekie, Nyong, and Soo	92.8%	79.9%
Nten (Dja and Lobo)	92.6	79.2
Kribi	92.5	83.0
Nyong and Kelle Sanaga Maritime	90.0	83.6
Haute Sanaga, Nyong and Moufou	92.3	66.7
Mbam	80.9	47.9
East		
Lom and Kadie	71.4	23.7
Haut Nyong	81.0	49.6
Urban Centers	87.9	70.5

SOURCE : *Enquêtè démographique au Cameroun: résultats définitifs pour la région sud est, 1962-64* (Paris: INSEE Service de Coopération, 1968), pp. 52-53.

TABLE 7-2 *Proportion of Literate Individuals Among Young Male Adults of West Cameroon (15-24 Years of Age) by Zone of Residence in 1964*

ETHNIC GROUP	RURAL	TOWNS	CITIES	TOTAL
Coastal	54.2%	100.0%	87.9%	56.2%
Balundu-Mbo	53.8	73.0	78.8	58.2
Forest Bantoids	44.7	75.0	87.8	56.1
Bamilekes	56.6	100.0	84.8	60.1
Bantoids of the Plateaus	44.1	48.7	72.5	46.2
East Cameroonians	55.1	85.3	77.6	71.5
Nigerians	22.8	48.9	69.3	42.6
Others	50.0	100.0	66.3	66.4

SOURCE: *La Population de l'ouest Cameroun* (Paris: INSEE Services de Coopération, 1968), p. 106.

(1) there are sharp differences in the relative participation of the distinct Cameroonian ethnic groups in educational structures; (2) these differences are not necessarily declining over time and in effect tend probably to increase during the early stages of the modernization processes; and (3) these differences are probably associated with parallel variations in the extent of other forms of selectivity — that is to say, the lower the overall participation of a particular ethnic group in educational institutions, the lower will be

TABLE 7-3 *Education Level of Douala Adult Male Residents by Ethnic Group in 1964 (Percentage Distribution)*

EDUCATIONAL LEVEL	ETHNIC GROUP							
	DUALA	BASSA	PAHOUIN-BETIS	BAMILEKE	NORTH-ERNERS	OTHER CAME-ROONIANS***	WEST CAME-ROONIANS	FOR-EIGNERS
Illiterates	26.9	29.7	29.8	40.7	66.0	44.6	49.4	45.6
Some Primary Education	46.4	47.2	41.9	45.3	13.8	39.9	5.2	17.5
Primary Education Completed	21.8	19.9	23.5	12.3	1.0	12.9	2.1	7.9
Went Beyond Primary Education	4.3	2.7	4.2	1.5	0.0	1.8	0.5	0.9
Educated in German or English*	0.5	0.3	0.4	0.2	0.6	0.5	41.7	25.2
Unascertained or Other Education**	0.1	0.2	0.1	0.0	18.6	0.2	1.1	2.8
Total	100.0	100.0	99.9	100.0	100.0	99.9	100.0	99.9
Number of residents	7,032	8,633	4,227	17,856	886	7,911	585	1,551

*Individuals educated in German attended German schools before World War I; they were between 55 and 63 years old at the time of the census.

**Includes Arab education.

***Includes the Kaka, the Banagantou, the Bamoun, the Pol, the Baya, the whole clusters of Mbam, Maka, Paleonegitic and Pygmy populations.

the relative enrollments of its female population and the more socially selective will be the recruitment of male students.[14]

The problem remains, of course, to determine the degree to which the Cameroonian Government is in a position to erode progressively the importance of the ethnic inequalities examined here. The coexistence of public, religious, and private educational sectors seems to have different effects along these lines. To be sure, the diversity of educational sectors might enable the government to adopt more flexible educational strategies in a variety of contexts, but these distinct schools do not necessarily share identical educational perspectives and goals and cannot, therefore, enhance the impact that educational processes should have on national integration. Further, these distinct sectors are not uniformly distributed throughout Cameroon. As far as the East is concerned, secular institutions tend to be both most numerous and most sizable in the largest cities of Douala and Yaoundé, where the demand for education is most significant. The question is, then, to determine whether such schools cater to a clientele mainly derived from ethnic groups with marginal educational enrollments or, alternatively, whether such schools recruit most of their students from the dropouts of already-educated ethnic groups who have not been able to hold their position in the public school system. Similarly, Protestant missions attract a proportionately larger number of students in the Center South region of the country than in the littoral or the western areas, whereas Catholic schools are more evenly implanted in the various parts of the country. Insofar as religious schools are not evenly spread, the distribution of the corresponding denominations tend to vary along ethnic lines. This particular pattern of interaction between ethnicity and European religion cannot but lower the contribution of private schools to national integration.

The government, however, can use other strategies to minimize the magnitude of ethnic inequalities in educational enrollments. It can impose ethnic quotas on the recruitment of students, though such a strategy is at variance with the universalistic and achievement-oriented ideology underlying educational enterprises. It can also establish schools in regions where enrollments are particularly low, a strategy that does raise two difficulties, however. It is not certain that the schools so created will recruit their students from local populations. Indeed, evidence available in Ghana suggests that schools recently opened in the northern part of the country tend to attract southern students with a relatively low quality of academic performance. The second difficulty is that such schools are not necessarily able to hire the most qualified teachers. Insofar as a teaching career depends at least in part upon the achievement of a teacher's students, he or she has few incentives for going to regions with low enrollments. Indeed, the eventual lack of success of the students in national examinations might jeopardize the teacher's own career. Moreover, the life of a teacher in marginal places is not necessarily a comfortable one.[15]

Another strategy to minimize ethnic inequities in enrollment consists of adapting educational curricula and organizational patterns to the needs and orientations of the population. Clearly enough, the Cameroon Government has made use of this particular technique. In the North, the academic calendar is different from that in the South as it corresponds more to the needs of the local agriculture. In spite of differences in the methods of socialization pursued by the two types of institutions the government has also attempted to establish organizational linkages between Islamic and public schools.[16]

To sum up, although the means that authorities can use to erode ethnic differentials are quite diverse, the efficiency of the strategies often remains doubtful. Such differentials result from economic and social forces that do not easily come under political control.

Ethnicity and the Recruitment of Teachers

In the previous section, we have discussed one particular contribution that formal schooling can make vis-à-vis national integration. Yet the problem is not only to allocate to the various ethnic groups an equal share of educational opportunities and, consequently, of economic opportunities. The problem is also to determine whether educational institutions can establish a curriculum — and a cultural and cognitive style — that overcomes the negative implications that derive from the cultural diversity of local peoples. Clearly enough, the fulfillment of this condition should depend upon the relative cosmopolitanism of the local teaching force as well as upon the degree to which teachers are recruited evenly from the various peoples of the country. Also, the diversity of the ethnic background of local teachers should remain the same in a variety of locales.

This condition, however, is far from being fulfilled in Cameroon (Table 7-4).[17] The ethnic background of teachers both at the primary and secondary level is more diverse: (1) in the larger city of Douala than in the capital Yaoundé; (2) among males than among females; and (3) at least in Yaoundé, in public than in private institutions. In other words, if the functions of an educational system are to overcome the negative effects of ethnic divisiveness, our data suggest that the contributions of such a system in this regard are not homogeneous.

TABLE 7-4 *Ethnic Composition of the Douala and Yaoundé Teaching Staff by Sector and Sex*

| ETHNIC ORIGIN | PUBLIC SECTOR | | | | PRIVATE SECTOR | | | |
| | MEN | | WOMEN | | MEN | | WOMEN | |
	DOUALA	YAOUNDÉ	DOUALA	YAOUNDÉ	DOUALA	YAOUNDÉ	DOUALA	YAOUNDÉ
Duala	24.3%	7.7%	57.3%	9.6%	15.1%	0.0%	25.0%	0.0%
Bassa	23.6	9.1	18.5	16.8	27.5	7.7	39.8	6.9
Pahouins	17.3	51.2	7.3	50.5	5.9	79.8	7.1	86.2
Bamileke	12.9	14.1	7.3	5.0	29.9	4.2	16.1	0.0
Others	21.9	17.9	9.6	18.0	21.6	8.3	12.0	6.9
Total	100.0	100.0	100.0	99.9	100.0	100.0	100.0	100.0
Number of Teachers	271	178	124	83	443	119	56	23

SOURCE: Derived from raw data of the Douala Census (1964) and the Yaoundé Census (1962).

These contributions are also made more problematic because of significant ethnic variations in the educational background of the male and female teachers of the two cities examined here. In the public system the number of male teachers with a post-primary education varies between a high of 69 percent for individuals with a Duala origin and a low of 29 percent for those who are derived from the Mbam area, from the eastern part of the country, or from northern peoples. Among their female colleagues, no less than 40 percent of the Bassa teachers have had some post-primary experience as against only 19 percent of those coming from either the Mbam cluster or the northern populations. Ethnic contrasts in the educational attainment of the private schools' teaching force tend to be more limited. Only 34 percent of the Duala male teachers and 15 percent of their Pahouin counterparts went beyond their primary schooling, but for women the corresponding figures range between a high of 21 percent for the Bassa to zero percent for the Bamileke.

In brief, the degree to which schools can overcome ethnic divisiveness is limited both by the ethnic diversity of the entire teaching force and by the uneven educational level of teachers with distinct ethnic backgrounds. Indeed ethnic variations in the choice of teaching as an occupation reflect the differential alternative occupational opportunities made available to the various ethnic groups of the country.

As economic development proceeds, however, signs already suggest that the most "Westernized" ethnic groups relinquish their initial dominance in the educational field and provide less advanced groups with the opportunity of entering teaching as an occupation. For example, about 26 percent of the older male teachers (over 35 years of age) employed by the public school system of Douala and Yaoundé have a Duala origin as against only 8 percent Bamileke. Among their youngest colleagues, the Duala proportion declines to 12 percent but the Bamileke contingent rises up to 28 percent. In other words, as teaching ceases to be defined as the most attractive job available in the urban labor market, ethnic contrasts in the composition of the teaching force should decline in degree — and the role of schools as a mechanism of national integration should increase in proportion.

The Impact of Ethnic Factors on Cameroonian Curricula and Educational Techniques

The contributions of schools to national integration does not only depend upon the ethnic diversity of their teachers, but also upon what these teachers teach. Insofar as it can be assumed that national integration requires the use of one single lingua franca, Cameroon is confronted with difficult choices.[18]

The first difficulty in establishing one lingua franca concerns the contrasting orientations of French and British colonial policies toward the use of vernaculars in the educational context. French officials always argued that no Cameroonian language was widespread enough to justify its use in the local schools. In contrast, and particularly in the northern areas of the British-dominated western part, the British initially encouraged the use of vernaculars in the primary system.[19] The reliance of many religious missions upon vernaculars has been accompanied by the development of written and systematized forms of seven local languages. Further, the geographic diffusion of languages such as Fulani, Hausa, and Pidgin has increased considerably. Under such conditions, it is easy to wonder whether schools should not rely more directly upon Cameroonian rather than European languages as instruments of communication. The use of one or several Cameroonian languages has obvious psychological and political advantages. It probably facilitates the inculcation of certain values and the acquisition of certain forms of traditional knowledge. Also, it enhances national pride and hence an active mobilization of the masses. It has, however, economic drawbacks in the sense that it might hinder the communication of local intellectual, political, and cultural elites with their counterparts in industrialized nations. Clearly, the Cameroonian Government has taken the view that it was more appropriate to stimulate the use of European languages in the educational context.

The second difficulty regarding a lingua franca in Cameroon is specific to the Cameroonian scene; it concerns the choice of which foreign language to retain. Officially, the government is devoted to the development of bilingualism, and French and English are equally encouraged on both sides of the country. In order to mix western and eastern Cameroonian students and to expose them evenly to French and English, two bilingual colleges have been created, one in Buea and the other in Yaoundé, at the secondary school level. Once again, however, one might speculate as to the real impact of government strategies in this regard. The development of a language is related both to the value attached to a particular form of schooling and to the implications of such forms of schooling on the future occupations of individual students. That is to say, English-speaking Cameroonians cannot be encouraged to attach equal importance to French and English as long as their academic future depends upon their performances on examinations administered by English universities. And of course, the reverse pattern holds true of their French-speaking counterparts. Yet because the economic integration of the country is dominated by French interests and because the economic value of a "French-oriented" diploma becomes higher than that of an English-oriented examination, it is clear that the learning of these two languages ceases to be evenly stressed. Though an increasing number of English-speaking Cameroonian students are eager to present simultaneously examinations administered by French and by British educational systems, their French-speaking counterparts are more frequently satisfied with presenting only a French-dominated examination. The bilingualism prevailing in the Cameroon, therefore, is most likely to become asymmetric. English speakers will become fluent in French, but their French-speaking compatriots are unlikely to go beyond basic English.

The same asymmetry is likely to characterize the relative diffusion of European languages and of Arabic in the northern regions. Changes in local patterns of social stratification and in the status of Islamic teachers do not only affect the composition of the populations attending Koranic schools but also the functions that Arabic plays as a system of communication between individuals and social groups.

Yet the contribution of schools to national integration also depends upon the formulation of a systematic national history, geography, and literature. Once more, Cameroon is subjected to divergent forces in this regard. The early educational development of the country led to the blossoming of a large number of intellectuals who have made their names in their own field. Authors like Oyono, Mongo, Beti, Francis Bebey have acquired a solid reputation in international literary circles and their texts are often used in local schools. Similarly, Engelbert Mveng has written a *History of the Cameroon* which has received widespread acclamation. Moreover, a relatively large number of printing houses in the country facilitate the diffusion of pedagogical materials. Having, then, the human and material resources for changing educational programs and making them more "relevant" to the needs of the local scene, the Cameroonian Government, particularly at the primary school level, has been anxious to implement the recommendations of the Scientific Council for Africa South of the Sahara regarding the necessity of "producing course textbook and audio visual materials especially designed to meet the needs of Cameroon."[20]

At the same time, three forces of uneven importance have contributed to limit the stress upon local culture and needs: expatriates, French universities, political unrest. A significant number of expatriates remain in the post-primary system and such teachers are not necessarily amenable to changes that would require further intellectual investment on their part. As for the French metropolitan universities, they continue to attract a large part of the student population graduating from Cameroonian secondary institutions, and for this reason any change from a metropole-based curriculum could be construed as limiting the opportunities of young Cameroonian graduates for upward mobility. Last, the efforts to alter the educational curricula, especially in the social science field have been limited by massive political unrest that plagued the country between 1954 and 1960. As this unrest pitted distinctive ethnic groups against one another, certain officials have been afraid that attempts to stress the significance of a Cameroonian history would be used to justify current ethnic particularisms.

It is not only by imposing a uniform curriculum, however, that educational institutions can overcome the divisive effects of ethnicity, but also by implementing pedagogical methods and techniques adapted to the diversity of local cultures. Surprisingly, there has been much more noise about the need for "Africanizing" the curriculum of schools, than there have been efforts to determine whether ethnic variations in cognitive styles are accompanied by parallel contrasts in the extent and the form of learning. Cameroon, however, has been making innovations in this field. For example, in the learning of French the Group of Applied Linguistics of the Yaoundé University has engaged in a systematic analysis not only of the kind of mistakes made by students in the last year of primary school, but also of the relationships between the distribution of these mistakes and the ethnic composition of the classes interviewed.[21]

To summarize, the functions performed by the curriculum and the teaching techniques of the Cameroonian schools with regard to national integration are perhaps less significant than one would like them to be. But this pessimistic evaluation reflects perhaps some skepticism as to the extent to which schools can really do something with respect to integration. In Cameroon, as elsewhere, there is no evidence to suggest in unequivocal terms that the school has a definite impact on the political socialization of students. Further, the origin of this potential impact often remains problematic. Is the impact of educational structures related to the origin of students rather than to the treatment to which they are exposed? Can it be attributed to the content of the courses taught, or does it rather reflect the formal and informal processes of interaction between teacher and student as well as between student and student?[22] Much research is needed to assess the intensity and the quality of the influence that educational institutions do exert in this regard. A first step in this direction would consist, for example, of assessing the degree to which students choose friends outside of their ethnic group and in determining whether this tendency varies with: (1) the proprietorship status of the school that they attend; (2) their status in the school, that is, whether they are boarders or day students; and (3) their academic standing.[23]

Conclusion

Our main objective in this chapter has been to delineate the variety of dilemmas with which educational institutions are confronted in their attempts to overcome the divisiveness of ethnic factors. Cameroon is an adequate laboratory for the study of these dilemmas, because the divisive effects of African ethnicity are enhanced by the divisive effects of the various colonial experiences to which the country has been subjected.

We have suggested that the potential contribution of African educational institutions to national integration is twofold. They must allocate equal shares of educational opportunities to the various local peoples, and they must expose their students to ideas, norms, values and techniques that transcend ethnic particularisms.

As far as the first function of schools is concerned, we have shown that ethnic disparities exist in enrollment rates and that these disparities are not necessarily likely to decline over time. We have shown further that ethnic inequalities are likely to be associated with other forms of inequities, for instance, of a sexual and socioeconomic nature. Finally, that the coexistence of various educational sectors in the country exerts diverging influence on ethnic enrollments, has also been demonstrated. This coexistence might increase the government's options in deploying strategies to reduce ethnic disparities in enrollments, but it might also accentuate competition among regions and ethnic groups.

As far as the second function of schools is concerned—to expose students to ideas and values unrelated to ethnicity—we have pointed out a variety of dilemmas confronting educational administrators. Though the instillation of a purely national perspective in the schools of the country might facilitate political mobilization, it might also isolate Cameroon from industrialized societies. Also, the historical dependence of the country upon German, French, British, and Arab cultures makes it difficult for local leaders to identify the national perspective most suitable to the country's educational and economic development.

It is possible to entertain doubt about the direct political impact that schools might have on their student populations, but it also remains possible to argue that schools overcome the divisive effects of ethnicity whenever formal schooling and educational attainment become the uniform criteria underlying the placement of individuals in occupational and social structures. Yet even in this sense, the contribution of Cameroonian schools to national integration remains fragile. Individuals who share similar educational experiences but do not have the same ethnic background often do not enjoy the same occupational status nor the same level of occupational attainment.[24] The government, however, could reduce inequalities in the rewards derived from similar educational attainment by imposing ethnic quotas upon employers. To do so, however, confirms the weakness of the effects of schooling on national integration. After all, a school is more the reflection of the social structure in which it is embedded than it is the creator or modifier of that structure.

Notes

1. For a further discussion of this particular theme, see Remi Clignet, "Patterns of Educational Development and Elite Formation" in *The African Experience*, ed. John N. Paden and Edward W. Soja (Evanston: Northwestern University Press, 1970), chap. 15.

2. A theoretical justification of this relationship is offered in William J. Goode's *World Revolution and Family Patterns* (New York: The Free Press, 1963), Introduction. Although the author does not necessarily imply any causality in the relationship, it remains clear that countries such as the Ivory Coast seem to view a nuclearization of the family as likely to promote modernization. Indeed, such countries have laws forbidding polygyny.

3. This approach corresponds to the development of political and cultural slogans focused on the theme of Negritude. For a discussion and critical evaluation of this approach, see Frantz Fanon, *Les Damnés de la Terre* (Paris: Maspero, 1961), parts 3 and 4.

4. For background information on Cameroon, see Victor LeVine, *The Cameroons from Mandate to Independence* (Berkeley and Los Angeles: University of California Press, 1964).

5. For a more complete treatment, see Manga Bekombo Priso, "Les Classes d'Age chez les Duala," in *Classes et Associations d'Age en Afrique de l'Ouest*, ed. Denise Paulme (Paris: Plon, 1971), pp. 286-307.

6. See Jean Hurault, "Les classes d'Age dans le système social des Bamileke," in *Classes et Associations*, op. cit., pp. 308-319.

7. For a full treatment see Renaud Santerre, *Pédagogie Musulmane d' Afrique Noire* (Montréal: Presses de l'Université de Montréal, 1973).

8. Further, insofar as such a group stirs strong feelings on the part of the remaining population, it is likely to be isolated from other peoples in the urban context. In turn, this relative isolation is likely to affect the quantity and quality of the educational facilities to which they have access. For a discussion of the relative degree of ethnic isolation prevailing in Douala and Yaoundé, see Remi Clignet and Frank Jordan, "Urbanization and Social Differentiation in West Africa: A Comparative Analysis of the Ecological Structures of Douala and Yaoundé," *Cahiers d'Etudes Africaines*, Vol. 11, No. 42 (April 1971), pp. 281-297.

9. A more complete discussion of the development of colonization on Cameroon is given by Le Vine, op. cit. See also H. Vernon Jackson, *Language, Schools and Government in Cameroon* (New York: Teachers College Press, 1967) and Willard Johnson, *The Cameroon Federation* (Princeton: Princeton University Press, 1970).

10. See Remi Clignet, *Liberty and Equality in the Educational Process* (New York: John Wiley & Sons, 1974).

11. See Remi Clignet and Phillip Foster, "Teachers as Potential Agents of Modernization" (Report submitted to National Institute of Mental Health, Bethesda, Maryland, 1972).

12. These figures are derived from *Evaluations et Projections Démographiques en République Fédérale du Cameroun* (Yaoundé: Direction de la Statistique, 1970), p. 101.

13. It is noteworthy that in the North, declines in the level of male participation in Muslim schools are associated with corresponding increases in female enrollments. While such changes in the composition of Muslim schools result from the growth of public institutions, they modify the functions traditionally assigned to a Koranic form of schooling and probably impede further changes in the role performed by both public and Muslim schools. See Renaud Santerre *Pédagogie Musulmane d' Afrique Noire,* op. cit., chapter 3.

14. Although I have not directly demonstrated this point in the case of Cameroon, this relationship is identifiable elsewhere, as, for example, in the Ivory Coast or Ghana. See Remi Clignet, "Ethnicity, Social Differentiation and Secondary Schooling in West Africa," *Cahiers d'Etudes Africaines*, Vol. 7, No. 26 (April 1967), pp. 360-378.

15. This lack of comfort is not assuaged by better pay. Salaries paid to teachers vary with their places of residence, but pay scales are higher in the larger centers than in the hinterland in spite of the fact that a modern life-style, usually adopted by teachers, is more expensive in rural areas.

16. While westernized public and private schools aim at enabling their students to fulfill a variety of roles in the modern sector of the economy, Koranic schools perform more specific religious and professional functions. Indeed there are many similarities between the climate of such schools (as described by Renaud Santerre in *Pédagogie Musulmane d' Afrique Noire*, op. cit.) and the atmosphere prevailing in the European schools of before the French Revolution (as described by Philippe Aries in *Centuries of Childhood*, New York: Knopf, 1926).

17. For a further discussion of this point, see Remi Clignet and Phillip Foster, "Teachers as Potential Agents," op. cit.

18. This theme is treated most forcefully by Johnson, op. cit., pp. 300-305.

19. See Jackson, op. cit., chap. 5.

20. Ibid., p. 20.

21. See, for example, Patrick Renaud, "Les Fautes de Français en CM2; Etude typologique et statistique" (Yaoundé: Université Federale, 1969), mimeographed.

22. For a discussion of the influence of such factors on the socialization of students see Michael Armes and Robert Youtz, "Western Education and Modernity," *American Journal of Sociology,* Vol. 76, No. 4 (January 1971), pp. 604-626.

23. I am currently starting the corresponding analysis on data constructed and gathered by Prof. Phillip Foster, Norman Haupt, and myself.

24. Remi Clignet, *Educational and Occupational Differentiation in the Cameroon,* in preparation.

Part IV

Language Policy, Communications, and Culture

Introduction

WITH APPROXIMATELY 2,000 languages being spoken in the countries of Sub-Saharan Africa, the linguistic diversity and fragmentation of the area is almost overwhelming. In precolonial times, when the borders of a state only occasionally extended beyond linguistic boundaries, this linguistic diversity posed only minimal problems. Although interstate communication was difficult and linguistic forces militated against the development of larger political units, state administration and viability were only rarely inhibited by linguistic factors. In terms of contemporary political geography, however, these 2,000 linguistic communities are grouped into 38 states, which means that most contemporary African states contain a multitude of linguistically fragmented segments.

Obviously, to state that 2,000 languages are spoken in Sub-Saharan Africa is not to assert that this area contains 2,000 linguistic islands whose members cannot communicate with one another. Bilingualism and even multilingualism were widespread in precolonial times, and are much more widespread today. In large part this has resulted from the natural desire and need for some kind of communication to take place across linguistic boundaries if commerce and other forms of interchange are to occur. Moreover, communication patterns within African states have been dramatically rearranged by the language and educational policies adopted both by colonial and independent governments. Each of Africa's colonial powers sought to impose its own language as a second language on its colonies' educated elite, largely to serve three purposes: to permit communication between the colonial administration and the local population, to facilitate communication among the various linguistic communities within the country, and to serve as a carrier of the particular brand of European culture the colonial power was seeking to disseminate.

In most cases, the independent states of Africa have seen little alternative thus far to the continuation of the basic language policies imposed by the colonial powers. Whether it is specifically designated or not as the official language, in the majority of countries the European language of the former colonial power continues to be employed for most official discourse. Even in a country like Swaziland, which traditionally enjoyed linguistic homogeneity, English is accorded official status along with Swazi. The only linguistically fragmented country in Sub-Saharan Africa that has aggressively promoted an African language as its national tongue is Tanzania, which has adopted Swahili.

In this introduction to the discussion of language policy in Ghana, Cameroon, and Nigeria in the three chapters that follow, it is useful to consider two fundamental questions:

1. How important to national integration is language policy and language usage?
2. What particular language policies are potentially most valuable in promoting the kinds of communication patterns and competence that can facilitate national integration?

The underlying issue of greatest importance, and in turn the one that arouses greatest controversy, is how aggressively a national government should attempt to promote a single national language as a means of combating linguistic fragmentation and overcoming the barriers these subdivisions erect to effective national communication. We would contend that the promotion of some means of national communication is of greater importance than has thus far been recognized by most of those who shape language policy in African states. This is not to assert that any existing language should be neglected or forgotten, nor that the citizens of a country should be encouraged to adopt a single mother tongue or first language. For the forseeable future, national communication in Africa will have to occur on the basis of near universal bilingualism or multilingualism. Nor are we prepared to prejudge the question of whether the language of national communication in a country should be an African language or the European language most widely spoken. But we are contending that national communication is of fundamental importance to the promotion of national integration and to the improvement of intergroup relations, and that the significance of national communication needs to be recognized in the formulation of national language policy.

The aspect of a nation's language policy most critically important in determining language usage and national communication patterns relates to education. The crucial decisions of a nation relating to language are those concerning the media of instruction at various levels of the educational system; what languages are to be taught as compulsory or optional subjects for study; what proportion of the school curriculum is to be devoted to a particular language or languages; and what standards of quality are to be sought and maintained in the teaching of these languages. Most of those who have written about language policy in Africa are linguists and educationists. Their viewpoints, and especially their attention to the welfare of school-children and to effective education, are obviously of enormous significance and should be given due regard in any policy decisions relating to language. Nevertheless, one needs at the same time to recognize that language policy has broader implications than the education of individual children. Language policy is of particular importance for nation-building, and specifically for national cohesion. One analyst has pointed out that "not to have a language in common with one's compatriot is to have a stranger for a countryman."[1] This consideration is one to which most linguists and educationsists have, unfortunately, accorded little attention.

Several analysts have assessed the impact of language on European nationalism. Karl Deutsch points out the close parallel between the growth of linguistic diversity in Europe from 1800 to 1937 and the growth in the number of sovereign European states over the same period.[2] Various studies have also shown the degree to which a shared language contributes to a sense of national identity and loyalty,[3] as well as the extent to which groups of persons who speak a particular language view themselves as different in kind from other groups.[4] Through a systematic comparison of 114 polities, 52 of which were classified as being linguistically homogeneous and the remainder linguistically heterogeneous, Arthur Banks and Robert Textor discovered certain significant features that differentiate these two types of states.[5] Many of these differences were found to be reduced in significance when the economic status of the various states was controlled statistically. Nonetheless, two distinguishing characteristics of linguistically heteroge-neous states continue to hold: (1) exaggerated sectionalism or interregional conflict, and (2) extreme difficulties posed by politically unassimilated minor-ities.[6] Dankwart Rustow has described language as being "to a modern society what money is to its economy: a universal currency of exchange."[7]

Australia,[8] Israel,[9] the Soviet Union,[10] and the United States[11] have all attempted to promote national cohesion through vigorous efforts to teach their citizens a common language. The approaches adopted by these four countries to achieve this end have varied considerably, but the effort has yielded handsome nation-building dividends for each. The United States, Israel, and Australia have all faced the problem of how to mold immigrant populations of diverse linguistic, cultural, and national backgrounds into a new national unit to which the new citizens would develop a sense of loyalty and identification. In each of these countries encouragement of immigrants to learn and use a common language was a critical step in this direction. The situation in the Soviet Union has been somewhat more comparable to that found in most parts of Africa. Because the Soviet Union is composed of settled but linguistically fragmented communities, the country's many language communities have been taught to speak Russian as a means of linking them to the national communication grid. Only 55 percent of the country's population speaks Russian as a first language, but intensive educational efforts have resulted in a high proportion of the remaining population speaking Russian as a second language.

Several instances of successful integration on an explicitly bilingual or multilingual basis can be cited. In Switzerland a sufficient degree of national cohesion has been engendered despite the fact that there are four national languages. The Swiss case is nevertheless instructive in pointing out that effective integration and national communication can occur in a multilingual situation only when a sufficiently high proportion of individual citizens are multilingual.

Languages indigenous to Africa represent approximately half of the total number of languages spoken by all mankind. Africa has a greater number of languages per unit of population than any comparable portion of the world.[12] Africa can only boast a handful of countries that even approach being monolingual. These facts not only indicate the difficulty of the nation-building task in contemporary Africa, they also suggest the urgency of each state encouraging one or more of the following: (1) the development of a truly national language; (2) an effective lingua franca; or (3) multilingualism sufficient to permit genuine national communication among different ethnic and language groups.

The linguistic situations in the three West African countries of Ghana, Nigeria, and Cameroon, which are discussed in detail in the next three chapters, reflect some of the common problems faced by most African states together with the uniqueness of each situation and the need for language policies appropriate to the particular circumstances of each state. All three countries are severely fragmented linguistically, but as a consequence of its peculiar colonial history Cameroon has its traditional linguistic geography overlaid by two European languages, which jointly enjoy the status of official national languages. The most hotly debated aspect of language policy in Cameroon relates to the respective roles to be accorded each of these languages and how to promote English-French bilingualism. Bernard Fonlon emphasizes how important it is for Cameroon to sustain national communication through the medium of these two European languages.

While no controversy surrounds the retention of English as the ascendant *European* language in both Ghana and Nigeria, discussions of increasing urgency are being conducted on whether English should continue to hold preeminent position as the official national language. Growing numbers of Nigerians and Ghanaians believe that English should either share its role as the national language or be supplanted by an African language indigenous to the country. Their position is based both on the nationalist sentiment that an African state needs to throw off its European legacy and adopt an African language and on the conviction that English will never be widely enough spoken in these countries to constitute an effective medium of national communication.[13] The major obstacle to the adoption of an African language as the national tongue in Nigeria and Ghana is bitter disagreement over which language should enjoy such a status. Paralleling the attack on the supremacy of English is the growing conviction that the role of all local languages should be reinforced, primarily through being accorded greater significance as media of instruction in the educational system. Unfortunately, those advocating this position often lose sight of the divisive impact equal emphasis given to many local languages can have on national communication processes. The Nigerian situation involves not merely the questions regarding the role of local vernaculars and the selection of a national language, but also the selection and use of regional languages to be used at the state level, giving rise to a three-tier or even a four-tier language policy. Ayo Banjo's discussion of Nigeria also demonstrates the interesting interplay between political and linguistic factors in Nigeria. He finds that language policy is not only generating political debate, but that the changing political structure of that country is altering language policy and language use.

Probably second only in importance to the educational system in implementing a country's language policy is the interconnection between language policy and the mass media. Given the fact that in most African states the mass media are operated by government agencies, their effective utilization constitutes a powerful mechanism for influencing language use. As a part of its effort to promote Swahili as an effective medium of national communication, the Tanzanian Government only permits radio broadcasting in Swahili and English. The Ugandan Government, on the other hand, has progressively augmented the number of languages in which radio programs are broadcast so that, as Aidan Southall reports in Part V of this book, daily broadcasts are now made in 16 different Ugandan languages, as well as English, French, and Arabic. Clearly, the Ugandan Government sees this linguistic proliferation as a means of increasing listener comprehension and as a way of offering psychological and political reassurance to a broad spectrum of ethnic groups regarding their place in the Ugandan framework. It also reflects the fact that Uganda has thus far eschewed the vigorous promotion of a national language.

But the importance of the mass media in promoting national integration far surpasses language issues,[14] and this has frequently been recognized.[15] As William Neher and John Condon point out in their chapter, effective utilization of the mass media can enhance governmental legitimacy, public comprehension of governmental structure and policy, and political socialization. An understanding of the actual and potential roles of the mass media is constrained, however, by the limited information available regarding the functioning of the mass media in Africa — one of the major topics that Neher and Condon address. The power of the mass media as potential instruments for political development also carries with it the inherent danger of exploitation for the purposes of thought-control and demagoguery. Government control of the mass media in most African states thus offers important opportunities for promoting national integration as well as inherent dangers, and the Neher-Condon chapter discusses the differing approaches to government control and exploitation of the mass media for nation-building purposes in Tanzania and Kenya.

Both the chapter by Neher and Condon and the chapter by Atta Annan Mensah emphasize the mutually reinforcing roles of the mass media and cultural activities. Some traditional cultural forms have played and continue to play important communicative roles, and they can be utilized for nation-building purposes. Moreover, the mass media can assist with the development and adoption of national cultural forms and thereby enhance national identity and pride. Most African states face serious problems in the cultural sphere, however, because cultural traditions in Africa almost necessarily involve local or subnational traditions; culture areas are rarely delimited by national boundaries.[16] In confronting this problem some states, like the Ivory Coast, have tended to downgrade particularistic traditions and lay emphasis upon new culture forms that are national in scope. Other states, like Mali, have selected a particular ethnic tradition and projected it to the national level, attempting to give a national definition to a previously particularistic tradition.[17] Ali Mazrui has articulated the remedy as "the commitment to indigenize what is foreign, idealize what is indigenous, nationalize what is sectional, and emphasize what is African. . . ."[18]

Mensah's discussion of Uganda and Zambia suggests that the preservation and elaboration of traditional forms need not be divisive, and that national cultural forms can develop alongside ethnic traditions, with or without government encouragement. He also suggests that while linguistic fragmentation in these two states inhibits to some extent the emergence of national literary, dramatic, and musical traditions, linguistic barriers are not insuperable obstacles to national and even continental cultural appreciation and expression.

Notes

1. Robert Jacobs, ed., "English Language Teaching in Nigeria" (Lagos: Ford Foundation, September 1966), p. 39, mimeographed.
2. Karl W. Deutsch, "The Trend of European Nationalism," in *Readings in the Sociology of Language,* ed. Joshua Fishman (The Hague: Mouton, 1968), p. 606.
3. Yehudi A. Cohen, *Social Structure and Personality* (New York: Holt, Rinehart and Winston, 1961); G. W. Skinner, "The Nature of Loyalties in Rural Indonesia," in *Local, Ethnic, and National Loyalties in Rural Indonesia,* ed. Skinner (New Haven: Yale University Southeast Asia Studies, 1959), pp. 1-11.
4. Sigmund Freud, *Group Psychology and the Analysis of the Ego* (New York: Bantam Books, 1960); Paul C. Rosenblatt, "Origins and Effects of Group Ethnocentrism and Nationalism," *Journal of Conflict Resolution,* Vol. 8, No. 2 (June 1964), pp. 131-146; Boyd C. Shafer, *Nationalism: Myth and Reality* (New York: Harcourt, Brace, 1955).
5. Arthur S. Banks and Robert B. Textor, *A Cross-Polity Survey* (Cambridge: MIT Press, 1963), no pagination.
6. Joshua A. Fishman, "Some Contrasts Between Linguistically Homogeneous and Linguistically Heterogeneous Polities," in *Language Problems of Developing Nations,* ed. Fishman, Charles A. Ferguson, and Jyotirindra Das Gupta (New York: John Wiley & Sons, 1968), pp. 63-64.
7. Dankwart A. Rustow, *A World of Nations* (Washington: The Brookings Institution, 1967), p. 47.
8. R. B. LePage, *The National Language Question* (London: Oxford University Press, 1964), pp. 23-24.
9. Simon R. Herman, "Explorations in the Social Psychology of Language Choice," *Human Relations,* Vol. 14, No. 2 (May 1961), pp. 149-164; Haim Blanc, "The Growth of Israeli Hebrew," *Middle Eastern Affairs,* Vol. 5, No. 12 (December 1954), pp. 385-392; and Judd L. Teller, ed., *Acculturation and Integration* (New York: American Histadrut Cultural Exchange Institute, 1965).
10. Elliot R. Goodman, *The Soviet Design for a World State* (New York: Columbia University Press, 1960), pp. 264-284; Vernon V. Aspaturian, "The Non-Russian Nationalities," in *Prospects for Soviet Society,* ed. Allen Kassof (New York: Frederick A. Praeger, 1968), pp. 143-198.
11. Joshua A. Fishman, *Language Loyalty in the United States* (The Hague: Mouton, 1966); and Judd L. Teller, op. cit.
12. Neville Denny, "Languages and Education in Africa," in *Language in Africa,* ed. John Spencer (London: Cambridge University Press, 1963), p. 40.

13. Pierre Van den Berge has contended that the promotion of a European language as the official language accentuates the divisions between the urban elite, who will be able to speak the language, and the less educated lower classes. See Van den Berge, "European Languages and Black Mandarins," *Transition,* Vol. 7, No. 34 (December-January 1968), pp. 19-23.

14. For consideration of the role of the mass media in the development process generally, see Daniel Lerner and Wilbur Schramm, eds., *Communication and Change in the Developing Countries* (Honolulu: East-West Center Press, 1967); Wilbur Schramm, *Mass Media and Development* (Stanford: Stanford University Press, 1964); and Lucien Pye, ed., *Communication and Political Development* (Princeton: Princeton University Press, 1963).

15. The recommendations formulated by the first international conference on television held in Africa stated that ". . . with the object of promoting national unity . . . African broadcasting authorities should use every appropriate type of television programme which can help to bind the nation together culturally, intellectually and economically." (UNESCO Report of Meeting on the "Introduction and Development of Television in Africa" [Paris, September 1964], p. 3.)

16. This problem is explored in J. F. A. Ajayi, "The Place of African History and Culture in the Process of Nation-Building in Africa South of the Sahara," in *Social Change: The Colonial Experience,* ed. Immanuel Wallerstein (New York: John Wiley & Son, 1966), pp. 606-616.

17. For a discussion of the differing approaches of the Ivory Coast and Mali in this regard see Aristide Zolberg, "Patterns of National Integration," *Journal of Modern African Studies,* Vol. 5, No. 4 (December 1967), pp. 449-467.

18. Ali Mazrui, *Cultural Engineering and Nation-Building in East Africa* (Evanston: Northwestern University Press, 1972), p. 278.

Chapter 8

Language Policy in Ghana

by David R. Smock

ETHNIC CONFLICT in Ghana has never reached the proportions that it has in Nigeria and Zaire. It exists, nonetheless, for Ghana is characterized by considerable ethnic and linguistic diversity, and the problems this diversity creates for national integration are serious. The sharpest division in the country is between the North and the South, with the northern population speaking primarily languages of the Gur subgroup of the Niger-Congo family and the southern population speaking languages of the Kwa subgroup of the Niger-Congo family. This North-South division is not confined to the linguistic sphere. It also marks the principal economic and cultural differences.

Oddly enough, the greatest ethnic conflict does not occur between the peoples of North and South, but among various southern communities. Despite, or maybe because of, the economic and educational underdevelopment of the North, the northerners have not clashed sharply with the southern population. In both precolonial and modern times, ethnic friction has most frequently occurred between such southern groups as the Ashanti, the Fante, the Gas, and the Ewes. In terms of political action, the Ashantis felt themselves to be persecuted and neglected during the Nkrumah era, while it was the Ewes who saw themselves as the exploited ethnic minority of Ghana under the Busia regime. Inter-ethnic alliances and hostilities shift with changing political and economic circumstances, but one can foresee continuing problems posed for national integration by ethnic diversity. Of considerable importance to the future character of ethnic relations in Ghana is the relatively recent development of a pan-Akan identity among the more than 40 percent of the population that speaks one or another Akan dialect as a mother tongue. In the past, some of Ghana's most bitter ethnic conflict occurred among such Akan subgroups as the Ashanti, the Fante, and the Akim, but since 1969 a new sense of Akan identity has developed, based largely on a recognition of linguistic and cultural similarities and underscored by common opposition to the non-Akan Ewes.

Though more than 40 percent of Ghana's population speaks one or another of the Akan dialects as a first language, the overall linguistic variegation and fragmentation in this country of 9 million people is considerable. According to the 1960 census, Ghana's population speaks 34 distinct, mutually unintelligible languages, and 15 additional languages are spoken by large numbers of aliens.[1] As indicated in Table 8-1, 13 of these languages have more than 100,000 native speakers.

A mere enumeration of the size of the country's various language communities as given in Table 8-1 only goes a certain distance toward portraying the complete language situation. Unfortunately, very little data are available regarding multilingualism in Ghana, which is an equally important aspect of the language picture. The follow-up survey of the 1970 census did include questions regarding multilingual competence, but

TABLE 8-1 *Numbers of Native-Speakers of Different Languages in Ghana in 1960*

1.	Twi-Fante (Akan)	2,657,020
2.	Ewe	876,230
3.	Guan	254,790
4.	Adangbe	237,440
5.	Ga	236,210
6.	Dagbani	217,640
7.	Dagarti	201,680
8.	Gureni	193,500
9.	Nzema	178,100
10.	Kusal	121,610
11.	Konkomba	110,150
12.	Mole*	106,140
13.	Yoruba*	100,560
14.	Anyi-Bawle	88,740
15.	Buli	62,620
16.	Hausa*	61,730
17.	Sisala	59,210
18.	Mamprusi	58,710
19.	Busa*	56,690
20.	Kotokoli*	51,020
21.	Tobote*	48,720
22.	Wali	47,200

23.	Lobi*	37,550
24.	Kasem	37,030
25.	Songhai*	35,930
26.	Bambara*	34,180
27.	Talene	32,780
28.	Bimoda	32,270
29.	Fula*	25,050
30.	Pilapila*	24,790
31.	Nabt	16,500
32.	Buem	14,900
33.	Chokosi	14,090
34.	Ibo	14,050
35.	Nanume	13,700
36.	Avatime-Nyangbo-Tafi	10,210
37.	Mo	8,830
38.	Akposo*	8,530
39.	Likpe	7,140
40.	Kru*	6,500
41.	Akpafu	5,370
42.	Bowiri	3,280
43.	Santrokofi	3,230
44.	Adele	2,900
45.	Lolobi	2,860
46.	Vagala	2,230
47.	Logba	2,090
48.	Akposo	1,780

*Most persons speaking these languages as their mother tongue are aliens, or non-citizens.

SOURCE: Extrapolated from B. Gil, A.F. Aryee, and D.K. Ghansah, *Population Census of Ghana, Special Report "E" Tribes of Ghana* (Accra: Census, 1964).

these data are not yet available. Probably an extreme case of linguistic diversity and of multilingualism is offered by Madina, a suburb of Accra that has been carefully studied in a sociolinguistic survey. In that small community 70 different mother tongues are spoken by its 2,000 residents. Ninety-six percent of Madina's residents are bilingual and 70 percent claim competence in three or more languages.[2] Thus, in spite of the extremely fragmented character of the suburb's linguistic situation, by means of multilingual competence considerable intracommunity communication can occur. And what is true of Madina applies to Ghana as a whole.

Even without precise survey data, one can assert with reasonable accuracy that Akan, or one or another of the Akan dialects, serves as the most widespread lingua franca in Ghana. At one time a Nigerian language, Hausa, was the lingua franca in the northern portion of Ghana because the commerce of the area was largely controlled by Hausa traders. However, Hausa seems to be losing currency and Akan appears to be supplanting it as a lingua franca in the North. It is unfortunate that no accurate statistics exist regarding the use of Akan as a lingua franca and the rate at which its use is increasing, because it is conceivable that with such statistics one might reasonably predict that within a specified number of years Akan will become nearly a universal lingua franca and thereby provide a medium of national communication, even without official government encouragement. Without accurate statistics, such an eventuality can only be posited with considerable uncertainty. It can be said with confidence, however, that more than half of Ghana's population currently speaks Akan as either a first or second language.

The Ghanaian Government, faced with the nation's linguistic complexity, has laid down certain guidelines concerning language use in particular situations to enable effective communication. These guidelines constitute the government's language policies. English is the language for official government communication, and when the National Assembly has functioned under civilian governments, English has been the language prescribed for the legislature. Official examinations are also conducted in English. Occasionally a government department may issue a statement for the public in one or more Ghanaian languages, but this is usually a simplified version of the official policy statement originally prepared and recorded in English.

A government agency, the Bureau of Ghana Languages, has responsibility for the preparation of local language literature, primarily for use in schools but also for public consumption. By government policy the bureau produces materials in eight different Ghanaian languages and dialects: Fante, Asante-Twi, Akuapem-Twi, Ewe, Ga, Nzema, Dagbani, and Kasem.

The government-run Ghana Broadcasting Corporation (GBC) offers programs in English, and in addition provides some programs each week in the following five languages: Ewe, Akan, Nzema, Hausa, Dagbani and Ga. The ratio of English programs to those broadcast in one or another of these five African languages is approximately 3 to 1 for GBC radio transmission and 14 to 1 for GBC television transmission.

Language Policy in Education

Ghana's language policy in the field of education has great influence on language usage and patterns of national communication. As noted in the Introduction to Part IV, the most urgent questions in the educational sphere are: What language or languages are to be taught as compulsory and optional subjects for study? What proportion of the school curriculum is to be devoted to which languages? What language or languages are to be used as the media of instruction at various levels of the educational ladder?

Schoolchildren study only the Ghanaian language which predominates in the locality where the school is located. Consequently, unless a child is resident in an area where his mother tongue is not the prevailing local language, he will not study a Ghanaian language other than his own. Thus, the teaching of Ghanaian languages has not generally been seen as a means of increasing communication across language boundaries, but of increasing competence in one's own language. Multilingualism in Ghana has resulted from individual efforts to learn other Ghanaian languages; it is not the product of official encouragement in the educational system or elsewhere. In November 1970 the then minister of education, R. R. Amponsah, stated that beginning in 1971 every pupil in Ghana's primary schools would be required to learn a Ghanaian language in addition to his mother tongue. The second language was to be either Ga, Nzema, Akan, Ewe, or Dagbani. Amponsah's was the first major government statement concerning the utilization of Ghanaian languages to increase national communication. Unfortunately, his policy statement was unrealistic in terms of the availability of teachers and teaching materials, and as a result no serious effort has been made to implement it.

The most frequently discussed question involving language policy in Ghana has been that of the medium of instruction. From the earliest days of formal education in Ghana, controversy has surrounded the question, and differing practices have been followed in different parts of the country and by different educational agencies. In the mid-nineteenth century, for instance, the Basel Mission employed Ga and Twi as the media of instruction in their schools,[3] while the Wesleyans, working in the coastal towns, used English.[4] Throughout most of Ghana's educational history both English and local languages have served both as subjects for study and as media of instruction, but their respective roles have been subjected to a series of policy fluctuations.

The report of the Phelps-Stokes Commission in 1922 was one of the earliest comprehensive reviews of education in West Africa, and its recommendations regarding language had considerable impact on the thinking of the colonial administration. The following statement summarizes its conclusions regarding the prominent role it believed local languages should be accorded in West African schools:

With full appreciation of the European language, the value of the Native tongue is immensely more vital, in that it is one of the chief means of preserving whatever is good in Native customs, ideas, and ideals, and thereby preserving what is more important than all else, namely, Native self-respect. It is the means of giving expression to their own personality. No greater injustice can be committed against a people than to deprive them of their own language.[5]

Basing its conclusions largely on the recommendations of the Phelps-Stokes Commission, the British Advisory Committee on Native Education in Tropical Africa recommended in 1927 that local languages serve as the media of instruction throughout the early primary years and that a whole year should then be devoted to slowly shifting to English as the medium of instruction for the final years of primary schooling.[6] These recommendations became British Government policy, and this position was strengthened by the British Education Committee Report of 1937-1941 and the 1944 Memorandum on Language in African School Education.

Significant revision of this policy came with the Accelerated Development Plan of 1951. It urged a gradual transition from the mother tongue to English as the medium of instruction in primary 2 (second grade), while at the same time stating that the aim of primary education in the Gold Coast should be to provide permanent literacy in both English and the mother tongue.[7] The Barnard Committee, appointed in 1956 to report on the use of English as the medium of instruction in Gold Coast schools, recommended that the mother tongue be employed as the medium for the first three years with a gradual transition to English coming in the fourth year.[8] However, these recommendations were largely neglected, and the government started to push for an increase in the proportion of time devoted to English.[9]

By 1960 only the first year of primary school was supposed to be taught in the mother tongue, with the transition to English taking place in primary 2. Once again in 1963 a committee of educators recommended that the mother tongue be given a more prominent place because of the scarcity of trained teachers competent to teach English,[10] but the government was pushing in the other direction. At approximately the same time the committee was making its recommendations, the minister of education declared in June 1963:

Where conditions permit, we insist that English should be used by both teachers and pupils right from the first year. A number of experimental schools have been opened throughout the country to test the efficacy of using English as the only medium of instruction right from the first year. Results achieved so far indicate that given the right type of teacher, all primary schools can conduct their teaching in English from Primary 1.[11]

In 1967 one once again witnessed a committee of educators advocating increased use of the mother tongue, while the government defended the existing policy. The Education Review Committee of that year recommended that "a Ghanaian language be used as the medium of instruction for the first three years of the primary course; the change to English as a medium of instruction should commence in the fourth year whilst the Ghanaian language continues to be studied as a subject."[12] The White Paper on the *Report of the Education Review Committee* stated:

> It is the view of the Government that arrangements for the medium of instruction should be flexible. Government considers, therefore, that a Ghanaian language should be used in the first year, and that a gradual change to English as the medium of instruction should begin in the second year with practical subjects such as number work, handwork, physical education, and games. More and more subjects should be progressively taught in the English medium. In the cosmopolitan areas, however, English may be used as the medium of instruction as early as the first year of school.[13]

The most recent policy statement by the Ministry of Education on this subject of when and where to teach in English and in a Ghanaian language came in November 1970 and largely accepts the recommendations quoted above of the 1967 Education Review Committee. It endorses the idea that the mother tongue should be used as the medium of instruction for the first three years of primary school, and that a transition to English as the medium should commence in the fourth year.

Despite the importance of the government's policy, it would be erroneous to assume that the teaching situation faithfully reflects its policy. Seventy-six percent of the primary schools reviewed by the Barnard Committee in 1956 did not use English as the medium of instruction at *any* level, despite the fact that according to government policy at that time English should have been introduced as the medium in Primary 2.[14] English is undoubtedly more widely utilized today than in 1956, but no reliable information has been compiled regarding actual practice. Whether the policy change in 1970 has had much impact on local practice is also unknown. The practices followed by particular schools depend upon several factors besides government policy, including the inclinations of the head teacher and individual teachers, the language area in which the school is located, and whether the teachers are fluent in the local languag .

As an illustration of local and individual variations in teaching practices, we have observed teachers introducing the same topic to primary classes 1, 2 and 3 in a school in a Ga-speaking area. The teachers of primary 1 and 3 used Ga, but the teacher of primary 2 introduced the topic completely in English. Though some flexibility might be expected, it would seem desirable that linear consistency and regularity be achieved by individual schools.

Moreover, consideration of changes in language policy is only meaningful if the government has both the intention and the capability of implementing whatever policy changes are decided upon.

The professional educators in advocating more extensive use of the mother tongue have understandably been influenced by their professional concern over the ease with which young children can absorb new information, and the difficulties they have in doing so in a foreign language. The educators have also been anxious that children appreciate local traditions, which can probably be done best in the language of the locality.

Counterbalancing the influence of the professional educators in shaping language policy for the schools have been the parents of schoolchildren, officials in the finance ministry, and Ghana's political leaders. Parents have been a strong lobby for English because command of English is considered the avenue to social and economic mobility. Ministry of Finance officials responsible for holding down government expenditure shudder at the enormous costs involved in training language teachers and producing sufficient teaching materials in a wide variety of Ghanaian languages. During the Nkrumah era, political leaders demonstrated considerable concern over the possible divisive impact of a mother tongue medium policy. Although English is a language alien to Ghana, they saw it as the best vehicle for achieving national communication and social and political unification. They also viewed English as important for international communication, not only with Europe and America but also with other African states in furtherance of African unity.

One aspect-of the Ghanaian social situation that has posed particular difficulties for the greater utilization of local languages as media of instruction is the degree of ethnic mixing in many parts of the country. The mingling of ethnic groups is manifested in both urban and rural schools and arises primarily from the frequency of internal migrations. In 1956 only 499 of the 1,652 schools surveyed by the Barnard Committee were pure language schools in the sense that all pupils spoke a single mother tongue, whereas 599 of the schools surveyed had more than five mother tongues "represented in fair numbers."[15] It seems likely that the ratio of one-language to mixed-language schools has even increased since 1956, but no substantiating statistics for this assertion are available.

What is both surprising and disconcerting about the continuing debate over the medium of instruction is that no significant research has been undertaken on the subject in Ghana, or for that matter in most other parts of the world. To some extent the debate over languages in the classroom cannot be resolved by research simply because proponents of one view or another have different value orientations. But the debate could move to a higher level of sophistication and the consequences of one policy or another could be much more clearly discerned if controlled experiments utilizing a variety of approaches were conducted.

Current Interest and Debate

With the government accepting the recommendation that a mother tongue be used as the medium of instruction in the first three years of primary school, professional linguists and secondary-school language teachers have recently become a lobby against the ascendant position of English in the higher grades. They want to assure the preservation of all Ghanaian languages and instill an appreciation for them among future generations of Ghanaians. They advocate that more classroom hours be spent on the study of mother tongues and that greater use be made of mother tongues as the media of instruction in the upper primary (grades 4 to 6) and middle school (grades 6 to 10) grades. Their principal interest, therefore, is not in increasing multilingualism but in improving facility in and the usage of one's mother tongue. When English was still officially the medium of instruction in the early primary years, these advocates advised switching to mother tongues.

While this effort to preserve and promote Ghanaian languages is in many respects a worthy and commendable one, the principal spokesmen for this point of view seem to disregard the possible implications of the policies they urge for multilingualism, national communication, and national integration. The danger exists that increased emphasis upon mother tongues will inhibit the growth of a lingua franca and reinforce the rigidity of existing boundaries between language communities. Interestingly enough, the chief advocates of preserving and promoting the multitude of Ghanaian languages are usually those who are the best educated and who have the best command of English. They tend to assume as a given the existence of English as a medium for national communication and then advocate policies aimed at strengthening individual Ghanaian languages. If the day comes when English or a Ghanaian language provides a truly national medium of communication, then their position would be defensible. But Ghana must yet go some considerable distance before its problems of national communication are solved.

Others are urging that Ghana have a Ghanaian language rather than English as the single official language for national communication. The degree to which this point of view has gained strength over the past decade among Ghana's intelligentsia is reflected in two surveys of students at the University of Ghana conducted with a 10-year interval between them. A survey in 1961 conducted by Gilbert Ansre, a leading Ghanaian linguist, revealed that 93 percent of Ghana's university students favored the retention of English as the official language.[16] A 1971 survey conducted by Audrey Smock among students at the university disclosed that only 30 percent favored the retention of English; 56 percent wanted a Ghanaian language as the national language.[17]

In May 1971 S.H. Addae introduced the following private member's motion to the National Assembly: "That in view of the importance of a national language as a factor for national unity in Ghana, this House requests the Government to set up a national committee of experts to promote and coordinate all efforts being made to evolve a common Ghanaian language or lingua franca."[18] It was not clear in the motion whether he proposed the creation of a new hybrid language or the adoption of an existing Ghanaian language as the official language. What was clear was that Addae was proposing a Ghanaian alternative to English. In his defense of the motion, however, Addae quite plainly advocated the adoption of an existing Ghanaian language rather than a hybrid, though he did not prejudge which language should be chosen. After three days of lively debate the following amended motion was adopted: "In view of the importance of a national language as a factor for national unity in Ghana, this House should take note of the necessity of a common Ghanaian language or lingua franca."[19]

Agreement on principle there was. But that was about all. Action on it was stymied by the difficulties involved in deciding which of Ghana's various languages should be adopted as the national language, and that has been the dilemma of most multilingual countries trying to pick a national language. Significantly, though, the public discussion of a national Ghanaian language recognized the importance of utilizing language policy to promote national integration.

Ghana's Policy Alternatives

Although neither of these movements against English represents a ground swell of public opinion, it is a fair certainty that Ghana's language policy will be the subject of continuing and increasing debate. Within the context of its need for improved intergroup relations and for greater national integration, what language policy alternatives does Ghana have? National cohesion requires some means of achieving effective intergroup communication, but the very complexity of Ghana's linguistic fragmentation will make this task extremely difficult.

We would suggest that there are four alternative approaches to effective national communication. The first is to encourage, or even require, schoolchildren to learn a Ghanaian language other than their own. The educational system could thereby contribute to greater inter-ethnic understanding and communication. Consistent with this idea, the National Redemption Council has recently exhorted all Ghanaians to learn at least one Ghanaian language other than their own.[20] Through extensive multilingualism, members of each language group could communicate with one another; there would be no common, national language of intercommunication. Ansre has proposed this approach as the only feasible one at the present time for breaking down linguistic and ethnic barriers,[21] and Bliss Ackuaku, a member of parliament, recommended it in a 1970 parliamentary debate.[22]

A more systematic approach toward the same end formulated by Kwamena Bentsi-Enchill would be to require that every Ghanaian schoolchild study another Ghanaian language, and then specify that all non-Akan speaking children study Akan as this second language. The Akan-speaking children would have the option of learning one or another of Ghana's remaining major languages. If this policy were to be systematically implemented, it would have the unstated effect of creating a certain level of competence in Akan among all those who have passed through Ghana's educational system. And the requirement that all Akan-speakers learn some other Ghanaian language precludes their being placed in a favored position vis-à-vis non-Akan speakers. Akan might through this process become the country's lingua franca, but it would not be designated as the official national language.[23] Whether it is realistic to expect a Ghanaian student to study his own language, learn English, and learn another Ghanaian language in addition to his other academic requirements would have to be explored. This approach, however, offers a particularly innovative and appealing, though partial, solution to Ghana's linguistic fragmentation.

Bentsi-Enchill has also recommended the systematic encouragement of linguistic borrowing among Ghanaian languages and the creation of a common orthography as a step toward the homogenization of Ghana's diverse languages. It is unlikely that a common language would develop in this fashion, but if the process succeeded, it would eventually prove less difficult for the speaker of one Ghanaian language to learn another.[24]

The second alternative toward achieving effective national communication is to improve the teaching of English within the schools. This effort can be made while working within the current educational framework and adhering to current language and education policies. One important means toward this end, although not sufficient in itself, would be the adoption of English as the medium of instruction as early as is educationally feasible and desirable; the precise timing of the transition to English as the medium of instruction can only be decided upon after carefully weighing the various factors enumerated in this chapter and in the Part IV Introduction. Such an approach would provide a basis for English to serve as the principal vehicle for national communication. In the recent parliamentary debate regarding the common Ghanaian language, one M.P. stated:

> I just want to say that a lot of things which were left us by the English people do not fit our status today; but their language which they left us is binding all the tribes and all the cultures which constitute Ghana as a nation into one. I think it is important to cherish the English language, develop and add to it, and make it our own, because it is the only thing which binds all of us together as one people.[25]

The third alternative is to choose one Ghanaian language as the vehicle for national communication. If a common national language were selected, it would need to be vigorously promoted by the educational system, and for this language to be given a prominent place in the curriculum the emphasis placed upon both English and the local mother tongue would have to be reduced correspondingly. One effective means of encouraging use of this particular language would be to make it the medium of instruction. Given its numerical predominance in the country and its prestige, Akan (Twi) would probably be the most logical choice for this national language.[26] Jack Berry, a British linguist with long experience in Ghana, has proposed that Akan be chosen as the common language for southern Ghana and Dagbani for northern Ghana.[27] To encourage different languages for these two portions of the country, however, would only widen the gap that already exists between North and South.

The fourth approach to effective national communication would be to maintain current policies as an interim arrangement while permitting one of Ghana's languages, through the natural process of selection, to become the lingua franca without official promotion. If one language clearly gained ascendancy, then it could be selected as the national language for use by schools and other institutions. Some linguists contend that such a process is inevitable; as one put it: "History has over and over again demonstrated that within sharply defined political boundaries the most influential vernacular does in time impose itself as a common or national tongue."[28] It seems doubtful that such an outcome is so assured, but it could happen. Some evidence exists to suggest that Akan is in fact gaining ground as a lingua franca, particularly in northern Ghana. Unfortunately, insufficient data have been gathered to make any definitive statement regarding such a trend. Although the 1970 census did contain questions on second language competence, comparative data suggesting trends over time will only be available following analysis of the 1980 census data.

Expectation that this process of natural selection would materialize seems implicit in the Nkrumah government's statement on language policy in 1961. Mrs. Sussana Al-Hassan, deputy minister of education, stated in a parliamentary debate: "It is the intention of Government to encourage the development of all our major national languages so that each of them may have an equal opportunity of attaining a standard which would improve its chances of being chosen as the national language when the time comes for such a decision to be taken."[29] A spokesman for the Busia government echoed this policy position 10 years later when he declared in parliament: "What the Ministry of Education is trying to do is to give equal opportunity to develop all the main languages in the schools, with the hope that in the long run one of them might emerge as the dominant language in this country, which can be accepted by all the people of this country."[30]

If it were to be decided that a single language should be selected and promoted as the national language, there would be certain obvious advantages to having this language a Ghanaian language. The selection of a Ghanaian rather than a European language would impart a sense of national uniqueness and pride, and a Ghanaian language would serve as a more effective vehicle for transmitting local and national culture from one generation to the next. Moreover, part of the population would already be familiar with it as a mother tongue.

The problems that would be encountered as the result of such a step, however, are equally evident. The initial and most serious difficulty would be faced when the government had to decide which of Ghana's many languages should be the national language. Few issues would arouse more intense intergroup hostility and conflict than the choice of one Ghanaian language as the national tongue. The 20-year controversy over an Akan orthography mutually acceptable to both Twi and Fante speakers suggests just how deep emotions can run on the issue of language. In the 1971 parliamentary debate on a motion to consider the selection of a national language, one M.P. warned:

> This motion, if adopted, will divide this country. It will be a risk which any Government will undertake if it tries to press this matter too hard. It will be interesting to get from the Hon. Member for Berekum the particular language we should be using as Ghana's lingua franca. I must remind him right from the outset that if he inflicts Ga on the people of Ghana as lingua franca, his own people will beat him up; and if he presses that his own language be accepted as the lingua franca the rest of the language groups in Ghana will get together and oppose him. Any Government which deceives itself that the

time is opportune to introduce a lingua franca in the country will be sitting upon a keg of gun powder. The motion can be described as a political dynamite....[31]

Only a few inconclusive studies have been undertaken in Ghana to assess people's attitudes toward the country's language policy. The Madina study reports that the diverse residents of that community have strong second language preferences. When asked which languages they like best, they accorded almost universal approbation to such foreign languages as English, French, Arabic, and Hausa. Of Ghanaian languages, residents preferred Akan and Ewe, although not as universally as the foreign languages mentioned.[32] In a survey of Ghanaian students, by D. K. Agyeman of the University of Cape Coast, 72 percent indicated a preference for English over a Ghanaian language as the medium of instruction, and Agyeman concluded:

> The people who opt for a Ghanaian language as a national language are the very people who are tribally inclined and would opt for their own tribal languages as a national language. Only 20 percent of all non-Akans interviewed opted for Akan as a medium of instruction. No Akan on the other hand opted for any of the other languages. All the Gur-speakers opted for a Gur language as a medium of instruction and as a national language.[33]

Audrey Smock's survey of students at the University of Ghana, mentioned above, revealed the same tendency for respondents to prefer their own language as the national language, although this preference was much more frequently the case for Akan-speakers than for non-Akan speakers.[34]

To select a single Ghanaian language as the national language would, of course, place another educational burden on the school system and on the children alike. Teachers would have to be trained in teaching the Ghanaian language, and too, an enormous quantity of new educational material would have to be prepared for its use as the medium of instruction. In those portions of the country where the national language is not spoken as the mother tongue, schoolchildren would have to contend with learning English as well as an additional Ghanaian language, both of which would be foreign to them. If the radical step of dropping English altogether were taken, then the three-language problem would not arise, although the national language would still constitute a second language in many places.

No attempt at language engineering would succeed unless incentives were built into the program to encourage people to learn and use the new language. The two most effective types of incentives would be: (1) the exclusive use of the national language in the mass media and for educational and civil service examinations; and (2) the existence of a body of literature in the national language that people wish to read. The availability of vernacular literature is of central importance to any attempt to promote vernacular literacy. The limited scope of vernacular literature in Ghana today is revealed in Table 8-2. This table includes all the books and pamphlets published in a Ghanaian language; obviously, little incentive is offered a Ghanaian to become literate in his mother tongue, much less in another Ghanaian language. Approximately 50 percent of the books available in Ghanaian languages are either school readers or are devoted to the subject of religion, the product of mission activity. A survey of books and pamphlets on the shelves of one of Accra's principal bookstores in 1968 indicated that a total of only 44 books written in Ghanaian languages were available, whereas several hundred were available in English.[35]

TABLE 8-2 *Literature Availability Analysis*

LANGUAGE	TOTAL BOOKS AND PAMPHLETS
Akuapem Twi (Akan)	267
Ga	191
Ewe	184
Fante (Akan)	126
Asante Twi (Akan)	108
Nzema	77
Adangbe	52
Dagbani	38
Kasem	25
Dagarti	22
Kusal	9
Mamprusi	9
Buli	8
Gonja (a Guan dialect)	7
Nanume	5
Wali	5
Bimoda	5
Konkomba	3
Gureni	1
Total	1,142

SOURCE: Efua Sutherland, " Textbooks for the Study of Ghanaian Languages" in *The Study of Ghanaian Languages,* ed. J. R. Birnie and Gilbert Ansre (Accra: Ghana Publishing Corp., 1969), p. 41. Used by permission of the publisher.

A vicious circle is created when there is not much incentive to become literate in a Ghanaian language because so little interesting or relevant literature exists in a Ghanaian language. In turn, few writers or publishers are prepared to work in a local language because so little demand exists for such reading material. In many countries, village people find literacy in the mother tongue useful because agriculture extension literature is published in local languages, but on only one occasion, in 1961, has Ghana's Ministry of Agriculture produced an extension bulletin in a language other than English. The English version of that bulletin proved very popular, but large quantities of the vernacular versions are still available. The 1960 census indicated that only 5 percent of Ghana's adult population is literate in a Ghanaian language but illiterate in English,[36] which means that there is a very small reading public for works written in a Ghanaian language. To adopt a Ghanaian language as the national language would require revolutionary changes in the production of literature and radical alteration of Ghanaian attitudes regarding vernacular reading material.

Teacher training poses a considerable problem no matter what policy is adopted. If a common Ghanaian language is selected as a medium of instruction, then all teachers would have to achieve fluency in that language before they could teach. It is often argued by those who oppose English as the medium of instruction that Ghana's primary school teachers do not have a sufficient command either of English or pedagogical techniques to be able to teach English well. In support of this contention, the high proportion of uncertificated and untrained teachers is often cited. Those defending this position, however, lose sight of the rapid rate at which the teaching force is being upgraded in Ghana. In 1969-1970 only 53 percent of Ghana's primary school teachers were fully qualified, but the figure rose to 60 percent in 1970-1971, and will rise to 85 or 90 percent in 1975. It could reach 100 percent by 1976-1977.

One nation-building by-product of using a national language as the medium of instruction, whether it be English or a Ghanaian language, could come through an ethnically mixed teaching staff because teachers can be moved to any part of the country. If local languages are extensively employed, then the teaching force at each school must be composed of a single ethnic group — the same ethnic group as the students, except for teachers who happen to have bilingual competence in the local language. Such an arrangement has in fact been recommended by the Education Review Committee.[37] Though this arrangement might have pedagogical advantages, it would not contribute to inter-ethnic contact and understanding. If English or a common Ghanaian language were used as the medium of instruction in all parts of the country, however, then the teaching force at any given school could be ethnically mixed, with consequent advantages for the development of ethnic tolerance among the student population.

Research Needs

The formulation of intelligent language policies in Ghana, or any other country, is so complex a process and has so many ramifications that the best research information possible must be provided to the policy-makers. But as mentioned above, it is surprising how little useful research has been done in Ghana.

Probably the most critical, but manageable, problem for research investigation is a controlled comparison of performance by primary school children subjected to differing media of instruction. Given the variety of practices followed by different schools in Ghana, it ought to be possible to find matched pairs of schools that are utilizing different media, or different combinations of media, and administer tests to determine how successful the schools have been in educating their pupils. If it proves too difficult to isolate the language factor from among all the other variables that might differentiate schools, then an experimental situation could be created in which matched schools would employ different approaches and their performances later compared.[38]

In addition to considering these experiments, it would also be useful to experiment with the mother tongue as the medium for certain subjects while using English as the medium for school subjects that more easily lend themselves to it. Valuable information could also be obtained by determining whether literacy in the mother tongue assists a child in learning how to read and write English. It would also be useful to measure the degree and nature of linguistic interference caused by the mother tongue in learning English or another Ghanaian language. Another relevant issue is whether extensive use of English as the medium of instruction in the early years of primary school has an adverse effect upon a child's competence in his mother tongue.

Equally important is the need to obtain more information on the burdens and blessings imparted to children pushed into multilingualism. Well-educated children in Ghana must of necessity become bilingual, but some of the language policies being considered in Ghana today would require children to become trilingual. How great an educational load does this impose on children, or can learning situations be created to promote multilingualism at an early age without children having to spend an inordinate portion of their classroom time on language study?

It would also be valuable to survey comprehensively the attitudes of parents, students, and teachers regarding the use of English and local languages as media of instruction, as well as their reactions to the idea of introducing a common Ghanaian language as the medium. Such a survey could be broadened to determine what people think about such other language issues as whether English is an acceptable national language, or whether a Ghanaian language should be selected and promoted for national communication.

The Madina project was an important pilot attempt to investigate the extent of multilingualism in Ghana and the languages most frequently used and most preferred as second languages. Wider investigations of the same issues could determine the extent to which English, Akan, and other languages already serve as effective media of communication across language barriers. Periodic surveys administered at set time intervals would indicate trends of language use and language competence, and the spread of a lingua franca.

It would be useful too, to have more information on the effects that language competence has on intergroup relations. For instance, if an Ewe speaks Ga as a second language, is this language competence likely to increase the frequency of his interactions with Gas and increase his understanding and tolerance of Gas? Answers to these questions might suggest the potential impact of the adoption of a national language on inter-group relations. Along the same line, it would be helpful to know whether an ethnically mixed teaching staff encourages greater tolerance of other ethnic groups on the part of the student body.

These are the kinds of data I would want at my disposal before recommending any radical changes in Ghana's language policies. In the interim Ghana would probably be well advised to carefully preserve the present reliance upon English in its educational system, and to find the means of improving the quality of language instruction for both English and the mother tongues. Ghanaian languages should be accorded their proper place within both the educational system and national life generally, but the importance of English in Ghana as a lingua franca and as a vehicle for international communication should also be fully recognized. Careful attention should be given to the trends of language use in Ghana, because if Akan or another language rapidly gains ground as a second language, it is of considerable importance for policy formulation. Possibly over time Akan will unobtrusively become a medium for national communication without its having to be energetically pushed by the government. At the present time the official declaration of a single Ghanaian language as the national language would give rise to a highly emotional and possibly violent reaction.

All those in Ghana who recommend policy changes in the language sphere must continually bear in mind the complexity of the issue and the multifarious ramifications of what they advocate. Given the current paucity of research data, it is a subject that must be approached with humility and flexibility, and without dogmatism.

Notes

1. Work since 1960 by Prof. Gilbert Ansre and Dr. John Callow has led them to conclude that the 34 languages enumerated in the 1960 census should be further subdivided, giving a total of 54 Ghanaian languages. Presumably in this new classification, some speech communities classified as dialect communities in 1960 have now been classified as distinct language communities, based on the definition of mutual unintelligibility. See Gilbert Ansre, "Language Policy and the Promotion of National Unity and Understanding in West Africa" (Paper presented at the Institute of African Studies, University of Ife, December 1970), p. 2, mimeographed.

2. Jack Berry, "The Madina Project: Ghana Language Attitudes in Madina," *Research Review*, No. 5 (1969), Institute of African Studies, University of Ghana, pp. 61-79.

3. Philip Foster, *Education and Social Change in Ghana* (London: Routledge and Kegan Paul, 1965), p. 88.

4. Foster, op. cit., p. 51.

5. *Phelps-Stokes Reports on Education in Africa* (London: Oxford University Press, 1962), p. 63.

6. Advisory Committee on Native Education in Tropical Africa, *The Place of the Vernacular in Native Education* (London: Colonial Office, 1927), p. 11.

7. Ministry of Education, *Accelerated Development Plan for Education in the Gold Coast* (Accra: Government Printer, 1951), para. 3.

8. G.L. Barnard et al., *Report on the Use of English in Gold Coast* (Accra: Government Printer, 1956), p. 37.

9. Ministry of Education, *Education Report for the Year 1956*(Accra: Government Printer, 1957), p. 1.

10. "Report of the Committee on Pre-University Education" (May-June, 1963), p. 19, mimeographed.

11. Ibid.

12. *Report of the Education Review Committee* (Accra: Ministry of Information, 1957), p. 55.

13. *White Paper on the Report of the Education Review Committee* (Accra: Ministry of Information, 1968), p. 6.

14. Barnard et al., op. cit., p. 27.

15. Ibid., p. 26.

16. Gilbert Ansre, "A Study on the Official Language of Ghana," in *Colloque sur multilinguism* (London: CCTA, 1962), p. 215.

17. Unpublished data obtained from Dr. Audrey Smock.

18. *Parliamentary Debates*, Vol. 6, No. 35 (May 3, 1971), p. 1514.

19. *Parliamentary Debates*, Vol. 6, No. 37 (May 5, 1971), p. 1606.

20. *The Charter of the National Redemption Council* (Accra: Ghana Publishing Corp., 1973).

21. Gilbert Ansre, "Language Policy for the Promotion," op. cit.

22. *Ghanaian Times*, March 24, 1970.

23. Personal discussion with Professor Kwamena Bentsi-Enchill.

24. Kwamena Bentsi-Enchill, "Ghana's Linguistic Challenge — What Do We Do To Meet It" (Paper presented to Centre for Civic Education Civic Club Leaders at Tamale, Ghana, March 31, 1971).

25. *Parliamentary Debates*, Vol. 6, No. 37 (May 5, 1971), p. 1583.

26. The choice of Akan has been proposed by E. A. Asamoa in "The Problem of Language in Education in the Gold Coast," *Africa*, Vol. 25, No. 1 (January 1955), pp. 60-78.

27. Jack Berry, "Problems in the Use of African Languages and Dialects in Education," in UNESCO, *African Languages and English in Education*, Educational Studies and Documents, No. 11 (Paris: Education Clearing House, 1953), p. 42.

28. Clifford H. Prator, *Language Teaching in the Philippines* (Manila: U.S. Education Foundation in the Philippines, 1950), p. 4.

29. From *Parliamentary Debates* (1961), as quoted by Ansre, "Study on Official Language," op. cit., p. 218.

30. *Parliamentary Debates*, Vol. 6, No. 37 (May 5, 1971), p. 1602.

31. *Parliamentary Debates*, Vol. 6, No. 37 (May 5, 1971), p. 1582.

32. Berry, "The Madina Project," op. cit., pp. 65-66.

33. D. K. Agyeman, "Ethnicity and Language Policy for our Schools," *Faculty of Education Bulletin*, University College of Cape Coast, Vol. 1, No. 2 (July 1970), p. 17.

34. Audrey Smock, unpublished data.

35. Efua Sutherland, "Textbooks for the Study of Ghanaian Languages," in *The Study of Ghanaian Languages*, ed. J.R. Birnie and Gilbert Ansre (Accra: Ghana Publishing Corp.,1969), p. 33.

36. Gil, Aryee, and Ghansah, p. lxvi.

37. *Report of the Education Review Committee*, op. cit., p. 54.

38. Some very rudimentary work of this nature is reported in Barnard et al., op. cit., pp. 58-73; P. Gurrey, "Report on Research into the Teaching and Learning of English in the Gold Coast" (Accra: Education Department, May 1953), p. 11, mimeographed; and in the "Annual Report of Curriculum Research and Development Unit, Ministry of Education, 1969-1970," p. 6, mimeographed.

Chapter 9

The Language Problem in Cameroon: A Historical Perspective

by Bernard Fonlon

I HAVE BEEN led to believe that culture is to a country what a soul is to a man, that is, the principle of life, of unity and continuity; and, therefore, that a nation is not just merely so many millions of people living on the same land or stemming from the same ancestral origin, but that a nation, thanks to its culture, is essentially a unit of thought and feeling and will and action. For communion of thought and feeling and will and action to be possible, there must be communication between the members of the national community. That is why a common language is such an effective instrument in forging national unity.

Theoretically, the human mind is supposed to think in ideas. But as a matter of practical fact, we think in words, and, this to the extent that, if we reflect as we think, we can actually hear ourselves thinking in a definite language. This language substitutes itself for ideas in our minds so much so that it becomes the very warp and woof of our mental life. Thus, the union that exists between people who share the same language must be very intimate indeed, because it creates in them a oneness in that which is the highest and the most essential thing in man, namely, the mind. Thus, the cry "One people, one language" that is heard in countries like Israel is not an empty political slogan.

What is more, among the owners of one language, this oneness of thought, feeling, and will is further reinforced by the fact that this language enshrines their common experiences through time and space, their achievements in letters, in the arts and the sciences, their common aspirations, their loves and hates, their hopes and fears. A communion of thought, a communion of feeling, a communion of will, a communion of behavior—surely those who say that there is such a thing as a national character, a national personality, are not just talking airy nonsense. Such is the unifying power of language that it not only binds together the people whose property it is, it not only gives them a distinctive personality, but when a language acquires the enviable fortune of becoming the medium of wider expression at the world level, it serves to bring closer together the far-flung peoples that use it.

In Africa, partly due to the failure of the great African empires to consolidate themselves and expand and endure, partly due to the constant movement of peoples, and most especially, to four centuries of the ravages of slave raiding and trafficking, no African languages, with the possible exceptions of Arabic and Swahili, have been able to impose themselves as dominant media of wider expression. And consequently very few countries today in Negro Africa can boast of linguistic unity. Nearly every independent African country is a patchwork of linguistic and ethnic groups. One of the major problems facing the leaders of almost every African country today is how to weld this motley mass into a harmonious, homogeneous whole; how to forge this communion of thought, feeling and will of which I have been speaking; in a word, how to create national unity.

Historical Setting

Cameroon, thanks to its geographical position, has the distinction of being the one spot on the black continent where all the African peoples meet: here you have the Bantu, who claim kinship with peoples as far south as the Cape; you have Sudanese peoples; you have the Fulani, whose kinsfolk are found as far West as Senegal and Mauretania; you have peoples like the Shuwa Arabs; and you have the pygmies of the equatorial jungle. It is in Cameroon therefore, that the confusion of tongues is worse confounded, where it has become absolutely impossible to achieve through an African language that oneness of thought, feeling, and will that is the soul of a nation. We are left with no choice but to strive to achieve this unity through non-African languages; and, to make things more difficult, the Federal Republic of Cameroon, being composed of the former Southern Cameroons (British administered) and the former French Cameroons, has inherited two of them—French and English. As a result, it has been obliged to become, constitutionally, a bilingual state.

The history of the influence of European languages in Cameroon is very interesting. The first contact that Cameroon had with the Western world was with the Portuguese. With the discovery of the New World and the rise of the slave trade, other adventurers followed in their wake. Notable among these were the Dutch, who founded a trading post at the mouth of the Rio dos Camarões; the Swedes; the Danes; the French; the British; and the Brandenburgers. Of all these Europeans, the first to make a marked and lasting linguistic impact on Cameroon were the British. By the beginning of the nineteenth century they had become the dominant power along the Nigerian and the Cameroon coast. In 1807 they declared slavery illegal, and in order to take effective measures to put it down in the Gulf of Guinea, they obtained permission from the Spaniards in 1827 to occupy Fernando Po and to establish a squadron there to control the shipping of slaves from the Bights of Benin and Biafra. They took advantage of their occupation of Fernando Po to encourage various Bristol and Liverpool enterprises to set up floating hulks as trading posts on the Cameroon River; and by 1830 they had established several stations along the coast and made agreements with native chiefs. The first vehicle, therefore, that brought English to Cameroon was trade. And as commerce is not a formal cultural medium, like education, the form of English that sprang up was the well-known Pidgin English.

After occupying Fernando Po with Spanish permission, the British brought there from Freetown a number of manumitted slaves. Their presence spurred a second factor that was to promote the spread of English in these parts, namely, the establishment of mission stations. In 1844 the Jamaican branch of the English Baptist Missionary Society landed 42 volunteers at Santa Isabel on Fernando Po where two churches had been founded a few years earlier. Later in the same year, under the leadership of Joseph Merrick, the society founded at Bimbia on the coast of Cameroon the first Christian mission in the country. The following year Alfred Saker, another missionary, followed by starting a second mission in King Akwa's Town in Douala. Later, in the 1870s, English-speaking American Presbyterian missionaries established themselves at Batanga on the southeastern coast; and from there they pushed inland as far as Ebolowa in the Bulu country.

Everywhere the missionaries elected to settle there sprang up the classic missionary trilogy of mission house, church, and school. In the West as well as in the Southeast the missionaries systematically studied the indigenous languages, Duala and Buly, reduced them into written form and taught them in school in order to use them in evangelizing. But English was also taught, and Cameroonians in these areas came under the permanent influence of spoken and written English through formal language training. Thereby, a more systematic and penetrating factor played a part in the introduction of English into Cameroon education.

As the number of British commercial houses grew, and as French and German firms came to swell their ranks, the relations between these firms and the people of Douala were not always friendly. It was therefore decided to establish in that town a Court of Equity to settle disagreements and to maintain peace. Cases that the court found difficult to settle were referred to the British consul who visited the town from time to time. Indeed, by the early 1880s such had become the authority of the consul that his recognition was felt necessary to consolidate the position of a native king. Several coastal chiefs became anxious to secure a British protectorate over the Cameroon coast and directed petitions to this effect to the British Government. Thus a third influence was brought to bear on the spread of English in Cameroon — politics.

Thanks to their naval power, their commercial enterprises, their educational efforts, and their political activities, the British presence became the most predominant European influence along the coast of Cameroon. English became the language of commerce, of the churches, of the schools, and of the Court of Equity. Its offshoot, Pidgin English, spread far afield. The largest number of words of European origin that have been assimilated into Cameroon languages, like Duala, Bulu, and Ewondo, are derived not from German or French but from English. If plans to declare a British protectorate had not failed by a matter of days, English would have become the only European language today in Cameroon. But that was not to be.

During the 1880s there was great rivalry between England and France in the Gulf of Guinea, and, if the British saw any threat to their growing hegemony they saw it in the French, not in the Germans. Yet for some time German traders, foremost among whom was Adolf Woermann of Hamburg, were already consolidating the German position along the coast of Cameroon. Early in 1883 the German Government began taking quiet steps for the occupation of Cameroon; and the following year they entered the race in earnest, and beat the British, it is said, by five days and the French by one week. For on July 11, 1884 Dr. Gustav Nachtigal, Bismarck's plenipotentiary, arrived in Douala. By the following day he had signed a treaty with King Bell and King Akwa establishing German rule; on July 14, 1884, Nachtigal hoisted the German flag and Cameroon became a *Schutzgebiet* of the Kaiser's Reich.

With the German take-over, a problem of communication arose between the Cameroonians and their newfound masters. And, by the very nature of the situation, the German administration, at the start, was obliged to use English. That, of course, could only be a transitional solution. For whoever rules Cameroon is confronted with a language problem that demands a definite policy, a definite decision, a definite, if not definitive, choice.

The language situation at the time when Cameroon became a German protectorate was this: There were, as I have said already, the numerous African languages. Among these some were beginning to establish themselves over sizable areas. In the North and down the grasslands, thanks to the roving, cow-rearing Bororo and thanks to the fervor and the might of the Jihad, and the consequent spread of Islam, the Fulani language was expanding far afield. In the South the Protestant missions had adopted and reduced into written form certain native languages, notably Duala in the South, Bali farther in the hinterland, and Bulu in the Southeast, as media for evangelization, and consequent on this these languages had begun to spread beyond their homes of origin. The German presence, oddly enough, put a premium on the further spread of Pidgin English. As a result of Germans' setting up military and administrative posts, commercial centers, and large plantations requiring labor by the thousands, an increasing number of Cameroonians began leaving their ancestral homes and mingled in the mixed communities created by these activities. In these heterogeneous centers, there could be only one answer to the language problem—Pidgin English.

In terms of missionary activity after the German annexation, the German Baptists left and the Basel Mission, with German and German-Swiss missionaries, took their place, expanded further inland, and established schools in which German and Duala were taught. In the Southeastern section the long-established American Presbyterian mission elected to stay on and was allowed to; but it had to replace English with German. In 1891 the first group of German Roman Catholic missionaries, the Pallottine fathers from Limburg, arrived in Cameroon. With the help of government officials, the Roman Catholic missions spread east and west and into the hinterland and strove to implant not only the Catholic brand of Christianity but also the German language through the establishment of churches and schools.

The setting up of German authority brought with it a new influence—in addition to commerce, the church, and the school—as a decisive factor in the spread of language: administration. At the start Germans did not seem to have a clear-cut idea of what should be done. However, initial hesitation, debate, and experiment soon gave way to an obvious and categorical choice—German. On the question of the official policy of the Reich's representatives on the language problem, Vernon Jackson, an authority on the history of education in Cameroon, has this to say:

The wisdom of German language instruction in Cameroon had been debated at the beginning of the German colonial period. Despite a fear that Cameroonians who were proficient in German might constitute a potential threat to German domination, the final consensus reached by government, educational authorities, and commercial houses was that the study of German should be intensified in order to reinforce German influence and to deepen the German-Kamerun connection as well as for the convenience of German administration, communication, and trade. The policy to supplant English with German and to limit dominant vernaculars was set.

Meanwhile the popularity of German among Cameroonians grew as German administration, military organization and police, trade, agriculture, research, commerce, communications, and social services increased and as employment and promotion in connection with these activities rose. German was becoming the social language among educated Cameroonians of different tribal backgrounds by the turn of the century when the first generation of German-instructed students reached adulthood.[1]

Curiously, pockets of resistance to German in favor of English persisted throughout the period of the Reich's political hegemony. The largely self-governing Protestant churches in Victoria and Douala, resentful of the Basel Mission, formed the Native Baptist Church and retained English and Duala. British firms continued to operate in English and court records in Victoria continued to be kept in English.

Sometimes we Cameroonians are led to speculate on what would have happened if the Reich had not been ousted from Cameroon. Many believe that, thanks to German know-how, energy, and drive, we would be economically and technically more advanced than we are today, though we might have ended with a South Africa on our hands. Culturally, we would have a scientific and philosophical language more deep-rooted and widespread in Cameroon than French and English are. Yet, this culture would entail a serious handicap—the danger of isolation at both the African and at the world level. For all its scientific and philosophic precision, for all its cultural wealth, its curious phonic charm, for all its weird beauty, German has no mission today for the gathering of peoples in Africa—or globally. This highly enviable role is reserved for English and French.

The First World War brought an end to the German *Schutzherrschaft* over Cameroon. And, after a brief period during which the territory was administered as a condominion by the Allied military administration, Cameroon was shared, very unequally, between France and Great Britain, the former receiving four-fifths of the territory while the latter got a bottle-necked strip of land wedged between Nigeria and the French share, running from the sea to Lake Chad. With the Allied take-over a curious thing occurred. Unlike what had happened at the beginning of the German administration, when English continued in use during a transitional period, German vanished almost overnight from the government offices, from the commercial houses, from the churches, from the schools, despite its having been assiduously implanted for three decades by government policy and by vigorous instruction. Obviously, it continued to live in the minds and on the lips of the thousands of Cameroonians who had imbibed it; but in spite of the fact that numerous Germans and German-Swiss later came back to exploit their coastal plantations and to run their mission stations, German in Cameroon was formally condemned to death and executed the day the Allies took over.

In their sector, the French set about, with great gusto and dispatch, replacing German with French, which they considered "la porte ouverte vers la culture, vers l'avenir, vers le progrès." French missionaries, both Catholic and Protestant, replaced the Germans in the mission schools and at once began teaching French to both teachers and pupils. There was a definite policy against encouraging the vernaculars. Not only was French taught as a subject by itself, but it was considered essential that instruction in the other subjects should be in French almost from the first day in school. Mission schools increased in number and the French administration, a fervent advocate at home of *l'école laïque,* set up nondenominational schools of its own. Before the Second World War secondary schools were completely absent, but between then and independence they mushroomed. The implantation and the growth of the French language was greatly speeded up and reinforced by the massive French physical presence: large numbers of French people came to live in Cameroon and were in daily contact with Cameroonians. During the last decade of the trusteeship, a new element was introduced: a scholarship program, thanks to which quite a sizable number of Cameroonians went to study in France. They created a Cameroon elite which produced authors of international repute like Alexandre Biyidi, more widely known as Mongo Beti, and the Cameroon writer-turned-diplomat Ferdinand Oyono.

As for the British, they further divided their slender slice of territory into two sections: Northern Cameroons, mostly Muslim, administered as part of Northern Nigeria, and Southern Cameroons, administered as part of the Eastern Region of Southern Nigeria. In comparison with the vigor of the French, the British effort to implant their own language was largely lackadaisical. Witness Vernon Jackson, an English Canadian, who has this to say:

> As far as written work was concerned, the local or native administrations were largely conducted in Hausa; federal and regional government departments used only English. Nevertheless, Kanuri, Shuwa Arabic, and Fulani were also spoken, although not written, according to local circumstances

and convenience. British and Nigerian officers of all government departments were financially encouraged to pass language examinations in
Hausa, Kanuri, or Fulani; in some cases, their promotions depended upon
their successfully passing such language examinations, both written and
spoken.

What were the effects of the change from a unified German government to the French and the British-Nigerian with regard to language and
schools? Both sides abruptly terminated the use of the German language
officially, in daily life, in available printed materials, and in the schools.
The French zone then developed a well-organized, though very selective,
educational system using French as the official language; the system
utilized both government and mission resources and included further
training in France. The work of the schools was enhanced by the presence
of a comparatively large number of French settlers, printing presses for
local publications in French, and a lack of tolerance for vernaculars that
encouraged learning French in school. In the British-Nigerian zone the
school systems virtually collapsed, and no language policy was emphasized
apart from the use of English by government officials arriving from Nigeria.
This was followed between the world wars by a resurrected, inadequately
financed, and slowly developing spread of primary education, mainly
through missionary organizations. English became the official language,
and although the government encouraged the use of vernaculars in schools,
this was to be followed by English after the first two years. Higher education for Cameroonians was available only in English-speaking Nigerian
institutions and was restricted numerically; study in Britain was possible
only for a handful of scholarship holders.[2]

With regard to the overall effects of the suppression of the energetic,
go-ahead, unified German administration, and its replacement by the
Franco-British divided mandate and trusteeship, Victor LeVine, has this
to say:

> The mandate ushered in a new phase of the Cameroons' development . . . .
> The two Cameroons under separate administrations moved off in different
> directions, propelled by the force of colonial policies often diametrically
> opposed to one another, The artificial bisection of the territory created the
> reality of two distinctly different Cameroons, with different social, eco-
> nomic, and political traditions. It would be thirty-five years, almost two
> generations, before the possibility of reunifying the two Cameroons could
> be raised as a meaningful issue.[3]

During the Franco-British period when the two sections of the country
were separated, Cameroonians on both sides never ceased to think of themselves as one. I know this from personal experience. In the 1940s, for
example, which I spent entirely as a student in Nigeria, wherever Cameroo-

nians were found they associated as brothers, and it was very seldom that the distinction was made that this one came from the French sector and that one from the English. During that period, and even before then, large communities of Cameroonians from almost every sizable group in the French Cameroons came to the British Cameroons, and never did it occur to their brethren indigenous to the British sector to consider them foreigners. On the other hand, no Cameroonians from the British sector, despite our 40 years of intimate political, administrative, and cultural association with Nigeria, ever considered themselves Nigerians. The division of our population into East Cameroonians and West Cameroonians is largely a cultural division. Such was the spirit of unity that animated us during the Anglo-French separation; such is the spirit that animates us today. When political activity began and parties sprang up, nearly all of them, on either side, had *Réunification* as one of their principal slogans; and the people heard it not as an idea completely new, but as the expression of a thought and aspiration that already pulsed in every heart and mind.

In the 1950s agitation for reunification came to a head, as evidenced by the vocalness and the energy with which it was given expression, the declarations made to the United Nations missions that visited Cameroon, and the number of petitioners that streamed into the Trusteeship Commission. In February 1961 the United Nations was obliged to test it by a plebiscite in the British Cameroons, which resulted in the northern portion joining Nigeria and the southern portion united with West Cameroon. It was thus that the Federal Republic of Cameroon came into being on October 1, 1961. Today, in spite of all the towering cultural, linguistic, administrative, and economic differences with which we have to battle, it is a pride to say that the Cameroon federation, which many considered doomed to fail, is the most successful experiment in federalism that Africa has yet seen. Indeed, not only is it notable for its stability, but year by year it is moving from strength to strength.

Current Language Problems

Communication being an absolute necessity between those governing and those being governed, whoever takes upon himself to govern Cameroon has a complex and ineluctable language problem on his hands. So have we today. In spite of the fervent will in every heart to cement this union, the native Babel persists. To make confusion worse confounded, we have inherited not one foreign language, as in the early days of the unofficial British

hegemony or when we were part and parcel of the Kaiser's Reich, but two —
French and English: French for four-fifths of the country, English for the
remaining fifth.

Faced with this many-sided problem, what is the stance of the government? Let me speak first about our myriad indigenous tongues. With regard
to our native languages, the federal constitution and the constitutions of
the federal states are mute. And there is no official policy insofar as these
languages are concerned. This constitutional silence on our languages,
however, does not wipe them out of existence nor weaken their influence.
They are asserting themselves as vigorous living realities. Indeed, there are
certain factors, religion especially, that are reinforcing the position of a few
of them. The head-long drive of the Muslim religion southward, the integration of the Fulani herdsmen into the savannah communities — these are having as a side effect the spread and the reinforcement of the Fulani language.
Especially in the savannah regions, Fulani is currently the most widely
spoken African language in Cameroon. In the South, especially among the
Ewondo-, the Bulu-, and the Duala-speaking peoples, the bring-the-liturgy-
down-to-the-people spirit born of the Second Vatican Council has obliged
the Catholic Church and other religious denominations to use these
languages intensively in their religious services. Their use is immensely
facilitated by the fact that they have already been reduced to writing, and
are used not only in translations of the Bible, of missals, hymnals, and
catechisms, but also in periodicals and other forms of literature.

To play this new role effectively, these languages will not only have to
be taught, they will also have to be studied and developed. The cultural
movement of which the *Cameroon Cultural Review, Abbia* is the spearhead
and the mouthpiece, has taken the stand that Cameroon languages, at least
the major ones, shall not die. Some of the Cameroon bourgeoisie, however,
especially those who are married to white wives or have spent long years
abroad, bring up their children speaking only French, or in the case of
West Cameroonians, let them drift and grow up speaking only Pidgin
English. In my opinion this is not right. For I believe that every human being
needs to feel that he belongs somewhere, else he will grow up into a rootless
person, living in permanent malaise. It is only by knowing his own language
firmly and fluently that an individual can acquire this feeling, this stabilizing
force. A foreign tongue, however well-possessed, cannot give it.

The constitution of September 1961, which brought the federation into
existence, says that French and English are the official languages — French
for the Federated State of East Cameroon, English for that of West
Cameroon, and both for such federal institutions as the federal government
and its ministerial services, the Federal Assembly, the Federal Court of

Justice, the Federal University, and the secondary schools. It has been laid down as official government policy that bilingualism will be extended to the primary schools at such a time as the means permit. Thus, de jure, Cameroon has become a bilingual state; de facto, however it is a highly diversified multilingual, multicultural country.

The reasons for the official choice of English and French are obvious. First, Cameroonians did not want what happened at the departure of the Germans to happen again — that is, that a highly technical and philosophical language like German, the vehicle for modern progress and culture, should be swept away overnight. To have eliminated French and English would have set the country back 40 years. Second, as I have implied above, these languages play a role that none of the indigenous languages fulfil, namely, they are the languages of science and modern technology, which are absolutely indispensable for our modern development. Third, by a hazard of history English and French have become, at the world and at the African level, languages of wider expression, and are, consequently, absolutely necessary instruments for world cooperation and for African unity.

A country like Somalia inherited English and Italian; but I am convinced that, by the fact that Italian has no world and African mission, it will by the very nature of things yield to English as the years go by. There are pessimists who moan that a similar fate will befall English in Cameroon, because it is the minor partner in our present cultural setup and will, therefore, gradually be ousted by its more extensive, more exclusive, and more militant partner — French. For my part, I do not think so. For one reason, the position of English has been secured by the constitution; for another, as a matter of practical daily official and private life, English is used and taught as the first language throughout West Cameroon. Furthermore, English is compulsory in all East Cameroon secondary schools, and in years to come will become so in the primary schools of that state as well. And finally, there is the influence of our giant English-speaking next-door neighbor, Nigeria, with whom contact, physical and cultural, is permanent. Before the Nigerian civil war, each of the national Nigerian papers had a Cameroon edition, and they were widely circulated and read in Cameroon. The educated West Cameroonian has, culturally speaking, 80 percent more in common with his Nigerian cousin than with his East Cameroon French-educated brother.

It is also very striking to note the enthusiasm of East Cameroonians to master English and the pride they take in using it. In fact, in terms of concrete linguistic achievement they have more to show than their English-speaking brethren. As a consequence of American university scholarship programs, quite an impressive number of East Cameroonians have university degrees in English. In contrast, in 1969 only two West Cameroonians had a *licence* from a French university. I am convinced that, thanks to our will and effort, thanks to the aid from countries like Great Britain, the United States, and Canada, English is here to stay. Such is the language situation in Cameroon today.

The language load that the average Cameroon child has to carry in school and college is necessarily heavy. Is it an impossible load? Will it mar his intellectual and psychological development? I do not think so. I do not think that it is impossible for a child to acquire two, three, or four languages *pari passu.* Daily experience proves that to us. I had a ministerial colleague who has a B.A. Honors English degree; he speaks and writes good French, speaks and writes Duala, and speaks with absolute fluency two other Cameroon languages. The secret is an early start, favorable surroundings, good teachers, good textbooks, good equipment, good teaching methods, determination, and enthusiasm.

Today in Cameroon our official position is clear: we are, de jure, a bilingual state. If we had all the money, all the teachers, all the textbooks, and all the equipment that we need, English and French would be taught today in our schools right from the day the youngster begins classes. Unfortunately, we are poor, and the implementation of our defined policy will take a long time. Fortunately, we are free from the violent language emotions that bedevil Canada, topple governments in Belgium, and rouse the frenzied fury that causes citizens to riot and hew each other down in India and Ceylon.

In the principal bilingual countries in the world, like Canada, Belgium, and South Africa, there are factors that militate not only against the successful acquisition of the two languages by the individual citizen, but also against the harmonious bilingualism of the state itself. One factor is that one of the two languages is not a medium of wide communication on a continental or a world scale. This is the case with Dutch and its variants: Flemish in Belgium and Afrikaans in South Africa. It is not the case with bilingualism in Cameroon. English and French are so important in Africa and in the world at large that this consideration alone should be enough to spur us on to pursue them with the utmost determination, with relentless energy.

A second factor weighing against peaceful bilingualism in some other countries is that each of their languages is the property of a national or racial group. They gave it birth. It is the vehicle of their culture, the seal of their identity, the expression of their distinctive personality, the root that anchors them in their past, and the umbilical cord linking them to their ancestors. Consequently, this language occupies a choice place in their hearts and minds and is the object of deep mental and emotional attachment. Any threat directed against it by the speakers of a rival language rouses violent passions. Witness the recent language disturbances that overturned a government in Brussels and touched off bombs in Quebec. When things reach this pass, there is stirred up not merely the resolve to defend the threatened language, but also the burning hostility against the rival partner language. In Belgium there are Flemings who won't speak French even if they know it perfectly. And yet there was a time when French almost conquered Flanders because it had become the language of the Flemish bourgeoisie. Popular reaction, however, reversed the tide and passed the legislation of 1932 that recognized Flemish as the official language in Flanders. How different the situation in Cameroon! Neither of the languages is our own. I can see little reason for any emotional involvement on the part of any Cameroonian with regard to English or French. It would be a queer Cameroonian who felt so strongly for English or French as to riot in its defense.

Bilingualism also faces severe problems where, as in Canada, the two-language state has come into existence as a result of war and conquest. For then we often witness overweaning insolence on the part of the conquerors, who strive to impose on the vanquished their culture in addition to their rule. Such efforts arouse in the conquered resolute rejection, which in French Canada has led to resentful isolationism. Unlike Canada, the bilingual Republic of Cameroon was brought into existence by the deep and fervent will of the Cameroon people. Cameroon bilingualism, therefore, has an atmosphere for its growth that is not marred by victor-vanquished friction.

I can hardly think of another country where everything augurs so well for bilingualism as in Cameroon. If we take note of these advantages and strive to strengthen them, if we set ourselves to the task with resolution, with verve, and with method, we may one day offer the Belgians and the Canadians an example of a nation composed of united and brotherly bilingual citizens.

The Future

But what sort of bilingualism are we aiming at, and what are the levels of bilingualism that we can achieve? The constitution makes Cameroon a bilingual state with English the language of the federated state of the West, French as that of the federated state of the East and both as the languages of the federal government. This situation is similar to what obtains in Canada where, out of 10 federated states one is French and the rest are English. Belgium, on the other hand, furnishes an example of a unitary state with two languages, French and Flemish. In spite of the fact that Belgium and Canada have been bilingual for a long time, however, the vast majority of

Canadians and Belgians remain monolingual. A bilingual state, therefore, does not necessarily imply bilingual citizens. But for us in Cameroon it would be singular blindness to remain satisfied with merely having created a bilingual state. The target for us to aim at should be not merely state bilingualism, but individual bilingualism. Every child who passes through the Cameroon education system should be able to speak and write both English and French.

In the teaching of English and French in our schools and colleges, we should aim at producing citizens capable of handling both languages with consummate skill, capable of producing in English or French works of art or science of the highest merit. Obviously, only a limited few will ever be able to attain such a height. But a linguistic feat of this kind is by no means outside the bounds of possibility. More numerous, however, will be those who hit the best lower target: the level of those who master one of the two languages consummately for artistic or scientific expression, and who possess the other language sufficiently to translate from it with skill and exactness, but cannot wield it themselves with the same measure of ease and grace.

The lowest level is within the reach of any child who, having been put through a well-organized and well-equipped language teaching course, is prepared to exert the minimum effort. Though unable to scale the higher reaches of vocabulary and phraseology, he will at least acquire in both languages fluent use of ordinary words and phrases. This level is the farthest that the general run of citizens will ever be able to attain. But it is well worth the effort. Of these three levels, each person will attain that to which his talents, aided by his energy, will bear him. But what is of supreme importance is that the education system should make sure that the linguistic knowledge and skill of those prepared to exert themselves to the utmost should be as thorough as possible.

My argument is that because language is so overwhelmingly important in life and in studies it is imperative to begin systematically teaching it to children as early as possible in their childhood. Language should be the central concern, the pivot around which all effort revolves in the primary school. If the importance of bilingualism in our national life has become so primordial, we must begin it early enough to see it through successfully. In other words, the teaching of English and French together should start right from the very first day that the child takes his seat in the infant school.

A reader may be inclined to ask: You sound enthusiastic and optimistic, but what results have you to show so far? After an experiment lasting only a decade, it would be too much to expect us to produce something spectacular. Both languages are taught throughout our secondary schools and the generation of students now finishing secondary school are expected to be able to read the second language, and thus have a basis upon which to build. When I said that the Cameroon ideal in the teaching of English and French should be to produce citizens capable of creating, both in English and French, works of art or science, I was envisaging this objective as something feasible in the far, far future. Yet, there are indications that these heights may be scaled a good deal sooner. Witness, for instance, the achievements of Cameroon's bilingual playwright, Guillaume Oyone Mbia, who has published highly praised works in both French and English. We can breathe no other prayer but that his promise should handsomely materialize and that many Cameroonians, now and in the future, should be stirred to emulate his example.

I cannot bring this chapter to a close without mentioning a special experiment that is currently being carried out in Cameroon in this field of bilingual education. In nearly every African country English or French is taught as a second language. Here it was felt that Cameroon, being constitutionally a bilingual state, needed to do something more. So the idea of the Bilingual Grammar School (le Lycée Bilingue) took birth. With the help of the French Government, the first was created in 1963 at Man O'War Bay, near Victoria, in West Cameroon. A couple of years later a second was started in Yaoundé and attached to the UNESCO-sponsored Ecole Normale Supérieure. The Canadian Government has undertaken to build, equip, and run a third in Douala. The aim of these bilingual grammar schools is to produce Cameroonians evenly fluent and efficient in the use of both languages.

The Man O'War Bay School is spearheading the experiment. Each year an equal number of choice students from each federated state is admitted into the school. In the first, second, and third forms they are taught in separate classes. The Francophones receive intensive courses in English, the Anglophones in French. At the beginning of the fourth form, they are rearranged into two grades, bilingual classes in which Francophones and Anglophones sit side by side and receive the same lessons. In addition to the continued language effort, some subjects are taught in French and others in English. Where a subject has a particular terminology, the school intends to facilitate its grasp in both languages by the preparation of special *lexiques*. To test this experiment, it is intended that the pioneering group of students will take the *Brevet* (a French secondary school examination administered at the end of the fourth form) and the GCE Ordinary level at the end of the fifth form. [4] Thereafter, the students can prepare for the Baccalaureat or the GCE Advanced level, or both, as they choose. Those with a bent for science or mathematics can go for sixth-form work to the College of Arts, Science, and Technology in Bamenda. This experiment would have been rendered easier if we had already created a uniform education system throughout the federation; but we have still to harmonize our syllabi, create common examinations, and negotiate their acceptance abroad.

Because of the heavy language load and because of the need to keep up standards in the other subjects, which is rendered more difficult by the fact that some of them are taught in the second language, this is an experiment fraught with problems. Its success will require far more than normal effort. The students understandably await the approaching Brevet and the GCE with doubt and fear. But I believe that an experiment of this nature is not doomed to fail. With careful planning and preparation, with thoroughness of execution, with cooperation, dedication, and spirit on the part of all concerned, we can see it through. If the first attempt succeeds, the organizers plan to begin the bilingual classes from the third or even from the second form.

If the bilingual grammar school experiment succeeds and is reinforced and extended, and when students from our bilingual secondary schools begin coming to the Federal University of Cameroon, that institution will become really bilingual, as it is intended to be by statute. Each cultural group will be adequately represented on the faculty; and each student will do his course in the language of the lecturer. At present the French element predominates in the university. There is, however, a British component, and a small but growing number of English-speaking lecturers. In the Department of Mathematics, for example, the foremost professor, Dr. Gregory Tanyi, is a non-French-speaking West Cameroonian who lectures in English to classes almost entirely composed of East Cameroonians.

Such have been the linguistic vicissitudes of Cameroon originating from our contact with the West; such are the language problems that plague us; such are the hurdles that our education system is striving to clear. We are faced with certain imperatives, which by the very nature of the situation in which we find ourselves, have become categorical. We need to preserve our African linguistic patrimony, not as pieces in a museum, but as living, active realities. True, some of our myriad dialects must die sooner or later. But the main Cameroon languages must live; for if they are completely supplanted by English and French, we will become a nameless and rootless race. This native patrimony being so heterogeneous, so hopelessly fragmented, and none of these languages being the vehicle of science and technology, we are forced, for all our pride, to seek unity among ourselves, to seek modern development through alien tongues. And our ambition should be to give to those of our children who are able the means to achieve great success in the use of these foreign languages, to possess over them the same mastery as their owners possess.

We are singularly happy and blessed by the fact that the languages we have inherited have become the main languages for communication between the peoples of Africa and the far-flung races of the world. In an Africa that seeks its unity, in a world where the need for an ever closer coming together is felt as an urgent need, we can become in our humble way a model state, a shining example of peaceful cultural integration, if we make ourselves masters of these two world languages.

Notes

1. Vernon Jackson, *Schools and Government in Cameroon* (New York: Teachers College Press, 1967), pp. 11-12.
2. Jackson, op. cit., pp. 15-18.
3. Victor T. LeVine, *The Cameroons from Mandate to Trusteeship* (Berkeley and Los Angeles: University of California Press, 1964), p. 35.
4. Denis L. Ropa, "Rapport sur l'expérience bilingue" (Victoria: Lycée Fédéral
. Bilingue, n. d.).

Chapter 10

Language Policy in Nigeria

by Ayo Banjo

EVERY COUNTRY, it would seem, has its language problems. In the older nations of the world these problems center around standardization, whereas in the newer nations they simultaneously center around standardization and the choice of a national language, with the attendant phenomena of bilingualism or multilingualism. In recent years greater attention has been focused on the language problems of developing countries.[1] Such attention is quite understandable. As Professor J. A. Fishman points out, they are "at an earlier stage in development" where "the problems and processes of nationhood are more apparent . . . and their transformations more discernible to the researcher." They have, as a consequence, attracted the attention of "those sociolinguists . . . interested in societal (governmental and other) impact on language-related behavior and on language itself."[2]

Problems of National Integration in Nigeria

Nigeria, the most populous black African country, has always been faced with seemingly intractable problems of national integration. Before the amalgamation of the country in 1914, the area had been governed as two units, namely, the Northern Provinces and the Southern Provinces, and now, many decades after amalgamation, the division between the North and the South has not disappeared. There is a sense, indeed, in which it can be said that the country falls naturally into two parts, culturally and linguistically, and these differences have tended to be exacerbated by party politics during the civilian regime. Hausa and Fulani, the two most influential languages of the North, belong to the Chad (Afro-Asian) and West Atlantic (Niger-Congo) groups of languages respectively, but Yoruba and Ibo, the two most influential languages of the South both belong to the Kwa (Niger-Congo) group of languages.[3] In terms of external cultural influence, the North has always looked toward the Middle East, whereas the South has always looked toward Europe and America.

The North, however, is more homogeneous than the South, in the sense that Hausa has become, to all intents and purposes, the lingua franca. The South, on the other hand, is more susceptible to ethnic conflict because it lacks a linguistic rallying force, and the minority languages of the South are much less willing to lose their identity. There are, in fact, many such minority languages in the North and in the South, though even the most elementary data on the subject are sadly lacking. Nevertheless, the great majority of the inhabitants of the North, whose population according to the 1963 census is approximately 30 million, speak Hausa as either a first or second language. In the South the two major languages are spoken by 9 million Yoruba in Western State and 7 million Ibo in East Central State. In addition, about 750,000 more people in Lagos State speak Yoruba as their mother tongue, while about 500,000 more people in Midwestern State also speak Ibo as their mother tongue. Over and above this, a large number of non-Yoruba Nigerians all over the country, and particularly in Lagos, Kwara and Midwestern states, speak Yoruba as a second language, while Ibo is similarly spoken as a second language in Rivers and Southeastern states.

Ethnic conflict has long been identified as the greatest danger threatening the existence of Nigeria as a nation-state. As a consequence, two diametrically opposed proposals have been offered in recent times regarding the political organization of the country. One proposal is that the country should be broken up into states in such a way that each state is linguistically heterogeneous. It is hoped that each ethnic group will thereby learn to tolerate the others and ultimately submerge its individual identity in a common Nigerian citizenship. The other proposal claims that such an arrangement can only accentuate the existing conflict and instability. As an alternative, it is suggested that the states of Nigeria should as far as possible, be linguistically homogeneous. This proposal obviously leaves open the question of minority languages whose speakers cannot possibly stand as single states on their own. The present 12-state structure can be seen as a compromise between these two proposals.

Language Policy and National Integration

To what extent, it may be asked, can Nigeria's political problems be justifiably attributed to its language problems? It is possible that the dilemmas of a monolingual state are fewer than those of a multilingual one, even though the latter has many advantages. In Nigeria, however, the facts have tended to point in the other direction, for in the prewar years the region with the greatest political problems was the West, a homogeneous Yoruba area. In comparison, the Midwestern Region, though not without its own problems, was quiet, and yet it was then the region with the largest number of languages in relation to its size. The case of the West suggests that it is possible to place too high a premium on a common language. It would appear that Nigeria's political problems in the past have been due at least as much to clashes of personality as to clashes of ethnic interests. The personal friction was compounded by the politicians' desire to get as much as possible for their own constituencies. The resulting conflict might have appeared ethnically based, but in the old Western Region it could be seen for what it really was.

Moreover, in Nigeria there has so far never been any really serious difficulty in inter-ethnic communication, thanks to the English language and Nigerian Pidgin. With the spread of education, more and more Nigerians are capable of speaking a variety of English that is understood at least within the country. At the same time, the language problem for a state like Midwestern is happily solved by the widespread use of Nigerian Pidgin. Other linguistically mixed areas have adopted precisely the same solution, with the notable exception of Benue-Plateau State whose lingua franca is, in effect, Hausa. These natural solutions have evolved without anyone doing anything about them. The real issue is that many people take exception to these solutions. English, to some people, still smacks of neo-colonialism, while Nigerian Pidgin, in spite of all the evidence. is still begrudged the status of a legitimate language. For this reason, a search is being made for a lingua franca among the indigenous languages of the country. The possible options in this regard are considered below.

The situation is further complicated because official policy presumes that the country's lingua franca is in fact English. All national events are conducted in English, which is the language of government, administration, the judiciary, broadcasting, and journalism. The large majority of the population who do not speak English — though a good proportion of these might be reached through pidgin — are therefore cut off from the mainstream of national life. Suggestions on how the official policy can be modified are made later in this chapter, but it would be well from the outset to recognize the two main aspects of the problem: the *practical* and the *nationalistic*.

The Language Situation in Nigeria

In Nigeria today, as perhaps in every other West African country, linguists tend to concentrate their attention on the problems of language in education — the establishment of orthographies to enhance literacy and, perhaps more important, the learning of the official (European) language in schools. The problems of an explicitly stated national language policy have been cautiously avoided because of their explosive political implications. But in recent years these problems have gradually begun to be faced.

The first step toward resolving Nigeria's language problems was the Ford Foundation Survey in 1966, which was conducted to take stock of the position of the teaching of English in Nigerian schools.[4] The immediate result of the survey report was to direct attention to the shortage of equipment, inadequacy of teaching methods, and lack of coordination in the teaching of English. But it also raised questions about the teaching of English itself. How soon or how late should it become the language of instruction? Why are pupils learning English? For what roles should English prepare them in the life of the country? Reactions to the survey included the feeling that school children should learn English at a very early stage; the educationists, however, objected to using it too soon as the medium of instruction. It was in this climate of disagreement that a Consulting Report, again sponsored by the Ford Foundation, appeared in 1969.[5] The report, prepared by Marjorie Lowry Shaplin and Judson T. Shaplin, lent support to the view that it would be best to defer the use of English as the medium of instruction until the secondary stage of education. An experiment to verify this viewpoint is today still going on at Ile-Ife under the auspices of the Institute of Education of the University of Ife.

Meanwhile, the general interest in the development of Nigeria's educational curriculum had led linguists and English language teachers to seek to define the role of the English language in the national life. To define such a role is not easy, primarily because any policy based on it is bound to be ad hoc until the real issue, that of the choice of a national language, is settled. English teachers themselves would be the first to admit that the teaching of English in Nigerian schools today is based, at worst, on wrong assumptions, and, at best, on inspired hunches. All the newly independent nations of Asia found it necessary to choose a national language; they then sought to give expression in their education policy to the resultant bilingualism — or multilingualism. It is generally believed that sooner or later Nigeria will follow the same course. Understandably, therefore, there is some skepticism about translating the status quo into an educational policy. But because it is not our place as a linguist to answer the political question relating to language policy, all we can do is offer suggestions in the light of our understanding of the current situation as it actually exists.

We must begin by recognizing, as already stated, that there is a great dearth of statistical information on the status of languages in Nigeria. The number of languages spoken has been variously put at between 50 and 100 plus. Though the actual figure remains unknown, the one mentioned depends on the mood of the speaker. As it is generally believed that the existence of numerous languages within a single country is a valid index of the backwardness of its nationals, those who wish to underline Nigeria's backwardness are happy to quote a figure well above 100. Nigerians themselves, to prove the opposite, are inclined to quote a much lower figure. All that one can say with certainty at this stage is that Nigeria is multilingual.

Part of the difficulty in obtaining exact figures stems from the difficulty in distinguishing between languages and dialects. As Hans Wolff has shown as a result of his studies in Nigeria, intelligibility depends largely on interethnic attitudes, and therefore cannot be relied upon to show whether two linguistic media are two separate languages or dialects of the same language. He explains the Nembe's claim that they and the Kalabari speak dialects of the same language (on the ground that the Nembe find the Kalabari intelligible) as follows:

> The Kalabari are by far the largest and economically most prosperous group in the eastern Delta. They regard the Nembe — and, for that matter, all other Ijaw speaking groups — as poor country cousins, definitely inferior to themselves. They alone, among eastern Delta groups, boast several large towns, such as Abonnema and Buguma; because of their proximity to Port Harcourt, and the shipping approaches to that harbor, they have access to much of the lively commercial activity in this area. Nembe and Brass — the two towns of the Nembe territory — have been reduced to the status of miserable fishing villages by the shifting sand-bars of the lower Niger. In other words, one might term the Kalabari an "up and coming"

society, enjoying an economic boom and having access to the more profitable features of civilization, despising the backwater Nembe . . . . Thus, the intelligibility evidence merely seems to underscore Kalabari ascendancy. Whether the Kalabari actually do understand Nembe and merely claim lack of intelligibility for prestige reasons, is, of course, irrelevant. Linguistic communication from Nembe to Kalabari, by means of the Nembe dialect, seems to be non-existent. [6]

The second example is that of Urhobo, a language of the Midwest, about which, says Wolff, "until recently there was general agreement that mutual intelligibility was relatively high among all Urhobo dialects." Wolff, however, remarks:

Lately, however, speakers of Isoko have been claiming that their language is different from the rest of Urhobo, and that intelligibility between Urhobo and Isoko is not sufficient for normal linguistic communication. This claim has coincided with Isoko demands for greater political autonomy and ethnic self-sufficiency. Surprisingly enough, the speakers of the Okpe dialects — almost identical with Isoko — continue to consider themselves ethnically part of the Urhobo area and claim mutual intelligibility with the majority of Urhobo dialects. [7]

In the light of such evidence, any determination of the exact number of languages spoken in Nigeria cannot completely escape the charge of arbitrariness. Census figures are unlikely to help either, partly because no reliable census has been taken in Nigeria for a long time, and partly because any information obtained from it must inevitably be tainted by ethnic attitudes.

One reason for this lack of exact information on the number of languages spoken in Nigeria is that the country operates in terms of "the three main languages of Nigeria" — Hausa, Ibo and Yoruba. Earlier in the century the colonial administrators had in addition sponsored Efik, but after the merging of the Efiks with the Ibos in the former Eastern Region, the importance of Efik nationally tended to decline. The choice of these former "Big Four" languages was, of course, a matter of administrative convenience for the colonial government. Hausa was — and still is — the language with the largest number of native speakers (about 12 million). There was, therefore, a natural desire on the part of the colonial administrators to develop it into a lingua franca for the whole of northern Nigeria. This desire was clearly translated into a language policy for that part of the country, for the colonial administration's Annual Report on the Education Departments for 1934 states that in northern Nigeria the language of instruction was Hausa for the most part. Where some other language was used in the first part of a school year, Hausa was nearly everywhere introduced later as a subject and before the end of the year became the medium of instruction. The result today, 40 years later, is that Hausa is widely spoken in 6 of Nigeria's 12 states, namely Northwestern, Kano, Northeastern, Benue-Plateau, North Central, and Kwara. In most of these states, Hausa shares the honor of being the official language in all but name with English, and a unique feature of the linguistic situation there is the large number of non-Nigerians who speak fluent Hausa. They have to speak it in order to survive socially and economically.

The pattern in the old Western Region was also similar, with the result that today one hears Yoruba spoken in Benin, Warri, and Sapele. But Yoruba never occupied anything like the strong position that Hausa has come to hold in the northern states. Presumably, the old North was little exposed to the Western European type of education and was left to evolve a partly indigenous, partly Arabic system of education. Today there are about 10 million native speakers of Yoruba in Lagos, Western, Kwara, and Midwestern states, and although the language is fairly widely spoken by other Nigerians — principally because of the position of Lagos — it is rare to find non-Nigerians who speak it, apart from the Yoruba of Dahomey, because in these states English serves as the sole official language.

In the old Eastern Region, as already indicated, both Ibo and Efik were cultivated by the colonial administrators. Of all the "Big Four," Efik was the one with the smallest number of native speakers (about 3 million today), but so important commercially at the time were the towns in which it was spoken — such as Calabar and Opobo — that the colonial administrators took an interest in the language. Ibo, on the other hand, is not a coastal language, and the interest in it must have derived from the larger number of its native speakers (some 9 million today). The attainment of independence in 1960 caused Efiks themselves to learn Ibo — unwillingly, it would seem, for no sooner had Calabar and Ogoja provinces been included in the old Eastern Region than a strong separatist movement was formed within them. As with Yoruba, it is rare to find non-Nigerian speakers of either Efik or Ibo.

The government position, then, has been to ignore smaller languages at the national level. Understandably, no trouble was ever taken to find out exactly how many there were. Within the original three regions, the degree of linguistic tolerance varied. In the North, Hausa became so deeply entrenched that, given enough time, it might have "killed off" the minority languages. In the West, on the other hand, the importance of Edo was always recognized, and Ibadan (Yoruba) and Benin (Edo) always provided two important linguistic focuses. In the East, concessions inevitably had to be made to Efik. One good result of the rudimentary language policy of the colonial regime is that it has produced a situation in which the great majority of Nigerians speak Hausa, Yoruba, Ibo, or Efik either as a first or a second language. Any future national language policy must build on this foundation.

With the splitting up of the old regions into 12 states, however, a new element has been introduced into the situation—one that illustrates the dependence of a national language policy on the political organization of a country. Prior to 1966 the great majority of Nigerians had come to accept the idea of "the three main languages of Nigeria": Hausa, Yoruba, and Ibo. In the North there was no opposition whatsoever on the part of the native speakers of other languages to learning Hausa. In the West an overwhelming majority of the inhabitants were Yoruba, and the rest, apart from a small minority of Ibos and Ijos, spoke one of the Edo group of languages. So the West operated in terms of Yoruba and Edo. The East similarly operated with Ibo and Efik. The current tendency is likely to be that each of the 12 states will want to establish its own lingua franca—causing problems as a result. What was accepted as a minority language in one of the old regions may now turn out to be a major language in one of the states, and its native speakers are apt to be quite unwilling to concede the honor of the state lingua franca to any of its rivals.

There are not likely to be any dramatic changes in the northern states, with the exception of Kwara where Yoruba may conceivably oust Hausa. In the South, Lagos and West are homogeneous Yoruba states, whereas East Central is a homogeneous Ibo state. Southeastern State is almost as fortunate, for although it is not a homogeneous Efik state, Efik is already, to all intents and purposes, the lingua franca in the area. Perhaps the state with the most acute language problems is Midwestern, rightly regarded as the microcosm of the Federal Republic itself. Apart from the Edo group of languages spoken by the majority of the citizens, there are at least three other languages spoken in the state, namely Ibo, Itsekiri, and Ijo. These three languages bear a close relationship to the major languages of three neighboring states, namely East Central, West, and Rivers. And it is precisely because the speakers of these minority languages within Midwestern State speak languages that are the lingua francas of other states (indeed, in two cases, two of the country's "three main languages") that the language problems of Midwestern are uniquely complex. Moreover, we must remember that not all the Edo languages are mutually intelligible.

It has never been seriously suggested that English should be completely abandoned in Nigeria. Rather, what is sometimes advocated is that it should be phased out as the country's official language and lingua franca and be replaced in these roles by a Nigerian language. Even though the choice would seem to lie between the three main languages, each time the debate has arisen the country's rulers, both civilian and military, have counseled caution in making it. They would rather adopt a practical, if procrastinating, approach. A strong body of opinion, nonetheless, opts for the nationalist line. Surprisingly, no compromise has been sought in Nigerian Pidgin, which has an English base, but its dialects are truly indigenous. Given the present rapid spread of formal education in Nigeria, however, the logical outcome of the present policy is that English will become not only the country's official language, but also its true lingua franca—a policy generally regarded as nationalistically untenable. The policy is not particularly hostile to pidgin, but the spread of English is likely to remove the necessity for pidgin.

Even though English dominates the press and radio, a few mother tongue newspapers are published, notably in Hausa and Yoruba, and all radio stations devote some broadcasting time to the Nigerian languages. It is, however, in its educational institutions that a nation's language policy can be seen most clearly. English is, of course, the undisputed language of higher education, but it does not prevail at the primary level. Apart from a handful of "international" primary schools where all instruction is given in English, every other primary school has at some stage to make a switch from a mother tongue to English as the medium of instruction, and the favored stage for this transition seems to be at the start of the fourth year. This policy has been challenged on two main grounds. First, critics point out that it produces considerable waste because pupils who drop out of school after the primary level tend to forget most of the English they learned and revert quickly to monolingualism. Second, critics argue that it is educationally unsatisfactory because English is being made to carry too great a burden too early.

On the other hand, there is the real problem of the inadequacy of many local languages in their present stage of development to serve as effective media of instruction. Of all the Nigerian languages, Yoruba probably has the largest volume and greatest variety of written literature, and yet those engaged in the Ife experiment are finding how difficult it is to make Yoruba serve as an effective medium of instruction. Western State is the only state in the federation, with the possible exception of one or two in the North, to make the teaching of the local mother tongue compulsory in all its schools. Other states, however, are also alert to their responsibilities toward local languages, and Rivers State, for example, is engaged in a project in collaboration with the University of Ibadan to produce local language readers for its primary schools.

On the campus, Yoruba, Hausa and Ibo are degree subjects at the University of Ibadan, whereas the University of Lagos also teaches Edo at a nondegree level. Research into Nigerian languages is pursued by most of the universities, as well as by such independent bodies as the Institute of Linguistics. Very recently, a committee sponsored by the Committee of Vice-Chancellors of the Nigerian universities looked into the problems of orthography for all Nigerian languages. Thus, interest is definitely mounting in the Nigerian languages. Even though there has been no explicit statement from the government on the role of these languages in Nigerian education, it can be inferred from practice that the intention is to strengthen the adult literacy campaign and to guarantee effective education during the first three years of primary school, both of which will give increased emphasis to Nigerian languages.

Toward a More Adequate Language Policy

An explicit language policy for Nigeria will have to take into account the political peculiarities of the country. The more political units there are, the more complex the national language policy. The division of Nigeria into three regions had, as we have seen, conditioned Nigerians to think in terms of three main languages. Now with 12 states, the country will almost certainly have to think in terms of a larger number of regional lingua francas. Already the Nigerian Broadcasting Corporation, which used to broadcast in English and the three main Nigerian languages, now broadcasts in English and 18 Nigerian languages.

If, as seems very likely, Nigeria is to follow the pattern already set in Southeast Asia, then one of the prerequisites of a comprehensive and long-term national language policy is the choice of a national language. And, quite clearly, that choice will be made from among the three main languages. To make a rational choice, it will be necessary to use the following criteria:

1. *Population:* How many people already speak the language as native speakers? Is there a standard variety of the language?
2. *Acceptability:* How acceptable is the language to the native speakers of other Nigerian languages? The number of its current speakers for whom it is not the mother tongue could provide an index to this question.
3. *Typology:* To how many other languages in the country is it related? The ease with which it can be learned may offer a clue here.
4. *International Standing and Cultural Considerations:* What are world attitudes toward the language and the culture it embodies? The selection should be in consonance with the image Nigeria wishes to project abroad.

5. *State of Development:* Does the language already have a standard orthography? To what extent can it express modern ideas?
6. *Literary Status:* What is the quantity and quality of the literature (bellettristic and otherwise) existing in the language?

None of the three main languages is likely to be superior to the other two on every one of these points, but it should be possible to determine which one, on balance, is preferable. It may not, of course, be easy to find a way of weighting these factors in relation to one another — an additional problem. Some believe that population should be the overriding factor, whereas others hold that the most important consideration should be acceptability. In practical terms, acceptability — which cannot be easily induced — would seem more important, for once a language is found acceptable by all, then the question of its propagation becomes relatively easy.

Bearing all these considerations in mind, the choice appears to lie between Hausa and Yoruba. They are the two best-known languages in Nigeria, and they are also both widely spoken outside the country, though Hausa is undoubtedly in wider use. Yoruba, even so, derives many advantages from the fact that it is the language of Lagos, and therefore the most modernized (some would say corrupted) of the Nigerian languages. Whichever language is selected, Fishman's distinction between nationalism and nationism is useful to remember.[8] The desire for a national language arises from nationalist considerations, insofar as the intention is to substitute an indigenous language for a world language as the official language of a country. At the same time, however, only nationist considerations can ensure that the wisest choice is made so that the new nation can be consolidated and all the energies of its people harnessed toward achievement of agreed-upon national goals. In a country as large and diverse as Nigeria, the decision should not be allowed to be based on Hausa nationalism, Yoruba nationalism, or Ibo nationalism.

Once the issue of the national language is settled, the other components of the national language policy have to be considered. Two questions in particular have to be answered. The first relates to the status of mother tongues, and the other to what is going to be the character of regional lingua francas. The fewer the regional lingua francas the better, from the nationist point of view, and it would be best to preserve the original "Big Four" as far as possible. The states where this solution might prove difficult are Midwestern and Rivers. If Edo for Midwestern State and Ijo for Rivers State are added to the list the total number of regional lingua francas becomes six. This would by no means be a perfect solution, because it leaves a state like the Benue Plateau without a lingua franca of its own, though the majority of its citizens already speak Hausa and its local needs could be satisfied by developing its various local languages. Most states would then operate in terms of four languages — the local language, the regional lingua franca, the national language, and English.

How can this policy be given expression within the educational system? The language of higher education in Nigeria is English, and no one, at the moment at least, appears anxious to alter this state of affairs. The language of the secondary school is also English. Over the long term, it will probably be necessary to make some changes at the secondary level, with instruction being given in the national language and English being taught as a subject. The languages of primary education will have to be the local mother tongue, the regional lingua franca, and the national language. Because learning of the national language would receive enormous reinforcement outside the school, it might be wise to make it the medium of instruction from the fourth year onward. What pattern is followed in the first three years of primary school might be allowed to vary from place to place. For example, the local mother tongue could be made the medium of instruction, with the regional lingua franca and the national language brought in as subjects. Where the local languages are very numerous, the regional lingua franca might be made the medium of instruction in the second and third years or even for all three years.

Reinforcement for the language policy adopted by the government could be expected to come from the press and radio. Both media can do much for the standardization of the national language, though Nigeria would likely find it necessary to have one English newspaper for purposes of communication with the outside world. The radio, though concentrating on using the national language, might at the outset broadcast news and some other programs in the six regional lingua francas. Because the current trend is for each state to have its own broadcasting station, broadcasting in the regional lingua francas and local languages can be left to the state radio stations.

Something should be said about the future of the English language in Nigeria. At the moment it is both the official language of the country and a restricted lingua franca for the educated classes. Because of its importance, there is a general tendency to use it as the medium of instruction as early as possible in the educational system. In some schools teaching is done in English from the first day of primary school. In all others, as already pointed out, it becomes the medium of instruction after three or four years. The poor results being obtained in English competence have stimulated a great deal of interest in the Ife experiment, where the experimenters hope to show that the best method of all is to wait until the secondary school before using English as the medium of instruction. Richard Noss, the UNESCO consultant in Southeast Asia, even takes a more extreme position:

When unfamiliar languages are to be taught by means of language courses only, the language instruction should be delayed as long as possible, being given just before the objective for which they are designed (e.g., general instruction in a new medium) comes into play. This takes maximum advantage of both the attrition rate and the compression factor. [9]

With the inauguration of the kind of national language policy described above, English would become a foreign language in Nigeria, but a foreign language in which educated Nigerians will want to have fluency. For the foreseeable future, English will be the language of higher education, and the possession of a world language is likely to become more rather than less of an asset as time goes on. One possibility is that once the present pressure on English slackens, the teaching of the language may actually improve. Indeed, the future position of English in Nigeria is adequately described neither by "English as a second language" nor "English as a foreign language." What is needed is a label for an intermediate position between these two.

The regional lingua francas, components of the language policy described above, will conceivably phase out after some time, leaving only the mother tongue, the national language, and English. But these regional lingua francas have a vital role to play in the transitional stage. While the national language is taking root, they can serve as official languages in the states, and also as a means of communication between the center and the states in national broadcasting. They do not really constitute too great an additional burden because they are already the local vernaculars in many parts of the country. They can also usefully help to preserve Nigeria's cultural diversity. Finally, their adoption may make the choice of a national language more acceptable to the other major language communities, thus, it is hoped, preventing the kind of language riots that India and other countries have experienced.

Notes

1. See for instance J.A. Fishman, C.A. Ferguson, and J. Das Gupta, eds., *Language Problems of Developing Nations* (New York: John Wiley & Sons, 1968); Dell Hymes, ed., *Language in Culture and Society* (New York: Harper & Row, 1964); R.B. Le Page, *The National Language Question* (London: Oxford University Press, 1964); Richard Noss, *Higher Education and Development in South-East Asia: Language Policy* (Paris: UNESCO, 1967); John Spencer, *The English Language in West Africa* (London: Longman, 1971); and idem, ed., *Language in Africa* (Cambridge: Cambridge University Press, 1963).
2. J.A. Fishman, "Nationality-Nationism and Nation-Nationism" in *Language Problems*, op. cit., pp. 39-51.

3. J.H. Greenberg, *Languages in Africa* (The Hague: Mouton, 1966).

4. Robert Jacobs et al., *English Language Teaching in Nigeria* (Lagos: The Ford Foundation, 1966).

5. M.L. Shaplin and J.T. Shaplin, *Selected Aspects of Primary and Secondary Schools Language Development in Nigeria with Recommendations* (Lagos: The Ford Foundation, 1969).

6. Hans Wolff, "Intelligibility and Inter-Ethnic Attitudes," in *Language in Culture*, op. cit., p. 442.

7. Wolff, op. cit., p. 443.

8. Fishman, op. cit., p. 43.

9. Noss, op. cit., p. 68. By "compression factor" Noss means the pay-off that comes from a short but very intensive period of language learning.

Chapter 11

The Mass Media and Nation-Building in Kenya and Tanzania

by William W. Neher and John C. Condon

KENYA AND TANZANIA have had contrasting experiences with inter-ethnic relations. Historically, Kenya has suffered more overtly from ethnic animosities, most recently and noticeably between Kikuyu and Luo. Tanzania, on the other hand, has enjoyed considerably more peace on this score. It is true, nonetheless, that there are ethnic feelings and occasional resentments toward certain groups in Tanzania, such as the Chagga and Haya, who have been considered favored with educational and economic opportunities. But the ethnic problems of Kenya have been more explosive, leading on occasion to violence. Divisions based on ethnicity in Kenya have been reinforced by divisions based on other criteria—regionalism, economic development, political loyalties. Even in the area of language policy, some partisans suggested that the adoption of Swahili as an official language of Kenya favored the Bantu Kikuyu over the Nilotic Luo.

The most dangerous period for Kenya in terms of ethnic relations probably came just before the parliamentary elections of 1969. The major posts in the Kenya African National Union (KANU) government were generally held by Kikuyu, and the opposition party, the Kenya People's Union (KPU) was identified with the Luo people and the prominent Luo politician, Oginga Odinga. Implications that Odinga and the KPU were somehow financed by Communist governments helped to further the division. The assassination of Tom Mboya, minister and secretary general of KANU, in the summer of 1969 quickly exacerbated ethnic tension.

In late October 1969 President Kenyatta went to Kisumu to dedicate a Russian-built hospital and to deliver a strong speech denunciatory of the

KPU. Kisumu, on the shores of Lake Victoria, is the major city in the area of the main Luo population concentration. The crowd, largely Luo and KPU members, was unruly and surged toward the president's motorcade as he left the ceremony. Some members of the escort opened fire into the crowd. Perhaps this whole event sobered some people while it certainly enraged others. At any rate, the KPU was accused of inciting the riot at Kisumu and was banned by the government. Parliamentary elections were then called for December, and though there were incidents, the election campaign and the balloting were generally peaceful. Many of the observations concerning Kenya in this chapter are from this troubled period of late 1969.

Tanzania's problem of national integration is of a somewhat different nature from that of Kenya's. Kenya must strive to prevent open hostilities, the manifestations of "tribalism," in building a national and cultural identity. Tanzania must strive to mobilize in terms of a national identity and consciousness, partially frustrated by the geographical separation of her populous regions. Both countries have some advantages in their efforts toward national integration. Swahili, an African language that is widely understood and that does not suggest favoritism toward a large or powerful ethnic group, is the national language of Tanzania and provides a means of overcoming linguistic barriers. Swahili has recently become officially a national language of Kenya as well. The communication media of both countries can therefore use Swahili and English without suggesting that either has official favor or cutting off access to mass media. The two countries also have well-known national leaders whose popularity by and large transcends ethnic identities. President Nyerere, however, has probably been more successful than President Kenyatta in avoiding identification with a specific ethnic group.

We are concerned primarily in this chapter with communication — specifically, the function of the communication media with respect to nation-building in the East African states of Kenya and Tanzania. Our focus is on the mass media, especially the press and radio, and such forms of traditional cultural expression as drama, literature, and dance are noted as possible media for creating an ambience for the emergence of a national culture. It is our contention that mobilization of a national consciousness, to supersede regional and ethnic consciousness, is partially a function of communication. It follows from this assumption that the effectiveness of communication depends upon the delivery of the message, that is, upon the channels of communication. In this light, media are defined as the channels of communication for inducing images of a national culture. What follows is an analysis of the main channels of communication, or media of communication, in Kenya and Tanzania.

The Study of Media in Africa

One important aspect of mass communication studies in developing countries has been concerned with the functional relationship between communication and national development and national integration. The writings of Lucien Pye, Daniel Lerner, and Wilbur Schramm are significant general summaries of this interrelationship.[1] These writers propose that the mass media can serve in two spheres, the political and economic (and a third sphere may be added—the cultural). The governments of new nations, faced with problems of validating their legitimacy and of creating a feeling of nationhood among disparate groups, can use the press and radio to further their ends. Rosalynde Ainslie puts forth a perhaps exaggerated assessment of the power of the mass media to effect political objectives by maintaining that the person or group that controls the mass media of an African country has a "terrible power"—the ability to create images of the world and of that country's government.[2] As for economic development, Schramm and Lerner argue that the mass media, especially radio, are essential to its success. In this regard, they assert that the mass media can widen individuals' horizons, raise expectations, and thereby create a suitable climate for economic growth.[3] More specifically, Schramm suggests that the function of mass communication is to contribute to a feeling of "nationness," to act as the "national voice of economic planning," to teach new skills, to extend markets, and to help prepare people to play new roles as economic development proceeds. [4]

The positive nature of these earlier views concerning the effectiveness of mass media in promoting economic growth may be overstated. The mass media can indeed raise expectations, but raise them so high that youth flock to the national capital in search of good jobs, only to be woefully disappointed and become, instead, a contributing factor to increased crime and unemployment levels. The optimistic view does not always take sufficient cognizance of the effects of group processes and informal networks of communication in modifying the effects of messages. Communications on cattle-dipping or destocking, for example, can expect to meet resistance among the Masai of East Africa regardless of the media campaign waged by development officers. Technical aid officials have reported failures to introduce innovations that seem to interfere with traditional functions or behaviors.[5] In addition, the development of mass media themselves is handicapped by lack of money and trained personnel, uneven terrain and inadequate transportation systems, and, sometimes, political obstacles.

More studies of the extent and nature of media development in the new nations of Africa are, of course, needed.

Ainslie devotes some consideration to the problems of media development in her survey, *The Press in Africa*, which deals mainly with English-speaking Africa but includes one chapter on *"l'Afrique noire."* She devotes most of her attention to newspapers, though radio and television are discussed in a chapter each. Ainslie concludes that the extent of mass media development depends upon such things as the pattern of colonization, the presence or absence of settlers, the policies of the former metropolitan power, and the political features of the new state. Because of the high rates of illiteracy and the difficulties of newspaper distribution, Ainslie suggests that radio is a far more reliable means of reaching people of Africa outside the urban areas. [6]

George Baker comes to similar conclusions about the importance of radio in his briefer survey of mass media in Africa. [7] He points out that although circulation figures for African newspapers may seem low, because papers are passed around and read aloud before groups of people, they may reach more people than previously realized. He estimates that there may be a readership (or listenership) of about ten for every one buyer of a newspaper. Nonetheless, radio is expanding rapidly in importance throughout Africa, reports Baker, much faster than in other developing areas of the world. The average number of radio sets per 1,000 population in Africa, for example, is nearly double that in India. [8]

John Condon, Lloyd Sommerblad, and Graham Mytton examine the development of the press and radio in East Africa. [9] Condon suggests that one of the most difficult problems of research lies in discovering the meaning that the media have for African people. [10] He argues that the social role of the media, as well as the content and extent of media development, should be investigated. Mytton and Sommerblad review the practical obstacles to the rapid development of either the press or radio in the countries of East Africa. Their research, indicating the social role of mass communications and the practical limitations on mass communications, serves to balance optimistic views of the relationship between mass media development and national economic and political development.

Media in East Africa — Traditional and Modern

According to legend, after a special council of Kikuyu elders drew up a new "constitution" for their people, they had to decide how to communicate its provisions to all Kikuyu. The council then formulated the new laws in songs and dances to be performed throughout the land. War dances of this kind, according to Kenyatta, were the most effective means of communication available to tribal leaders. The provisions of the new laws were embedded in the rhythm and movements of the dance.[11] This legend attests to the fact that forms of mass communication exist in the world that may not be recognized as usual in America or Europe. Dance as one traditional form of media in Africa, still provides communication as well as entertainment for large numbers of people. It serves to reaffirm social solidarity and to provide excellent learning devices. The Swahili word, *ngoma*, which originally referred to drums or drumming, is now used to refer to this type of dancing. In *ngoma*, songs, music, drumming, and rhythmic clapping are all considered part of a unity.

Dances, or *ngoma*, are sometimes employed in East Africa for communicating political or developmental goals. It has been suggested that ngoma can serve the general purpose of transmitting a new national culture to people and can help build and bind a people's culture. The ngoma can also explain governmental policy, the meaning of *ujamaa* ("family-hood"), or new farming techniques.[12] Those being taught are actively involved in the instruction, as they engage in the clapping and dancing.

Dances are also used in demonstrations of public support for national policy or political leaders. In a typical example, the main speeches at a political rally in Uhuru Park in Nairobi, just prior to the national elections in 1969, were preceded for nearly an hour by singing and dancing by Kamba, Ganda, and others. The songs accompanying the dancers praised the policies of *Harambee*[13] and the wise leadership of Kenyatta. Condon has described similar *maandamano* ("demonstrations") to signify support for the 1967 Arusha Declaration in Tanzania.[14] On occasions such as the celebrations for *Jamhuri* ("Republic") Day in Nairobi, traditional forms of ngoma are presented along with the modern forms of demonstrations such as military reviews and overflights by aircraft.

Thus the dance is a traditional medium of communicating contemporary messages. Ngoma may function to further national integration by the consolidation of a new national culture, although this purpose requires a nationally organized troupe that follows a coherent policy or guideline for the amalgamation of traditional forms. It should be noted that traditional dancing is also used for partisan political ends; troupes of traditional dancers accompanied candidates in the 1969 Kenyan national elections.

Oral literature is another form of traditional communication that has been adapted as a contemporary medium for transmitting political messages. Concerning its traditional use, Taban Lo Liyong disagrees with commentators who have suggested that the sole purpose of oral literature was entertainment. He maintains that stories once served to instruct the young in the cultural premises and codes of conduct of a society and also pointed to the wisdom of possible choices of action.[15] When Venable suggests that story-telling can be employed for furthering economic development and national integration, he is indicating a function for such literature similar to the one it traditionally had. Small drama groups, organized locally, performing plays based on traditional stories, have been found to be effective for conveying educational messages to people in remote parts of the interior of Tanzania.[16] Modern film techniques could also be adapted to this end.

Group singing is another important medium of communication in Africa. The singing of songs like *"Kanu Yajenga Nchi"* ("Kanu Builds the Nation") or *"Mungu Ibariki Afrika"* ("God Bless Africa") has become a means of communicating political solidarity and legitimacy in political parties in Kenya and Tanzania. Candidates in Kenyan elections have songs composed for their campaigns, indicating what they propose and what they promise to do if elected. Songs in political campaigns are particularly important in countries like Kenya and Tanzania because political advertising over the national mass media is either prohibited or prohibitively expensive.

Leonard Doob, in his discussion of "basic" media, refers to clothes or fashions of dress as also a traditional means of communication in Africa.[17] Fashions can serve to convey political attitudes, for example. Letters to the editor of East African newspapers frequently urge women to adopt the "national dress," rather than to follow European trends. The Tanganyika African National Union (TANU) Youth League's campaign against miniskirts has become well known. Attire, however, can have the disadvantage in the eyes of national leaders of being associated with one identifiable ethnic group and not the nation as a whole. The astute national leader, therefore, is careful not to advocate the clothing styles unique to a single group. President Nyerere adopted the collarless shirt in an effort to avoid both Western and distinctive tribal dress, although some saw the fashion as a nonverbal sign of favor for the Chinese. President Kenyatta usually wears a suit and a KANU tie, but for ceremonial purposes he sometimes dons an old leather jacket evocative of his years in detention.

Family and community networks of communication, or grapevines, can also be used for political communications. The TANU cell system in Tanzania represents an attempt to co-opt and make use of community and primary group relationships for such communication.

Ngoma, songs, stories, dress all represent traditional forms of media that can be used for modern political and development purposes. They complement the modern forms of mass media—newspapers, radio, television —which, as indicated above, have been more amenable to systematic research. East African governments reflect a belief that these modern forms of media can provide short-run benefits for national integration and development. The press and radio, after all, can communicate cultural material like songs and fashions of dress over vast distances—thus can one medium become the message of another.

The function of the media depends upon their distribution and use among intended audiences. Several studies of communication flows and effects were carried out in East Africa in the latter half of the 1960s that bear upon the question of the impact of various media.[18] One of the most complete surveys of the communication environment of Tanzania was completed under the direction of Condon while at Kivukoni College of Tanzania in 1967. The survey was completed several years ago, but the depth, scope, and geographical distribution of respondents recommend the value of its findings in indicating the distribution and use of communication media in Tanzania and possibly in other developing nations. There were 1,023 respondents to the survey questionnaire located in Dar es Salaam and throughout the country as indicated in Table 11-1.

TABLE 11-1   *Tanzanian Communication Survey*

LOCATION OF RESPONDENTS	NUMBER OF RESPONDENTS
Dar es Salaam and environs	397
Songea and environs	262
Tabora and environs	105
Mwanza and environs	52
Moshi and environs	61
Bukoba and Westlake	19
Mbeya, town and region	77
Newala and Mtwara Region	50
Total	1,023

The 55 questions in the survey dealt with language preferences, media contact, and understanding of political and rhetorical terms used in the media. Certain items in the questionnaire bear upon the questions considered here about the mass media. For instance, the sources of information for local, national, and world news were investigated. Respondents were asked to indicate their first, second, and third sources of information about local news and events. These results are shown in Table 11-2.

TABLE 11-2 *Tanzanians' First Source of Local News*

News Source	Number of Responses	Percentage of Responses
TANU cell leader	325	36
Radio	311	34
Friends	78	9
Public meetings	51	6
Newspapers	32	3½
Schools and teachers	32	3½
Other	79	8
Total	908	100

Newspapers are obviously not a very important first source of information for local events in Tanzania. This result is not entirely surprising: the papers are unable to carry very much news about local areas outside Dar es Salaam except to note the visits of Cabinet ministers and other officials to the interior for the dedication of new public facilities. The TANU cell leader and the radio, however, are important sources of local information. This finding appears to indicate that the national ruling party, TANU, at least in the late sixties, was able to either locate opinion leaders or confer opinion leadership on those selected as local cell leaders; TANU, in other words, has had an excellent opportunity to present its point of view at the local level.

For those who listed a second choice for local news information, newspapers appeared much more often than they did on the first-choice list. Thirty-one percent of those giving a second choice cited newspapers as their source of information. The party cell leader continued to get 36 percent. Only 597 respondents indicated a third choice, and 51 percent of these gave the radio as the source for local information. Public meetings and friends tended to be the only other two sources of information that were mentioned an appreciable number of times. Public meetings received 13 percent of the responses as a third choice, and friends 15 percent. Public meetings generally refer to party gatherings or *baraza*—meetings held by an official such as the area commissioner or a development officer.

The respondents were then asked the same question concerning their sources of national news. The findings here indicate that radio is significantly more important as a source of national news than any other medium. Table 11-3 reveals that more than three-fourths of those surveyed cited the radio as their first source of information about national events. No other source received as much as 10 percent of the responses.

TABLE 11-3 *Tanzanians' First Source of National News*

NEWS SOURCE	NUMBER OF RESPONSES	PERCENTAGE OF RESPONSES
Radio	373	77
Public meetings	33	7
Newspapers	29	6
TANU Cell Leader	24	5
Other	24	5
Total	483	100

For those who gave a second source of information about national news, newspapers were the most important medium, accounting for 37 percent of the selections. In the Dar es Salaam area, the telephone was also identified as a second choice. Among third choices for sources of national news, the party cell leader again became prominent, receiving a little more than 32 percent of the responses. The survey bears out the notion advanced by Ainslie and Baker that the radio is the most important source of information about the nation in many African countries. The pattern of responses is very similar for sources of information about international news: radio and newspapers are far and away the main sources.

The Condon survey of the media in Tanzania is more illustrative than definitive. It does, however, provide some notion of the distribution and impact of various forms of mass communications, and underscores the importance of other variables — party cell leaders, friends, visitors — in communicating information and ideas. The following sections consider those forms of the mass media that have importance in communicating information and news to large numbers of people in East Africa: the press, radio, and television.

The Press

Many West African nationalist leaders have been described as journalists. [19] Although journalism may not have been their vocation, many leaders of nationalist movements found it necessary to engage in journalistic activities. As early as the 1870s James Brew published a nationalist newspaper in the Gold Coast, as did Caseley Hayford not much later. John Payne Jackson, who published the *Lagos Weekly Record* from 1891 to 1915, was perhaps the foremost of the anti-imperialist journalists of this period. These men, and others like them, helped to establish the tradition followed by Nnamdi Azikiwe, Obafemi Awolowo, and Kwame Nkrumah in West Africa. In part because of the large and influential settler populations in East Africa, its history of journalism has differed from that of West Africa's. Except for Kenyatta's editorship of *Muigwithania,* a Kikuyu nationalist organ from 1928 to 1930, nationalist journalism has had little significance.

The first important newspaper in East Africa, the forerunner of the present *East African Standard,* was founded in Mombasa by A. M. Jeevanjee in 1905. In a short time, Jeevanjee was bought out by an English partnership and the paper moved to Nairobi where it is still published. The *East African Standard* subsequently became associated with settler rather than African nationalist interests. Partly as a result of this tie-in between settlers' points of view and newspapers in East Africa, national governments now seek a measure of control over the press. In Tanzania party newspapers are published directly by the ruling party, TANU. There are no official or party newspapers in Kenya, but the *Standard* group of papers and the *Nation* group, which are the most important on a national level, voluntarily adopt the government's stance on most issues.

Considerations of profit and loss also account for the relationship between governments and newspapers in East Africa. The costs of paper and equipment and of training and hiring competent personnel, the scarcity of advertising in a developing nation, and problems of distribution are such that most newspapers presently cannot afford to operate without the backing of government or a wealthy overseas firm.[20] Under these conditions, it is not surprising that a newspaper will tend to represent the government's viewpoint, whether the paper is run directly by the government or the party in power or by expatriate organizations that fear nationalization or banning. Furthermore, especially in Tanzania, journalists tend to suggest that newspapers have the duty of advocacy rather than of merely reporting the news. Concerning African journalists in general, Nkrumah in a speech to the Second Conference of Pan-African Journalists in Accra declared they have a duty to express views that "move the revolution forward." [21] The editors of the *Nationalist* in Tanzania have set forth similar ideological guidelines for the "true Afro-Asian journalist." [22] The *Nationalist* has also charged that the privately owned newspapers of East Africa are "devil's advocates" of neo-colonialism.[23]

Ownership of the newspapers in Kenya has remained largely in private hands, and such explicit ideological stands are usually not taken. The owners of the *East African Standard* in Nairobi also own the *Uganda Argus,* the Kenyan Swahili language paper, *Baraza,* and did own the *Standard* of Tanzania. The *Nation* group of papers consists of the *Daily Nation* and the Swahili *Taifa Leo* in Kenya and the *Taifa Empya* printed in Luganda in Uganda. For a time, the *Nation* group also owned part of *Mwafrika,* a Dar es Salaam Swahili weekly newspaper.

The impact that the main newspapers of Kenya and Tanzania have on the national public depends first upon their distribution. It is difficult, however, to determine the extent and nature of readership of East African newspapers. To rely simply on the number of papers printed and sold is probably misleading because, as Baker and Condon have pointed out, newspapers are passed around and read aloud. Readership figures are often a guess based on multiplying times number of papers sold number of readers assumed for each paper. The editors of the *Standard* of Tanzania, for example, estimated that their paper had a readership of about three to one, meaning that for 17,000 papers sold on an average day, about 51,000 presumably read it.[24] Felice Carter estimates that the *East African Standard* had a readership of about 37,000 in 1968.[25] The *Daily Nation* has become a strong competitor: its circulation doubled between 1966 and 1968, reaching an estimated "over 30,000" readers in 1968.[26] In 1969 the *Daily Nation* claimed to have surpassed all other Kenyan newspapers in circulation. Its Swahili language companion, *Taifa Leo,* claims to reach more than 33,000 people in both towns and rural areas. The readership of the *Sunday Nation* is estimated at 38,000, whereas its competitor, the *Sunday Post* has a claimed circulation of around 16,000.

The Tanzanian communication survey probed the question of the distribution and function of newspapers in the nation. Respondents were asked first whether they bought any periodicals—newspapers or magazines. Of those responding, 67 percent said they did. It should be noted that 91 percent of those living in or near Dar es Salaam answered yes. People were then asked how often they regularly received periodicals; their responses are given in Table 11-4.

The geographical distribution of the responses in Table 11-4 indicates that, as expected, people are more likely to receive newspapers and periodicals on a regular basis if they live in or near a large urban center. The periodical most often listed in the survey was *Ngurumo* (33 percent of responses), a privately owned Dar es Salaam daily that at the time was a small, inexpensive newspaper filled mostly with neighborhood information and gossip. Other periodicals mentioned by significant numbers of people

TABLE 11-4 *Tanzanians' Responses to the Question, "How Often Do You Get Periodicals?"*

FREQUENCY	NUMBER OF RESPONSES	PERCENTAGE OF RESPONSES
Nearly every day*	396	55½
Two-three times a week	78	11
Once a week	62	9
Once in two weeks	22	3
Once a month	41	6
Less than once a month	3	½
Do not receive periodicals regularly (or no response)	111	15

*83% of those responding "nearly every day" live in the Dar es Salaam area.

were *Uhuru*, the Swahili language TANU organ (18%); the *Standard* (7%); *Mwenge*, a journal of Kivukoni College (7%); and *Kiongozi*, a Swahili language paper published at Tabora (6%). In addition, 16 percent of those responding said they read a foreign, English-language newspaper rather than a Tanzanian paper. Among second periodicals listed, *Ngurumo* was again most often named, receiving 32 percent of second responses. For those who gave a second periodical, *Uhuru* received 21 percent and the *Standard*, 4 percent. Non-Tanzanian, English-language newspapers were listed by 21 percent of those noting a second periodical.

The picture presented by these figures, supported by our observations in Kenya and Tanzania, is that newspapers do not reach a majority of the population on a regular basis and that papers are distributed among and used most by those with some formal education. It also seems true that English newspapers, particularly foreign ones, have some prestige value, and may have been mentioned partly for that reason. On the other hand, there is the popularity of *Ngurumo*, which in price, language, and format is accessible to a wider audience, particularly in the area of the capital city.

The impact of newspapers on audiences for campaigns of national development depends upon the image of the nation and the world presented to readers. Condon has examined such a "news geography" for four Tanzanian newspapers.[27] He attempted a quantitative content analysis of the amount of newspaper space devoted to particular areas of the world, including Tanzania, in news coverage. Such an analysis can provide some indication of the way in which the world is presented to the readers of the chief newspapers of a country. Not surprisingly, the content analysis of Tanzanian papers revealed that news about Tanzania dominated the news in terms of amount of space. In the Swahili papers, more than half the total news reported concerned Tanzania, whereas in the English-language dailies the figures were slightly less than half. The analysis also revealed a heavier emphasis on international news in the English-language press as compared with the Swahili press. In one 15-day period, for instance, Condon found that a reader of *Ngurumo* was not exposed to as much world news as was the reader of the *Standard* in one day. In the English-language press, most of this international news concerned areas in Africa. Of areas outside Africa, Great Britain received the most coverage.[28]

A similar content analysis of daily newspapers in Kenya was carried out in 1969. Neher counted the number of Nairobi newspaper lines devoted to news stories from various parts of the world and the nation between October 27 and November 10, 1969. The resulting figures, as shown in Table 11-5, are averages of lines per day over this 15-day period. The newspapers measured were *Daily Nation, East African Standard,* and *Taifa Leo.* In addition, the following weeklies were also counted: the *Sunday Nation, Sunday Post,* and *Baraza.*

TABLE 11-5 *News Geography in Kenyan Daily Newspapers October 27, 1969-November 10, 1969*

AREAS OF NEWS ITEMS	EAST AFRICAN STANDARD	DAILY NATION	TAIFA LEO
Kenya	1,540	1,270	940
East Africa (except Kenya)	220	140	35
Rest of Africa	280	95	35
United Kingdom	55	20	0
United States	90	85	10
Other International	415	290	10
Total International	1,060	630	90
Total News Linage	2,600	1,900	1,035

The "news geography" for the Kenyan press is comparable to that presented in the Tanzanian press. The Swahili press tends to focus on national or local items with heavy emphasis on speeches by government officials and other political figures. The overwhelming emphasis in the newspapers of both languages in both countries is on news from or about their own country. One is tempted to conclude that the newspapers of Kenya and Tanzania are doing what they can, purposely or otherwise, to foster a sense of national consciousness among their readerships. Unfortunately, it is precisely this cause-and-effect relationship that is so difficult to explore, to prove or to disprove. It is possible to study the short-run effects of some newspaper advertising campaigns in fostering name recognition, for example, or to find out how familiar people are with certain political slogans. But to determine the long-range effects of the messages from the press media is difficult not only in Africa, but in nearly any country or setting. The problem lies in formulating a research strategy to discern long-term, broad effects on national or cultural attitudes. The safest kind of generalization that seems warranted by our discussion of the press in Kenya and Tanzania is that the effects of newspapers are limited to certain groups by education or geographical distance from distribution points. Whether these people in turn influence others, as a multi-step flow of mass communications would suggest, has not yet been investigated. It also seems safe to conclude that newspapers will continue to have less effect on the outlooks of national audiences as a whole than a medium like radio, which can overcome distance and limited literacy.

Radio and Television

Radio will remain for the foreseeable future one of the most important means of mass communication in Africa—because of low rates of literacy. In rural areas, especially at appreciable distances from towns, radio represents what is often the only means for obtaining outside news or information. A radio receiver is probably one of the first luxury items that Africans purchase.[29] In East Africa radio service in local areas before independence had the purpose of entertaining and informing European settlers or administrators stationed there. In Kenya this service dates from 1927. Uganda and Tanzania, however, which had much smaller white settler communities, had to wait until the early 1950s for local broadcasting facilities. During World War II, when all Africa witnessed a great expansion of radio, Kenya began broadcasting in some local languages, a step toward the development of Swahili radio programming in both Kenya and Tanzania.

Although Kenya and Tanzania show contrasting patterns of public and private ownership and operation of newspapers, neither deviates from the standard African practice of state ownership and control of radio broadcasting. This practice is due partly to the pattern of radio control in colonial times. Additionally, there is a belief throughout Africa that radio is a powerful instrument of political control and that possession of the broadcasting facilities confers legitimacy on the regime in power.[30] Possibly as a result, radio reflects governmental policy more unquestioningly than do newspapers. For instance, when Oscar Kambona, former secretary-general of TANU, sharply criticized President Nyerere, no mention of the attack was made on Radio Tanzania though the news was carried in the Tanzanian newspapers.[31] Similarly, in Kenya the seriousness of the violence at Kisumu in October 1969 was not discernible in early radio reports; only after the reports appeared in the newspapers the following morning could it be gauged by the public.

In Kenya the Associate Business Consultants recently completed a survey for the Kenyan Ministry of Information and Broadcasting which found that there were about 750,000 radio sets in Kenya, or one for every 13 persons, and that there were approximately 4.5 million listeners to the Voice of Kenya (VOK).[32] Even the Ministry was surprised to learn that so many Kenyans in very remote areas had radio receivers.[33] Obviously, radio is important for communicating information and political programs throughout Kenya.

Two broadcasting services are transmitted most of the day in Kenya— the National Service in Swahili and the General Service in English. The English-language service devotes more air time to international news than the Swahili service. For example, it picks up the daily British Broadcasting Company (BBC) analysis of world events. National and African affairs tend to dominate the news portions of the Swahili-language service. Both Kenya and Tanzania have introduced policies for reducing or eliminating altogether broadcasting in regional or tribal languages. In 1969-1970, VOK still had programs in Kamba, Hindustani, Masai, Kimeru, Kikuyu, Somali, Kalenjin, Kuria, Luhya, and Dho-Luo, though they were regionally rather than nationally broadcast. At present, Radio Tanzania does not broadcast in any regional or tribal language.

Just what languages are used by the press and over the airwaves, then, attests to the importance of sociolinguistic considerations in rhetorical or political communications in East Africa. The process of language selection is primarily a rhetorical decision, determining the nature of the audience for and response to media messages. Both the printed and the broadcast media reflect decisions made about audiences for English and Swahili materials. The Swahili media are usually more nationalistic than the English press and radio, even though both are controlled by essentially the same authorities. Obviously, the decision to eliminate broadcasting in local languages is aimed at diminishing ethnic identification and propagating a national culture through a national language. Swahili is the language of political effectiveness in Kenya and Tanzania, and political speeches are generally in Swahili. Even in the English-language media, certain Swahili terms are never translated. The word *wananchi,* for example, is always used in referring to citizens or the people in news broadcasts (*"Wananchi* were told today of a new program. . .").[34] Clearly it is necessary to study two different national media, English and Swahili, and to be aware of the possibly different consequences of political messages, depending upon the language used. There may be different outcomes for people exposed to the English-language media in contrast with those exposed primarily to the Swahili-language media.

Condon's survey of Tanzania's communication systems indicates that radio is probably the country's most important means of disseminating news. In the survey 61 percent of the respondents said they had radio receiving sets, and 95 percent said they regularly listened to radio broadcasts. There appears to be no regional variation in the exposure to radio, as there were no significant differences in the percentage of people responding yes to this question from region to region. In answer to the question on their favorite kind of radio program, 55 percent said news. Music programs were picked by 32 percent of the respondents, with announcements and local news being the only other items receiving significant percentages of responses.

The difficulties of operating radio services — for example, the cost of facilities, the scarcity of trained personnel — are magnified for a country trying to operate a television service as well. Tanzania does not yet have a television service, although there are plans for a transmitter at Arusha. Kenya, on the other hand, was one of the first countries of tropical Africa to have a national television service. Ainslie says that there were 5,100 television sets in Kenya in 1963, all within a 25-mile radius of Nairobi.[35] Six years later the survey conducted by the Associate Business Consultants for the Kenyan Ministry of Information and Broadcasting found that there were 23,000 television sets in Kenya, and that the number of viewers was about 220,000.[36] Most African governments that want national television service justify its expense by pointing to the benefits it will bring in national development and integration. At least in part, television is seen as a potentially powerful medium. After laying out the cost of installing television facilities, however, African governments may find only enough money left to run packaged entertainment from Europe or the United States.

In Kenya, where early television service was designed for the amusement of the white settlers, the emphasis on entertainment over educational programs is still marked. Even had television in Kenya not had this history, the costs of new facilities and programming would have prohibited local production of effective educational programs for some time. As a result, the media of film and television will not greatly aid national integration as long as visual programs are packaged Western entertainment. In Tanzania the government has held back development of television service partly out of a desire to wait until it has the capacity for local production. Similarly, Tanzania is trying to foster a national film industry.

In summary, television is still at an early stage of development in Kenya and Tanzania. Radio, however, is the most vital medium of mass communication in East Africa. Lionel Cliffe reports that Tanzanians learned more about their candidates in the 1965 elections through radio than any other medium.[37] Radio was equally crucial as a source of information about the 1969 elections in Kenya. People have relatively easy and ready access to radio broadcasts and are not cut off by distance, illiteracy, or difficult terrain from this source of information. There are, nonetheless, real problems of staffing and financing effective radio production in both Kenya and Tanzania. Of the two, Kenya with a longer tradition of radio broadcasting may overcome these difficulties more easily than Tanzania.

A seminar held at University College, Dar es Salaam, in 1969 concluded that a general "lack of media" restricted the development of Africa. This lack of efficient communication media, the seminar reported, "hindered the people in Africa from making use of the results of other people's achievements."[38] The seminar reflected the belief that the mass media can play an important part in national development and political integration, but it warned against the adoption of "Western journalistic practices" and of an "entirely Western" culture in the development of the mass media. This concern about Western culture also reflected the belief that the mass media function to construct an image of a nation's society and culture. In the same vein, Pye concludes that the general communication process, referring primarily to the use of the mass media, can structure the "political climate" in a developing state. The communication process determines how the citizenry will relate themselves to political action, Pye says, since "it gives them a basis for understanding, interpreting, and evaluating political developments."[39] The process of political integration can be understood, from one point of view, as a process of communication. Those media which are characterized by immediacy — radio, television, film — can be most effective in the political process.

The emphasis of this chapter has been on print and electronic media in East Africa, partially because of their immediacy in bringing messages to people and partially because they have been more amenable to present methodologies of communication research. However, the less immediate media — those more traditional in the cultures studied — may be worth further government support simply because drama, *ngoma*, and literature require far less in capital input and technical training.

The ultimate question here in regard to media and national integration is what effect mass communication has in furthering the creation of a national cultural identity for the people of Kenya and Tanzania, or any other developing country. This question requires the exploration of the effect of mass communication on the attitudes and cognitions of the people who are to be influenced. The extent to which images presented in the mass media successfully alter the beliefs and behavior of people is not easy to determine. At present, there is uncertainly about effective research strategies for studying the persuasiveness of the mass media. General research goals should be formulated to determine how effective mass communications are in East Africa. What kinds of impact they generate must be isolated and related to specific types of media and specific types of messages. For example, to what extent are newspapers and radio pronouncements believable? To what extent are people able to recall messages from the press, radio, or other media? To what extent, if at all, do people perceive images of their world as presented in the media? Do cognitive tests indicate that the media contribute to the understanding of political slogans and ideologies? Or are slogans learned just as slogans?

All these questions relate to the receiver of the media's messages. But they are not the only questions that relate to the mass media and nation-building. There are others that pertain to the sender. Who makes the decisions concerning what appears in the mass media? How are such decisions made? What purpose are they to fulfill? To what extent are images consciously created by those producing the mass communication messages? Do these images differ from those perceived by the people? Are there consciously determined strategies to use radio, film, or other media to further national sentiment or culture?

Notes

1. Lucien Pye, ed., *Communication and Political Development* (Princeton: Princeton University Press, 1963); Daniel Lerner, *The Passing of Traditional Society* (New York: The Free Press, 1958), and Daniel Lerner and Wilbur Schramm, eds., *Communication and Change in the Developing Countries* (Honolulu: East-West Center, 1967); and Wilbur Schramm, *Mass Media and National Development* (Stanford: Stanford University Press, 1964).
2. Rosalynde Ainslie, *The Press in Africa: Communications Past and Present* (London: Victor Gollancz, 1966), p. 7.

3. Schramm, "Communication Development and the Development Process," in *Communication and Political Development*, op. cit., pp. 30-56; Daniel Lerner, "Toward a Communication Theory of Modernization," ibid., pp. 327-350.

4. Schramm, "Communication Development, " op. cit. pp. 37-50.

5. See Ithiel de Sola Pool, "The Mass Media and their Inter-personal Social Functions in the Process of Modernization," *People, Society, and Mass Communications*, eds. Lewis Anthony Dexter and David Manning White (New York: The Free Press, 1964), pp. 429-433.

6. Ainslie, op. cit., p. 152.

7. George Baker, "The Place of Information in Developing Africa," *African Affairs*, Vol. 63, No. 2 (1964), p. 213.

8. Ibid., pp. 213-214.

9. John C. Condon, "Nation Building and Image Building in the Tanzanian Press," *Journal of Modern African Studies*, Vol. 5, No. 3 (November 1967), pp. 335-354; E. Lloyd Sommerblad, "Problems in Developing a Free Enterprise Press in East Africa," *Gazette*, Vol . 14, No. 2 (June 1968), pp. 75-78; and Graham R. Mytton, "Tanzania: The Problems of Mass Communication Development," ibid., pp. 89-100.

10. Condon, op. cit., pp. 342-343.

11. See Jomo Kenyatta, *Facing Mount Kenya* (London: Oxford University Press, 1938), pp. 192-193.

12. A. Venable, "Development and National Culture," *Mbioni: Journal of Kivukoni College*, Vol. 3, No. 8 (January 1967), pp. 66-76.

13. *Harambee:* national slogan of Kenya; English translation: "Let us pull together."

14. John C. Condon, "Communication and the National Community," *Mobioni: Journal of Kivukoni College*, Vol. 3, Nos. 8 and 9 (January 1967), pp. 54-55 and 57.

15. Taban Lo Liyong. *The Last Word: Cultural Synthesism* (Nairobi: East African Publishing House, 1969).

16. Venable, op. cit., pp. 72-73.

17. Leonard Doob, *Communication in Africa* (New Haven: Yale University Press, 1966).

18. See John Condon, "The Arusha Declaration: Spreading the Word," *Mbioni: Journal of Kivukoni College*, Vol. 3, No. 10 (1967), pp. 28-41; idem, "The Group as a Focus for Change in a Developing Nation," *Today's Speech*, Vol. 17, No. 1 (Winter 1969), pp. 27-34; William W. Neher, "Contemporary Public Address in Kenya: A Study in Comparative Rhetoric" (Ph.D. diss., Northwestern University, 1970).

19. Ali A. Mazrui, "Political Censorship, Intellectual Creativity, and Nation Building," *East African Journal*, Vol. 3, No. 9 (December 1966), p. 34.

20. Sommerblad, op. cit., pp. 77-78; Ainslie, op. cit., pp. 213-214.

21. Kwame Nkrumah, *The African Journalist* (Dar es Salaam, 1965).

22. *The Nationalist* (Tanzania), Dec. 16, 1966, p. 4.

23. The term "devil's advocate" is not used here in the usual sense of testing a theory

or person, but that the private newspapers advocate the "devil's," or neo-colonialist's, position. *The Nationalist* (Tanzania), Dec. 10, 1966, p. 4.

24. Condon, "Nation Building and Image Building," op. cit., p. 336.
25. Felice Carter, "The Press in Kenya," *Gazette*, Vol. 14, No. 2 (June 1968), pp. 85-88.
26. Ibid, p. 86.
27. Condon, "Nation Building and Image Building," op. cit.
28. Ibid., p. 342.
29. John C. Condon, "Some Guidelines for Mass Communication Research," *Gazette*, XIV, 2 (June, 1968) p. 147.
30. Ainslie, op. cit., p. 152.
31. Mytton, op. cit., p. 99.
32. VOK news broadcast, Nov. 19, 1969.
33. *East African Standard* (Kenya), Nov. 20, 1969, p. 5.
34. See Carol M. M. Scotton, "Some Swahili Political Words," *Journal of Modern African Studies*, Vol. 3, No. 4 (November 1965), pp. 527-541.
35. Ainslie, op. cit., p. 177.
36. VOK news broadcast, Nov. 19, 1969.
37. See Lionel Cliffe, ed., *One Party Democracy* (London: Oxford University Press, 1967).
38. *East African Standard* (Kenya), Dec. 17, 1969, p. 3.
39. Lucien Pye, "Communication Patterns and the Problems of Representative Governments in Non-Western Societies," *Public Opinion Quarterly*, Vol. 20, No. 1(Spring 1956), p. 250.

Chapter 12

Cultural Activities and the Mass Media in Uganda and Zambia

by Atta Annan Mensah

THE EMERGENCE OF independent states in Africa led to a new consciousness of identity and created a widespread desire to rescue African values from the destructive influence of foreign rule and to protect these values for the future. This new consciousness prompted African governments to commit funds to national and international festivals of African performing and visual arts, for these were seen as repositories of African values as well as definers of the African essence of being, and it was considered important to give them a new lease on life.

This search for values and the essential African quality has been linked with the effort to assert and bring to the level of universal recognition the special character of the personality and world of the black man. A few terms and slogans remind us of the varying emphases laid by the pioneer searchers for identity: the black-and-white keyboard, Pan-Africanism, Soul, Negritude, and African Personality. The cry in all cases ultimately spelled the phrase "Back to Africa," which set off far-reaching reverberations across the continent. As Taban Lo Liyong's heraldic introduction to his poems of a later date, *Frantz Fanon's Uneven Ribs*, declared: "Epics of Kintu-type await encasement in eternity of Homeric *Illiad* or *Odyssey*. . . . When will the Nile basin find a Dickens?. . . Will the skyscraping Kilimanjaro, acquire lyricists, poets, musicians to sing to them?. . . No more flute to be piped from the island for coastal dancers . . . . Katwe [awaits] an Alan Paton for a John Kumalo setting. . . ."[1] These lines from a Ugandan depict a high confluence of nationalism and a wider search for identity. The tide precipitated a variety of actions that included not only the inauguration of festivals, but also the establishment in many places of African studies in centers of higher learning and the formation of national dance troupes. Thus in 1966 the Zambian Government opened a Department of Cultural Services, which immediately organized a national dance troupe for the First World Festival of Negro Arts held in Dakar, Senegal, that year. During the previous year the former Rhodes-Livingstone Institute, an active center for social research established 28 years earlier for the whole of Central Africa, was transformed into a Centre for African Studies by the new University of Zambia.

The phrase "cultural activities" was widely used as a label for the performances of both the new dance troupes of Africa and those of many similar private organizations that subsequently sprang up. But frequently the meaning of the term was extended to include all activities and social institutions that depicted the essence of African life and thought. In this sense the phrase embraced, at least by implication, all the products of man in Africa, thereby encompassing what anthropologists and sociologists consider the elements of culture.

In the actual response to the urge to express African values in terms of cultural activities, only a fraction of Africa's cultural products were portrayed in any one presentation, and this fraction very largely, and often exclusively, embraced the performing arts characteristic of precolonial Africa. It may be useful to note at this point that the division of cultural activities into dance, drama, and music should be regarded in Africa as no more than a matter of convenience. Traditional African societies not only blended the three in their performances, but also incorporated the visual arts — sculpture, weaving and clothmaking, beadwork, ceramics and ironwork, and so forth — in the form of masks, costumes, and other "stage" properties. Twentieth-century African creations in these expressive media are largely blends of these arts, with varying degrees of innovation and including artistic motifs derived mostly from the Western performing arts. Byron Kawaddwa's play *Wankoko* for instance, set in a king's palace in Buganda during the mid 1960s, is a musical featuring *banaggunju* ("court dances"), royal drums, choruses, and solos of Kiganda and Kitoro courting songs composed or arranged by Henry Serukenya. The musical props include drums and a *nsege* ("raft rattle"). The orchestra accompanying from the "pit" consists of an amadinda ("xylophone"), *bakisimba* drums, *endere* ("flute"), and rattle. The full orchestra accompanies dances and plays interludes. Sometimes the xylophone accompanies singers alone; occasionally, instead of the traditional rapid reticulated style this instrument simply spells out the melody of singers on stage. Most of the singing is in the Kiganda style of rapid syllable utterance, but frequently it slows down and the unison breaks into parts in Western choral style. The entire style of presentation also conforms to modern conventions derived from Western theater. Through such expressive elements creative men like Kawaddwa and Serukenya build a national language of theater for Uganda.

Toward Pan-Ethnic Harmony through Traditional Arts and Music

Through the medium of theater and with adopted conventions familiar to audiences from diverse ethnic backgrounds, African playwrights and play directors have addressed themselves with complete success to what could be described as sample national audiences. Thus artistic elements originally from particularistic ethnic sources gradually move to the plane of national artistic expression. Because the performing arts in Africa are often the basis for presenting the other arts and because all these together are fully integrated within the wider context of living, these developments are of considerable significance. Some indications suggest this approach to cultural activities is an escape from an uneasy present into a past — a past that certain forces simultaneously seem to be driving Africa to reject. But other forces stress the present. The effect of these forces is clearly seen in the field of music where, in obvious response to demand, recording, radio, and television services devote far more resources to twentieth-century African pop music than to any other musical genre. Government-owned mass media in Uganda and Zambia, as elsewhere in Africa, allocate some time to African traditional arts, but those responsible for radio and television programming are compelled by popular demand and limited resources to maintain this imbalance between those arts that take their genesis from the twentieth century and those of precolonial Africa. Nevertheless, it should be recognized that the new music, like other arts of twentieth-century Africa, mirrors not only African societies and their ways of life, but also African aesthetics and other African cultural values rooted in the past.

In response to the needs of nightclub life, therefore, Ugandan musicians in Kampala have evolved a new form of pop music based on rhythms of the bakisimba dance of the people of Buganda. Although this type of music has an ethnic basis, it is enjoyed and patronized by non-Baganda users of Ugandan barroom jukeboxes. So are Alick Nkhata's compositions that are based on adaptations of traditional songs from various parts of Zambia. If the development and sharing of a common artistic heritage are important aspects of social cohesion, these examples should be regarded as a small but important step toward national integration.

Inter-ethnic appreciation of cultural achievement is widespread in Uganda. Baganda observers often point, for instance, to the greater musical diversity of the Basoga, who they say have furnished Buganda with a large part of her musical heritage. These same observers also hail the Acholi for their achievements in the field of dance. In Zambia the *vimbuza* dancer delights everyone with his dances and his costume. The Zambian Government has endorsed this nationwide appreciation by depicting him on a postage stamp. Considering the inter-ethnic mistrust that politics tends to breed, these observations suggest a possible important new source of cross-ethnic harmony in Uganda and Zambia.

Annual Ugandan Schools Arts Festivals bring ethnic dances to mixed audiences from every part of the country and the impact underscores the promise the arts hold for national integration. The next step is for the planners of these festivals to draw up programs that will require performers to compete in all the distinctive ethnic dances making up the national repertoire. If schools have before them, say, a three-year syllabus in which the dances, songs, and musical instruments of different ethnic groups are prescribed items, inter-ethnic cooperation would be stimulated and the artistic resources of the nation would circulate faster. Moreover, every national region would eventually find itself in possession of the combined artistic heritage of the whole nation.

Literature

In another expressive medium where an imbalance of interest and patronage between the old and the new may be noticed, the cause of national integration is nevertheless being served. In literature Uganda and Zambia both seem to lay emphasis on modern forms. The effect of the impetus given by the Makerere University Department of Literature and the University of Zambia Institute for African Studies to fieldwork in oral literature seems to lie in the future. What remains visible is a strong leaning toward Western concepts of literature. The contents of *Short East African Plays in English* edited by David Cook and Miles Lee,[2] for instance, all seem geared to the proscenium arch. Other literary forms, with very few exceptions, are also cast on Western models. But in many cases the themes are African, and in this way they relate to the search for an identity that can unite the nations within themselves and unite African nations with one another.

The effect on national integration of setting African material within Western literary forms must now be assessed. It should first of all be determined whether the nonliterate groups that form the majorities in African nations have been affected. It goes without saying that all written material goes over the heads of these majorities and so its effect on the nonliterate population is practically nil — but not completely. Some of the impact written material exerts is radiated toward the nonliterate folk, because a tendency exists for those in this group to look up to their educated kinsfolk for guidance in nontraditional matters, nationhood being one of these. Nevertheless, written material tends to widen the gap between literate and nonliterate groups by progressively extending the horizon of the first while bringing little compensating benefit to the second. It thus carries a serious divisive effect that can only be removed by more and more literacy. The sustained drive toward universal education in Uganda and Zambia offers some hope for the future in this sphere.

Fine Art

Fine art among all the arts in Africa offers perhaps the greatest prospect for promoting national integration. Carvings, weaving, and basketry reflect a bit of the authentic artist-craftsman responding to the needs of tribal life, and the extensive borrowing and wide sharing of artistic motifs as may be seen, for instance, among carvers at Livingstone, Zambia, suggests a unity of basic concepts, even if this unity does not proclaim a definitive national cultural unity. But academy-oriented artists carry this potential to an even greater degree. George Kakooza's abstract formalism in sculpture spells out themes with close relevance to Ugandan life but with hardly any hint of his Kiganda background. Augustine Mugalula Mukiibi's cubistic painting harks back to African resources without reflecting particularistic ethnic origins.

The most faithful representation of ethnic themes and forms in Ugandan art is perhaps Eli Kyeyune's art, and the farthest removed from academy orientation is certainly Jack Katarikawe's, both painters of international repute. Kyeyune's characters appear to be stereotypes based on the features of Bantu-speaking facial types, which throw into the strongest light the elements he chooses to vary and thus to remove any possibility of equivocation in what he wishes to portray. His themes stand out as pan-ethnic even when rooted in ethnic legends, as they often are. Katarikawe is an entirely self-taught painter without even primary school education. He achieves the most astounding effects with all the things considered anathema in art schools. His success lies partly in his deep concentration on human themes and partly on a technique of bringing out psychical currents in his portraits. Such nonethnic, twentieth-century currents pervade whatever he produces.

His patrons in Uganda include people of diverse ethnic backgrounds, and he enjoys wide patronage among nonliterates as well as school-educated people.

Performing Arts

The performing arts — with their persuasive powers, their wide symbolic and direct communicative resources — have great potential as an instrument of national integration in Africa. Ugandan composers and playwrights are constantly demonstrating this potential. Uganda's Mbabi-Katana's opera, *The Marriage of Nyakato* (1968); Kawaddwa's musical, *Wankoko* (1970); Robert Serumaga's *Renga Moi*; and Zambia's George Kasoma's *Black Mamba* not only use the universal silent language of theater, but also draw freely from varied ethnic resources. In these productions folklore, song, and dialogue in various languages unite in depicting the fortunes and destinies of ordinary folk, warriors, kings, national leaders, princes, and princesses to mixed audiences who focus on the unfolding story and are not baffled by the switch from one musical idiom, dance idiom, or spoken language to another. Programs of Uganda's Nyonza Singers consist of songs in Luganda, Runyankole, Acholi, Lumasaba, and other languages, and audiences feel drawn to the range of a national song repertoire.

The University of Zambia's drama-training program, in an experiment tried at a workshop organized in 1970 at Chipata, demonstrates another kind of effort to promote national integration. In this experiment Lady Gregory's *Spreading the News* was transposed to a Chewa village scene and then to an Ngoni village scene with the addition of key lines in Chichewa and Ngoni and with local music and dance. The production completed the process of setting the play in various local idioms by replacing the Irish place names with local ones. Thus, through a foreign art form, and an example of that form, the possibilities of circulating ethnic-oriented ideas at the national level were demonstrated. The University of Zambia Dramatic Society picked up the idea and used it with success in play after play and in one musical after another.

Oral Traditions

The use by writers of themes from folklore has already been mentioned, and the underlying unity of these themes commends them to more intensive exploitation by creative artists concerned with the processes both of national and continental integration. The appearance of Kintu as the legendary founding patriarch of a number of ethnic groups in Uganda is an outstanding example. Folktales, proverbs, riddle-solving contests, and kindred verbal arts present even more fruitful possibilities. Amos Tutuola's *Palm-wine Drunkard* reads like an Akan or Ibo folk fantasy, though drawn from a Yoruba background. Similar themes can be illustrated in Ugandan and Zambian folktales. The problem of the unmarried daughter described in various ways in diverse oral literary traditions furnishes an example of shared concerns and interests among disparate ethnic groups. In Teso (Uganda), Namugoya's prospects of marriage are blocked by her own failure to recognize any virtues in the suitors coming forward. In Toro (Uganda), Nyamurunga's father faces the crisis of keeping his word and giving away his daughter to an unknown suitor under disturbing circumstances. In Zambia the recurrence of bird characters in folktales may suggest other unifying themes.

Mass Media

Oral traditions and other art forms thus hold considerable potential as great resources for national integration. The question keeps returning, however, as to how to exploit their potential. Music, dance, and literature as well as sculpture and painting have already been cited as promising vehicles. The communicative powers of all these can be boosted by the mass media. But Ugandan and Zambian newspapers carry only occasional features on the arts. Radio and television do much more and arouse considerable interest among listeners and viewers in their musical and play productions. With more than 4 million listeners, Uganda radio, for instance, can be a crucial factor in forging a national consciousness through the musical and verbal arts of Uganda. The wide popularity of radio in Zambia was clearly demonstrated by the response to a competition organized by Graham Mytton (a research fellow of Zambia Radio attached to the University of Zambia) in June 1970. The competition was of a type that unwittingly excluded most nonliterate listeners, but it was clear even so that the listenership was very wide indeed. "The audience is far less separated than we might think," Mytton observes.[3] Mytton's competition revealed a clear periphery of listeners who were not native speakers of the language. As he notes, "People listen to Tonga broadcasts in other areas, and often they are members of quite different language groups."[4] The same applies to broadcasts in Bemba, Nyanja, Kaonde, and other languages. For the most part, opportunities suggested by this situation still remain untapped, although efforts are being made. One of the most popular instances of mixed-language programming is to be seen in the program, *Tiyende Pamodzi* ("Let us move forward together"), which was among the five most popular programs, according to Mytton's analysis of the competition.[5] Participants (usually three in number) in the program discussed topical and other matters, each making his contributions in his own language. On a smaller but nevertheless significant scale, television and film (largely through productions of the ministries of information and broadcasting) make their contribution, but a large unexploited potential remains.

Conclusion

In sum, as far as Uganda and Zambia may be regarded as typical, African countries have some way to go toward full utilization of cultural activities to enhance national integration. But both Zambia and Uganda are full of promise in this regard. Though the search for identity leads to particularistic ethnic values as the most truly African heritage, there are great opportunities for this ethnic artistic heritage to be projected at national levels. This heritage blends with new pan-ethnic values and shows an infinite capacity for being propagated widely through the modern mass media. Uganda and Zambia are instances in Africa of a steady progression, often beset by political hurricanes, toward increasing national integration through cultural activities.

Notes

1. Taban Lo Liyong, *Frantz Fanon's Uneven Ribs* (London: Heinemann, 1971), p. 2.
2. David Cook and Miles Lee, eds., *East African Plays in English* (Nairobi: Heinemann, 1968).
3. Graham Mytton, "Report on 'Special Competitor No. 1'" (unpublished manuscript), pp. 1-2.
4. Ibid., p. 23.
5. Ibid., p. 17.

The Current State of the Integration Process

Introduction

OUR ANALYSIS in Part V of the current state of the national integration process in four African countries—Senegal, Cameroon, Somalia, and Uganda—explores the degree to which ethnic conflict and fragmentation have constituted dominant themes in the modern political histories of African states. These chapters exemplify the divisive character of ethnic conflict and illustrate the variety of ways that ethnic conflict manifests itself in Africa. In addition, the discussions of these four states describe the divergent approaches that governments have adopted to cope with ethnic conflict and promote national integration.

The four chapters of this section also make it clear that the dynamics of ethnic interaction and the character of ethnic conflict vary in important respects from state to state. Though Senegal, like most other African states, is composed of a multitude of ethnic groups, its ethnic situation is fairly unique. In many other states ethnic distinctions tend to coincide with and be reinforced by such other communal distinctions as religion and regional identification. But not in Senegal where many cross-cutting communal affiliations exist. The same holds true for class status and ethnic identity, because in Senegal class and ethnic community boundaries do not generally coincide. Although membership in particular Muslim sects constitutes an important source of primordial cleavage, the fact that 90 percent of Senegal's population is Muslim also means that the vast majority of Senegal's ethnically diverse population shares a common religious identity. Finally, unlike most other states in Africa, where particularistic ethnic identities have remained firmly implanted, the colonial and postcolonial periods in Senegal have witnessed a broad movement toward assimilation by the Wolofs of other ethnic groups, thus leading to the Wolofization of many segments of Senegalese society.

Cameroon's principal social and political cleavage has been the division between its two regions, West and East, which were under the colonial control respectively of Britain and France and were only rejoined to constitute a single state in 1961. Conflict between particular ethnic groups has

251

certainly not been absent, and the ethnic identities of the populations of these two regions have constituted a significant barrier to their effective amalgamation. But the different European languages and the different colonial experience of the populations of the two regions have provided the most tangible bases for sub-national identities. Now that the federation has been dismantled and the country structurally unified, it is quite possible that these regional identities will assume less salience, but integration may be further impeded by more particularistic ethnic identities taking on new importance.

The people of Somalia are rather singular in Africa in that they share a common language, a broadly homogeneous culture, and a single religion. And yet as I. M. Lewis states in his chapter, "The linguistically and culturally distinct divisions that threaten the fragile cohesion of most African states are here replaced by kinship-based ties which, though they lack the trappings of cultural uniqueness, are arguably even more deeply entrenched and paralyzing in their effects." Somewhat ironically, effective political solidarity in this segmentary society has moved to much lower levels in recent years, intensifying what Lewis terms "small group particularism." This development has resulted from the success recent regimes have had in achieving accommodation with Ethiopia and Kenya over the Somali irredentist movement, and from the roughly equal opportunities the current military regime has given the larger clan divisions to participate in the ruling councils. The reduction of conflict at higher levels has thus in a sense generated intensified conflict at lower levels.

Aidan Southall's discussion of the colonial period in Uganda demonstrates how ethnic identities there tended to rigidify as a result of the colonial experience. More importantly, the colonial era left Uganda saddled with the practically insoluble problem of how to incorporate the privileged Buganda into a unified state. In this context of ethnic hostility, President Obote came to rely more and more heavily on his own ethnic brethren, the Lang'o. Resentment over growing Lang'o predominance in the army and elsewhere helped provoke the military coup which brought General Amin to power. Under Amin other ethnic groups have attempted to attain ascendance in the ongoing ethnic tug-of-war. Even the sharp governmental attack on Uganda's Asian minority failed to stimulate any lasting cohesion among Uganda's black population. As Southall writes, "At present Ugandans still have a strong tendency to interpret conflict in ethnic terms, and so tend to precipitate it."

Variations among these four states in the dynamics of ethnic interaction are paralleled by differing approaches to the promotion of national cohesion and intergroup accommodation. Donal Cruise O'Brien considers "political clientelism" the most effective integrating force in Senegal. Muslim saints gather around themselves clients whose interests they represent with the bureaucracy and with the political leaders in Dakar. This extra-institutional arrangement permits appeals for assistance from the periphery to be heard by those at the center; it also provides channels through which patronage can flow. These patron-client linkages do not constitute a basis for the equitable distribution of benefits, but as O'Brien explains, "Representation along these lines, while perpetuating and even reinforcing communal inequalities paradoxically seems to give the state enough popular support to contain communal strife."

Victor LeVine's discussion of Cameroon focuses upon the establishment of the unitary state in May 1972. He sees this event as a dramatic illustration of Cameroon's approach to integration, which has emphasized the use of state power and even coercion to promote what he calls integration by absorption. The Cameroon effort, according to LeVine, has been relatively effective in state-building, but without comparable attention accorded to nation-building.

The military government in Somalia has managed to achieve equilibrium among the country's major clans by equitably sharing key government posts among them. The regime has felt inhibited, however, from capitalizing on Somalia's cultural unity for fear that arousal of Somali nationalism would rekindle the irredentist movement and thereby engender renewed conflict with Kenya and Ethiopia. As Lewis points out, the current situation of extreme lineage particularism "highlights the ambivalence of a cultural heritage that promises unity only at the price of division." It is too early to assess whether recent efforts by the military leadership to create a mobilization state of a Maoist type will promote the kind of organic unity that the regime seeks.

A recurrent theme in the approaches adopted by Uganda's governments to national integration has been the need to eliminate the special privileges enjoyed by a particular ethnic or racial group under the preceding regime. The Obote government, through the centralization of power and other measures, tried to incorporate the semi-autonomous Buganda into the state, while President Amin has confronted the pockets of privilege seemingly enjoyed by the Asian community and by Obote's own ethnic group, the Lang'o. Southall's concluding assessment is that Amin's "military regime has enforced a passive national integration at increasing cost."

It is clearly difficult, if not impossible, to generalize about the state of national integration in Africa as a whole. One can certainly point to some hopeful signs in the past few years. Nigeria has recovered from its civil war. In the Sudan, after years of insurgent activity by southern groups against northern control, a political settlement seems to have been achieved. The Somali irredentist movement has become relatively quiescent. Yet recurrent strife between Hutus and Watutsis in Burundi shows no sign of abatement. The absence of overt ethnic conflict in other states is often the result of firm, even repressive, military or one-party control rather than intergroup accommodation. Certainly the resurgence of ethnic conflict during the Second Republic in Ghana indicates that periods of ethnic calm under repressive one-party or military governments may be followed by renewed ethnic tension when competitive politics are reintroduced. The experience of states like Somalia and Nigeria also suggests that when strife among a country's major ethnic groups is reduced, the segmentary structure permits the locus of conflict to move to lower levels with tension increasing among ethnic subdivisions. Discord among ethnic subgroups generally constitutes a less severe threat to the state, but it nevertheless poses obstacles to effective national integration. Thus evidence can certainly be cited to demonstrate that many of Africa's multi-ethnic states are becoming increasingly viable, and yet the persistence of considerable ethnic conflict, both manifest and latent, indicates that the integration process in Africa is far from complete.

Chapter 13

Clan, Community, Nation: Dimensions of Political Loyalty in Senegal

by Donal B. Cruise O'Brien

The Political Clan

"The clan is a Senegalese evil, which has been with us for long generations, constantly denounced by the party, but always increasing in strength."
This official verdict by former Minister of the Interior Cissé Dia reflects
an unofficial consensus, that "clans" are the effective units of political
competition in the Senegalese single-party state. He added: "In almost
every region, we witness passionate confrontation, occasionally armed
struggle, between clans which all claim affiliation to the governing party."[1]
It should perhaps be made clear at the outset that the "clan" in local Senegalese parlance has nothing or very little in common with the normal usage
of the term among social anthropologists. The modern political clan in
Senegal is not defined by kinship, real or imagined, although kinship relations may exist and may help to reinforce political solidarity within a given
clan group. There is no requirement for a common revered ancestor; no
clanic name; no shared taboo; no rule of exogamy. The clan is a political
faction, operating within the institutions of the state and the governing
party. It exists above all to promote the interests of its members through
political competition, and its first unifying principle is the prospect of the
material rewards of political success. Political office and the spoils of office
are the very definition of success.

The prevalent practice of clan politics in Senegal makes for a type of
situation quite familiar to political scientists, that of the spoils system.[2]

The patron-client relationship, which is at the core of the clan, is also one which has been very widely discussed in other countries. Some scholars even claim a more or less universal applicability for the model of political clientelism. The factional politics decried by the Senegalese Minister of the Interior certainly does not constitute a specifically Senegalese problem. But situations of a broadly similar type do retain a particular local character, and it is the purpose of this chapter to deal with the social context that has produced clan politics as the particular Senegalese form of spoils-oriented factionalism. The character of Senegal's communal divisions, broadly and narrowly defined, helps to explain among other things the moral dimensions of a superficially amoral situation. Clan politics may then be interpreted not as a mere problem of party organization (the official view), but as a reflection of the real bases of social solidarity within the Senegalese state.

There are a number of important problems in the study of this form of political factionalism which should be mentioned here. The first of these lies in the informal character of the clan, the official disapproval to which it is at least nominally subject, and the consequently rather furtive character of clan allegiances. For political actors, clan solidarity is normally seen to be only characteristic of their opponents; although in dealing with the opposition, one may look to friends, protectors, or clients in an identical manner. A further problem lies in the instability and shifting character of the clan group. The clan is not a political institution in any acceptable sense; membership may change quite rapidly with political fortune, and the effective factional unit is defined by a situation of competition which depends on the availability of a prize. Hierarchical organization within party and state means that clans at any given level seek alliances at other levels, and these alliances also tend to shift with political fortune. The clan is thus subject to powerful strains on the political ties between equals or unequals. But for all the instability of any given clan group, one cannot but remark on the overall durability of the clan as a form of political organization in Senegal — denounced (as Cissé Dia points out) for more than 50 years, and still going strong.

Clan politics is here understood as factionalism at each level of the state and party hierarchy, and not particularly, as central government politicians would have it, as the problem of the localities.[3] The center also has clan alliances and its sectional contacts with local notables, so that factionalism should properly be seen as a broad principle of political action within the Senegalese state. Seen in this manner, and with regard to the communal social basis of political life, the examination of clan politics may yield a positive understanding of the phenomena conventionally labeled as "corruption" and "nepotism." Where these last have become general principles of political action, it may be more fruitful to see them as such, rather than as deviations from an officially proclaimed norm that is honored above all in the breach. Corruption and nepotism correspond fairly closely to patronage and factionalism, and the stigma attached to the former pair of terms can obscure serious analysis. Clans in particular may be seen as the democratic dimension of the Senegalese state, as a means for local notables (and indirectly their followers) to assert claims on the governing elite. Possible access to patronage in this manner helps to explain the otherwise surprisingly docile attitude of peasants in the face of bureaucratic exploitation. Some peasants do benefit substantially from government handouts, under or over the counter, especially through the intermediary Muslim saint.[4] It is also the case that handouts go above all to those geographical areas from which the government extracts most revenue—the peanut zone — a weighted proportional allocation with its own standards of equity. But of course it would be very wrong to attempt to idealize such a situation. Clan politics provides an accurate reflection of the social and economic inequalities that exist within the Senegalese state, inequalities within and between the communities that make up Senegalese society. In reflecting such inequalities, factionalism certainly tends to their preservation. It also, as will be argued, does much to reinforce the fragile political institutions of the Senegalese state.

Communities

Patrons and clients, operating in groups and with shifting alliances, are the stuff of Senegalese politics. This situation implies that social inequalities are expressed in political terms primarily in competing alliances, each of which draws recruits from several levels in the hierarchy of power, wealth, and prestige. No analysis of "class" tendencies in Senegalese society, such as I have attempted elsewhere,[5] can afford to disregard this major political fact. The Wolof peasants, for example, do indeed have definable economic interests which set them at odds with the Senegalese state, but in political terms it remains crucial that the Wolof are not united, and that in this latter regard, they are not alone among Senegal's ethnic groups. Segmentary conflict appears stronger than nascent class antagonism. The argument here is that segmentary conflict cannot be fully understood in patron-client terms, but must be seen against a background that includes the broader bases of social differentiation in Senegal. Clientelism at a political level works within a context of social communalism. An extension of this argument is that the particular character of political clientelism in Senegal is in some measure shaped by the character of community divisions within that state. This point will be argued in several ways, but in the "class" perspective it should be noted that in this case one does not find any significant tendency for class and community boundaries to coincide—politically a most explosive combination in all postcolonial states.

A study of communal allegiances is politically crucial in that it establishes the boundaries of subjective identification within Senegalese society. To identify these boundaries as "subjective" is not to argue that they are in any sense illusory, in contrast with the "objective," antagonistic interests of social classes. The subjective categories of community correspond to real differences and potential antagonisms, whether in political or economic terms. Several dimensions of community loyalty must be examined here — notably those of ethnic group, of religion and locality — in understanding the plural or polycommunal character of Senegalese society. Each of these dimensions is relevant to the Senegalese citizen in his response to the fundamental question, Who are my people? And if the answers to this question may still appear illusory to some in the light of emerging class divisions, it can only be said that this is one illusion that can lay claim to universality. It is characteristic of Senegal, as of other postcolonial states in Africa, that the boundaries of the state do not as yet coincide with those of national identity. But it shall also be argued that the elements of a "Senegalese" consciousness are present within the multiplicity of communal allegiances. It may indeed be the partial reality of Senegalese nationhood that makes possible the full efflorescence of communally inspired clan politics.

The linguistic and cultural groupings labeled as "tribal" ("national" being a term pre-empted by the postcolonial state) are, of course, of primary significance among communal affiliations. The sense of a shared history, in precolonial and colonial times, may reinforce communal solidarity. But the elementary fact is that people in the rural areas speak the language of their own ethnic group and are seldom very proficient in any other tongue. Linguistic barriers necessarily inhibit contacts, let alone a sense of mutual solidarity, between such groups. The 1960-1961 Senegalese census distinguishes seven major ethnic categories[6] with populations exceeding 100,000, as indicated in Table 13-1, and nine minor ones. Such communal diversity has its roots in precolonial history, when several of the major ethnic groups had the rudiments, in varying degrees, of a centralizing political and institutional structure, and when contacts between such polities were often antagonistic and military in character. But it is important to stress the manner in which colonial rule not only increased pacific contact between these groups, but also developed new forms of inequality between them. The growth of new colonial cities, centers of commerce and even of some light industry, offered a range of employment opportunities, the best of which went to those who could secure an education in the French language. The extension of commercial agriculture through the hinterland, which was most marked in those areas in reasonable proximity to the railway line, enabled the cash-cropping areas to develop while the subsistence-farming (or pastoral) zones tended to stagnate. Each of these broad tendencies — urban and rural — promoted new forms of inequality in general, but in specific terms they worked especially to the advantage of the Wolof people.

TABLE 13-1 *Principal Tribes in Senegal, Population 1960-1961*

	1960-1961	PERCENTAGE OF TOTAL
Wolof	1,116,000	36.0
Serer	431,000	13.9
Fulani	356,000	11.5
Tukulor	310,000	10.0
Diola	214,000	6.9
Mandinka	146,000	4.7
Bambara	127,000	4.1
Other	356,000	(12.9)*
	3,056,000	100.0

*Includes non-African
SOURCE: *Area Handbook for Senegal* (Washington: U.S. Army, 1963), p. 62.

The Wolof are by far the largest of Senegal's peoples — about 1.4 million in the early seventies, or more than one-third of the nation's total — and they have been fortunate in occupying both the littoral, where the colonial government established the major administrative and commercial centers, and a large part of that interior zone which was accessible to the railroad and suitable for peanut farming.[7] The Wolof in these circumstances got ahead in economic terms. They were, furthermore, the beneficiaries of a favorable colonial stereotype, being regarded by the French as "reliable" and "cooperative" as well as "intelligent," so that they tended to be recruited preferentially to the colonial administration.[8] With the extension of structures of elective representation after 1945, and with the promotion of Africans to the higher administrative levels, the Wolof again gained. These last gains, in terms of political power and influence, were, of course, directly those of the elite, but, as will be seen, with the trickle-down effect of patronage structures there were also gains even for some Wolof peasants.

Since the French conquest, the Wolof have indeed become so dominant, both in the market economy and in politics, as to occupy something of a position of cultural hegemony in Senegal. Wolof is now the lingua franca of trade; it is spoken by the great majority of town dwellers and, in varying

degrees, is familiar to an estimated two-thirds of Senegal's total population.[9] There has been, especially in the coastal towns, a tendency toward
"Wolofization" of other peoples, who find it attractive or expedient to adopt
the Wolof language and culture as their own. And Wolof dominance now
penetrates within the institutions of the dominant party and the state, despite
efforts to ensure at least the public appearance of an ethnic balance at the
top.

A second dimension of communal identification, arguably as important
in Senegal as ethnic categories, is that of religion. As revealed in Table 13-2,
the great majority of Senegalese — four-fifths or more — are Muslims; there is
a small Catholic minority and a substantial pagan one. Muslims are in turn
divided by their adherence to three large Sufi brotherhoods, which between
them account for almost all the followers (census estimate 97 percent) of
Senegalese Islam. A majority of Muslims — some three-fifths — are members
of the Tijāniyya brotherhood, with the Qāadiriyya and Mourides each
accounting for approximately another fifth. The political significance of
membership in a brotherhood has been buttressed by the practice of successive Senegalese governments, both colonial and independent, of using
Muslim leaders as the effective indirect agents of rural administration.
Brotherhood loyalties, as well as adherence to Roman Catholic or pagan
beliefs, may again correspond to certain differences in economic success
and political influence. Mourides, for example, tend to be concentrated at

TABLE 13-2 *Religion in Senegal, 1960-1961*

	MEMBERSHIP	PERCENTAGE OF TOTAL POPULATION
Muslim	2,500,000	78.5
(Tijāniyya	1,400,000)	
(Qādiriyya	415,000)	
(Mourides	575,000)	
(Other Muslim	60,000)	
Roman Catholic	107,000	3.5*
Traditional	540,000	18.0 †

*Including Europeans and Lebanese
†Probably overestimated.
SOURCE: *Area Handbook for Senegal* (Washington: U.S. Army, 1963), p. 181.

the lower levels of the urban occupational hierarchy, largely due to their
resistance to "French" education, whereas Catholics, for the opposite
reason, do well.[10] Interdenominational animosities, notably directed
against Mourides and Catholics, do exist and can become politically signif-

icant. But religious loyalties and boundaries, although sometimes overlapping with ethnic ones, do on the whole tend to follow a rather different pattern. Thus, although nine-tenths of Mourides are Wolof, most Wolof are of Tijāni affiliation; and although nine-tenths of Tukulor are Tijāni, a majority of this latter brotherhood are Wolof.[11] This pattern of cross-cutting allegiances helps to reduce the explosive potential of particular communal groups or ties.

The third significant dimension of Senegalese communalism is that of allegiance to regional or local groups. Some of the significant local groups have a basis in precolonial politics or states, as, for example, the individual states of the Wolof people (Kayor, Jolof, Walo, Baol, and Saloum). These states were suppressed and dismantled under French colonial rule, but loyalty to each given area persists even with the continuing absence of political institutions at the old state level. Other powerful localisms must be seen as the direct outcome of colonial rule. The multi-ethnic Casamance area in southern Senegal, for instance, came to develop a sense of its common existence as the French administrative *Cercle* of Ziguinchor. And a sense of identification with particular colonial towns — most notably Saint Louis, is equally a product of colonial history. Local identifications become the potential basis of political animosity when the substantial economic differences that obtain between them are taken into account. As Table 13-3 shows, government statistics suggest, for example, that per capita income is 50 percent higher in the region of Sine-Saloum than in that of Casamance. Relative prosperity in rural areas has tended to coincide with the degree of

TABLE 13-3 *Regional Population (1960-1961) and Average Per Capita Income (1965), Senegal*

	POPULATION (IN THOUSANDS)	AVERAGE PER CAPITA INCOME* (IN THOUSANDS OF FRANCS CFA)
Cap-Vert (Dakar)	397	—
Casamance	529	13·0
Diourbel	502	14.4
Fleuve	342	18.1
Oriental	151	16.0
Sine-Saloum	722	20.5
Thies	406	18.0

*Includes a value for subsistance produce.

SOURCE: Louis Verrière, "La Population du Sénégal," (Doctoral thesis, University of Dakar, 1965), p. 73; and Conseil Economique et Social, *Note Sur La Situation Agricole du Sénégal* (Dakar, 1966), Annexe 31.

involvement in commercial (peanut) agriculture. Subsistence farming and pastoral zones are poorer not only by reason of their meager production, but also in consequence of the preferential allocation of government revenue, colonial as well as postcolonial, to the peanut zone.[12] A sense of grievance, even of partial exclusion from the Senegalese political system, has developed in the most disadvantaged regions. In Casamance and Oriental provinces, for example, the people talk of a trip to the northern and western areas as "going to Senegal." The sense of regional (or local) loyalty has provided some effective mass basis for opposition parties and groups. Thus the left-wing *Parti du Régroupement Africain* (1958-1966) drew much of its support from Casamance, while the Marxist-Leninist *Parti Africain de l'Indépendence* (1957-1960) had some small success in Oriental Senegal and a more substantial success in the town of Saint Louis, particularly at the end of the 1950s, the time of the transfer of Senegal's capital from Saint Louis to Dakar.[13]

A tendency toward the communal fragmentation of the Senegalese state may appear to be implicit in the plural nature of Senegalese society. Senegal, like other postcolonial states in Africa, suffers difficulties in the construction of an effective framework of political institutions, and this in a context where "national" loyalties are present in widely varying degrees among the communities under the state's control. With the economic stagnation and decline of the post-independence decade, one might perhaps have expected communal bitterness to become more marked. Any such inclination toward fragmentation has to date been quite effectively contained, however, notably by the already mentioned tendency for the dimensions of communal loyalty to cut in different directions. The three crucial dimensions of particularism — ethnic, religious, and local — have not been mutually reinforcing to any significant degree, the tendency being for at least one dimension to cut across the other two. The fissile potential of particularism in these circumstances has been reduced; this is clear in principle, but it is also apparantly effective in fact.

In addition, its tendency toward fragmentation, a second and critically important characteristic of Senegal's plural society concerns the character of the dominant local people, the Wolof. Senegal's urban culture, that of one-fifth of the population, is a Wolof culture. Urban migrants of other ethnic groups, within a quite short space of time, may come to be considered by themselves and others as Wolof. Wolof dominance is the less resented because membership in the group is so open. Indeed, it may be said that the Wolof have very successfully practiced an assimilation policy on a mass basis where the French never succeeded. The practice of the French colonial administration, which never institutionalized and reinforced ethnic loyalties (as did the British elsewhere in Africa), must have been important in maintaining relatively open cultural boundaries.

The third notable feature of Senegal's pluralism is the unquestioned dominance of a Muslim majority whose internal divisions are contained within a shared commitment to Islam. Disputes do indeed arise between brotherhoods, or segments of brotherhoods, but the disputants themselves characteristically emphasize that "We are all Muslims, one Book, one Prophet." There is thus a common pledge to an overarching religious ideology on the part of four-fifths of the country's people, despite differences of brotherhood prayers and saintly heroes, and this commitment also helps to explain the relatively nonantagonistic character of Senegal's communal divisions.

The nonantagonistic nature of broad communal divisions is important in the social background of political struggle as it provides some basis for the construction of a viable Senegalese national polity. But it should also be borne in mind that "politics" within the framework of the state and the governing party remains essentially an activity of the Senegalese elite, principally of literate urban dwellers and their rural agents and intermediaries. In the context of political intrigue within the elite, communal segmentation — although extremely important in itself — tends to be divided and subdivided into social categories. Thus, the ethnic identification in politics, for example, is less significant than identification with a more or less extended family grouping — in certain cases, a true anthropologist's clan claiming common descent from a revered ancestor.[14] Identification with a Muslim brotherhood subdivides into local lodges, or clusters of lodges, which are nominally teaching centers but in practice also points of social and economic power. Regional identification breaks down to smaller localities, even to small towns and administrative units — *préfectures,* for example. Political identity, of course, can shift with changes in the situation and the case at issue, and loyalties to subunits do not preclude others to larger groups. This is the logic of segmentary politics, perhaps indeed of politics in general. But it remains notable in Senegal that the "larger" loyalties have seldom been mobilized.[15]

Communal division and subdivision are partly responsible for the manner in which political factions perceive their divergent interests. But they do not by any means fully explain the solidarity that obtains within a given faction. These factions are each composed of patrons and their clients, and the inherent inequality of the patron-client relationship dictates at least a mention here of the most crucial form of political inequality. Many forms of inequality — in social prestige, in wealth, and in acquired skill — are of significance in the establishment of relations of political dependency. But the major inequality in political terms in Senegal can also be seen as a broad one between the countryside and the town. Wealth and power are concentrated in the urban areas, especially in the capital city of Dakar, which has long been a powerful center of attraction for rural migrants. As noted previously, Senegal's urban dwellers — those who live in concentrations of 10,000 inhabitants and more — account for more than one-fifth of the total population; of these, more than half live in Dakar (Table 13-4). The political situation remains one in which political (and economic) power radiates from the capital city to the regional center, and then to the countryside.

TABLE 13-4 *Urbanization in Senegal (1960-1961)*

Total urban population (concentrations of more than 10,000):	686,600
Total rural population:	2,423,400
Urban percentage of total population:	22.1

Towns of more than 30,000:

Dakar	374,000
Rufisque-Bargny	50,000
Kaolack	70,000
Thiès	69,000
Saint Louis	49,000

Estimated urban growth (in 1960-1961): 200 percent in 30 years.
Estimated rural growth (in 1960-1961), 80 percent in 30 years.
SOURCE: Louis Verrière, "La Population du Sénégal" (Doctoral thesis, University of Dakar, 1965), p. 40.

Factional politics is above all a matter for urban activists. They in turn seek alliances with rural notables, but power within such alliances remains weighted on the side of urban bureaucrats or party functionaries. The centralization of the peanut trade under government control since independence, has eliminated many regional centers of private trading, wealth, and power. Government expenditure is almost all allocated from the center. There is no institutionalized local control over the amounts involved, although some influence remains over the specific use of funds. The state, centralized at Dakar, now effectively holds the purse strings for the entire territory of Senegal.

The predicament of the rural people of Senegal, and in particular of the peasants who produce the majority of the country's wealth, is thus in political terms one of weakness, internal division, and dependence. Peasants are indeed exploited as a socioeconomic category, while they remain marginal — and sometimes irrelevant — to the political operation of the state of which they are subjects. Yet it is also true that the workings of patron-client politics do permit a minority even of peasants to gain in determinate ways if they give their support to a local leader with influential connections in the city. Any nascent sense of class solidarity among peasants is thus at odds not only with broad communal divisions and relative inequalities, but also with clan political clientelism.

Rural notables, clan leaders in contemporary terms, are as indispensable to the present government of Senegal as they were in the past to the colonial administration. And they are indispensable intermediaries for what is essentially the same reason: the inadequacy of formal institutions in organizing support at a mass level. The saints of the Muslim brotherhoods in this context remain the principal actors. The leading saints are in a position to demand many favors, as they do in general remain the popularly recognized authorities in rural Senegal. Peasants benefit from the political patronage which their holy men can procure, and saints with good political connections recruit new followers on this basis. The mechanism is thus self-reinforcing. Government leaders see that preferential access to administrative favors is given to those saints who are deemed to have a large body of disciples, and the saints then use this patronage to recruit more disciples.

Without religious leadership and organization, peasants in all likelihood would simply be helpless victims of government exactions. The hostility of rural people to the state and its urban controllers is, however, tempered by the hope that they may be among the lucky ones if their local patron plays his cards right. Where this hope is consistently disappointed, in the last resort they may (and do) change their allegiance to a more favorably placed local leader. No saint can afford a record of failure in his intrigues with the national or local government authorities. The Senegalese tradition of clan politics, as it functions in the rural areas, thus provides an effective channel for patronage redistribution from the center to the localities. The existence of such structures of patronage politics, parallel with the formal or bureaucratic institutions of state administration, serves not only to soften the exploitative features of the state in rural areas, but also to provide, partially in consequence, some of the basis for a viable polity in Senegal.

State and Nation

To conclude this chapter it seems above all necessary for the author to present certain of his own judgments. An author's normative view will be present even where it is not made explicit, and there are many good reasons to make it explicit — of which the first and sufficient in this case is to avoid the appearance, if only by omission, of simply endorsing the morality of Senegal's governing clan politicians. The relevant areas of enquiry treated here in conclusion are the economic consequences of the operation of this style of politics and the principal consequences of this style in terms of the likely political future of Senegal.

The politics of patronage and communal representations, of a type broadly similar to that found in Senegal, have been found in other countries to involve certain costs in economic development. Economic stagnation, in the view of some, is the price of political stability — and the price in this sophisticated conservative view is well worth paying.[16] Senegal is indeed economically stagnant: World Bank estimates of the country's per capita "growth" rate in the 1960s are set at an annual average of −0.1 percent. But any "political" explanation for this meager performance seems of small significance when set against the harsh facts of Senegal's economic predicament: dependence on a single export crop (peanuts), the value of which has fallen fairly consistently over the past decade; the paucity of alternative agricultural produce adapted to the poor soils of most of the country; the virtual absence of mineral wealth; and a population growth estimated at 2.5 percent per annum. One may strongly doubt whether any government bent on a firmer political discipline, whether that government be one of military officers or left-wing revolutionaries, could achieve substantially more than that of President Léopold Senghor's in the face of such a bleak economic situation. The question of "stagnation as the price of political stability" at present simply does not arise in Senegal.

While clan politics appears to be little more than marginally relevant to the important problem of economic stagnation, it does seem to offer a number of very significant advantages in building a polity equipped to cope with the communal realities of Senegalese society. In the first place, modern (post-independence) clan politics represents the effective fusion of two distinct political traditions, one rural and the other urban. The historic factional political practices of Senegal's four colonial communes have persisted to the present, only superficially changed; they have now incorporated, however, the established hierarchies of the rural hinterland — in particular, the Muslim brotherhoods. As already indicated, there is a political bridge across the urban-rural gap, and the cash does cross, albeit unequally, in both directions.

Clan politics provides for existing social realities in enabling some form of representation for the various communities that make up the Senegalese state. This representation is indeed perversely proportional in giving most political weight to those communities in rural society that are most involved in the money economy upon which the state depends, and also in favoring those communities that are most effectively organized. Representation along these lines, while perpetuating and even reinforcing communal inequalities, paradoxically seems to give the state enough popular support to contain communal strife. And it is in this last area that the actual and potential achievements of clan politics can be recognized most clearly. For African states in their present phase, the dangers of communal strife seem much more immediate than the prospects of any revolutionary political solution that could render communal inequalities irrelevant by a rigorous political discipline imposed from the center. Indeed, the haunting recent history of Nigeria suggests that any such attempt to override communal realities is likely to be illusory; it will act to the immediate benefit of those communities best represented in the central government, and thus provoke hostilities in excluded communities with an outcome in violence and destruction.

Senegal at present appears to have a good chance of avoiding such a human disaster. Not only have communal antagonisms been rather well contained within the framework of clan competition, but some sense of a Senegalese national identity has emerged. This identity centers around Dakar, around the governing elite, and also, importantly, around the personality of the head of state. The political skill of President Senghor is certainly not a negligible factor in the relative stability that Senegal has enjoyed since independence. His status as member of a minority people (Serer) and a minority religion (Catholic) appears to make him an acceptable mediator for the larger communities. It is true, of course, that a "Senegalese" identity has developed to different degrees in different areas, being strongest in the northern and western areas, weakest in the southern and eastern. But it is, again, a vital element of this emergent identity that the Wolof, dominant in the larger towns and cash-crop areas of the northwest, are no ethnic exclusivists.

To consider Senegalese politics a relatively viable mechanism for the reconciliation of divergent group interests should not be to ignore the extent to which it operates to the exclusion of certain individuals and groups. There are political losers in Senegal, as elsewhere. Opposition parties, it is true, have in general been incorporated into the governing party rather than simply suppressed; but the use or threat of the state stick has been accompanied by the carrot of office. Even so, and in at least two very important instances, the banning, since 1960, of the Marxist-Leninist *Parti Africain de l'Indépendance* and the 1962-1974 detention of ex-Prime Minister Mamadou Dia, the apparatus of state repression has been used by President Senghor and his colleagues to devastating effect. The government reacts with particular decisiveness, and occasional brutality, against those of its opponents who present themselves as leftists—trade unionists and students in the Dakar disorders of 1968, for example. And there are also ideological divisions, which might be broadly categorized in left-right terms, within the governing elite itself. It must be said, however, the extragovernmental left — urban, small, and divided — scarcely at present constitutes a credible political alternative in Senegal.

The limits of Senegal's achievement have been recognized, and they are important: economic stagnation and the social inequalities of various kinds that have been perpetuated or accentuated. But the positive achievements also deserve full recognition. Senegal's present political style may appear unedifying, but it has permitted social peace and the gradual emergence of a viable national state. Senegal's political order is indeed partial and largely' extra-institutional, but it does appear to work.

Notes

1. Both quotations are drawn from a speech by Cissé Dia, then Minister of the Interior. See *Dakar-Matin,* May 17, 1967. Léopold Senghor much earlier expressed himself in similar terms: "Le népotisme est un mal Sénégalais." See *Condition Humaine,* May 2, 1950.

2. For a discussion of the spoils system, see Carl H. Lande, *Leaders, Factions, and Parties: The Structure of Philippine Politics* (New Haven: Yale University, Southeast Asia Monographs, 1966). The most useful introduction to the phenomenology of political situations such as that of Senegal is Fred Riggs, *Administration in Developing Countries* (Boston: Houghton Mifflin. 1964).

3. Francois Zuccarelli, in the only full-length study of the governing Union Progressiste Senegalaise, on the whole endorses this government view. Zuccarelli, *Un Parti Politique Africain* (Paris: Pichon et Durand-Auzias, 1970), p. 171, and throughout.

4. See D.B. Cruise O'Brien, *The Mourides of Senegal* (Oxford: Clarendon Press, 1971), pp. 262-284.

5. D. B. Cruise O'Brien, "Cooperators and Bureaucrats," *Africa,* Vol. 4, No. 4 (October 1971), pp. 263-278.

6. Of these seven, four may linguistically be treated as two only. Fulani and Tukulor, Mandinka and Bambara, are pairs effectively representing a single language.

7. A 1960 report estimated that two-thirds of the inhabitants of the peanut-growing zone were Wolof, one-quarter Serer. République du Sénégal, *Rapport General sur les Perspectives de Développement du Sénégal* (Dakar: CINAM, 1960), p. 1-1 (27).

8. Sheldon Gellar, "The Politics of Development in Senegal" (Ph. D. diss., Columbia University, 1967), p. 12.

9. This estimate is advanced in G. Wesley Johnson, *The Emergence of Black Politics in Senegal* (Stanford: Stanford University Press, 1971), p. 9.

10. Educational differences by religion are quite significant. The Dakar Census of 1955 found that among African male Christians, 76 percent spoke French and 55 percent were literate in French. Comparable figures for the Tijâni were 49 percent and 33 percent; for Mourides 30 percent and 15 percent. From *Recensement Démographique de Dakar (1955)*, Vol. 1 (Paris: Haunt Commersariat de la République, 1958), p. 37.

11. Cruise O'Brien, *The Mourides,* op. cit., pp. 242-243, provides statistical detail.

12. On inter-regional competition for government spending, and resentment of preference given to the peanut zone, Gellar, op. cit., p. 170.

13. Prior to independence in 1960, Saint Louisians monopolized the best government jobs open to Africans. Johnson, op. cit., p. 36.

14. On Wolof kinship, the best available published material is still that of D. P. Gamble, *The Wolof of Senegambia* (London : International African Institute, 1957). Abdoulaye Diop of Dakar University, whose research on the Wolof is nearing completion, will doubtless provide a wealth of information on this subject.

15. The most significant "larger" communal loyalty probably remains that of the relatively deprived southern region of Casamance, although the political sense of regional deprivation was softened with the incorporation of Assane Seck and much of the Casamance leadership into the governing party in 1966.

16. See Myron Weiner, ed., *Modernization* (New York: Basic Books, 1967), pp. 167-168. Also, Aristide Zolberg, *Creating Political Order* (Chicago: Rand McNally, 1966), pp. 73-77.

Chapter 14

Political Integration and the United Republic of Cameroon

by Victor T. LeVine

ON MAY 20, 1972, what had been the Federal Republic of Cameroon became the United Republic of Cameroon — an event that marked the ostensibly successful end of a 12-year experiment in federation unique to contemporary Africa. On the constitutional level, a unitary state replaced a federal one; on other, less tangible levels, several processes of long historical duration — political, social and economic — culminated in the reunification of two parts of what had once been the German protectorate of Kamerun, and brought to an end the separate identities of territories with widely differing political, social, administrative, and cultural traditions.[1] The event would seem to mark the victory of integrative forces at work in both territories. But did it? Whether it did or not, the event does provide an important instance wherewith to examine at close hand the workings of the so-called processes of national integration. Thus, it becomes highly instructive to inquire if what has transpired is indeed an example of national integration, or of something else, perhaps less evocative but more common on the African scene.

Within the limited ambit of this chapter, we propose, first, to examine briefly some analytical problems inherent in the concept "national integration"; second, to provide a short historical account of the steps to unification, and, third, to consider the nature of integration along several dimensions: constitutional, institutional-structural, associational, and, finally, sociopolitical. The exercise may then help to give at least a tentative answer to the question posed above.

"National Integration": Problems of Definition and Analysis

We begin with what is undisputed fact: that insofar as they use analogous language, the political leaders of Africa all espouse "national integration," whether they use the term itself, or speak of "national unity," *ujamaa* ("familyhood"), "national authenticity," or some other variation on the theme. As a political symbol, the term is rich in positive general connotations; particularly, it evokes a sense of purpose for the achievement of common, empathic links above and beyond the parochial ties of family, clan, village, or tribe. And precisely because the term is ambiguous, it has considerable instrumental value in the mobilization of support for national goals and programs. Yet beyond its general use as a term symbolizing the achievement of social and political commonalities, it has, in practice, a widely varied content. The formal literature on "political integration," though providing better-sounding definitions, does little to lessen the term's basic ambiguity. Because of limitations of space and circumstance, we cannot here review that literature.[2] Suffice it for our purposes, however, to point out several common elements stressed by leading commentators on the subject:

1. National integration is most commonly understood either as a goal or as a process, or both. The second meaning has received the greatest attention in the literature.

2. Seen as a process, its most important component is the growth or development, or both, of identifications and loyalties whose foci are national rather than parochial. That growth, seen as development toward the goal of national integration, cannot be forced, but can be — and usually is — stimulated and programmed by national governments anxious to create stable support for their policies.

3. Manifest indices of national integration may include not only such matters as levels and degrees of institutionalization, but also levels and degree of active popular support for national political groups (including parties), leaders, policies, and programs. Insofar as people are willing to be mobilized for national purposes, they can be said to be involved in the process of national integration, or at least displaying one of the salutary consequences of the process itself.

Implied in the above formulation is the proposition that national integration requires durable and largely voluntary attitudinal change, and that the term applies most specifically to societies with considerable, politically salient diversities, be they ethnic, religious, or cultural. If these implications are also seen as assumptions underlying the study of national integration, the analytical problems involved are then in clearer perspective. Two important questions must be answered before analysis can proceed: first, Is the polity plural (heterogeneous, diverse) in some consequential fashion? and, second, What evidence can be adduced to demonstrate that "integrative" attitudinal change has taken place or is taking place on a sufficiently large scale to permit the observation of a visible effect on the national polity? With respect to Cameroon, we can anticipate the answer to the first issue: clearly, Cameroon is a plural — or as Willard Johnson has put it, a "fragmentary" — society.[3] The second issue is the focus of most of the rest of this chapter.

Steps to Unity: A Historical and Contextual Summary

The key to an understanding of Cameroon politics and history is its extraordinary cultural, ethnic, economic, and political diversity. Its 6.2 million people constitute a mix of more than 150 linguistically identifiable ethnic groups, the majority of which are clustered in the southwestern quadrant, along the Cameroon mountain and plateau chain, historically an ethnic shatter zone dividing the Niger and Congo river basins.[4] Historically, interethnic cleavages in Cameroon have presented a formidable array of social, political, and economic tensions, of which the most important, and politically fissiparous, have been those between the northern Fulani and their southern neighbors; between various elements of the ethnically related Bamiléké Tikar-Bamoun-Bangwa configuration of groups; between the coastal Duala and their proximity inland neighbors; and, within the last 30 years, between the aggressive and active Bamiléké and the various peoples with whom they have come into contact in the process of their dispersal south and east from their highland homes in the southwest. An important political fact of life is that the long-festering rebellion (1955-1965) led by the Marxist Union of Cameroon Peoples (UPC) party found a focus and finally spent itself in the Bamiléké homeland. To ethnic fragmentation must be added such crosscutting cleavages as those of religion (Muslim north vs. southern Christian; Muslim vs. animist; Christian vs. animist; and so forth); economic modes (pastoral vs. agricultural); economic development (considerable primary and secondary industry in the south vs. little in the north); plus those significant differences of language, education, administration, and political style that are directly attributable to the different colonial experiences of the former West Cameroon (under British rule) and East Cameroon (under French rule).

The dimensions of these various cleavages and differences, and their resultant tensions and conflicts, are more fully examined in the several volumes dealing with Cameroon politics and economy.[5] The point here is that the fragmented nature of Cameroon society has had important ramifications for the country's politics and, as we shall see, has made the integrative efforts of its leaders exceedingly difficult.

Cameroon's colonial past unquestionably affected and undoubtedly contributed to its sociopolitical fragmentation. Between 1884 and 1916 the then Kamerun was a German protectorate. The victorious Allies of the First World War proceeded to partition the territory between them in 1916: two noncontiguous segments in the west, along the north-south Cameroon mountain line and making up one-fifth of the former Kamerun's area, came under British administration, and the rest, under French rule. In 1922 the League of Nations made "C" mandates of the two territories, imposing what turned out to be only nominal international supervision on the two colonial administrations. In 1947 the League's successor, the United Nations, converted the mandates into Trust Territories and therewith placed upon the administering states a new set of obligations directed toward eventual self-determination and possible self-government by the peoples in the two territories. In a 1959 United Nations-supervised plebiscite in the Northern Cameroons section of the British Cameroons, the voters rejected union with neighboring northern Nigeria and deferred the question of such attachment until both Nigeria and the French Cameroon became independent. On January 1, 1960, the French Cameroon became an independent republic, and on October 1, 1961, as a consequence of another U.N. plebiscite held in the British Cameroons (this time, in both parts), the Federal Republic of Cameroon came into existence, "re-uniting" the Cameroon Republic (which became the East Cameroon state) and the former British Southern Cameroons (which became the West Cameroon state). Another result of the plebiscite, a result received with ill grace in the republic, was that the former Northern (British) Cameroons became a part of the Sardauna Province of Northern Nigeria. The Federal Republic of Cameroon challenged that latter outcome in the World Court, but failed to reverse it. In any case, in 1961 the first bilingual federation in Africa was born, bringing together peoples whose separate colonial experiences provided marked contrasts not only in language, law, administration, and education, but also in such less tangible matters as political style and expectations. The situation called for restraint by leaders on both sides. The size of the vote in Southern Cameroons against joining the Cameroon Republic (29 percent) made it clear to President Ahmadou Ahidjo and his colleagues that complete "federalization," that is, imposition of national controls over the wide range of matters specified in the 1961 Constitution, would have to be a gradual matter so as to avoid the impression of an "Eastern takeover." Moreover, many West Cameroon politicians, including some ardent supporters of the new federation, were concerned about their own political future, were worried about preserving West Cameroon institutions in which they had a stake, and fretted about the fate of British traditions (including the English language) to which most West Cameroonians had become accustomed, if not attached.

This initial phase of the new republic—to some, the "honeymoon period"—lasted until 1966, when upon forceful initiative from the federal government in Yaounde all the surviving political parties in East and West Cameroon merged into the single Cameroon National Union (CNU). The merger turned Cameroon into a de facto (if not de jure) single-party state. Also, by 1966 most of the important governmental functions that had not come under federal jurisdiction in 1961 but remained "provisionally" under state control, were themselves "federalized". In effect, the unitary political die had been cast, despite the constitutional survival of separate state and national governments, official policies of "bilingualism," and tributes to the vitality of the separate eastern and western cultures.[6] All that was left to be done was a political mopping-up operation and preparation for the creation of a unitary state.

In October and November 1971, the country's three trade unions dissolved themselves to permit the formation of one central trade union within the framework of the Cameroon National Union.[7] Finally, on May 20, 1972, a national referendum approved the new constitution of the United Republic of Cameroon, 3, 217, 056 votes to 158.

Constitutional Integration

A venerable political tradition has it that there are two kinds of constitutions, the *constitution octroyée,* that is, handed down from on high, and the *constitution évoluée,* that is, the product of some sort of political development. The distinction is not unimportant for being old; it serves to remind us that constitutions, particularly those of the latter variety, often embody the values, goals, and aspirations of those that write them as well as reflect crucial political bargains struck by their authors. In this sense, the Cameroon constitutions of 1961 and 1972 are interesting mirrors of the country's changing political realities as perceived by its leaders in those two years.

The 1961 Constitution represents an uneasy compromise between the centralizing efforts of President Ahidjo and his eastern colleagues and the desire of western politicians led by Prime Minister John Ngu Foncha to retain as much political identity as possible for the English-speaking western state. Foncha, to be sure, had campaigned for reunification, and his party, the Kamerun National Democratic Party (KNDP), had carried the former Southern Cameroons into federal union in the 1961 plebiscite. There is, however, further evidence to show that Foncha's support for the federal option came not only late in the game but somewhat reluctantly, and that he and his colleagues had also considered other alternatives, such as independence and prolonged trusteeship.[8] This evidence notwithstanding, Foncha did support federation with the French East and he did support the 1961 Constitution, which, among its other provisions, permitted him to become vice president of the new republic. It had other provisions designed to gain the West's support, too: bilingualism was entrenched ("The Official Languages of the Federal Republic shall be French and English")[9]; by virtue of a statement on population, 10 of the federal legislature's 50 members had to be from the West; and separate elections were to be held for all three legislatures — those of the federal government and the East and West states. The constitution provided for separate eastern and western legislatures, for separate state executives, for the maintenance of the West's House of Chiefs and established a federal legislature, a federal executive, and a complete range of federal ministries. There was, moreover, provision for an odd sort of unit veto on federal legislation that could be exercised by the West's deputies to the Federal Assembly if it seemed on the verge of passing legislation contrary to the West's vital interest.[10] However, given the composition of the Federal Assembly (almost all the West's deputies were Ahidjo's men), the provision was never invoked. The capstone of these constitutional guarantees, of course, lay in the fact that the federal president and vice president could not come from the same state; in practice it meant that the East would provide the president (Ahidjo), and the West, the vice president (initially, Foncha and later, Solomon Tandeng Muna).

Ahidjo and his colleagues, nonetheless, got enough constitutional wording to permit their vision of political reality to become a self-fulfilling prophecy. In retrospect, it is now evident that Ahidjo had few illusions about the eventual relationship between the two states: the eastern state 10 times the size of its western partner, with almost five times its population, immeasurably greater resources, and a much higher level of economic development, had to be the dominant element in the new union. Thus, the federal government, inevitably dominated by eastern politicians, would by sheer force of circumstance become the fulcrum of increasing national power. The 1961 Constitution, accordingly, gave the federal president the power to constitute or dismiss state governments, made him a legislator in his own right, and (true to Ahidjo's preference), set him up as an active, powerful chief executive instead of a mere figurehead. In addition, the constitution was so worded as to permit an increase in federal jurisdiction to the point that most important internal matters would, within a short time, come under federal jurisdiction (which, indeed, did come to pass by 1966). Finally, the power of the purse rested squarely in federal hands, which meant that with the exception of limited local taxation for local purposes levied by local administrations, all moneys for major projects and development would come from the federal government.[11]

In sum, then, the 1961 document had all the hallmarks of a constitution évoluée: it bore ample testimony to a set of important political compromises thrashed out in lengthy conferences. The 1972 Constitution, in contrast, is close to being a constitution octroyée. It appears to have been worked out within federal precincts by men who, given the single-party state and the neutralization of western champions of states' rights (like Foncha and former western Prime Minister Augustin Jua), were able to fashion a document reflecting the centralizing views of President Ahidjo and his closest associates. To all intents and purposes there was no national debate on its provisions; the pre-referendum campaign was designed to secure an overwhelming turnout in its favor rather than to provoke discussion on its contents. The official view is that the Constitution of 1972 and its massive popular approval represent the final triumph of national integration; a less charitable view, expressed to us at the time in a letter from a West Cameroonian, is that "irresistible political power has now forced integration upon us."[12]

The 1972 Constitution eliminates by omission the office of vice president (considered superfluous), the prime ministers and cabinets of the states, the two state legislatures, and the West's House of Chiefs. It is also fairly unambiguous about the location of power: "State authority shall be exercised by the President of the Republic, and the National Assembly."[13] Most of the effective power, however, resides in the president. He appoints and dismisses all ministers, and despite a list of legislative powers reserved to the unicameral National Assembly, the president may enact ordinances that have the force of law and that execute provisions of the constitution not otherwise spelled out therein. He is also, by implication, the principal source of legislation. Given the duration of the assembly's sessions—two of 30 days each, with opening dates decided by the president—and the fact that only the CNU is represented in the assembly, it seems unlikely that it could be anything more than a periodic convention assembled to endorse the government's proposals. In only one respect does the constitution recognize the country's bilingualism: the official languages are French and English, though interestingly enough the document also stipulates that only the French text of the constitution is "authentic."[14] Also missing from the new constitution is the Federal Economic and Social Council,[15] a body that never had much active life or power, but that did manage to give some additional representation to the country's diverse interests. In short, one valid conclusion that can be made about Cameroon so far as its new constitution is concerned is that its once-flourishing political pluralism has seen its last days.

Is the constitution evidence of national integration in Cameroon? Obviously, it *is* evidence of the integrative desires of the country's active political elite, and its approval by 98.7 percent of those voting in the May 20 referendum could well signify the kind of nationwide support necessary to achieve national integration. But whether such evidence is *sufficient* to prove that support is another matter. Other data, of a less aggregate and inferential variety, is needed.

Institutional-Structural Integration

We are here concerned primarily with those institutions and structures of government whose impact is most likely to be directly felt by the citizen. These include local authorities, police and gendarmerie, tax collectors, service agencies, and state enterprises. To what extent have they been integrated, and how does such integration relate to the broader issues of widening parochial loyalties, of promoting structural changes that catalyze widespread attitudinal change?

To begin with, under the terms of a presidential decree issued on June 8, 1972, outlining the general organization and responsibilities of the new unitary government, all aspects of all governmental activities throughout the country have been firmly placed under national control.[16] The 1961 Constitution permitted, insofar as it gave governmental functions to the state governments, a limited degree of political devolution. For example, the West Cameroon prime minister controlled the legal and judicial departments and the state police. Various of his secretaries of state (ministers) were responsible for state development (including the activities of the Cameroon Development Corporation), community development, public services, natural resources, lands and surveys, primary education, local governments and customary courts, prisons, lotteries, and cooperatives. Even though these functions were in fact also subject to federal supervision, at least between 1961 and 1966, the West Cameroon government exercised some real authority in these areas. No longer. The June 8 decree put everything under direct national control, from kindergarten education and town planning to sports associations, from the "development and diffusion of culture" to the certification of "the wholesomeness of animal foodstuffs."[17]

Consonant with the new centralization, local administrative organs have undergone their third major change since 1961—all away from local autonomy. More accurately, the major changes have been in the former

West Cameroon; centralized administration has been a fact of life in East Cameroon since the days of French rule. Before 1972 a variant of the classic French prefectural system operated in East Cameroon, with each of some 30 departments headed by its own prefect, who was in turn responsible for the lesser jurisdictions under his control, the *sous-départements* and *sous-préfectures*. This system operated jointly with another involving urban and rural communes and an array of major and minor chieftaincies, the latter being holdovers from the colonial period. The nature of the relationships between the chiefs and the government's agents was supposed to be one in which the chiefs were subordinate; in practice, however, it depended on their real powers, their influence in Yaoundé, and whether the government needed them for its own purposes. Thus, the sultan of Foumban and the lamidos of Rei-Bouba, Garoua, and Ngaoundéré tended to exercise a great deal of autonomous power. In West Cameroon, the prefects replaced the district officers, the principal local officials before federation; unlike the prefects in East Cameroon, however, who derived their full authority from and reported only to federal sources, those in West Cameroon continued to be responsible to the West's secretary of state for the interior and to the western prime minister in some matters while being subject to federal control in others. The prefects in both states reported to federal inspectors— there were five inspectorates in the East, and the West constituted one single inspectorate—who in turn were responsible directly to the federal minister of state for territorial administration.

Of particular note in these arrangements was the position of the federal inspector in West Cameroon. Constitutionally, as noted above, the western prefects operated with somewhat divided loyalties. In fact, it became very clear within five years of federation that the real power lay not with the West Cameroon government, but with the federal inspector in Buea. Significantly, the occupants of that office were all from the East; the last incumbent made a point of speaking only French, though it was said he spoke good English. "The Federal Inspector in the West makes his point well," one Cameroon teacher wrote us, "the power lies East, and if you want to talk about important things, you must talk French."[18] The power and importance of this functionary, it need hardly be added, was a source of irritation to many West Cameroonians still jealous of their state's identity. They felt that an "eastern viceroy" in Buea violated the terms and spirit of federation.[19] The net effect of these arrangements, as Johnson points out, "was to progressively deprive West Cameroon of an autonomous administrative structure at the district or local level."[20]

Creation of the unitary state provided the impetus for finishing the job of centralization with respect to local, district, and regional institutions.

On July 24, 1972, a presidential decree set up seven provinces (South Central, Eastern, Coastal, Northern, Northwestern, Western, and Southwestern, the latter two constituting the former western state), each of which is divided into *départements* (39 in all), subdivisions (*arrondissements*), and districts. The provinces are headed by governors, the departments by prefects, the subdivisions by subprefects, and the districts by heads. In one minor respect, some older structures remain in the new arrangement: in the ex-East Cameroon area, *communes* (comprising three types of local governments) continue to function, and in the ex-West Cameroon, local councils continue to enjoy limited authority. Of significance is the fact that not much, save some nomenclature, has changed formally from the system that operated under the federation; however, the reality of power has changed: the eastern system now prevails throughout. As before, the whole governmental apparatus falls under the jurisdiction of the minister for territorial administration.

Is Cameroon experiencing national integration? In the formal sense, there has unquestionably been institutional-structural integration, but like Cameroon's constitutionally mandated territorial integration, it is integration largely by initative from the top. It is not, in any case, evidence of changes in attitudes or loyalties, though in time these structural changes may well engender habitual relationships that in turn affect basic, parochial identifications.

Associational Integration

Though the new constitution specifically permits political parties and groups to operate, Cameroon's once thriving pluralism of political parties and groups came to an effective end in East Cameroon in 1962, and in the federation as a whole in 1966. Before independence some 117 political parties and groups existed in East Cameroon, and at least two dozen in British Cameroons. By the time of federation in 1961 those numbers had been reduced to a mere handful — five in the East, three in the West — through a complex set of processes including disintegration, attrition, and proscription on the one hand, and absorption, integration, and amalgamation on the other. We have set forth the details of that story elsewhere;[21] suffice it for our purposes to note that by 1961 only two parties really mattered, and these were the governing parties of the two states, the KNDP (Kamerun National Democratic Party) in the West, and the *Union Camerounaise* in the East. The other groups were in opposition, but their opposition was both ineffectual and short-lived. In 1962, by imprisoning the heads of the four remaining eastern opposition parties for an alleged plot against the state, President Ahidjo effectively, if not formally, created a single-party regime in the East. Four years later the leaders of what was left of the eastern opposition—including three of the four who had been imprisoned in 1962—agreed to merge into the single national party, the Cameroon National Union. Similarly, the remnants of the western opposition, having seen either the light or the handwriting on the wall, together with the KNDP, joined the CNU at the same time. Since then the CNU has been the only party in Cameroon, and it incorporated under its trade-union wing, but without separate identity, the country's three trade-union federations.

With the exception of religious bodies, Cameroonian groups that operate outside the country, and such organizations as the chamber of commerce, all social, cultural, professional, and commercial associations are now expected to fall, however loosely, under some branch of the CNU. Those functioning outside Cameroon include the remnants of the exiled wing of the *Union des Populations du Cameroun* (UPC) party and Cameroon student organizations in Europe and the United States; these groups have virtually no influence in Cameroon itself.

Not only has the CNU achieved almost complete associational integration in Cameroon, but it now fully reflects a characteristic aspect of other single-party states: on the leadership level, the party is virtually identical with the state. Of the 24 ministers appointed to the Cameroon Government on July 3, 1972, 10 are members of the CNU's National Political Bureau, another 10 occupy high positions in the national and regional CNU hierarchies, and the remaining four are local party leaders. And of course, Ahidjo, president of the United Republic, is also national president of the CNU.

Before 1966 there was some debate in Cameroon elite circles about whether the country ought to have a "unified" political party (*parti unifié*) or a "single" party (*parti unique*)—a vague amalgam of groups under a single banner and doctrine or a party that, having digested all other parties, stood alone. Ahidjo for good tactical reasons declared himself in favor of the parti unifié, but it was the parti unique, under the pressure of events and with the assistance of Ahidjo and his colleagues, that came to pass.[22]

Sociopolitical Integration

We come now to the key question: Given the reality of centralization on constitutional, institutional, and associational levels in Cameroon, to what extent has this centralization been matched by the growth of supportive, supraparochial attitudes throughout the country? Note that the question does not imply the necessity of ideological consensus, or even broad agreement on national goals. Cameroon continues to tolerate a high degree of cultural pluralism, and the political system, by incorporating a variety of political orientations with a minimum of coercion, has shown itself capable of considerable flexibility. The question refers to the growth of attitudes that recognize the primacy of the larger Cameroonian national symbols, and that make possible the mobilization of support for the goals and programs of the regime.

The data on this issue are fragmentary, but highly suggestive. For one thing, on the elite level, the system has achieved marked integration. Almost all the influential forces in Cameroon have been incorporated or co-opted into the system, and almost all the important political factions feel they have reasonable access to the power center. The regime has brought into its ranks a number of the heads of the former UPC, and other onetime opposition leaders have either been absorbed by the party or government — or been given opportunity to join. The regime has also been able to mute, though not dispel entirely, the fears of West Cameroonians over being oppressively dominated by their eastern brethren.[23] The very real economic benefits conferred by unity upon West Cameroon — new roads and railway ties to the East, the revival and stimulation of its agriculture, participation in the country's 9 percent growth rate — and a high degree of administrative efficiency have all contributed to allaying uncertainty in the West. The evidence of the vote for the new constitution, though it attests to a considerable degree to the organizational effectiveness of the CNU, also indicates — because of a noticeable lack of coercion in getting out the vote — that the symbols of unity do have a hold on the voting population.

All these manifestations of integration notwithstanding, doubts still linger in West Cameroon about the intentions of the national leadership. These doubts are given some substance by the sense of isolation felt by western leaders with positions in Yaoundé, by the cavalier and quite one-sided manner in which bilingualism was implemented at the Federal University, by what has been perceived by some as the arrogance of federal officials in West Cameroon, and by the hastiness with which some westerners believe the unitary state was achieved. Then, too, disturbing instances of ethnic conflict, particularly between the Bamiléké and their neighbors, continue to recur.

Further, grumbling in the north about the marked economic imbalance between north and south continues to raise hackles in the national legislature, despite progress with the Transcameroon Railway, which was partly designed to bring the two sections closer together. Divisive tensions still exist in Cameroon, in other words, and ethnic, economic, and political particularism still pose serious, though not insoluble, problems for the national leadership.[24]

Finally, it is not inappropriate to observe that the CNU, despite its pretensions to being a truly national party, has failed to become a genuine mass party in which power emanates from the people. It remains very much a party of elites, given the widely-observed lethargy of its local cadres and the general lack of enthusiasm, not to mention militancy, of its adherents. In this respect the party has failed to implement one of its prime goals, that of becoming the associational catalyst of national integration. Instead, the party appears to have become a secondary auxiliary of the state, its cadres behaving more like government agents and civil servants than mobilizers of popular support. In effect, the task of national integration has become the charge of government, not that of an active, dynamic party.[25]

Conclusion

The above review of the state of Cameroonian integration, admittedly both summary and impressionistic, nevertheless suggests several possible answers to the question posed at the beginning of our essay regarding its direction and scope:

1. Cameroonian leaders have sought integration through the processes of state-building and not nation-building. They stressed initially the construction of stable administrative and economic institutions as a firm base for the exercise of the regime's power rather than the development of a mass base of popular support. Popular support, the regime's actions imply, will flow from the success of a stable government.

2. The political integration of West Cameroon has been integration by absorption, much more than it has been integration by persuasion. By successfully using the instrumentalities of national power (including coercion) at several crucial junctures during the past 10 years, the national leadership has both reduced West Cameroon's "state's rights" politicians to impotence and eroded, then finally eliminated, what local political or economic autonomy remained to it after 1961.

3. The process of integration by absorption in Cameroon is almost unique to Africa, though not uncommon elsewhere. Only one federal system, the Nigerian system, now remains in Africa, and it seems hardly likely to move

toward greater unity in the near future. In other African states, there has certainly been constitutional absorption, but very little evidence of genuine integration on the social and attitudinal levels: Eritrea continues to give Ethiopia political indigestion, and Zanzibar remains a contrast to mainland Tanzania.

Finally, let it be said that the Cameroonian political experiment—first creating a federation and then dismantling it in favor of a unitary state— has served to enhance rather than undermine Cameroon's enviable political stability. Blessed with firm and pragmatic leadership, a comparatively good economic resource base, a generally loyal and supportive citizenry, excellent interstate relations in Africa, and overseas friends with investment capital, Cameroon could well serve as a model for some of its less fortunate neighbors.

Notes

1. German Kamerun once comprised not only what is now the United Republic, but also the former British Northern Cameroons (which became part of Northern Nigeria's Sardauna Province in 1961), plus some 107,000 sq. miles of what had been the French Congo, ceded to Germany in 1911 in a deal with France. This latter area returned to French control in 1916 at the conclusion of World War I hostilities in Kamerun. The rest was divided into French (3/5ths of the territory) and British (2/5ths) League of Nations Mandates. In 1946 these became UN Trusteeships.

2. Of particular relevance to our discussion are: Philip E. Jacob and J. V. Toscano, eds., *The Integration of Political Communities* (Philadelphia: Lippincott, 1964); Myron Weiner, "Political Integration and Political Development," in *Political Modernization: A Reader in Comparative Political Change*, ed. Claude E. Welch (Belmont, Calif.: Wadsworth, 1967), pp. 150-166; Karl Deutsch, *The Nerves of Government* (New York: The Free Press, 1963); and Claude Ake, *A Theory of Political Integration* (Homewood, Ill.: The Dorsey Press, 1967). Willard R. Johnson discusses the problem of political integration as it specifically affects Cameroon in his *The Cameroon Federation* (Princeton: Princeton University Press, 1970).

3. Johnson, op. cit.

4. For fuller treatments of the Cameroon population and ethnic situation, see this author's *The Cameroons from Mandate to Independence* (Berkeley and Los Angeles: University of California Press, 1964), pp. 5-14, and *The Cameroon Federal Republic* (Ithaca, N.Y.: Cornell University Press, 1971), pp. 45-49.

5. See Victor LeVine, *Cameroons from Mandate to Independence*, op. cit., pp. 52-69; idem, *The Cameroon Federal Republic*, op. cit., passim; Neville

Rubin, *Cameroun* (New York: Praeger, 1971), pp. 143-168; Michel Prouzet, *Le Cameroun* (Paris: R. Pichon & R. Durand-Auzias, 1974), pp. 23-84; Hans F. Illy, ed., *Kamerun, Strukturen und Problemen der Sozio-ökonomischen Entwicklung* (Mainz: Hase & Koehler, 1974), pp. 13-36, 65-86, 145-172; Johnson, op. cit., pp. 135-167.

6. See particularly, Rubin, op. cit., pp. 143-168.

7. *L'Unité*, Nov. 19-25, 1971, p. 10. *L'Unité* is the official organ of the CNU.

8. LeVine, *Cameroons from Mandate to Independence*, op. cit., pp. 206-211.

9. 1961 Constitution, Sec. 1:3.

10. Ibid., Part 4, Sec. 18.

11. For a discussion of this matter, see H.N.A. Enonchong, *Cameroon Constitutional Law* (Yaoundé: Centre d'Edition et de Production de Manuels et d'Auxiliaires de l'Enseignement, 1967), p. 124.

12. The author of the letter, dated June 18, 1972, wished to remain anonymous.

13. 1972 Constitution, Sec. 4. See also the analysis of the 1972 Constitution by Joseph Owona, "De l'Etat fédéral à l'Etat unitaire," *Revue juridique et politique, indépendance et coopération* (1973) No. 1, pp. 3-40.

14. Ibid., Secs. 1:4 and 44.

15. 1961 Constitution, Sec. 37.

16. The decree is summarized in *L'Unité*, June 25-30, 1972.

17. Presidential decree, Secs. 7, 10, 15, 14, and 8.

18. R. Elangwe, letter to author, Aug. 10, 1971.

19. See Johnson, op. cit., pp. 207-210.

20. Ibid., p. 209.

21. See LeVine, *Cameroon Federal Republic*, op. cit., pp. 95-136.

22. Johnson, op. cit., pp. 250, 252.

23. An excellent treatment of West Cameroon in the federation is by Jacques Benjamin, *Les Camerounais occidentaux: La minorité dans un état bicommunitaire* (Montréal: Les Presses de l'Université de Montréal, 1972).

24. On obstacles to and the problems of integration see Rubin, op. cit., pp. 143-186; LeVine, *Cameroon Federal Republic*, op. cit., pp. 152-185; and Prouzet, op. cit., passim.

25. The point is documented by J.F. Bayart in his "Cameroun: l'illusion du parti unique," *Revue Française d'Etudes Politiques Africaines*, No. 65 (May 1971), pp. 40-49, and made by Michel Prouzet, op. cit., pp. 342-353.

Chapter 15

The Nation, State, and Politics in Somalia

by I. M. Lewis

MOST AFRICAN COUNTRIES, as is now glaringly obvious, are states rather than nations. They generally lack any uniform national culture to serve as an effective basis for a fully fledged patriotism transcending their numerous internal ethnic divisions. On a popular level, African politics has become virtually synonymous with "tribalism"; in erudite circles, the euphemistic if more comprehensive term "pluralism" to describe this ethnic-tribal fragmentation is currently enjoying a vogue. It is easy to exaggerate and oversimplify, but there is little doubt that most African states have witnessed an intensification of their internal divisions — ethnic and otherwise — since independence. In these circumstances, the Somali Republic appears at first sight as a striking anomaly. For in contrast with her neighbors, she owes her very existence to the sense of common identity and destiny that the Somalis display as a people and that, if sharpened by colonization, was certainly not created by colonization.

This sense of community among the Somalis is anchored in the possession of a broadly homogeneous and largely pastoral culture, a common language, and a fervent and deep-rooted devotion to Islam which reached their shores more than a thousand years ago. These attributes in Somali eyes distinguish them clearly from other neighboring ethnic groups in Northeast Africa. Thus, self-determination has always meant Somali-determination. As I have argued previously, the pan-Africanism that has enjoyed most support among the Somali follows the principle that charity begins at home, and concentrates on the areas that surround Somalia.[1]

On the basis of this traditional cultural unity, in 1960 the former British

Somaliland Protectorate and the United Nations Trust Territory of Somalia (administered by Italy) joined together as the northern and southern regions of the Somali Republic. The formation of this new state left hundreds of thousands of Somalis outside the fold and still under foreign rule—in eastern Ethiopia, in northern Kenya, and in French Somaliland, known since 1967 as the French Territory of the Afar and Issa. The republic was thus from the outset incomplete, containing only part of the total nation.

Not surprisingly, the first aim of the new republic was to expand the state so that it fully comprehended the nation; nationhood had already been achieved and awaited its political fulfillment in a single all-embracing Somali state. This desire to continue and bring to fruition a process that had received international sanction with the formation of the republic seems perfectly natural to the Somali; but it was, of course, the basis of the "Somali Dispute" with Ethiopia, Kenya, and France. This irredentist policy was pursued with varying degrees of militancy, if with little result, by successive Somali governments in the period from independence until 1967, for these countries were as reluctant to cede territory and subjects as the republic was anxious to acquire them.[2]

In this context the fact that the Somali people—today estimated to number some 4-5 million—did not form a single, united political group in the precolonial era is scarcely relevant (except, perhaps, to those who confound the concepts of state and nation). The significant thing is that they possessed a vigorous sense of cultural nationalism, of a kind familiar to students of nineteenth-century European nationalism, which in the colonial period gained new political meaning. It is worth emphasizing that here we see an example of the politicization of an existing cultural identity. This is the reverse of the familiar manufacture of ethnic identity as a basis for political and economic interests which, already well known to historians, has received a great deal of attention in recent discussions of politics in the Third World.[3]

The Nation and Its Traditional Subdivisions

If then, as I argue here, the Somali people are to be considered a nation, part of which has achieved independent statehood in the republic, does this mean that their national, cultural homogeneity has saved them from the vicious tribal factionalism that plagues the political life of other African states? Somali nationalist politicians certainly do not think so. Indeed, since the birth of modern political parties in Somalia in the early 1940s, these leaders have consistently denounced the sectarian evils that have so often jeopardized their efforts to unite. These divisive and constricting forces are identified as "tribalism" and equated with similar particularistic attachments in other African states. If, however, the effects of these forces are much the same, the institutions that produce them differ. The linguistically and culturally distinct divisions that threaten the fragile cohesion of most African states are here replaced by kinship-based ties which, though they lack the trappings of cultural uniqueness, are arguably even more deeply entrenched and paralyzing in their effects.

It is thus "clanship" in the technical sense, rather than tribalism, that commands allegiance and frustrates the achievement of much that is in the national interest. Strictly, all the units of people referred to here are conceived of by the Somali as lineages based on common descent, traced in the male line, from an eponymous ancestor. I use the terms "clan-family," "clan," and "lineage" for convenience to indicate groups of descending size and to emphasize that these analytical distinctions refer to essentially relative levels of lineage activity.

These kinship ties, moreover, are the more crippling in that they are embedded within the existing structure of nationhood. They represent the price Somalis have to pay for their "pre-formed" national identity because their traditional cultural unity is founded upon these very divisions. The effect of kinship ties is further complicated by the fact that each individual is bound not merely to one specific clan group, but to an almost infinite series of such groups, and his loyalties ebb and flow between different levels of lineage allegiance according to the context in which he is acting.

The patrilineal genealogies that record these kinship ties are thus not conserved simply for antiquarian or historical reasons. Their significance is primarily political, and their function is to "place" the individual socially and politically in a world of transient and shifting loyalties. Clan and lineage genealogies define friend and foe, and the character of the relations between people is in principle a direct reflection of their closeness or distance genealogically — of the "number of ancestors counted apart," as Somalis express it. At the highest level, the genealogies each Somali child learns at his father's knee converge in a single national pedigree. Hence, the entire Somali nation can be represented on a single all-embracing family tree.

Beneath the highest genealogical level, the most significant groups are six large "clan-families." Of these, the Dir live in the Northwest, extend into French Somaliland, and have one small pocket in southern Somalia. The Isaq occupy the center of the ex-British northern region. The Darod, who alone number well over a million, form a bridge between the former British Protectorate and northeastern Somalia, and also extend in force into eastern Ethiopia and northern Kenya. They are at once the largest and most widely distributed Somali group with the most direct stake in the pan-Somali campaign, a fact that has not passed unobserved by hostile governments in Ethiopia and Kenya seeking to refute Somali nationalist claims. The Hawiye, who live in a wide area in and around the capital, Mogadishu, also occur again in the South of the republic and extend into Kenya. The people of these four groups are traditionally and still overwhelmingly pastoral nomads, herding sheep, goats, camels, and in some areas cattle over vast expanses of territory. Produce from this pastoral economy provides the bulk of Somali exports.

The remaining two groups in the national genealogy are the Digil and Rahanwin, who occupy the comparatively fertile area between the Juba and Shibeli rivers — the only permanent watercourses in this otherwise largely arid land. Theirs is a mixed economy with an emphasis on cultivation. The region in which they live provides Somalia's other main export, the plantation banana crop. These two clan-families speak a distinctive dialect of Somali and retain special cultural features that set them somewhat apart from the rest of the nation. But the significance of their distinctiveness is offset because, unlike their nomadic countrymen, they are of very mixed origin. They represent a synthesis of old cultivating stock and more recent but once nomadic immigrants from the other Somali clans. Almost every other Somali lineage has an offshoot living among them. This mixed heritage gives the Digil and Rahanwin potential ties with the other four clan-families. And such unity as their heterogeneous structure possesses has been further eroded by legislation adopted in 1960 maintaining the right of every Somali to live and farm where he chooses, irrespective of his relationship with the local people. This official abolition of the status of foreign client has thus encouraged many partially assimilated lineage groups to assert their original identity and to participate on this basis in national politics.

These clan-families are the main social units within the nation. In their traditional setting, however, they were generally too large and too widely dispersed to act as effective political units, albeit they represented a largely unrealized political potential. Within these six groups, individuals identified with and acted as members of smaller units that can be usefully distinguished as "clans," which had a maximum population of some 100,000 though they were often considerably smaller. Clans in turn did not exist on a permanent footing; rather, in Chinese-box fashion they comprised a series of smaller lineage subdivisions which might be mobilized at any level of grouping. This fluid pattern of shifting loyalties, well adapted to the exigencies of the nomadic life which discouraged the formation of permanently established units, was accompanied by an equally loose and highly democratic process of government. Whenever, at any point in the series of segments, a lineage was mobilized, its policy was determined in ad hoc assemblies attended by all the adult men concerned, or their representatives. Men of energy, valor, and wealth, as well as sagacity and wit, were highly respected; and these and other factors enabled certain individuals to build up temporary followings and spheres of influence. Some clans, admittedly, had leaders (sometimes dignified with the Arab title "sultan"), but these were essentially mediatory and ritual figureheads. With the general exception of the southern Somali cultivators—the Digil and Rahanwin—there was no clearly defined hierarchy of established chiefly offices. This circumstance, of course, did not prevent the colonial administrations from appointing salaried headmen and "chiefs" at various levels of lineage division.

Nevertheless, as in other highly egalitarian cultures, traditional Somali attitudes toward power and authority were decidedly ambivalent. For all their hardy republicanism and individualism, and perhaps indeed because of the very difficulties involved in wielding effective power under such unpropitious conditions, the figure of the tyrant and despot seems always to have held a curious fascination for the pastoral nomads. To some extent this respect for power is also a facet of the martial character of traditional Somali society where the display of force, however brutal and merciless, is associated with manly virility whereas weakness, even though it is held to possess a certain, compensating mystical virtue, is despised.

In this generally turbulent society with its mercurial political formations, a certain stability was provided in the basic traditional political unit, the so-called *dia*-paying group. Rarely boasting more than a few thousand warriors, these groups consisted of closely related patrilineal kinsmen who had combined together for mutual support and who were parties to a specific *heer* ("treaty"), which contained many features comparable to those of the social contract of the political philosophers. The crucial bond here was the common obligation to act in concert in order to pay and receive damages for injury or death (Arabic, *dia*). If one member of a group was killed or wounded, his comrades rallied together until revenge or satisfactory damages had been exacted. Fighting, when it occurred, tended to spread rapidly, however, soon involving the members not only of the dia-paying groups directly responsible, but also those of more distant kin and allies. With such quickly escalating hostilities, where group identities were constantly being enlarged as the more inclusive levels of lineage patriotism became involved, whole clans would eventually be mobilized to defend their component lineages against their foes.

In this context of interclan conflict, constituent dia-paying group loyalties would be set aside for the duration of the wider confrontation. As soon as fighting between clans ceased and tension at this level abated, these units would again fall apart into their component lineages. In such a conflict-ridden culture, peacemakers clearly had an important role to play. And here, appropriately, religion came to the aid of a divided society. Local Muslim leaders were expected to intercede not only between men and God, but between men and men. These sheikhs symbolized the transcendental brotherly love of the Islamic community, and although ultimately forced to rely on traditional lineage ties, they were ideally committed to the furtherance of peace between warring clans and lineages. The complementary character of their two roles is reflected in traditional Somali view that mankind is divided into two fundamental categories: men of the sword and men of God.[4]

This segmentary political system continued after independence to provide the basic framework within which modern Somali political organizations operated. Where, for example, the government was still the main employer, but no national pension scheme existed and material conditions were precarious, clansmen naturally continued to regard their traditional kinship ties as their ultimate safeguard and protection. Consequently, despite the existence of an unusually well-trained and effective police force, fights and feuds in the rural areas remained a characteristic feature of life, and towns were not immune from their politically polarizing consequences. Only the rich could sometimes afford to disregard these lineage bonds, and more typically sought to employ them selectively to advance their own personal interests. Even so, they had to be prepared to come to terms with the claims inevitably made on their resources by less successful clansmen.

The principle that, regardless of education or ability, kinship ties should be recognized and honored permeated all aspects of Somali life. It affected the composition and working of political parties and intruded forcibly into every government department and private enterprise. It also cut completely across the largely nominal division between urban and rural society. Hence, before the 1969 coup, cabinet ministers and wealthy urban merchants were still strongly bound to their rural cousins who looked to them for employment and preferment. The merchants and ministers in turn benefited from this rural support in situations — such as elections — where they needed it. Equally, fashionable as it had become to invest in banana plantations, rich and powerful men often continued to maintain profitable livestock interests— and therefore viable social and political connections—in the rural economy. The wealthy townsman was frequently a nomad not only at heart but also in pocket. In urban life, too, of course, kinship continued to play an important role. For instance, in the absence of any system of comprehensive motor insurance, the traditional (dia-paying) procedure of restitution was extended in the towns to cover traffic accidents. In this and many other respects the continuities between town and country were more binding and significant than the differences.

Understandably, however, the enduring appeal of these traditional imperatives posed serious problems for those seeking to overcome their divisive implications and to replace them by a steady attachment to the transcendent nation. How, in other words, could a formula be found to elicit and express clan identity that was both compatible with modern nationalist aspirations and, at the same time, in tune with the realities of clanship. Where members of the elite maintained that clanship was as dead as the dodo, it was clearly impossible to employ the old brusk challenge "What is your clan?" in order to establish a person's most basic political affiliation. This difficulty was tackled with typical Somali ingenuity; clanship was kept at arm's length by consigning it to the past. And so in the heady days prior to independence it became fashionable to speak of a man's "ex-clan," the English word "ex" even being adopted into the Somali language expressly for this purpose! Nationalist solidarity had become at least a *façon de parler*.

Party Politics before the 1969 Coup

These were the political conditions with which party politics and bureaucratic government had to come to terms if they were to relate meaningfully to social and political realities. Immediately prior to independence and the formation of the republic in 1960 by the union of the two former colonies, there were four main political parties. In the South (the Italian sphere) the Somali Youth League (SYL), originally founded in 1943 during the British military administration of Somalia (1941-1950), held a secure monopoly of power and represented a loose consortium of all the main clan groups. Its chief rival was the Digil Mirifle Party (HDMS), which catered to the separatist interests of the Digil and Rahanwin clans and had no following outside that area. Though the SYL also had adherents at this time in the North (British Somaliland), the principal parties there were the Somaliland National League (SNL), with a tradition going back to 1935, and the more recently formed United Somali Party (USP). The SNL represented the Isaq clan, which had dominated the life of the British Protectorate since its inception. The USP appealed to the interests of the Dir clans of the West and the Darod of the East. Although far apart geographically and scarcely interacting at all, these two clans had at least one thing in common: the joint political maxim that one's enemy's enemy is one's friend.

When the republic was proclaimed on July 1, 1960, the two legislative assemblies in the British and Italian territories combined to form a single national assembly at Mogadishu with 123 seats: 33 for the North, and 90 for the South. The southern assembly president, Adan Abdulle Osman, a Hawiye politician of great esteem and experience, was elected provisional president of the republic, and confirmed in office by a referendum held a year later. Dr. Abidirashid Ali Shirmarke, a prominent member of the Darod leadership of the SYL, was appointed prime minister and formed a coalition cabinet containing SYL, SNL, and USP members. The new government included four northern ("ex-British") ministers, two of whom were Darod and two Isaq.

The identity of the northern region as a whole was reflected in the existence of the two northern parties, neither of which had any direct support in the South. The separate interests of the main northern clans, the Isaq on the one hand and the Dir and Darod on the other, were faithfully mirrored in their two distinct parties. In the South, apart from the HDMS, comparable particularistic clan interests were catered for within the omnibus SYL.

The creation of the republic radically altered the position of the northern regions, and also affected the balance of power between opposing clan groups in the state as a whole. The capital both of politics and of business was now in the South, and northerners were forced to adjust to this situation and to adapt their British colonial experience to fit the Italian pattern in the South. The resolution of the inevitable problems which this process involved, and particularly that posed by the northerners' attachment to English and that of the southerners to Italian, was to some extent eased by the 10-year period (1941-1950) of British administration which the South experienced after Italy's defeat in East Africa during World War II. Nevertheless, there was initially considerable friction between the exponents of these two rival colonial traditions. The northern political, administrative, and commercial elite did not immediately accept the fact that to further their interests they now had to work through Mogadishu.

The first two years of the republic's life were consequently marred by many signs of northern discontent and disaffection. The most dramatic was a short-lived and unsuccessful coup staged by a group of young Sandhurst-trained officers. By 1963, however, the North had come to accept the republic as an established framework within which to pursue its interests. The political parties, which had become more and more out of touch with current political realities, now adjusted to this situation. The uneasy SYL-SNL-USP alliance fell apart with the formation of a new party called the Somali National Congress (SNC), which was led jointly by a former Isaq minister and a prominent ex-SYL politician of the Hawiye clan. The USP was disbanded, its members joining either the SNC, the SYL, or a more radical new party called the Somali Democratic Union (SDU).

This alteration in party alignments was highly significant. The formation of the SNC on a basis of Isaq, Hawiye, and Dir elements, represented a new attempt to capitalize on the close genealogical relationships of these three groups in opposition to the Darod-led SYL. (See Figure 15-1.) It

Figure 15-1. *Groups, Parties, and Personalities*

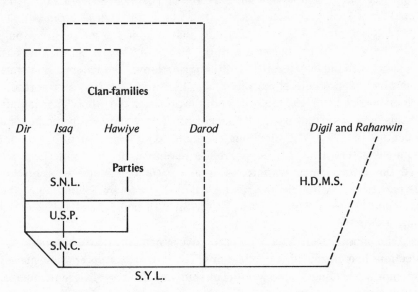

Personalities

Abdirashid Ali Shirmarke
Darod: premier, 1960-1964; president, 1967-1969; assassinated, 1969.
Adan Abdulle Osman
Hawiye: president, 1960-1967; arrested, 1969; released, 1973.
Abdirazaq Haji Husseyn
Darod: premier, 1964-1967; arrested, 1969; released, 1973; appointed permanent representative, United Nations.
Mohamad Haji Ibrahim Egal
Isaq: premier, 1967-1969; tried and sentenced to 30 years further imprisonment 1974.
General Mohammad Abshir
Darod: first commander of the Somali police; 1969 forced to resign and placed under house arrest at the time of the coup; released, 1973; re-arrested and detained without trial 1974.
General Jama Ali Korshell
Darod: commander of police from 1969; and made vice president of Supreme Revolutionary Council; denounced as a "traitor" and arrested, 1970.
General Mohammad Siad Barre
Darod: army commander, 1965-1969; led coup and became president of Supreme Revolutionary Council, 1969.

signified the collapse of the northern-southern regional political axis, and indicated the common commitment of all the political leaders to the republic as a unitary state. Further, it demonstrated that the Isaq and Dir of the North now recognized that they shared common interests not only with the southern Dir but also with the Hawiye.[5] This recognition was all the more striking because prior to the formation of the independent state there had been no effective contact at all between the Isaq and northern Dir on the one hand, and the Hawiye of the South on the other. The viability of this new pattern of party allegiances was put to the test in the general elections of 1964. The elections coincided with a period of maximum nationalist fervor, when the republic's perennial dispute with Ethiopia had flared into open warfare. A total of 973 candidates representing 21 parties ran in the elections, which the SYL won by gaining 69 of the available 123 seats. The SNC won 22, the SDU 15, while the HDMS secured only 9 seats.

The new Somali Youth League government formed after the 1964 elections had far-reaching implications. The previous premier was replaced by another leading Darod politician, but one from a different lineage. Again the new government contained northern as well as southern ministers, and representatives of all the main Somali clans. But the split in the ranks of the Darod leadership of the SYL had profound consequences, which were all the more embarrassing to stable administration because they existed within the government party itself. Here it is necessary to appreciate that, except on special issues, voting in the assembly was usually conducted by secret ballot, which allowed individual deputies great freedom of manoeuver and immense power, thereby hampering the maintenance of party discipline. Members of parliament who had promised their support for the government might, in fact, not give it if they found sufficient encouragement to do otherwise. The government of 1964 was severely harassed in this fashion and, despite a number of cabinet changes, actually resigned in 1966 following its defeat over an unimportant issue. With the encouragement of the president, however, it was reappointed, and a determined effort was made to patch up the party's persistent internal differences. But the respite which this brought was brief. The fact that the SYL could now count 105 members in the assembly (after defections from other parties) paradoxically only compounded its many difficulties.

Matters came to a head with the election by the assembly of a new president of the republic in 1967. The existing Hawiye incumbent was supported by the Darod premier and opposed by the latter's Darod predecessor, Shirmarke, who was now campaigning in alliance with the Isaq ex-leader of the SNC. This experienced politician, Mohammad Haji Ibrahim Egal, had in fact recently joined the SYL and was one of those siding with Shirmarke in opposition to the premier, Abdirazaq Haji Husseyn. Shirmarke turned the tables on his opponent and was elected president by the national assembly. So the 1964 government resigned and Egal was summoned to replace it with a new team of ministers.

These developments greatly reduced the significance of the SNC. For the first time a northerner was premier and his government, like all its predeccessors, was built on the tacit principle of clan balance. The Dir-Isaq-Hawiye alliance represented by the SNC was now decisively shattered with the continued division of the Darod bloc within the SYL. Indeed, these large groups had temporarily lost their significance in party politics, and effective allegiance had fallen back to the smaller constituent lineages that were now combining across their parent divisions. The hostilities and animosities between the smaller lineage groups, which had necessarily been suppressed to some extent during the period of wider national solidarity against Ethiopia and Kenya, had now come again to the fore.

This reemergence of small group particularism coincided with growing disillusionment among the urban elite about the effectiveness of the methods that had been used to secure the missing Somali territories. Egal, therefore, at once embarked on a policy of détente with his powerful neighbors, arguing that if he could first secure the friendship of Ethiopia and Kenya, his government would be more likely to meet with success in furthering Somali nationalist claims. This new policy initially aroused hostility at home, but with considerable financial resources at his disposal the new premier was soon able to secure a favorable balance of cautious support. Though he was obviously vulnerable on this ground, his personal position vis-à-vis his main Darod opponent—the ousted premier, Abdirazaq Haji Husseyn—was entirely secure (the president, Shirmarke, being Darod, the premier must of necessity belong to a different clan).

The elections of March 1969 confirmed all these trends. Despite new electoral regulations designed to discourage one-man lineage parties, 62 parties—mainly of this type—fielded 1,002 candidates, a record even for Somalia.[6] The SYL won 73 seats, and the emasculated SNC only 11. The Digil and Rahanwin, whose cohesion had been progressively eroded through their members' increasing participation in other parties (especially the SYL), gained only three seats for their local party, the HDMS. With such intense competition involving an unprecedentedly large number of senior civil servants who had resigned from their posts to enter the lists, electoral expenses had been unusually heavy, and those who had succeeded in gaining a seat in the national assembly were naturally anxious to recover their costs at the earliest possible opportunity. In a country where the annual budget was running at approximately £15 million, some candidates are estimated to have spent as much as £15,000.

When the Darod president, Shirmarke, again summoned his Isaq ally, Egal, to form a government, and Egal again selected a group of ministers representing the main clan blocs, no one imagined that this new administration would founder for lack of support in the national assembly. Yet few could have anticipated the enormous enthusiasm with which the new government was received. For at the very first meeting of parliament, all the opposition members, with the sole exception of Abdirazaq, crossed the floor to join the SYL government. If this haste to demonstrate their unqualified support for Egal and his colleagues appeared unseemly to some critics, those deputies concerned could protest, not without truth, that they knew where the interests of their constituents (as well as their own) lay. Thus, with surprisingly little fuss or clamor, the Somali Republic had at last joined the ranks of African one-party states.

The Military Revolution of October 1969

The republic was now completely dominated by the longest-lived and most comprehensive party organization in Somali political history; obviously, the big clan blocs had, for the moment at least, lost much of their political identity. Two factors seem of major importance here. First, the republic's markedly improved relations with Kenya and Ethiopia had greatly reduced the external pressures bearing on the state as a whole, and thus tended to encourage the mobilization of loyalties at the lowest levels of lineage organization. Second, within the state the schism in the ranks of the Darod elite and the fact that the head of state was drawn from this group reinforced the same trend. For as long as the leading Darod politicians were incapable of working together there was little incentive for those of other equivalent lineage blocs to unite against them. It would be a mistake to assume, however, that "tribalism" in its special Somali form had also disappeared.

With its 122 deputies, the SYL government was bursting at the seams. It could not, however, be anything more than an extremely heterogeneous assemblage of competing personal, family, and lineage interests. The maintenance of any semblance of unity under the circumstances would clearly prove a most costly business.[7] Further, as successful as the SYL government appeared at that first session of parliament, with only one member in opposition, there were political storm clouds on the horizon — one of the darkest being the election itself.

Stability has never been a conspicuous feature of Somali governments. On no previous occasion since independence, however, had the internal forces favoring instability been so many and so menacing. Shortly after the elections, it became obvious that though the government had not completely rigged them, numerous irregularities had occurred. Disturbances hushed up during the electoral campaign were now reported to have accounted for as many as 40 deaths — although this figure may be exaggerated. The chief of police, the widely respected General Mohammad Abshir, had himself resigned before the elections in protest at increasing political interference in his work. And under its newly appointed president, the Supreme Court now conveniently reversed a previous decision and denied that it had the authority to judge the mass of electoral petitions alleging irregularities which complainants had brought before it.

In the ensuing backlash of discontent and frustration the president steadily consolidated his position by every means at his command. The premier acted in the same fashion with little regard for the steadily mounting public criticism that his actions encouraged, one of them being his policy of détente.

The government's increasingly cordial relations with Kenya and Ethiopia did not seem to bring Somali unification any nearer and certainly offered a convenient stick with which to assail Egal. Finally, official corruption and nepotism seemed to be flourishing on a scale hitherto unknown in the republic. Some previous governments (and particularly that led by Abdirazaq) had attempted to curtail these activities, but there was little sign that either the premier or the president were unduly disturbed by their persistence.

This complacent abuse of power, as it seemed to many critics, enraged some of the country's leading intellectuals, particularly those who were not closely associated with the government or who had failed to secure a seat in the last elections. The democratic parliamentary system, which had seemed to combine so well with traditional Somali political institutions and had begun with such verve and promise, was turning distinctly sour. The national assembly was no longer the symbol of free speech and fair play for all citizens. On the contrary, it had been transformed into a sordid marketplace where deputies traded their votes for personal rewards with scant regard for the interests of their constituents. Its members were ferried about in sumptuous limousines bearing the magic letters A.N. (*Assemblea Nazionale*), which the inveterate poor of the capital translated with bitter humor as *anna noolyahay* — "I'm all right, Jack". When even such an enlightened and inspired politician as Abdirazaq Haji Husseyn had tried to improve the governmental system and had failed, more drastic remedies seemed the only possible recourse. In the view of the most disillusioned critics, democracy had lapsed into commercialized anarchy, and strong rule of a new type was desperately needed if the state was to be rescued from its present morass of poverty, insecurity, and inefficiency, and set on the road to progress. It was inevitable, therefore, that rumors of military intervention should be in the air.

The immediate precipitants of the impending coup were, however, entirely unexpected. While the premier was out of the country traveling abroad, Shirmarke, the president, was assassinated by a policeman on October 15, 1969. The murderer belonged to a lineage that had long nourished a grievance against the president, and it sought revenge rather than revolution — or so at least it seemed.[8] Nor was the death of Shirmarke followed immediately by a coup. The next event in the rapidly unfolding drama was the hasty return to Mogadishu of the premier to mastermind the national assembly's election of a new president who would safeguard his own position. Naturally, a Darod candidate was put forward — an old campaigner whom the government's critics saw as sharing most of the vices of his predecessor. When the party caucus reached agreement at a late-night meeting on October 20 to support him as their official candidate, and it was thus virtually certain that he would be elected by the assembly the next day, those army officers who had been closely watching the situation decided to act.

In the early hours of October 21, 1969, the army occupied key points throughout the capital. With the aid of the police, the army rounded up members of the government and other leading politicians and personalities.[9] The national assembly was closed, political parties were declared illegal, and it was announced that the state would be governed by a Supreme Revolutionary Council. Corruption and tribalism would be eliminated, and true justice and democracy restored. While declaring that it would honor existing treaties, the military regime also stated that it would support national liberation movements and the struggle for Somali unification. As an earnest of its intentions, and as a symbol of its hopes, the country would henceforth be known as the Somali Democratic Republic.

The membership of the Supreme Revolutionary Council was announced on November 1. Predictably, its president turned out to be General Mohammad Siad Barre, commander of the army, who was supported by 24 other officers, listed in descending order of rank from major general to captain. Of the two initial vice presidents, one was General Jama Ali Korshell,

Abshir's successor as police commandant. These members of the SRC were to be assisted by a 14-man civilian secretariat whose members were to fulfill much the same function as previous civilian ministers—but without their power. The appointments initially announced were certainly promising, and included a high proportion of the ablest civil servants in Somalia.

Insofar as it is possible to discern any public response to these dramatic events, which had taken place very quickly and apparently without a single shot being fired, the sudden and triumphal entrance of the army onto the political stage appears to have been greeted with cautious optimism and with a mixture of respect and fear. The army had previously played no direct part in the internal affairs of the republic; its leaders had their links with politicians, but the army had never been directly employed to support any of the previous civilian governments. Its significance lay primarily in external affairs—as a shield against the Ethiopians and Kenyans, and as a symbol for the vigorous pursuit of the Somali unification struggle. It had been in action against Ethiopia in 1964, and it had also participated more or less clandestinely in the Somali guerrilla campaign in northern Kenya, though it is only fair to point out that much of the day-to-day border patrolling was carried out by special units of the armed, carabinieri-style police force.

We must now consider more closely the relationship between the police and the army. Historically, the army is largely an offshoot of the police, formed initially in 1958 and strengthened after independence by the incorporation of the former British Somaliland Scouts unit. As with the police, its officers have been trained in Italy, Britain, Egypt, and Russia, and sometimes in several of these countries. Both forces probably contain an equally representative cross section of the Somali population, though each has few recruits from the southern Somali cultivators.[10] Their distinctiveness as separate armed organizations with different roles was accentuated by the fact that the first commander of the army was a Hawiye whereas Abshir was drawn from the Darod. These differences bred a tradition of comradely rivalry between the two forces, and made it seem perfectly logical that while the United States (until 1969) should be the main source of arms and support for the police, Russia should fulfill the same role for the army. This arrangement, of course, did not prevent both forces from jointly drawing on further aid from other friendly countries, including Italy, Egypt, Britain, and Germany.

Despite its explicit emphasis on efficiency, self-help schemes, and the value of work, and despite repeated appeals and threats to all and sundry by the new president, the military government has found the task of social reclamation arduous and unrewarding. As an armed authoritarian regime, it can dispense with the niceties of parliamentary government, and it can command obedience. Nonetheless the SCR, like the republic's preceding governments, has come to recognize the intractable character of the problems Somalia faces: poverty, climatic uncertainties, limited natural resources, and a turbulent, predominantly nomadic population whose divisive clan and lineage attachments are as stubbornly unyielding as the stark physical environment.

In attempting to deal with these impediments to progress, General Siad has developed his own rough-and-ready brand of socialism, which he sees as the necessary alternative to Somalia's parochial conservative forces. On the first anniversary of the revolution on October 21, 1970, for example, he publicly declared that henceforth Somalia would be dedicated to socialist goals and to the complete eradication of "tribalism." He also declared that the positions of government-stipended tribal chiefs and headmen would be abolished, that the practice of paying blood-money would be forbidden, and that those who indulged in "tribalism" would incur serious penalties.[11] These exhortations were followed in December 1970 and in early 1971 by public demonstrations in the nation's main centers during which "tribalism, corruption, nepotism, and misrule" were symbolically buried and thus eliminated. In some cases effigies representing these evils were also burned. More pragmatically, the regime promised to provide funeral expenses for those who died in the towns without relatives at hand who could perform these services. This innovation was aimed at providing an official substitute for one of the functions served by lineage ties in the urban centers.

The regime's unremitting struggle against traditional conservative forces—including many of its religious leaders—is accompanied at a more intimate—and less observable—level by General Siad's personal battle with the hidden "tribal" enemy within the Supreme Revolutionary Council itself.[12] For, as the new president has himself scornfully declared, the general public tends to regard the SRC as it did previous civilian governments, and expects it to be equally representative in lineage composition. The council is indeed largely assessed in terms of the lineage identities and assumed loyalties of its members, and changes in its ranks are interpreted in the light of this all-pervasive logic. If, for example, the SRC dealt less strictly than might otherwise have been expected with former politicians of the Digil and Rahanwin groups, then that was reportedly because they were underrepresented on the council.

Similarly, when the former police commander and first vice president, Korshell, was abruptly arrested and charged with organizing an "imperialist" counterrevolution, local commentators interpreted this as a shrewd move devised to correct the SRC's supposed overrepresentation of senior

Darod members. And those critics who at the time of the coup smugly asserted that Siad was a "mere-Negib" who would be swept from power into obscurity once the real militants of the revolution—the young majors and colonels—came to the top, have since found it necessary to revise their opinions. For the astute maneuvers within the SRC which led to the appointment as army commander of one of Siad's closest dependents, and to the expulsion or neutralization of many of his potential rivals, have greatly enhanced the Head of State's reputation as a master of political strategy, and contributed to his personal image as an outstanding example of the Somali conception of the "Big Man." Further evidence of General Siad's political adroitness can be seen in his creation in November 1971 of a personal advisory board, or cabinet, of three leading members of the SRC to debate policies before their submission to the council as a whole.

Those who adopt this traditionalist approach in analyzing the fortunes of members of the SRC in terms of an internal power struggle along lineage lines, see confirmation rather than contradiction in the charges employed to discredit council members who have fallen from grace. Few Somalis take at face value the accusations of "failing in revolutionary zeal," which have accompanied some unexpectedly abrupt demotions. The rapid turnover in the first two years after the revolution of vice presidents on similar counterrevolutionary charges[13] also tended to reinforce the public's impression of a cut-throat struggle for power, which, though conducted in a tougher style, recalled the endless factionalism of previous civilian governments. Speculations of this sort, however, are now best kept secret, because the airing of any opinion that can be construed as hostile to the regime is a serious offense. The inveterate tea-shop gossip, with its scandalous accounts of the latest escapades of the republic's leading politicians— so much a feature of the urban scene in the "bad old days" of civilian rule— has disappeared.

Siad's vigorous espousal of a form of socialism that he finds fully compatible with Islam seems likely to place Somalia more definitely among the Arab states. In inter-African affairs and in the OAU, the republic is playing a more effective role than it used to. Thus, in 1974, the Organization held its Eleventh Summit Conference in Somalia and President Siad became OAU chairman for 1974-1975, the Somali foreign secretary narrowly missing being elected secretary-general. Contrary to what might have been expected of a military government, the new regime not only continued to follow Egal's conciliatory path in seeking to build stronger and more effective links with both Ethiopia and Kenya, but has displayed little evidence of adopting a more militant stance on the issue of Somali unification. This policy is perhaps not so paradoxical as it may seem; it is perfectly understandable that those who gained power by force should fear to lose it while their attention is diverted in skirmishes on the Ethiopian and Kenyan borders. Indeed, it seems most significant that of the many accusations made against Korshell, one of the most damning was that he was allegedly intriguing to create trouble with the Ethiopians—open evidence of General Siad's private nightmare and, it must be presumed, the hope of some of his opponents.

The third anniversary of the revolution (on October 21, 1972) seemed to inaugurate a new phase in the policies of the Supreme Revolutionary Council. The Maoist-style cult of the leader (who successfully maintains a public image of accessibility and humility) was now well established in the main urban centers, receiving its strongest support from those sections of the population that had least benefited from previous civilian governments. The dynamic new secularism, which challenged traditional Islamic assumptions about the authority of men over women and of elders over the young, was not without appeal, especially in the towns, and energies that had previously been wastefully dissipated were now being channeled more purposefully into a series of "crash programs," one of the SRC's favorite incantations. These programs depended for their effectiveness upon energetic grass-roots organization, provided by the locally recruited people's militia — *ghoulwaddayaal* ("vigilantes") — who wear green uniforms and can be seen marching through the various quarters of towns directing community projects. Their emblem is an unblinking Orwellian eye, and because they are assumed to be in close contact with the secret police, their instructions and advice are not to be dismissed lightly. The possibility always exists that those not prepared to cooperate readily in civic projects will be spirited away to join other malcontents in the republic's "ninth region," as prison was euphemistically known before the new administrative divisions were introduced in 1974.

Foreign delegates attending the 1972 celebrations were no doubt most impressed by Somalia's well-timed and remarkably successful mediation in the dispute between Tanzania and Uganda. But an even more impressive measure of the SRC's achievements — indicating its new self-confidence — was the momentous decision to convert Somali into a written language using the Roman script. This choice of script amounts to a critical test of governmental effectiveness in Somalia. All the previous civilian governments had, understandably enough, not felt able to make and implement this decision, which involved choosing among the three rival contenders — Arabic, Osmania (a Somali invention), and the Roman script — each vociferously supported by different sections of the population. Having picked the most technically feasible candidate, the SRC launched a highly successful mass literacy program in the towns. Officials were given three months in which to become proficient in the new written Somali and were warned that they might lose their jobs if they failed to achieve the necessary standard of literacy. The new script now enjoys wide popularity, serving as it does as a vehicle for Somali nationalism, and has had a highly significant leveling effect. For once an uneducated nomad has mastered the script, he often finds he is more articulate in his native language than those of his formerly privileged countrymen who have enjoyed an education overseas. Some indication of the public enthusiasm generated by this daring innovation can be seen in the fact that less than six months later the SRC considered the time had come to release most of the civilian political leaders who had been held in detention since the coup. So, without warning, on April 1973, Radio Mogadishu announced to its astonished listeners that all but six of the 25 detainees were to be freed immediately. The remaining six were brought to trial in October 1974, former Premier Egal being sentenced to 30 years imprisonment.

It would be both premature and presumptuous to try to judge at this time whether the authoritarian means adopted by the Supreme Revolutionary Council are justified by the ends to which they are directed. That is a matter which must be left to Somali historians of the future, who may have better evidence at their disposal than is available in the mid-seventies. It suffices to note now that many of the regime's difficulties follow inevitably from the army's assumption of power. Having assumed a political role, SRC members have naturally become increasingly subject to political pressures, and the old civilian party leaders whom they supplanted must view their plight with a certain ironic satisfaction and, perhaps, even sympathy. The very fact of ruling plunges them headlong into the uninviting maelstrom of clan and lineage rivalries with which, as we have seen, they are wrestling valiantly — if not yet victoriously. The legitimacy and the stability of previous civilian governments depended essentially on the extent to which they were judged to be satisfactorily representative of the major lineage interests in the country at large. The only additional claim to legitimacy that the present military administration can make is that of reformist zeal; and as long as its social objectives remain incompletely realized in tangible benefits for the whole population, the old yardstick of clan representativeness must remain a critical factor.[14]

The extreme fragmentation of lineage ties which obtained at the time of the coup is further encouraged by the absence of external pressures from Ethiopia or Kenya, by the inclusion in the council of members belonging to all the major clan-families, and by the regime's evident concern to distribute its punitive measures as evenly as possible among the various groups. Most major groups have officers in power in the SRC — and civilian politicians in detention. If enemies are to be made, the SRC apparently reasons, it is best that they be made on all sides. But if this balancing act seems to add up to a successful exercise in stability, it does not take the regime very far in the direction of its declared reformist aims. Here the problem is to retain stability and, if possible, to secure a greater measure of independent legitimacy in order to draw more effectively and constructively on the state's unique endowment of traditional cultural nationalism. This task, however, requires a great delicacy of judgment and skillful manipulation, because an excess of nationalist fervor might well stimulate ungovernable pressures that could thrust the republic into a militant campaign to retrieve the missing territories in Ethiopia and Kenya. When the ambitious mass literacy campaign for the nomads was launched in August 1974 at an estimated cost of £10 million, it was already apparent that the introduction of written Somali in the towns has led to a quickening of nationalist sentiment.

We are thus led back to the issues raised at the beginning of this chapter, on the political implications of Somalia's unusual position as a state based upon traditional national identity and culture. I continue to regard this feature as a particular instance of John Stuart Mill's general principle that such circumstances permit — if not actually encourage — a democratic political system that, because of its cultural stability, can tolerate the open expression of dissent. Of course, the same factors could be employed to sustain and reinforce an oppressive tyranny. It seems to me significant, however, that Somalia's shift from multi-party democracy to one-party rule and finally to military control coincides with a general movement from wide-ranging national solidarity to extreme lineage particularism. The simultaneous failure, at least up to the present, of the military to overcome lineage divisions, again reveals how deeply entrenched these traditional imperatives are, and poignantly highlights the ambivalence of a cultural heritage that promises unity only at the price of division. Democracy is also a deeply rooted Somali political principle which continues much as usual in the more remote parts of the nomadic interior. How long it will be before it reasserts itself in the central political life of the state remains to be seen. Here attention will naturally focus on the character of policy-formation and public debate within the new state political party introduced in January 1975 when Somalia was desperately wrestling with its worst drought in recorded history.

Notes

1. I. M. Lewis, "Pan-Africanism and Pan-Somalism," *Journal of Modern African Studies*, Vol. 1, No. 2 (August 1963), pp. 147-162.

2: In 1967 and 1968, however, Somalia signed treaties with Kenya and Ethiopia which produced a détente and greatly improved relations between the three states. See Catherine Hoskyns, *The Ethiopia-Somali-Kenya Dispute, 1960-67* (Nairobi: Oxford University Press, 1969); I. M. Lewis, *The Modern History of Somaliland* (London: Weidenfeld, 1965), and "Integration in the Somali Republic" in *African Integration and Disintegration*, ed. Arthur Hazlewood (London: Oxford University Press, 1967).

3. In the work of Africanist anthropologists this theme is particularly marked in the writing of Abner Cohen, notably in his *Custom and Politics in Urban Africa* (London: Routledge and Kegan Paul, 1969).

4. For a detailed account of the traditional political system and its initial response to modern developments, see I. M. Lewis, "Modern Political Movements in Somaliland," *Africa*, Vol. 28, No. 3 (July 1958), pp. 244-261; and idem, *A Pastoral Democracy* (London: Oxford, 1961).

5. For details on the political integration of the two parts of the state, see I. M. Lewis, "Nationalism and Particularism in Somalia," in *Tradition and Transition in East Africa*, ed. P. H. Gulliver (London: Routledge and Kegan Paul, 1969), pp. 339-362. For an analysis of the legal problems engaged in this process, see Paolo Contini, *The Somali Republic: An Experiment in Legal Integration* (London: Cass, 1969).

6. The total number of candidates happened to be roughly equivalent to my estimate of the number of dia-paying groups in the republic. But I think that this is a coincidence, because most candidates were representing coalitions of these groups.

7. According to a detailed statement made after the 1969 coup by a spokesman of the Supreme Revolutionary Council, said to be based on a close study of the accounts of the premier's office, Egal expended £500,000 of public funds in payments to members of the assembly in the period between January and October 1969.

8. See *Anglo-Somali Society Newsletter*, Vol. 67 (September-October 1970), for a report of the trial of the culprit who was found guilty and sentenced to death.

9. Those arrested included Egal, his opponent Husseyn, and Adan Abdulle Osman, once the head of state. This oddly assorted party of politicians and dignitaries was confined in the presidential guesthouse at Afgoi, outside the capital. The ex-Police Chief, Abshir, was placed under house arrest. He was later released and then imprisoned without trial.

10. From earliest days of colonization, the bulk of recruits for the police, and indeed for other government employment, has come from the nomadic elements of Somalia. This selective recruitment is a direct reflection of the pressure of population on resources in the most nomadic regions of the country.

11. In January 1971, for instance, a district court in a remote northern part of the republic sentenced a number of people to 18 months' hard labor for "fostering tribalism."

12. Some of Siad's speeches are conveniently collected together in an official publication entitled *My Country and My People* (Mogadishu: Ministry of Information and National Guidance, 1970). A series of informative pamphlets covering all aspects of development in Somalia were issued by the Ministry of Information in June 1974 at the time of the OAU meeting.

13. Following Korshell's disgrace in May 1971 General Mohammad Ainanshe (another vice president) and General Salad Gavaire were arrested and charged with engineering a plot "to kill the revolution." They were tried by a military tribunal and publicly executed on July 3, 1972.

14. For a provisional and personal assessment see, however, I.M. Lewis, "Somalia's Leaders Go Forward with Confidence," *New Middle East,* No. 51 (December 1972), pp. 9-12. An interesting account of developments since October 1969 by an Italian communist is found in L. Pestalozza, *Somalia, Cronaca della Rivoluzione, 21 Ottobre 1969,* Bari, 1973.

Chapter 16

The Current State of National Integration in Uganda

by Aidan Southall

NATIONAL INTEGRATION remains the primary concern of most of those African countries that experienced the full impact of colonialism. Not only are dangers of secession ubiquitous, they are particularly serious because they involve territory. The colonial era and the recent period of national independence meant a vast increase in scale, from numerous small societies to fewer and larger units. [1] Though it is certainly necessary to consider the dangers of sectional or class conflict, and of regional economic rivalry and deprivation, it is nonetheless true that an account of national integration must at present concentrate upon the problems involved and the successes achieved in building nations out of many languages and cultures.

Uganda has so far managed to avoid the horrors of full-scale civil war, like those that have ravaged Nigeria, Zaire, Sudan, Rwanda, and Burundi. Yet her ethnic problem is one of the most severe in Africa, partly because of the basic linguistic and cultural situation and partly because of the way in which British colonial policy myopically treated it. Great Britain won the support of the Kingdom of Buganda and with the assistance of Ganda armies gained control of a territory four or five times its size on the cheap. But as a reward, the British had to confer a status upon Buganda that was obviously incompatible with the formation of a viable larger whole. At the time, such a problem seemed remote, and as a result it was shelved — until it was too late.

Ethnic and Historical Background

National integration for most new African states involves greatly enlarging their spatial, territorial, and social scale by welding many small units into a single large new entity. The boundaries of this new entity — with its framework of new and more specialized institutions — are usually recognized to be derived from the historical accidents of colonial partition and not from rational considerations. Nonetheless, it is necessary to consider briefly what experience and capacity for territorial and social scale the precolonial societies had. The fact is that an almost continuous process of transformation[2] has been going on from remote precolonial times, which are coming to be seen as less static than has often been assumed, through the colonial and into the independence era. The peoples, cultures, and societies of precolonial Uganda were highly diverse in size and scale, in economy and political structure. Though it is recognized that empirically these peoples, cultures, and societies represented a continuum, they can only be explained briefly by dividing them into the artificial categories of unitary states, segmentary states, and stateless segmentary societies.[3]

When Arabs, Asians, and Europeans first reached this part of the world they were most deeply impressed with Buganda, and secondarily with Bunyoro. Buganda was advantageously placed in relation to the dominant east coast route, but Bunyoro was significant in relation to penetration from the north by Sudanese traders and by the Egyptian interests whimsically expressed through Gordon, Baker, Emin Pasha, and other European adventurers. Bunyoro-Kitara had been for centuries the dominant political and cultural influence in the region, supplying subsidiary rulers to wide areas in all directions around it. It was a segmentary, not a unitary state,[4] and its boundaries could be defined in many different ways according to the precise criteria chosen: direct political sovereignty, ritual suzerainty, religious cult community, language group, and so forth. Each of these constellations of factors has a different distribution, and an attempt at general definition can only produce distortion and nebulous results.

Even so, Buganda was definitely ascendant by the nineteenth century and had established a centralized territorial jurisdiction and clear-cut, well-defended frontiers, which put it well within the category of unitary states.[5] Explorers, missionaries, traders, administrators — all were impressed with Buganda, and by establishing themselves around the kabaka's court and supplying firearms, literacy, and new ideas they further stimulated its development. With quite economic use of direct force the British were able to gain control of Buganda and to use it as an effective instrument for expanding their colonial rule. Thus gradually emerged an enlarged Uganda in which the Ganda, after whom it was named, were only a numerical minority, however politically dominant. Through this Ganda-British alliance most of south Uganda was brought under effective British control, with more or less serious military campaigns and punitive expeditions undertaken from time to time against major enemies, or recalcitrant pockets, in Bunyoro, Lango, Toro, Ankole, Bukedi, Bugisu, Teso, and elsewhere. After the first phase, Nyoro agents were used in a similar way in parts of the uncharted north. Of course, for a while the early Uganda Protectorate included the huge eastern province of Kavirondo, Uasin Gishu, and Turkana, all of which were transferred to Kenya in 1902 and so will not concern us.

A much more adequate understanding of the real problems of national integration in Uganda may be obtained if the true nature of the component ethnic groups is grasped. They have been almost universally misrepresented as primeval tribes, each with its distinctive language, culture, sense of identity, and clear-cut boundaries. There is no evidence that the peoples of Uganda — or for that matter the rest of Africa — could ever be so categorized, until the exigencies of colonial administration forced some of these qualities upon them. This fact has been dimly realized by some historians but never clearly stated. Rather, they blunder on, talking indiscriminately of tribes and clans with no clear meaning attaching to either.[6]

When Baker marched through the Sudan into northern Uganda in 1864 he found no identifiable peoples called the Acholi. He only mentions individual chiefdoms such as Obbo, Faniquara, Farajoke, Fallibek, Fabbo, Faloro — all easily identifiable *political* units.[7] Nor does Baker mention Alur or Jonam, but only chiefdoms such as Koshi, Foquatch, Farakatta, Faigore. Ten years later, however, Emin Pasha was referring to the Shuli, whom the Nyoro called Gani, and the Shefalu (Jo Pa Lwo), whom the Nyoro called Chope.[8] The present name Acholi developed from Shuli, which may have been a corruption of Collo, the correct name of the Shilluk, perhaps applied to the Acholi by Arab travelers who sensed the similarity of their language. Gani was a Bantu corruption of the Lwo *gang'* meaning "fence," "village," "homestead," "home."

The Lugbara acquired this name only about 1885, when Arabs coming first upon the small Lugwari clan in the north extended their name to a much larger area. The Kiga were never regarded as a bounded group before colonial administration crystallized them into one. The term simply means "highlanders" without any specificity. An early British administrator seeking his way through hitherto uncharted and little understood ethnic complexities produced a truly practical rule of thumb saying: where agriculturalists are ruled by Tutsi (Rwanda) they are Hutu; where they are ruled by Hima (Ankole) they are Iru, where they are ruled by no one they are Kiga.

The Gisu of Mount Elgon have at different times and places preferred to be called that or else Masaba, but neither was a general name accepted by them in precolonial times. H. H. Johnston, in a rather uncomplimentary vein, remarks: "They do not themselves recognize this name, which is one applied to them by the Baganda, and is a convenient general term for a group of wild mountain tribes that have no general designation of their own."[9] And as examples of these component groups, he mentions the Bapobo, Bangoko, Bakonde, Bagesu, Basokwia, and Bosia, which are recognizable today as maximal lineages[10] or regional clusterings of them.

Although the Banyankole are universally regarded as an identifiable ethnic group today, there was no such entity before 1901. There were some dozen territories which the British welded into counties of the new Kingdom of Ankole by persuasion, threats, and punitive expeditions.[11] Five had actually been parts of the small and ancient kingdom of Nkore (Kaaro-Karungi). One was the Bunyoro-oriented tiny kingdom of Buhweju. One was Buzimba, a fraternal kingdom to Buhweju. Five others had been part of the Kingdom of Mpororo, which was breaking up during the nineteenth century: two of these became semi-autonomous kingdoms ruled by sons of the King of Mpororo, one was given by the latter to the King of Nkore as a marriage gift, another came gradually under Nkore influence, and the fifth came under the rule of Babito princes ultimately derived from Bunyoro.

Busoga was a purely ecological area, regarded as an island, bounded by the Nile, Lake Victoria, Lake Kyoga, and the Mpologoma River. It contained two quite large states (Bugabula and Bulamogi) and half a dozen others of moderate size in the north, and numerous smaller petty states or principalities and even areas of localized segmentary lineages free of any monarchical institutions in the south.

Toro was a splinter from Bunyoro, made independent by rebellion in about 1830. It was purely Nyoro in language and culture and would probably have been reconquered by Bunyoro if it had not been artificially bolstered up by Lord Lugard and his successors as a divide-and-rule bulwark against the threatening power of Bunyoro.

The Bakedi were the most ridiculous group of all. The term had been derogatorily applied, in the sense of "naked people," by the Baganda to those living in the vague unbounded area to the north and east of them.

When transformed by the British into a "district tribe" after the Ganda General Kakunguru had conquered the area for them, it consisted of the Nilotic-speaking Jopadhola, the Bantu Samia and Gwe, the Nilo-Hamitic Tesyo in the east and Teso of Palissa in the north, the Bantu Nyole and Gwere. All these had been completely independent of one another. The Padhola, Nyole, Samia, and Gwe were segmentary lineage systems, the Teso and Tesyo had age organization, and the Gwere comprised three small states of Interlacustrine type (though the rulers of the largest were in fact Bantuized Teso). Not suprisingly, the Bakedi gave trouble throughout the colonial period. Despite their absurd artificiality, they are still regarded as a tribe by most Ugandans unfamiliar with the area, and were actually treated as such in the Marriage Commission of 1964.

If we take the average conventional definition of the term *tribe*, as commonly used, to be a politically autonomous group with its own distinctive language and culture, name and sense of identity, with a near-subsistence economy, simple technology, and no writing, it can easily be seen that while the last three characteristics were broadly true of most tropical African peoples before the colonial conquest, the first five characteristics were not fulfilled. Partly, it was a case of mistaken identity. Foreigners were not able to understand the complexities of the actual situation, so they had to simplify it for themselves. They could not cope with a multitude of small, interlocking and often overlapping groups, so they had to amalgamate them into new fictitious units of larger size, which under pressure of colonial administration eventually took on a life of their own, and acquired strong vested interests.

After the settlement with Buganda, the subjugation of Bunyoro, and Kakunguru's eastern conquests, the districts of south Uganda began to take shape: Mengo, Masaka, and Mubende (the "lost counties" taken from Bunyoro) making up the province of Buganda; Bunyoro, Toro, Ankole, and Kigezi in the west; Busoga, Bukedi, Bugisu, and Teso in the east; and in the north, eventually, Lango, Acholi, West Nile-Madi, and Karamoja. As we have seen, Buganda had already achieved unitary statehood; the application of the tribal concept to it can only be explained as an expression of the same kind of intellectual racism that produced the Hamitic theory that all highly organized African states must have been created by invaders from the north because Africans could not have been capable of it. Bunyoro was the rump of the old Bunyoro-Kitara segmentary state, as severely pruned down by the British, especially by the strengthening of Toro as a completely separate kingdom-district. The convenient myth of Uganda as composed of Buganda and twelve other district-tribes took strong hold. Of course, administrators directly concerned knew to their cost that this was a travesty in the case of Bukedi; they knew that there were Banyarwanda as well as Bakiga in Kigezi; Konjo and Amba in Toro; Sebei in Bugisu; Dodoth, Jie, and Labwor in Karamoja; and Alur, Lugbara, Madi, Okebo, and Lendu in West Nile, as well as many other small groups elsewhere—Kenyi and Ligenyi in the Kyoga swamps, Tepes on the Karamoja mountains, Batwa in the Kigezi forests, and so on. But to the general public, including the masses of population, the districts were tribes. This cherished illusion was a potent force in bringing the myth nearer to reality.

Language, Population, and Traditional Structures of Ethnic Groups

The number of ethnic groups recognized in the Uganda census has never been constant. Under "native population" in 1921 we find more than 30 groups listed. Several of these overlap, or appear twice under different names, but more than 20 may be regarded as functional. Under "races or tribes" of the indigenous population in 1931 we find more than a dozen new groups added. Some of these were immigrant groups and others had not previously been distinguished from larger groups with whom they were very similar or by whom they had been dominated. The 1948 census cut the total of "main tribes" to 22, each with more than 50,000 people. The 1959 census, with greater statistical sophistication, brought many small groups back again, but this time for the new reason that they were fighting their last desperate battle for recognition. By 1969 the census discreetly omits all mention of "tribes," although the 15 largest still live on in the names of Buganda Region and the districts.

In Table 16-1 Uganda's ethnic groups of the 1959 census, together with their populations, are arranged according to the regions and districts in which they are mainly situated; and 1969 census figures for the populations of the administrative areas are shown. Groups which are primarily immigrant are given separately below. These groups are conventionally classified by language into Bantu (B); Western Nilote (WN), formerly called Nilote; Eastern Nilote (EN), formerly called Nilo-Hamite; and Sudanic (S). There is a rather palpable division between the Bantu south and the Nilotic and Sudanic north, fairly accurately demarcated by the swampy, ramifying Lake Kyoga drainage system, which cuts across most of the middle of the country from Lake Albert (Oneg Bonyo in Nilotic, and renamed Lake Mobutu in 1972) in the west to Mount Elgon in the east.

Most of the Bantu speakers of the south belong to the group best known as Interlacustrine Bantu and markedly characterized by the development of centralized political institutions, hereditary rulers, elaborate state rituals, and some degree of administrative bureaucratization.

As we have seen, Buganda and Bunyoro were the two dominant structures, whose relative fortunes had been gradually changing and were drastically altered by the differential impact of the colonial system upon them. Toro and Ankole were also built up as kingdoms by the colonial regime itself, and Busoga with its many components, large and small, struggled to achieve the same status and almost succeeded. But the Bantu were not by any means all organized in kingdoms. The Kiga in the southwest; the Amba and the Konjo in the west; the Gisu in the east; the Nyole, Samia, and Gwe in Bukedi, together with similar pockets in Busoga, constituted a large population mainly organized on the basis of localized agnatic groups with a segmentary structure. In the north the Madi and Lugbara were also organized in localized agnatic groups, while the Acholi and Alur had superimposed lines of hereditary rulers, although their states were themselves segmentary and rather small in size. The Karamojong and Teso had a framework of age organization, within which their patrilineal groups were more dispersed, and the Lang'o were somewhat similar, with small sections of different clans united in local religious congregations and defended by an egalitarian, achievement-oriented military organization.

The division between Bantu south and Nilotic north has certainly been accentuated by colonial administration and by the course of post-independence politics. Before the colonial conquest there was a great deal of movement and interchange to and fro across this apparent language barrier, with extensive borrowing of language, social institutions, and cultural features, sometimes in one direction, sometimes in the other. But the largest political structures of the south were stronger than anything comparable in the north and this supremacy had its influence upon the spread of language and culture. Generally speaking, the Sudanic and Nilotic peoples have been moving south in Uganda during relatively recent times, and the Bantu have received a substantial Nilotic infusion. The picture conveyed by the whole of modern literature is much too clear-cut and the rich ebb and flow of reality has been forgotten. The Nilotic origins of the Babito dynasty of Bunyoro kings have attracted a good deal of interest, but the innumerable blending processes occurring in many parts of the country remain very little known. For example, one section of the Eastern Nilotic Irarak clan adopted Bantu speech as Ba-lalaka, began to practice a marginal type of Interlacustrine hereditary rule, and founded a small state that came to be known as Bugwere and is generally regarded simply as part of the Interlacustrine Bantu area.

TABLE 16-1

PROVINCES AND ETHNIC GROUPINGS, 1959		REGION AND DISTRICT POPULATIONS, 1969	
Buganda (Kingdom)	1,834,128	Buganda Region	2,667,332
Baganda (B)	1,048,642		
Eastern Province	1,872,949	Eastern Region	2,817,066
Teso (EN)	524,716	Teso District	570,628
Kumam (WN)	61,459		
Bagisu (B)	329,257	Bugisu District	397,889
Badama (Padhola)(WN)	101,451	Mbale Town	23,544
Bagwe (B)	36,130		
Bagwere (B)	111,681	Bukedi District	527,090
Bakenyi (B)	23,707		
Banyole (B)	92,642		
Basamia (B)	47,759		
Basoga (B)	501,921	Busoga District	896,875
		Jinja Town	52,509
Sebei (EN)	36,800	Sebei District	64,464
Karamojong (EN)	131,713		
Labwor (WN)	6,278	Karamoja District	248,067
Tepeth (EN)	4,363		
Suk (Pokot) (EN)	21,850		
Western Province	1,497,510	Western Region	2,432,550
Bakiga (B)	459,619	Kigezi District	647,988
Batwa (B)	2,592		
Banyankore (B)	519,283	Ankole District	861,145

Batoro (B)	208,300		
Baamba (B)	34,506		
Bakonjo (B)	106,890	Toro District	571,514
Banyoro (B)	188,374	Bunyoro District	351,903
		Northern Region	1,631,899
Northern			
Alur (WN)	123,378		
Jonam (WN)	27,422		
Lugbara (S)	236,270	West Nile District	573,762
Kakwa (EN)	37,828		
Lendu (S)	4,744		
Madi (S)	80,355	Madi District	89,978
Acholi (WN)	248,929	Acholi District	463,844
Lang'o (WN)	363,807	Lang'o District	504,315
Immigrant Peoples			
Banyarwanda	378,656		
Barundi	138,749		
"Jaluo" (Luo)	37,648		
Kikuyu	914		
Kenya (other)	43,255		
Tanganyika (other)	33,570		
Congo (other)	24,296		
Asians (1969)	74,308		
Europeans (1969)	9,533		

B: Bantu; EN: Eastern Nilote (Nilo-Hamite);
WN: Western Nilote (Nilotes); S: Sudanic.

SOURCE: Uganda Census, 1959 and 1969.

My own studies on the Nilotic-Bantu borderland of Alur, Jonam, Acholi, and Bunyoro have shown that there existed in it a great deal of common ground in political institutions (despite considerable differences in scale), in religious ideas and practices, and in symbolic and cognitive structures,[12] which language diversity hid effectively from foreigners and which the linguistic standardization accompanying the colonial process tended to drive even further out of sight.

Administration, Mass Communication, Education, Religion, and Law

The needs of the British colonial administration in the broadest sense, and in its many diverse branches of school teaching, missionary work, and mass media, all tended toward the encouragement of larger, harder, and more clear-cut ethnic units that inevitably became the basis for political maneuver. Though national or central interests have developed that are generally committed to the transcendence of ethnic divisions, it is also inevitable that tempting political support can be picked up from time to time by promising some new kind of recognition or privilege to small groups whose influential members see advantage in winning a distinct identity for themselves.

Nowhere is this more strikingly revealed than in the development of radio, where the number of local languages catered for has continued to increase right up to the present time. Uganda Radio, with its limited resources for program production and vast task of communication, now has daily programs in Swahili, Luganda, Lwo (sometimes read in Acholi, sometimes in Lang'o), Runyankore-Rukiga, Runyoro-Rutoro, Rukonjo, Lusoga, Lumasaba (Gisu), Lugwe, Ateso, Karamojong, Kakwa, Lugbara, Madi, Alur (sometimes in Jonam), Dhopadhola, and Kupsabiny (Sebei) as well as the predominant English programs with some pioneering Arabic and French. In the past different parties and regimes have favored different languages, though all have had to come down on the side of English as the official language. Until recently, the prospect of an African national language in Uganda has never seemed realistic. Luganda is certainly the most widely understood indigenous language, but its adoption as a national language has been out of the question, within present perspectives, because of the fear of Ganda domination. When Ganda influence has been low, it has sometimes seemed that Swahili might be adopted at least as a second national language—somewhat paradoxically with the support not of the

Bantu to whom Swahili is linguistically closest, but rather of the non-Bantu. And, indeed, in 1974 Swahili was declared the *national* language while English remains the *official* language.

Obviously, this linguistic situation has created enormous difficulties for the educational process at the deepest level, as well as at the practical level of organization, administration, and training. These difficulties were reflected in the local and regional organization of the Christian missions. The English-dominated Church Missionary Society has successfully transformed itself into the national Church of Uganda in the international Anglican Communion and the World Council of Churches. Its priesthood and hierarchy is completely Ugandanized and it has hardly any foreign missionaries attached to it except in specialist or advisory tasks such as Bible translation, nursing training, and hospital administration. But communication between the different dioceses and parishes of the Church of Uganda is by no means easy, except at the highest level. Nor, strangely enough, does the Church of Uganda have a structure coinciding with the boundaries of the national state, for it is organized as the Province of Uganda, Rwanda, Burundi, and Mboga-Zaire, transcending three international frontiers (which are frequently closed or difficult to cross), under a Ugandan archbishop from the Western Region.

The Roman Catholic Church has added to the linguistic diversity of Uganda a further diversity of European tongues, with the White Fathers in the center and west predominantly French, the Mill Hill Fathers in the east Dutch and English, and in the north the Italian Verona Fathers. The Catholic hierarchy is somewhat less Ugandanized, although there are now a number of Ugandan bishops and an archbishop as well as many priests.

After independence the Ministry of Education succeeded in taking over ownership, control, and, of course, financial responsibility for the school system from the competing missions that had established most of it, thus creating the structure of a nationally integrated system of education, which takes by far the largest ministerial slice out of the national budget.

Uganda's linguistic and cultural diversity have implications in all fields of social activity, but one of the most important in which efforts at integration were made during the first decade of independence was in that of the law where a unified legal system was developed. The main inconsistencies in Ugandan law involved the special powers of the courts in Buganda and the local diversity in customary laws of the family, marriage, and inheritance. The Buganda courts were brought within the national system when the whole structure of the Buganda Kingdom was dismantled after the violent confrontation in 1966 between Milton Obote as prime minister of the national government and Sir Edward Mutesa as king of Buganda and head of state. The local customary courts are being gently drawn along a path of convergence through centralizing and improving the training of the lowest leyel of professional magistrates. At the same time, the national government is allowing informal and officially unpaid court moots to continue hearing cases and arbitrating disputes for large numbers of litigants who still accept their decisions, from which they can always appeal to the formal courts if they so desire. Apart from constitutional changes, the main body of the laws of Uganda remains rather antiquated, having been laid down during the colonial period and reflecting the condition of English law in the early twentieth century without the more recent reforms subsequently effected in it.

Political Problems of National Integration before Independence

As administrative penetration proceeded, two conflicting processes were at work. The infrastructure of roads, railways, and waterways, the production of cash crops, the establishment of retail trading, and the growth of migrant labor brought far more people from distant localities into touch with one another than had ever been the case before. Yet at the same time the progressively elaborate institutionalization of district administration hardened the social and cultural and even linguistic boundaries of districts, bringing them nearer to the tribal stereotype than ever before. The seal was set on this process by the British treatment of Buganda, the Ganda reaction to it, and the game of make-believe that both sides played to their sectional advantage for more than half a century.[13] The myth was that the Ganda invited the British to come and advise them in their sudden confrontation with the outside, Westernizing world. When the Ganda had received enough advice they would say thank-you and good-bye and the identity of Buganda and Uganda would be restored. The myth was shattered ironically by the most intelligent, enlightened, liberal, and in some ways popular governor Uganda ever had—Sir Andrew Cohen, whose unpleasant duty it became to explain for the first time in unequivocal terms that British advice could not be rejected. So the kabaka went into exile in 1953, but returned with unprecedented glory and prestige in 1955. The Ganda experience rubbed home the lesson to most ethnic groups in Uganda that in the British scheme of things prevailing in Uganda they had to have their own district and it had to have a monarchical ruler after the model of the kabaka. Toro, Ankole, and, much later, the black sheep Bunyoro had succeeded in setting up their own districts and rulers under agreements with the British that were pale echoes of the Buganda Agreement, conferring far fewer privileges. The next strong candidate was Busoga, which never quite achieved a hereditary monarch but came extremely close. Its people developed a new honorific title—*Isebantu Kyabazinga*—as an obvious echo of *Sabasajja Kabaka*, the incumbent being recognized as the ceremonial head of Busoga. Thus it was no accident that when the kabaka of Buganda became the first president of Uganda, the kyabazinga became its first vice president. Busoga also received the unique distinction in Uganda's Independence Constitution of being classified as a territory, next to the kingdoms of Buganda, Ankole, Toro, and Bunyoro, whereas all other parts of Uganda were simply called districts. During the hectic jockeying for position in the last years before independence, many other ethnic groups which felt deprived made frantic final efforts to assert themselves: in West Nile the Alur had long been struggling for a district of their own, while the smaller groups of Okebo and Lendu demanded at least a subcounty or division named after them; in Toro the Bakonjo of the Ruwenzori foothills, tired of Toro rule, revolted and maintained guerrilla operations in the mountains, declaring themselves as the separate state of Rwenzururu for many years; only the Sebei in Bugisu actually succeeded in winning a new district for themselves.

Thus at independence every district had its own ceremonial head, seen by his "subjects" as conferring upon them some approximation of the status and privilege that seemed to flow from the kabaka of Buganda. Besides the latter, there was the mukama of Bunyoro, the mukama of Toro, the mugabe of Ankole, the kyabazinga of Busoga, the rwot adwong of Lang'o, the laloyo of Acholi, the agofe-obimo of West Nile, the kingoo of Sebei, and the umuinga of Bugisu.

This ceremonialism assuaged the wounded feelings of many areas at what seemed a very cheap price, though in other ways it boded ill for the future. It had flowered as a direct and immediate accompaniment of the kabaka's triumphant return in 1955, and it was carried even further in 1958 and 1959 when many of the districts whose ceremonial heads had been at the same time chairmen of their district councils were removed from this executive position to a purely ceremonial role. In West Nile, for example, the agofe-obimo became ceremonial district head, while yet another awkward portmanteau title, combining the Alur and Lugbara languages (the bili-ipi/jadipu) was created for the chairman of the council. All these maneuverings were very important, for the colonial power had already agreed in principle to independence. The problem, however, was to devise a constitution that could somehow accommodate the unwieldy Buganda Kingdom and at the same time convince the other districts that they were being given a sufficiently fair share of power to win their approval. This reconciliation of divergent aspirations was the major task of the Uganda Relationships Commission.[14] The approval of all districts was sought to a basically unitary national parliamentary democracy embodying some federal features and combined with democratically elected councils in each district and kingdom. One of the many paradoxes was the long drawn-out refusal of Buganda to participate in this national democracy. Although Buganda was the first to be offered fully democratic elections, in the end she rejected them; it was all the other districts and kingdoms that first participated in national parliamentary elections on the basis of universal suffrage, whereas Buganda insisted on electing its members of the parliament indirectly through its own *lukiko* ("council").

In the final round of bargaining for the independence settlement, the game was intricately balanced. Obote and his party could not at that time survive without the backing of the kabaka and Buganda. The latter were fighting for independent powers of taxation, maintenance of a separate court system, and their own police force and even army. It would have been suicidal for Obote to give in to these demands, but Buganda was promised a large subvention from the national government to finance its little *imperium in imperio* and maintain its special courts and ministerial system with its large control over education, health, agricultural and other services in Buganda, but not to finance its own army and police force, which had been desired and which, as events later proved, was indeed the crux of the matter. The financial provisions were sufficiently ambiguous to lead to constant dispute. Buganda succeeded in winning a continuance of the special position she had had, but not really enough to make it secure for the future, though quite enough to be a constant source of irritation to Obote's administration.

National Integration in the Independence Decade

The choice of the kabaka of Buganda as first president of independent Uganda solved the problem of Buganda's insistence, through its own sectional political party, *Kabaka Yekka* ("the kabaka alone"), that no commoner should ever be placed above the king on the soil of Buganda. The supreme rank belonged to the kabaka-president, but the supreme power in effect belonged to Prime Minister Obote, a Lang'o from north Uganda and leader of the dominant Uganda People's Congress (UPC) party. When Obote took a Muganda girl of good family as his wife, the ritual and symbolic point counterpoint was complete. Baganda proudly remarked that they had the head of state *and* the prime minister's wife. But the balance was very uneasy. Obote's UPC with its socialist orientation (though many prominent party members were involved in capitalist enterprises) could only rule with the support of Kabaka Yekka (KY) which represented the wealthy, capitalist oriented elite of Buganda. Despite a strong basis of peasant prosperity in the country, the government of independent Uganda was inevitably too preoccupied with political tightroping to carry through defined policies of economic development effectively. Obote's energy notwithstanding, the international image of Uganda remained blurred and ambiguous. The internal contradictions were so great that Uganda could not present a very coherent stance.

From the point of view of national integration, contradictory tendencies were at work in the immediate pre- and post-independence periods. Before independence the colonial administration had the power to ensure the ultimate unity and integrity of the country and was also rapidly developing centralized national institutions, manned increasingly by Ugandans. Furthermore, the mere presence of colonial power imposed a certain common purpose on the African population in the struggle for independence, even though in practice the Uganda independence movement was rather notoriously disunited.[15] The development of democratic institutions of local government facilitated and even legitimized the expression of local, regional, and ethnic rivalries and hostilities, but also provided a potential arena for the operation of nationalist parties. After independence the colonial power that had held the ring and enforced the rules of the game was gone. The uneasy coalition of the UPC and KY manifested itself in the uneasy relationship between the president and the prime minister. Britain's colonial autocratic practice proved a far more influential example than her democratic precepts. No one seemed to realize the inevitability of this at the time, although it is commonplace now.

The colonial government left a legacy of almost insoluble problems: not only the manifest absurdity of trying to fit four kingdoms into a would-be socialist democracy, but the dispute over the "lost counties" between Bunyoro and Buganda. These areas had clearly been confiscated from Bunyoro to punish her for the resistance of Kabarega to the British and to reward the Baganda correspondingly for their support. The Banyoro had steadfastly kept the issue alive and the pre-independence period, when all ethnic groups were feverishly jockeying for position, was obviously the moment for a supreme effort.

Looking back, of course, events seem to have moved with a relentless inevitability. The dynamite that threatened to blow up the fragile edifice of the independent state was clearly the relationship of Buganda with the national government and the rest of the country. The explosion was detonated by the smoldering fire of the Bunyoro lost-counties dispute.

The Molson Commission[16] had before independence recommended the immediate return of Bugangaizi and Buyaga counties to Bunyoro, but Buganda entirely rejected this proposal and no constitution for independence could be agreed upon without the consent of Buganda, both because of British treaty obligations and because Obote's government depended upon the support of the Kabaka Yekka. To avoid an intolerable postponement of independence, a dangerous compromise was adopted, which washed the British Government's hands of responsibility but left the wound festering. The two counties were to be under central instead of Buganda administration and a referendum was to be held to settle the matter finally after a period of two years.

Although an administrator was appointed, the two counties remained effectively under Buganda control. In April 1963 the kabaka led a large hunting expedition to the area which remained there indefinitely. Buganda announced plans to settle thousands of Ganda ex-servicemen in the two counties in the hope of building up enough votes to win the referendum.

One Nyoro member of the National Assembly, seeing that the only hope for Bunyoro lay in Obote and the UPC, crossed the floor to join the UPC, thus very significantly giving Obote's party a bare majority for the first time. The assemblyman's switch began the snowballing progress of the UPC toward control of a one-party state. Other ministers came out in favor of Bunyoro; and other dissatisfied groups, such as the Baamba and Bakonjo, struggling to win their independence from administration by the kingdom of Toro, also threw their weight behind the UPC. Likewise, some of the KY ministers in Obote's cabinet began to find their interests more closely tied to the national government than to Buganda secessionism and proposed to merge with the UPC. The Kabaka Yekka denounced them as traitors, but in June 1963 six of 21 KY members and two Democratic Party (DP) members joined the ranks of the UPC in the National Assembly. The KY was angry at the growing support from the UPC for Bunyoro over the lost counties, and the KY actually opposed the UPC in a Busoga by-election, thus threatening the foundations of the UPC-KY alliance. In August 1963 Obote formally abrogated the alliance. Defections to the UPC continued and by 1965 the UPC had 67 members in the National Assembly against 14 KY and 10 DP members.

Meanwhile another storm was blowing up. In January 1964, sections of the Uganda Army mutinied for higher pay and increased Africanization of higher posts. Obote called in British troops from Kenya and on his orders they stormed the Jinja barracks, but without casualties or a shot fired. The pay of lower ranks in the army was then more than doubled. Obote was shaken, nevertheless, by the experience and remarked ominously that "we cannot be expected to let the people the nation pays to protect us, turn themselves into dangerous elements to terrorize us."[17] It was seven years to a day after the assault on the Jinja barracks that the army took power in Uganda. The closely interlocked chain of events that followed the Jinja barracks raid was in a markedly centralizing direction and to this extent could only further the process of national integration—provided it did not cause reactions that would be too strongly counterproductive.

Two years after the Jinja attack there was an acceleration of these reinforcing processes.[18] In February 1966 serious charges were made in parliament implicating Obote and other prominent figures in illicit profiteering on gold, ivory, and coffee from Zaire, and support for a commission of inquiry began to grow. On February 22 Obote used the police to arrest and imprison five of his ministers at a cabinet meeting, accusing them of conspiracy. Two days later he suspended the constitution and took over as president and head of state himself.

On March 3 Obote abolished the former offices of president and vice president, accusing the kabaka, as president, of stockpiling arms, seeking outside help from Britain and the United Nations, and instigating a rebellion in Buganda. Next day the kabaka countered, charging Obote with breaking the constitution and of arrogating totalitarian powers to himself. With the country in a very disturbed state, Obote drew up a new constitution which, with a walkout by KY and DP members, was passed in the National Assembly by 55 votes to 4. The hereditary rulers were still recognized but were to hold no other public office. Members of the National Assembly from Buganda were no longer to be appointed by the lukiko but elected by popular vote. Control over appointments to public office was centralized, thus depriving the kingdoms of control over their local chiefs.

Buganda, understandably, was in an uproar over Obote's power plays and on May 20 the Buganda lukiko passed a resolution requiring the national government to withdraw from the soil of Buganda by the 30th. For the government to withdraw would, of course, have cut Obote off from his capital and from all the central institutions of the state. He could hardly be expected to tolerate the order, but such resolutions had been passed by the lukiko under the British and tactfully ignored.[19] This kind of ritual game could no longer be played under the old rules, however. As Erisa Kironde wrote: "a tiny, tiny tribe trying to hold to ransom a small, landlocked country in the middle of Africa could live in the world of political fantasy under a benign, alien imperial power with extensive global resources. Under a national government with very limited resources this just could not be sustained."[20]

Unrest in Buganda was reaching the proportions of a rebellion and by

May 23, 1966, insurgent forces were undertaking widespread action, blocking roads and capturing some police posts. Next day Obote sent the army to take the kabaka's palace and the "Second Battle of Mengo" began. There was considerable loss of life; the palace was sacked; the kabaka, his chief minister (katikiro), and many others escaped into exile; a state of emergency was declared; and the army took reprisals against the Baganda in various parts of the country.

Obote had at last succeeded in centralizing the state, at the cost of a much greater dependence upon the army and deeply antagonizing the largest, wealthiest, and most highly educated ethnic group, which dominated the very heart of the country. He could no longer even trust the support of his own party members, despite their complete dominance of the National Assembly. There was great temptation to gather civil power into his own hands, relying upon the ultimate military force of the army. When this move appeared too dangerous, he tried to develop a counterforce through the General Service Unit and the Special Force. It is generally believed that both these paramilitary forces, but especially the latter, were preponderantly recruited from Obote's own Lang'o people, thus giving the lie to his public fulminations against tribalism. This is not necessarily to suggest that Obote was insincere in his public statements, but it does suggest that this leader, who earnestly desired to achieve national unity, was forced, tragically, by his own feelings of insecurity and by his determination to retain power into ultimate reliance on his own ethnic group, thereby effectively sabotaging his own efforts.

The succeeding years were spent in working out and consolidating the new constitution and in coordinating and controlling all major fields of social activity through the development of centralized and UPC-oriented umbrella organizations such as the National Union of Youth Organizations (as a nationwide auxiliary of community-development programs), the National Union of Students of Uganda, and the Uganda Council of Women's Organizations. Factions or movements among Muslims and in the Church of Uganda were built up to support the UPC and counter hostile Ganda influence. UPC forces were mobilized in each district to weaken and intimidate local pockets of resistance among chiefs, DP branches, teachers, and cooperatives. These years were also spent in planning the Move to the Left, the Common Man's Charter, and the nationalization program; in designing a complex new scheme for general elections aimed at mixing and neutralizing ethnic forces; in trying to redress the balance of economic development away from Buganda and especially toward the north; and in developing a more positive stance in international affairs.

The assassination attempt of December 19, 1969, had a devastating effect on Obote, heightening his suspicions and intensifying his insecurity, making him even more unapproachable and driving him into further reliance upon henchmen of his own ethnic group and on the ever expanding network of intelligence agents. Yet the official formula was "government by discussion," with diffuse appeals to the people over the heads of legislators and constitutional organs.

In May 1970 it was announced that the government would acquire a 60 percent holding in banks, insurance, transport, Kilembe copper mines, and industry generally. This move exacerbated the flight of foreign capital which had been going on for some time.[21] The Asians, who still dominated wholesale and retail trade, had been the major factors in the removal of funds. The Trade Licensing Act of 1969 was an effort to squeeze them out gradually by reserving major trading areas to Uganda citizens. The law operated rather slowly and ineffectively because many mechanisms of circumvention were devised, and there was the further difficulty that while a fair number of Asians were citizens and therefore not affected by it, awkward problems were created by considerable numbers of noncitizen Africans in business.

During the second half of 1970 an active campaign was conducted in all districts to put across to the public the detailed implications of the Common Man's Charter and to explain the intricate voting scheme in preparation for a general election in 1971.

The Rise of the Army and the Military Coup

The army mutiny of 1964 and its solution had brought Idi Amin and S.O. Opolot to the highest ranks in the army. with the latter as senior commander. But by 1966 Amin had ousted Opolot from the senior position. Amin had been directly concerned with the operations to assist the rebel forces in Zaire and had been linked with Obote in the charges of smuggling gold and ivory. Through the capture of the palace at Mengo and the army control of Buganda, he saved Obote from the danger of being ousted from leadership of the party and the government. But the relationship between these two, who stood on the top of two parallel and potentially rival power hierarchies, political and military, was inevitably uneasy. In 1969 Obote accused Amin of responsibility for the murder of Brigadier Pierino Okoya and his wife, and seven persons were arrested and said to have been tortured to induce them to make incriminating confessions.

This inflammable situation was ignited while Obote was at a Commonwealth Conference in Singapore, when, it is alleged, Lang'i and Acholi soldiers were selected by the commander of the mechanized battalion to go to the armory and get arms and ammunition, then disarm those of other ethnic groups and arrest their officers. But the rest of those in the battalion got wind of the plan and demanded that they should have arms too. Amin gained control of the battalion and through it dealt with pockets of resistance in the army one by one, having also seized strategic points in Kampala and other towns.

Thus military rule was inaugurated in Uganda on 25th January 1971. The soldiers' spokesman announced 18 reasons why they had taken power. They included detention of innocent people without trial, continuation of the state of emergency, lack of freedom of speech, insecurity and loss of life and property from *kondoism* (robbers bearing rifles and machine guns), proposed national service, corruption in high places, failure to hold elections, bad economic policy leading to unemployment, high and burdensome graduated sales and social-security taxes, low crop prices, expelling Kenyans and Tanzanians, creating an ever richer elite class in the false name of socialism, mismanaging the army and setting up a rival army of Lang'o and packing its top positions with Lang'o, and favoring Lang'o with development projects.

At first the military government seemed to have carried national integration a definite stage further, both by making central control more absolute and by reconciling the defeated Baganda with the wider nation. At the same time the major sources of dominant power had changed, first from the immediate post-independence threat of dominance by Buganda traditionalism and capitalism, then under Obote to dominance by the socialist and Lang'o-based UPC, and lastly to an increasingly Kakwa-Nubi-Muslim-dominated army.[22]

Recent Events

The military government of Uganda is not only quite different from any government the country has had before but is also quite different in style and technique from any other military regime in the rest of the continent. It took over in a blaze of popularity and relief from the most obnoxious features of the previous regime, and since then it has adopted a number of dramatic measures that have largely tended to maintain this popularity, particularly in the central parts of the country. However, severe and prolonged reprisals have been taken against the Lang'o and Acholi groups, which were associated with the previous regime, to such an extent that every one of their families mourns the loss of some relative. This ethnic struggle has also continued on and off in various army units, so that the loss of life has been heavy and the turnover in the officer corps particularly serious, with practically every unit commander now belonging to the Kakwa-Nubi-Muslim group.

The military head of state himself has very successfully adopted the pose of a man of the people, identifying himself with the common soldiers rather than the officers, visiting every part of the country, addressing large open-air assemblies, mingling warmly with the crowds, and moving about with little sign of tight security precautions.

Yet at the same time many prominent figures have mysteriously vanished. Whatever the actual reason for their disappearance, many people are now afraid for their lives. There is, as a result, a high degree of conformity with government orders as well as constant public expressions of adulation from individuals and organizations throughout the country.

The expulsion of the Asians was undoubtedly a highly popular move with the masses, which seemed to remove at one dramatic stroke one of the deepest grievances of many decades. The results will take a long time to show. Many small entrepreneurs are getting the chance of a lifetime to acquire property and businesses on the cheap. But doubt continues as to whether the larger enterprises can be effectively manned in the short run, and many of the more prominent and wealthy citizens who might have the best chance of doing so seem afraid to come forward. All the channels of trade, internal and external, have been severely disrupted and increasing shortages are feared. What might not have been anticipated is that such critical and persistent shortages would develop in products produced by Uganda herself, such as salt and sugar. Recent indications are that the price of basic local foodstuffs to the common man may have risen as much as 500 percent. This inflation might not be so serious if it were part of an effective attempt at making the economy stand on its own for the sake of future strength whatever the present hardships. But this is not so, for paradoxically the declared aim is openly capitalistic and clearly dependent upon large infusions of foreign-aid investment and technical experts, although some of the major sources of both have now been cut off.

A much reduced level of commercial and industrial activity seems inevitable for some time to come, with a vicious circle of reinforcing effects from higher unemployment and greatly reduced income from taxation. It is difficult to see how, as a consequence, the regime can avoid incurring unpopularity, even though it will blame its economic dilemma on a neo-colonialist, Zionist and imperialist conspiracy. The army may well retain power for a long time, even with changes of personnel at the top, because there is no other serious competitor. If the program of free capitalism leads to an increasing polarization of rich and poor, as seems inevitable, it may ultimately provoke a revolutionary movement which, while requiring dedicated leadership of a kind not yet in sight, would involve the masses in a more far-reaching transcendence of ethnic differences than has yet occurred—and which would thus provide a more thorough solution to what has hitherto been the major problem of national integration. At present Ugandans still have a strong tendency to interpret conflict in ethnic terms, and so tend to precipitate it. Such ethnic conflict could lead to new coalitions and mitigate direct class conflict for a while, if we assume an absence of direct foreign intervention, which indeed seems highly unlikely.

In 1973 a total administrative reorganization was announced, including a complete redrawing of regional or provincial boundaries and district boundaries, as well as the dismissal and reselection of the many thousands of chiefs at the county, subcounty and parish levels in each district. This reorganization was carried out in 1974. It was the biggest administrative upheaval since the colonial administration was first established sixty to seventy years before. The chiefs were selected by mixed civilian and military boards in each locality. Some previous chiefs were retained but most were new.

The four regions (called provinces during the colonial era) were divided into ten new units to be called provinces once again but under governors instead of the former provincial commissioners. These in turn were subdivided into thirty-eight districts instead of the previous eighteen. Approximately half the new provinces and districts were able to make use of already existing administrative buildings. The rest had to make shift in minimal substitute accommodation such as community development centers. The reorganization is bound to involve a considerable enlargement of the administrative civil service, including eventually the specialized services: police, medical, agricultural, veterinary, education, community development, co-operatives, credit banks and so forth. The increased number of administrative units could be seen as a rational reflection of population growth. It does not have any clearcut ethnic implications. Thus, it could not be said that favored ethnic groups were administratively recognized and others not. Because provinces and districts are smaller than before, some of the smaller ethnic groups coincide with such boundaries for the first time, while larger ones are inevitably subdivided. Thus, Busoga is a province for the first time and the Alur approximate to a district for the first time. But Amin's own Kakwa are joined with a section of the Lugbara to form North West Nile District, and such ethnic groups as Teso, Lang'o, Acholi, Ankole, Kiga, Nyoro, which formerly corresponded to single districts, are now divided into two or even three districts.

It is too early to tell what the practical day-to-day effects and implications of this wholesale reorganization have been.

TABLE 16-2

1969 REGIONS	1974 PROVINCES	1974 DISTRICTS
Buganda Region:	North Buganda Province:	Mengo, Kyagwe, Luwero, Mubende.
	South Buganda Province:	Buddu, Sese, Kyotera.
	Central Province:	Kampala, Entebbe.
Eastern Region:	Eastern Province:	N. Teso, S. Teso, Central Teso, Bugisu, Bukedi, Sebei.
	Busoga Province:	Jinja, S. Busoga, N. Busoga.
	Karamoja Province:	N. Karamoja, Central Karamoja, S. Karamoja.
Western Region:	Southern Province:	S. Kigezi, N. Kigezi, E. Ankole, W. Ankole.
	Western Province:	Toro, S. Bunyoro, N. Bunyoro, Semuliki, Rwenzori.
Northern Region:	Nile Province:	South West Nile, Central West Nile, North West Nile, Madi.
	Northern Province:	East Acholi, West Acholi, East Lang'o, West Lang'o.

To sum up the present situation from the point of view of national integration it is obviously necessary to weigh a number of factors. Presumably, any military regime, if it is at all successful, must tighten centralized control. The question is whether the price is worthwhile and whether it is counterproductive in the long run. It may be said that Uganda's military regime has enforced a passive national integration at increasing cost. If in the fullness of time a strong alternative movement develops, transcending narrow ethnic loyalties, a more positive national integration may with much suffering emerge.

Notes

1. Compare the use of this concept by Godfrey and Monica Wilson, *The Analysis of Social Change* (Cambridge: Cambridge University Press, 1945).
2. See for example, Aidan Southall, *Alur Society: A Study in Processes and Types*

of Domination (Cambridge: Heffer, 1956); republished: (Nairobi: Oxford University Press, 1970).

3. Aidan Southall, "Stateless Society," *Encyclopedia of Social Sciences,* Vol. 15 (New York; Macmillan and Free Press, 1968), pp. 157-168; also *Alur Society,* chap. 9.

4. J.H.M. Beattie, *The Nyoro State* (Oxford: Clarendon Press, 1971), pp. 28-29.

5. L.A. Fallers, ed., *The King's Men* (Oxford: Oxford University Press for East African Institute of Social Research, 1964).

6. Aidan Southall, "The Illusion of Tribe," *Journal of Asian and African Studies,* Vol. 5, Nos. 1-2 (January-April 1970), pp. 28-50.

7. Samuel Baker, *The Albert N'yanza* (1866; London: Sidgwick and Jackson, 1962), front end papers.

8. George Schweitzer, *Emin Pasha, His Life and Work* (London: Constable, 1898), Vol. 1, p. 75.

9. H.H. Johnston, *The Uganda Protectorate* (London: Hutchinson, 1902), Vol. 2, p. 724.

10. J.S. La Fontaine, *The Gisu of Uganda* (London: International African Institute, 1959), p. 25.

11. H.F. Morris, "The Making of Ankole," *Uganda Journal,* Vol. 21, No. 1 (1957), pp. 1-15.

12. Aidan Southall "Cross-cultural Meanings and Multilingualism," in *Language Use and Social Change,* ed. W.H. Whitely (London: Oxford University Press for International African Institute, 1971); and also idem, "Twinship and Symbolic Structure" in *The Interpretation of Ritual: Essays in Honor of A.I. Richards,* ed. J.S. La Fontaine (London: Tavistock Publications, 1971).

13. Anthony Low and R. Cranford Pratt, *Buganda and British Overrule* (Oxford: Oxford University Press for East African Institute of Social Research, 1960).

14. *Report of the Uganda Relationships Commission* (Entebbe: Government Printer, 1961).

15. Anthony Low, *Political Parties in Uganda,* University of London, Institute of Commonwealth Studies, Commonwealth Papers No. 8 (London: Athlone Press, 1962).

16. Molson Commission, *Report of a Committee of Privy Councillors on a Dispute between Buganda and Bunyoro,* Cmd. 1717 (London: HMSO, 1962).

17. Quoted by Donald Rothchild and Michael Rogin, "Uganda," in *National Unity and Regionalism in Eight African States,* ed. Gwendolen M. Carter (Ithaca, N.Y.: Cornell University Press, 1966), p. 388.

18. For an account of the events see M. Crawford Young, "The Obote Revolution," *Africa Report,* Vol. 11, No. 6 (June 1966), pp. 8-16.

19. The Buganda lukiko had in 1960 expressed the determination of Buganda "to be a separate autonomous State" and had declared, as it were, with tongue in cheek, that "other parts of Uganda are absolutely free to seek the attainment of their autonomy through whatever means they think fit." It also made it quite plain that Buganda aimed at having its own army and complete indepen-

dence from the rest of Uganda in foreign affairs and finance. D.A. Low, *The Mind of Buganda: Documents of the Modern History of an African Kingdom* (London: Heinemann, 1971), pp. 200-207.

20. Ibid., pp. 225-228.

21. For a critical commentary see Selwyn Ryan, "Uganda: A Balance Sheet of the Revolution," *Mawazo* (A publication of the Faculties of Arts and Social Sciences, Makerere University, Kampala), Vol. 3, No. 1 (June 1971), pp. 57-59.

22. The Nubi are the descendants of the irregular troops recruited in the Southern Sudan by Emin Pasha in the 1880's and brought by him to Wadelai, in what was later to become Uganda, when forced to retreat south in escape from the Mahdi. When Emin Pasha was rescued by Henry Stanley, the Nubi were left marauding in Uganda, living off the country as best they could. To relieve the population from their ravages and put them to good use, Lugard recruited them into his forces in the 1890's and a few years later they became the core of the newly established Kings African Rifles, which eventually became the Uganda Army. The Kakwa were among the Southern Sudanese peoples from whom they were originally recruited, so that a Kakwa Muslim who serves in the army is, in effect, a Nubi. The Nubi virtually amounted to a hereditary military caste in Uganda and General Idi Amin is their most famous son. [See Southall, "General Amin and the Coup: Great Man or Historical Inevitability?" *Journal of Modern African Studies,* Vol. 13, No. 1 (April 1975).]

Index